NEW SECOND EDITION
LEADERSHIP
FOR TODAY'S
HEALTH CARE
PROFESSIONALS
Concepts and Cases

EDITED BY

LOUIS G. RUBINO, PHD, FACHE

Professor and Chair of Health Sciences Department, California State University, Northridge

SALVADOR J. ESPARZA, DHA, RN, FACHE

Associate Professor, California State University, Northridge

YOLANDA S. REID CHASSIAKOS, MD, FAAP, FACP

Clinical Assistant Professor, Pediatric David Geffen School of Medicine, UCLA
Director, Klotz Student Health Center, California State University, Northridge

JONES & BARTLETT
LEARNING

World Headquarters
Jones & Bartlett Learning
5 Wall Street
Burlington, MA 01803
978-443-5000
info@jblearning.com
www.jblearning.com

Jones & Bartlett Learning books and products are available through most bookstores and online booksellers. To contact Jones & Bartlett Learning directly, call 800-832-0034, fax 978-443-8000, or visit our website, www.jblearning.com.

Production Credits

VP, Product Management: Amanda Martin
Director of Product Management: Michael Brown
Product Manager: Danielle Bessette
Product Assistant: Tess Sackmann
Director, Relationship Management:
    Carolyn Rogers Pershouse
Senior Marketing Manager: Susanne Walker
Manufacturing and Inventory Control Supervisor: Amy Bacus
Composition: codeMantra U.S. LLC

Project Management: codeMantra U.S. LLC
Cover Design: Kristin E. Parker
Text Design: Kristin E. Parker
Rights & Media Specialist: Merideth Tumasz, John Rusk
Media Development Editor: Shannon Sheehan
Cover Image (Title Page, Chapter Opener):
    © liuzishan/Getty Images
Printing and Binding: McNaughton & Gunn
Cover Printing: McNaughton & Gunn

Library of Congress Cataloging-in-Publication Data
Names: Rubino, Louis, author. | Esparza, Salvador, author. | Chassiakos, Yolanda Reid, author.
Title: New leadership for today's health care professionals / Louis G. Rubino, PhD, FACHE, Professor and
    Chair of Health Sciences Department, California State University, Northridge, Salvador J. Esparza, DHA,
    RN, FACHE, Associate Professor, California State University, Northridge, Yolanda Chassiakos, MD, FAAP,
    FACP, Clinical Assistant Professor, Pediatric David Geffen School of Medicine, UCLA, Director,
    Klotz Student Health Center, California State University, Northridge.
Description: Second edition. | Burlington, MA: Jones & Bartlett Learning, [2019] | Includes bibliographical
    references and index.
Identifiers: LCCN 2018040495 | ISBN 9781284148640 (paperback)
Subjects: LCSH: Health care reform—United States. | Leadership—United States. | Public health
    personnel—United States—Administration. | BISAC: LAW / Health.
Classification: LCC RA410.6 .N49 2019 | DDC 362.1/04250973—dc23
LC record available at https://lccn.loc.gov/2018040495

6048

Printed in the United States of America
22 21 20   10 9 8 7 6 5 4 3 2

I dedicate this book to my wife of 33 years, Judy, and my children, Rebecca and Nicholas, who make me proud every day.

−Louis Rubino

I dedicate this book to my wife, Caroline, for her constant love and support throughout my career.

−Salvador Esparza

I dedicate this book to E.G. and Effie Stassinopoulos for their inspiration and motivation, and to my husband, Anastasios Chassiakos, for his patience and support.

−Yolanda S. Reid Chassiakos

Contents

Chapter 4 Creating a Culture of Professionalism 69

Keith Benson and Chris Hummer

Chapter 5 Human Resource Considerations at the Top 87

Mary Helen McSweeney-Feld and Nancy Rubin

Chapter 6 Strategic Thinking Leaders 107

Thomas F. McIlwain and Michael Ugwueke

Chapter 7 Building a Successful Leadership Team . . . 127

John Shiver and Craig Nesta

Foreword

Leaders in healthcare organizations have consistently stated that healthcare management is one of the most challenging yet rewarding professions. Organizational leaders face numerous issues, such as complying with increased regulations, fostering employee engagement, creating a positive patient experience, and maximizing revenue. The work of healthcare leaders is not only vital but gratifying. Serving people in times of great need and vulnerability provides significant intrinsic motivation for healthcare leaders. However, the dynamic nature of healthcare organizations and their environments necessitates new leadership thinking and practice.

The growth in the number of healthcare management programs and their increasing enrollments underscore the key role educational programs play in the preparation of future healthcare leaders. The education of leaders is critical to advancing the field of practice. The editors have crafted the update of this book with one goal in mind: to provide students with updated concepts, strategies, and practical skills to develop and perform as effective leaders.

While the impact of healthcare leadership is widely acknowledged, the practice of healthcare leadership is in a state of flux. It is clear that leadership is multidimensional. Organizational leaders are faced with a tough balancing act: meeting the needs of their patients and communities while achieving desired organizational metrics. These challenges are shaping new thinking about healthcare leadership, and, as a result, best practices in healthcare leadership are evolving. To fully understand today's best practices, students need to gain the perspective of the practitioner, and providing that viewpoint is a unique and key contribution of this book. The book's chapters on leadership concepts and practices are written by co-authors representing both academia and management practice; this novel approach provides a rich and balanced assessment of the current state of healthcare leadership.

This text fills an important gap in available resources for educating healthcare leaders. Being an effective leader in health care requires exhibiting the knowledge, behaviors, and practices to lead staff to the desired level of performance. As this book insightfully describes, leading others begins with leading oneself, which includes assessing and developing one's own knowledge and skills and building on personal strengths. Much has been written recently about the importance of leadership and the desired competencies of effective leaders in healthcare organizations. The knowledge base is expanding with new research that identifies the success healthcare leaders have had in transforming their organizations into high performers, and the strategies and tactics used to achieve these results. The chapter authors of this book highlight important updated healthcare leadership concepts and practices. For example:

- *Cultural competency.* Organizations are becoming more diverse in terms of professional and support staff and the populations they serve. Leaders must fully embrace this trend and create effective relationship management with key internal and external stakeholders.

- *Teamwork.* Effective delivery of care requires staff to work closely and interdependently. This process begins with the establishment of a leadership team that shapes an organizational culture of teamwork, collaboration, and engagement.
- *Patient- and family-centered leadership.* Patient- and family-centered care and the patient experience have been shown to impact patient satisfaction as well as quality and outcomes and are now a key factor influencing reimbursement. Leadership in healthcare organizations is instrumental in achieving patient- and family-centered care and a positive patient experience.
- *Community outreach.* Healthcare organizations fundamentally serve the community. Leaders must conceptualize and act on strategies and approaches to effectively engage in community outreach and development.
- *Physician collaboration.* Positive relationships with physicians are critical to healthcare organization success. Leaders must work effectively to engage the medical staff in implementing clinical best practices, organizational strategy, and strategic marketing, and create opportunities for physicians to serve as organizational and system leaders.

The academic and practice communities are in agreement that healthcare leadership must continually adapt, as organizations respond to external challenges and internal needs. This book's call for new leadership by today's healthcare professionals is a needed and welcomed invitation. This updated edition of the book duly challenges those of us who teach in healthcare management programs, as well as our students, to reconsider the changing practice of healthcare leadership.

Jon M. Thompson, PhD, FACHE
Professor Emeritus and Director Emeritus
Health Services Administration Program
James Madison University
Harrisonburg, Virginia; and
Adjunct Professor
MHA Program
Department of Health Administration
Virginia Commonwealth University
Richmond, Virginia

Preface

The second edition of *New Leadership for Today's Health Care Professionals* was driven by our desire to create a textbook that meets the needs of undergraduate students in the field of healthcare management and administration. The first edition was published after the successful passage of the Patient Protection and Affordable Care Act (ACA), and many of the concepts and cases reflected the ACA's directions and guidance. Newer regulations and legislation have impacted the ACA guidelines, and ongoing efforts to modify, revise, repeal, and replace the ACA continue at federal and state levels. This dynamic evolution demands healthcare leaders who are knowledgeable, flexible, and responsive to continuous and rapid change: leaders who are able to address the salient elements of persisting legislation and adapt to modifications and amendments. Our book provides an update and overview of this evolving landscape and helpful information to provide up-and-coming leaders with a foundation that will promote resilient leadership in an environment of change.

Published books on successful leadership in a variety of fields, including health care, are plentiful. Some of these texts have been penned by researchers presenting rigorous empirical analyses; others were produced by industry practitioners who brought an experiential perspective to the presented material. Some books have been written with senior leadership in mind, and others target newly minted managers. Academic tomes tend to include complex theories and models, whereas workbooks may present simpler algorithms or formulas to demonstrate management approaches. All of these texts strive to capture the general nature of outstanding leadership, its significance, and its contribution to organizational effectiveness—with variable success. As professors of health administration and health services management, we have often struggled to find texts that are well-suited to undergraduate students. Many textbooks are written at a level of content best suited for graduate students or readers with experience as practitioners in the field. For undergraduate students in health administration using this textbook, we therefore endeavored to select readings and references that would provide meaningful and understandable information, appropriate and valuable for their level of expertise.

The majority of undergraduate students we have encountered have had similar interests, needs, and profiles. These enthusiastic students are typically only 2 to 3 years beyond high school, have had little work experience, and have a minimal or nonexistent frame of reference as we dive into the complex and dynamic structure and function of healthcare management and administration. A smaller number of our students are healthcare professionals with an associate degree, license, or certification in a clinical field such as nursing, radiologic technology, or respiratory therapy. These students have started on the pathway to management in the healthcare workforce and are seeking the necessary leadership knowledge, training, and degrees that will promote their progress. Finally, a few of our students are aiming for professional schools in medicine, nursing, or pharmacy and are pursuing an undergraduate degree in a healthcare field as a first step in the pipeline. Finding a health administration text that can effectively address the educational needs of these diverse populations can be challenging.

To tackle that challenge, the editors set out to acknowledge and merge academic and practitioner perspectives and to develop a textbook that would combine the highlights and best practices from both critical worlds, creating a synergistic collaboration. They invited renowned professionals in academia and industry to partner in producing each content area, so that the information, theories, and models provided are both academically rigorous and practically applicable. For this second edition, many of the same distinguished academics and practitioners revised and updated their chapters to reflect the evolving healthcare landscape. To address these dynamic changes, contributors wrote new cases for this edition, and updated graphs, charts, and figures to include more current data or information. Finally, with the ongoing and expanding globalization of health and health care, a chapter and case were added about global healthcare leadership.

Textbook content, which addresses administration and leadership across the full breadth of healthcare disciplines, is presented in language and formats easily understandable by and relevant to these diverse groups of health administration undergraduates. Our research and experience have demonstrated that leadership knowledge and skills must be developed in a sequential fashion, beginning with the foundation of "leading oneself," and then moving step-by-step to the higher echelons of leading other leaders. Our model of leadership development is shown in **FIGURE 1**.

Using this model as a basis for promoting leadership development in our text, we begin Chapter 1 with a call for modern leadership, and provide the foundation and skills (such as self-assessment) required for entry into the world of management. Chapter 2 relays information on how healthcare leaders are developed today and explores the characteristics of leadership excellence. Chapter 3 completes the

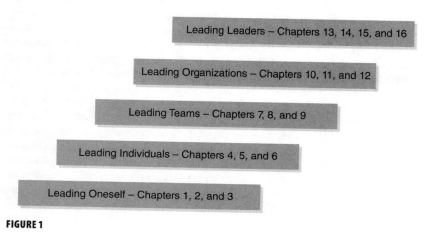

Leading Leaders – Chapters 13, 14, 15, and 16

Leading Organizations – Chapters 10, 11, and 12

Leading Teams – Chapters 7, 8, and 9

Leading Individuals – Chapters 4, 5, and 6

Leading Oneself – Chapters 1, 2, and 3

FIGURE 1

basic instruction by introducing the culturally competent leader and the strategies used to promote cultural competency and inclusion in the healthcare setting.

The next step in the model promotes skill-building for future leaders. Chapter 4 establishes the importance of creating a culture of professionalism, which transcends individual responsibility and underscores the value of organizational responsibility. Chapter 5 examines the strategies associated with effective personnel management and the human resource implications of their implementation. Chapter 6 discusses the value of strategic leadership in promoting an organization's success in the modern healthcare environment.

How to build and lead outstanding teams becomes the focus of Chapter 7; Chapter 8 addresses the need for effective teamwork to successfully implement quality initiatives and continuous performance improvement. The skills and attributes of collaborative leadership, essential in the healthcare field, are highlighted in Chapter 9.

Chapter 10 offers a review of how leading organizations utilize transformational leadership via leaders who are change agents. Chapter 11 explores the new concept of patient- and family-centered care and the social and financial benefits for an organization that adopts this model. A detailed discussion of organizational financial management in Chapter 12 outlines the basics of this critical leadership function.

To be able to approach and understand the highest levels of leadership, students must learn how leaders can train and lead other leaders both within and outside of their organizations. Physician leaders are an important and unique constituency in healthcare organizations and are discussed in Chapter 13. High-level health administrators must also successfully interact with and answer to a governing body, such as board of directors or trustees, as reviewed in Chapter 14. The critical role of external relationships and community outreach for organizational success is explored in Chapter 15.

Expanding on the concept of external relationships and communities, Chapter 16 is a new addition to the textbook that explores leadership in the context of global health. Finally, addressing our era of groundbreaking healthcare reform that was launched in 2010, Chapter 17 is written with the understanding that our students will be entering the healthcare industry in a time of rapid, dynamic, and continuous change. This chapter presents current trends in healthcare delivery and their impact on and implications for leadership.

Additionally, to demonstrate the practical applications of the leadership principles presented in each chapter and promote interactive student learning, the chapter authors provide case studies based on their industry experiences that give students a glimpse of the current working environment. Accompanying instructor resources can help teach the concepts presented.

As the editors of this book, we have researched and reviewed the requirements for quality leadership in a variety of modern healthcare settings. We have ourselves served both as experienced administrators and academics, as well as currently practicing healthcare leaders, and we have assembled a group of respected contributors who have the academic understanding and the practice 'know-how' necessary for excellent leadership in today's healthcare industry.

Our students will take on the mantle of healthcare leadership in the coming decades and will have the opportunity to enhance our healthcare system for the benefit of our country and our population. We hope the strong foundation we provide in this book will help our students to develop into the outstanding healthcare leaders our country seeks and needs.

Louis Rubino
Salvador Esparza
Yolanda S. Reid Chassiakos

Acknowledgments

Our thanks go to our esteemed colleagues who contributed their time, talent, knowledge, and experiences to this work. It has been a privilege and an honor to work with each and every contributor. This project would not have been possible without their dedication to the field of health administration education.

Louis Rubino
Salvador Esparza
Yolanda S. Reid Chassiakos

About the Editors

Dr. Louis G. Rubino is Professor and Chair of the Health Sciences Department at California State University, Northridge (CSUN). In the community, he serves as a governing board member at St. Francis Medical Center and is Chair of their Quality and Patient Safety Subcommittee. Prior to academia, Dr. Rubino served for 20 years as a hospital administrator and health system executive. Dr. Rubino holds a master's degree and PhD in Public Administration from the University of Southern California. His expertise is the study of integrated systems with special emphasis on the operation of acute hospitals, international comparative studies in hospital administration, and leadership. He is a recertified Fellow in the American College of Healthcare Executives. He is the coeditor of *Collaboration Across the Disciplines in Health Care.*

Dr. Salvador J. Esparza has been teaching full-time in the Health Administration Program at California State University, Northridge since 2006. Prior to this time, Dr. Esparza was a practicing healthcare executive with extensive experience in hospital and ambulatory operations for a variety of healthcare organizations within and outside of California. He is a board-certified executive and Fellow of the American College of Healthcare Executives. Dr. Esparza started his career as a registered nurse and as a result has a great appreciation for the role and contribution of clinicians in healthcare organizations and the strategic value they provide for the effective delivery of healthcare services. He serves on the board of a local, not-for-profit medical foundation and has contributed his governance expertise to other organizations in his community.

Dr. Yolanda S. Reid Chassiakos is the Director of the Klotz Student Health Center at California State University, Northridge, and a Clinical Assistant Professor of Pediatrics at the David Geffen School of Medicine, UCLA. She is a Fellow of the American Academy of Pediatrics (AAP) and the American College of Physicians and serves on the Executive Committee of the AAP Council on Communications and Media. Dr. Chassiakos has also served as the Assistant Head of the Ambulatory Branch of the Department of Pediatrics at the Naval Hospital Bethesda, as the Project Director of the Preventive Services Initiative at the Office of Disease Prevention and Health Promotion in the U.S. Department of Health and Human Services, and as the Chair of the Medical Staff at the Ashe Health and Wellness Center, UCLA. She is the co-editor of *Collaboration Across the Disciplines in Health Care.*

Contributors

Hildegarde B. Aguinaldo, JD, MPH
Attorney
Lewis Brisbois Bisgaard & Smith LLP
Los Angeles, CA

Frankline Augustin, DPPD, MSHA
Associate Professor
Health Sciences Department
California State University, Northridge
Northridge, CA

Keith Benson, PhD, MHA, MBA
Professor
Department of Management and
   Marketing
Winthrop University
Rock Hill, SC

Nancy Borkowski, DBA, CPA, FACHE, FHFMA
Professor
Department of Health Services
   Administration
University of Alabama at Birmingham
Birmingham, AL

Dale Buchbinder, MD, FACS
Clinical Professor of Surgery
University of Maryland Medical
   School
Vascular Surgeon, Maryland Vascular
   Specialists
Lutherville, MD

Sharon B. Buchbinder, PhD, RN
Professor and Program Coordinator,
MS in Healthcare Management
Stevenson University Online
Owings Mills, MD

Marsha Choy Chan, PharmD, MBA, FACHE
Chief Administrative Officer
Cynosure Health

President
MCC Healthcare Consulting
La Cañada, CA

David E. Cockley, DrPH
Associate Professor of Health
   Administration
James Madison University
Harrisonburg, VA

Barbara Perez Deppman, MSM, FACHE
Principal
Deppman Strategic Alliances, LLC
Miami, FL

Ethel Elkins, DHSc
Associate Professor
Health Services/Health
   Administration
University of Southern Indiana
Evansville, IN

Brenda Freshman, PhD
Associate Professor
Health Care Administration
   Department
California State University, Long Beach
Long Beach, CA

Andrew N. Garman, PsyD
Chief Executive Officer
National Center for Healthcare
   Leadership
Professor and Associate Chair,
   External Relations and Business
   Development
Rush University
Chicago, IL

Linda Joyce Gunn, PhD, CPHRM, ACC
Course Faculty
College of Health Professions

Western Governors University
Salt Lake City, UT

Mellisa Hall, DNP, ANP-BC, FNP-BC, GNP-BC
Family Nurse Practitioner
University of Southern Indiana
Evansville, IN

Christopher R. Hummer, MHA
President, Southern Division, Atrium
    Health
President, Carolinas HealthCare
    System-Pineville
Charlotte, NC

Mary Lynne Knighten, DNP, RN, NEA-BC
Adjunct Faculty
University of San Francisco and Azusa
    Pacific University
Principal
Knighten Consulting
Los Angeles, CA

Christy Harris Lemak, PhD, FACHE
Professor and Chair
Department of Health Services
    Administration
School of Health Professions
University of Alabama at Birmingham
Birmingham, AL

Sandra Lundahl, MPH, MA
Faculty Development Instructional
    Design
Health Education
Ellicot City, MD

Thomas F. McIlwain, PhD, MPH
Professor and Director
MHA Program
Clayton State University
Morrow, GA

Mary Helen McSweeney-Feld, PhD, LNHA, FACHCA
Associate Professor
Health Sciences
Towson University
Towson, MD

Carol Molinari, PhD, MBA, MPH
Professor
Health Systems Management
University of Baltimore
Baltimore, MD

Craig Nesta, JD, MBA, MS, FACHE, FHFMA
Consultant
Performance Improvement and
    Healthcare Practice Management
Boston, MA

John A. Orsini, CPA
Senior Vice President and Chief
    Financial Officer
Northwestern Memorial HealthCare
Des Plaines, IL

Victoria A. Parker, DBA, EdM
Associate Professor
School of Public Health
Boston University
Boston, MA

Carrie Pullen, EdD
Assistant Professor
Health Sciences Department
California State University, Northridge
Northridge, CA

Timothy Putnam, DHA, MBA, FACHE
President/CEO
Margaret Mary Community Hospital
Batesville, IN

Beverly Quaye, EdD, RN, NEA-BC, FACHE
Assistant Professor
Nursing Department
California State University, Fullerton
Fullerton, CA

Anne Rogers, MS, CIH, CSP
Manager of Industrial Hygiene
Occupational Health Department
CSX Transportation, Inc.
Jacksonville, FL

Nancy Rubin, MS
Retired Vice President of Human
    Resources

Motion Picture and Television Fund
Woodland Hills, CA

Laurie Shanderson, PhD, MPA
Dean
School of Health Sciences
Northcentral University
San Diego, CA

John M. Shiver, MHA, FACHE, FAAMA
Assistant Professor
Department of Health Administration
  and Policy
George Mason University
Fairfax, VA

Melanie P. Standish, BS
Project Coordinator
Leadership Competencies Research
Rush University

Michael O. Ugwueke, DHA, FACHE
President & Chief Executive Officer
Methodist Le Bonheur Healthcare
Memphis, TN

Brian O. Underhill, PhD
Founder and CEO
CoachSource LLC
San Jose, CA

Michael L. Wall, MHA, FACHE
Chief Executive Office
Antelope Valley Hospital
Lancaster, CA

Donghai Wei, PhD
Vice President
Guangzhou Medical University

© liuzishan/Getty Images

CHAPTER 1

A Call for New Leadership in Health Care

Salvador Esparza, Louis Rubino, and Yolanda Chassiakos

LEARNING OBJECTIVES

By the end of this chapter, the student will be able to:

- Understand how leadership can respond to the evolving changes in modern health care.
- Describe the difference between leadership and management.
- Know the shared models of leadership.
- Explain the importance of understanding yourself and others for effective leadership.

KEY TERMS

C-suite
Ethics
Healthcare value
Leadership competencies
Leadership models
Learning organization
Medicaid
Medicare

Mental models
Patient Protection and Affordable Care
    Act (ACA)
Psychological contract
Single-payer
Succession plan
Will-Ideas-Execution

▶ Introduction

We are living in challenging times. Healthcare delivery systems are rapidly evolving, the cost of health care continues to rise, and the healthcare needs of our diverse population continue to grow. Legislators are attempting to address issues that include providing access to low-cost, high-quality health care for all Americans through a variety of options presented via political platforms. Healthcare organizations are using strategic thinking and planning to meet the needs of their customers and employees, and to promote the success and sustainability of their operations. Communities and advocacy groups are partnering with health service providers to expand and enhance services. Federal and state agencies that provide healthcare leadership and guidance are implementing measures to research, evaluate, analyze, and review quality of care, and to encourage clinical and fiscal accountability in health care. Healthcare leaders in this dynamic, constantly changing environment are tasked to play a critical role to address the issues and concerns identified and to partner with multiple stakeholders, including healthcare consumers, to ensure that our population achieves its "Healthy People" objectives.

The **Patient Protection and Affordable Care Act (ACA)**, enacted in 2010, was upheld in June 2012 by the U.S. Supreme Court and was implemented in 2014. The ACA had been envisioned as a catalyst for additional reforms of our healthcare delivery system and, by some, as the first step on a pathway to **single-payer** health coverage (e.g., "**Medicare** for all"). For example, the ACA addressed quality and cost-effectiveness of care; public health, including disease prevention and wellness; the healthcare workforce; fraud and abuse; long-term care; biopharmaceuticals; elder abuse; and Indian Health Services (McDonough, 2012). New frameworks and structures, such as accountable care organizations, patient-centered medical homes, foundations, and health insurance exchanges, were developed and implemented to enhance healthcare services and quality (McLaughlin, 2011).

The objective of these changes was to improve American **healthcare value** and accessibility. Even though the ACA did not provide universal healthcare coverage, it did increase the availability of health insurance for most Americans, allowing more people to seek out and obtain medical care. By 2016, almost 25 million additional Americans had been covered by an expansion of **Medicaid** eligibility, and through the development of new individual insurance markets that provided subsidized premiums for eligible applicants. "Value of services provided" remained a more elusive goal, however. Cost-effective services, that is, the provision of high-quality care at lower cost, are difficult to achieve, but critical to successful healthcare reform (Wachter, 2012).

Opposition to the ACA in Congress led to several attempts to repeal the act in 2017, none of which were successful. However, legislators did take steps to undermine the ACA's implementation and operation. Medicaid was not expanded in 19 states. Insurance subsidies (cost-sharing reduction [CSR] payments) were cut, along with appropriations for transitional financing to support insurance exchanges. Premiums increased and options for low-cost insurance were reduced. Enrollment periods were halved, and advertising budgets were significantly cut. Enforcement by the Internal Revenue Service of the ACA mandate for universal participation was limited, allowing individuals, many of whom are likely to be healthy, to avoid buying insurance and contributing to the funding pool. Meanwhile, efforts to support and/or provide alternatives to the ACA continue in Congress, as well as in state legislatures.

In this period of dynamic change, outstanding leadership is necessary to guide us well. Strategies must be developed to achieve the performance benchmarks and financial stewardship needed to survive in this new healthcare environment.

Potential barriers to successful adaptation for healthcare organizations and their leaders include limited economic resources and increased government regulation. The healthcare workforce will be looking to their leaders and managers to steer them safely through these churning waters. Stakeholders from within and from outside healthcare entities will demand leadership that can appropriately address interests and concerns such as fiscal stability and sustainability. Healthcare reform will provide new opportunities for graduates entering the healthcare workforce who have the confidence, abilities, and skills to effectively lead under these challenging conditions.

▶ Leadership as a Course of Study

In this environment of growing demand and finite resources, today's healthcare leaders must transform the way their organizations operate (Gabow, Halvorson, & Kaplan, 2012). A Robert Wood Johnson Foundation symposium in 2012 included the cultivation of new leadership to promote a healthy society as one of the four key areas needed to improve national health in the next two decades (Japsen, 2012). In its discussion paper, *A CEO Checklist for High-Value Health Care*, the Institute of Medicine also included governance priority as one of its foundational elements, recommending visible and determined leadership by healthcare CEOs and board members (Cosgrove et al., 2012).

In order to meet this need for new and dynamic leadership in the healthcare industry, educational institutions will need to expand programs to develop modern leaders. Leadership training should be included in all health professional training curricula; effective leadership skills can be taught and learned. Early exposure to leadership principles will better educate and prepare our future managers and supervisors, and teach them to conduct ongoing personal assessments and to reflect on their successes and their failures, or, better termed, "learning opportunities."

Health professionals have frequently been promoted into leadership positions without formal instruction in health administration. Lack of adequate training, for example, could lead new managers to spend most of their time on tactical problem-solving rather than strategic decision-making, diminishing their effectiveness. With trained leaders who possess the competencies proven to promote success, the healthcare industry will be in a better position to address the challenges in this environment of reform.

▶ Leadership Versus Management

Leadership and management aim for similar outcomes: getting people to achieve organizational goals through specific acts and behaviors. A main difference, though, is that in management, this is accomplished through processes (i.e., organizing, staffing, controlling, planning, etc.), and for leadership, through influence. Another defining feature is orientation. In general, managers maintain more of an internal focus, concentrating on the issues associated inside the organization. Leaders display more of an external focus, concentrating on issues outside of the organization, which can impact the organization and its stakeholders.

A commonly debated question in the first session of any basic leadership course is: Can good leaders be good managers, and can good managers be good leaders? And, is there a differentiation of duties between leadership and management? Yes, some leaders can be good managers, and some managers can be good leaders—depending in large part on their training and skills.

Good leaders typically rise to their position of influence through the ability to successfully lead others toward achieving a mutually agreed-upon goal. Without others willing to be led, however, there can be no leaders. "Followership" is complementary and essential to leadership (Atchison, 2003). Not everyone has the skills or inclination to be an effective leader; successful leaders need capable followers to be able to achieve their organizations' goals.

Katz (1955) conducted primary research on leadership and managerial effectiveness, and determined that successful leaders and managers utilize three distinct sets of skills: conceptual, interpersonal, and technical skills. Conceptual skills include being able to work with ideas and concepts, critical to strategic planning for senior leadership. Interpersonal skills are needed by both leaders and managers. Technical skills are predominantly utilized by managers for operational functions, but can be valuable for senior leaders who are tasked with accountability data analysis. Different skills are critical to leadership versus managerial success.

Further distinctions between leadership and management foci are made by Manion (2011). Building on the original premises presented by Bennis (1989), Manion points out that those in charge must look differently at situations depending on their administrative level and position. For example, leaders are more concerned about effectiveness (*if* the task gets done), whereas managers are more concerned with efficiencies (*how* the task is done). Leaders are focused on "what" and "why," whereas managers are more focused on "how." Leaders are more concerned with people and relationships; even though managers are more concerned with organizational structure, people and relationships are also critical to good management. Leaders are focused on innovation and managers on "maintaining the status quo." Most importantly, whereas managers are typically eyeing "today's" bottom line, leaders look toward the horizon to help move the organization forward (see **TABLE 1.1**).

TABLE 1.1 Leader Versus Manager Focus	
Leader Focus	**Manager Focus**
Effectiveness	Efficiency
What and why	How
People and relationships	Organizational structure
Innovation	Status quo
Horizon	Bottom line

▶ History of Leadership in the United States

Over the past century, leadership has been influenced by social and cultural contexts (see **TABLE 1.2**). From the industrial revolution to the 1920s and 1930s, the "Great Man" theorists believed that the best leaders had inherent traits such as strength, firmness, and male gender. During the 1940s and 1950s, after the devastation of World War II, leadership theories shifted toward considering relationships in addition to getting tasks done. In the 1960s and 1970s, the emergence of social consciousness led to situational approaches wherein the dynamic nature of relationships was examined, the needs of subordinates were considered, and the styles of leadership were assessed relative to subordinates. Path–Goal and Contingency are examples of two such theories. By the 1980s, the transformational approach became prominent. Recently, this theory has had a renaissance of sorts as the healthcare industry experiences paradigm shifts. Some recent examples are the evolution from value-based care to a value-based delivery model (Chatfield, Byrd, Longenecker, Fink, & Gold, 2017), the population health management shift (Caldararo & Nash, 2017), and patient experience being touted as the "new heart" of healthcare leadership (Wolf, 2017).

TABLE 1.2 Leadership Theories in the United States

Period of Time	Leadership Theory	Leadership Focus
1920s and 1930s	Great Man	Having certain inherent traits
1940s and 1950s	Style Approach	Task completion and developing relationships
1960s	Situational	Needs of the subordinates
1970s	Contingency and Path–Goal	Considers style and situation
1980s	Transformational Approach	Raises consciousness and empowers followers
1990s	Team Leadership	Team development and performance
2000s	Authentic, Servant, Spirituality, and Emotional Intelligence	Leading with a purpose, serving others, and being empathetic
Contemporary Theories	Adaptive, Discursive	Concentrates on follower problem-solving and communication

Modified from Buchbinder, S., & Shanks, N. (2012). *Introduction to health care management* (2nd ed.). Burlington, MA: Jones & Bartlett Learning.

In the 1990s, team building and leadership were heralded. In the 2000s, an appeal to the "helping" mission became popular in health care. Authentic leadership invites people motivated by leaders who follow their internal compass of true purpose and associated values. Servant leadership rests on the principle that leaders and followers are motivated by the desire to serve others: followers to serve clients and leaders to serve the employees who implement the organizational mission. Spiritual leadership tends to be a good fit for an industry that is often sponsored by religious organizations. Emotional intelligence, with its five dimensions of self-assessment, self-regulation, self-motivation, social skills, and social awareness, can provide healthcare leaders using any of these leadership styles with a tool kit from which to draw strategies and solutions that respect both leaders and subordinates (Rubino, 2012).

In the 21st century, a number of contemporary approaches have been developed. Two pointed out by Northouse (2019) are adaptive leadership, which encourages followers to adapt by confronting and solving problems, challenges, and changes; and discursive, in which leadership is created through communication practices that are negotiated by the leader and the follower.

Individual Leader Perspective

In healthcare organizations, there are many opportunities for leadership. For example, the **C-suite**, especially in larger organizations such as hospitals, contains several high-level executives who are responsible for the entire entity, or multiple affiliated entities (e.g., Chief Executive Officer, Chief Operating Officer, Chief Quality Officer). Other leaders might supervise specific groups of associates (e.g., Chief Nursing Officer and Chief Medical Officer) or have critical administrative and operational responsibilities (i.e., Chief Financial Officer and Chief Information Officer). All the department leaders are expected to work together as a leadership team to ensure the alignment of action with the organization's strategic plans and mission. Smaller healthcare organizations, such as nursing homes, clinics, and home health agencies, also identify leaders for their units, but, having more limited human and financial resources, may provide fewer opportunities for the development of functional leadership teams and collegial camaraderie.

Healthcare organizations tend to be hierarchical. Professionals who provide patient care are typically supervised by physicians or advanced-practice nurses. In hospitals, a physician is usually elected or appointed Chief of Staff and oversees the breadth of clinical operations that are organized and provided as per the hospital's medical staff bylaws. Subdivisions and units such as Surgery, Pediatrics, and Obstetrics will usually have a physician leader who has been trained in the unit's specialty to supervise the unit's specialists and advanced-practice nurses. Nursing units are typically supervised by experienced senior nurses, many of whom have master's or doctorate degrees. Physicians or nurses may be elected to serve as the Chairs of Quality Improvement and/or Patient Safety Committee and monitor the quality of care provided.

There is a breadth of leaders in many other healthcare organizational units/departments/divisions (imaging supervisors, laboratory scientists, business office managers, etc.), who have similar roles and responsibilities for their various specialties. In healthcare sectors that are not provider based, such as pharmaceutical, medical supply, and insurance companies, many other leadership positions can be identified. The **leadership competencies** needed to be successful in these roles are transferable across multiple types of healthcare organizations.

▶ The Leadership Competencies

Competencies are a set of skills, knowledge, and abilities. An alliance of associations representing healthcare leadership groups—the American College of Healthcare Executives, the American Association for Physician Leadership, the American Organization of Nurse Executives, the Healthcare Information and Management Systems Society, the Healthcare Financial Management Association, and the Medical Group Management Association—collaborated to determine the set of competencies needed by successful healthcare leaders.

Leadership was identified as the central domain that intersected with four other domains: (1) communication and relationship management, (2) professionalism, (3) knowledge of the healthcare environment, and (4) business skills and knowledge. Within the area of leadership, the important competencies identified were leadership skills and behavior, organizational climate and culture, communicating vision, and managing change. The American College of Healthcare Executives (ACHE), as well as the other associations, now uses this set of competencies to help its members conduct self-assessments of their leaders' practices (ACHE, 2012).

A few other competencies are recognized as being important for healthcare leaders today. With the changing demographics of our society, we must produce culturally competent healthcare professionals to respond to patients' unique needs with the goal to reduce health disparities (Abrishami, 2018). Leaders must demonstrate this competency and instill it in their organizations. Humble leaders confess if they make mistakes and ask for patience in correcting them (Kaissi, 2017). And resilient leaders address not only the everyday challenges that occur but also those faced in crisis situations (Bowen, 2018). With the rising incidence of burnout among health professionals (Perlo & Feely, 2018), leaders need to demonstrate resiliency for success.

The demands of U.S. healthcare reform for improved quality of care and cost-effectiveness have inspired a renewed examination of the competencies needed by healthcare executives who are preparing their organizations for change. A recent survey of hospital and other healthcare systems attempted to assess the promotion and adoption of these competencies in organizational leadership development programs (Awo Osei-Anto, 2011). Though leadership development programs were variable from organization to organization, the study demonstrated a correlation between leadership training in best practices and improved performance. These training programs must be coupled with a true **succession plan** to ensure the organization has consistent and effective leadership at all times (Walker, Fineran, & Giella, 2018).

▶ IHI Framework for Leadership for Improvement

A more specific framework for leaders to achieve better performance is provided by the Institute for Healthcare Improvement (IHI; Reinertsen, Bisognano, & Pugh, 2008). Acknowledging the pressures healthcare leaders are facing, the IHI developed a roadmap that leaders who wish to improve their organizations can follow. The core elements of this model are **Will-Ideas-Execution**. Successful leaders must develop the organizational will to achieve results, generate or identify effective ideas or strategies for improvement, and then execute those ideas. In addition, setting

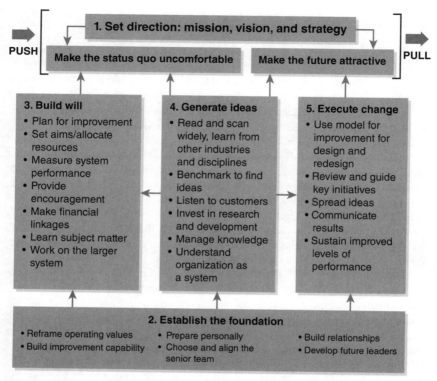

FIGURE 1.1 IHI Framework for Leadership for Improvement

Reproduced from Reinertsen, J.L., Bisognano, M., & Pugh, M. D. (2008). *Seven leadership leverage points for organization-level improvement in health care* (2nd ed.). Cambridge, MA: Institute for Healthcare Improvement. (Available on www.ihi.org.)

direction and establishing the foundation will help spread the ideas across the organization and sustain them over time. A push–pull type of response is typical in organizations implementing this model: building will and generating new ideas make the status quo uncomfortable, but the implementation of good ideas will make the future attractive. The IHI Framework for Leadership for Improvement includes 24 elements and provides a helpful perspective regarding the steps needed to achieve success in today's healthcare environment (see **FIGURE 1.1**).

Healthcare reform in the United States will demand a different skill set from leaders to ensure ongoing success. Bolster and Larrere (2012) present six areas in which senior leaders will need to develop expertise in this new era: having political savvy, being influential, having the ability to lead during change, being adaptable, exhibiting excellent communication skills, and being a true visionary. All of these areas depend on the development of successful and effective interpersonal skills.

Models of Leadership

As mentioned previously, a model is a construct that helps us better understand and address a situation or environment. **Leadership models** can help us understand why leaders act the way they do and which leadership actions are most likely to lead to successful outcomes. Because different situations call for different leadership approaches, leaders must avoid getting stuck using only one type of model. Two well-regarded models that address common leadership challenges are the *Managerial Grid* and the *Four Framework Approach*.

Managerial Grid

The Managerial Grid, also known as the Leadership Grid, was developed by Blake and Mouton (1985), and it is based on two dimensions or axes, each of which has a range from 0 to 9: The axes are the extent to which there is a "concern for people/relationships" and the extent to which there is a "concern for results/production."

Data or observations collected for each leader are plotted on the grid (see **FIGURE 1.2**). Most leaders fall somewhere in the middle of the two axes (i.e., middle of the road). When we look at the extreme quadrants of the grid, however, we find four classic types of leaders:

- Impoverished—low concern for people and results
- Country Club—high concern for people, low concern for results
- Authoritarian—low concern for people, high concern for results
- Team Leader—high concern for people and results

Impoverished Leader

Leaders demonstrating this style detach themselves from their workforce and tend to allow their team or group members to do whatever they want. Lacking commitment to either group maintenance or task accomplishment, they generally "delegate and disappear."

Country Club Leader

Leaders demonstrating this style shy away from exerting authority or implementing disciplinary measures in the quest for improved outcomes because they fear jeopardizing the positive interpersonal relationships with their workforce. Instead, these

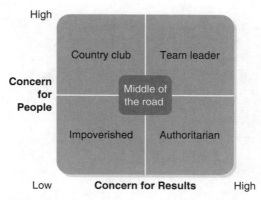

FIGURE 1.2 The Blake Mouton Grid

Reproduced from Blake, R. R., & Mouton, J. S. (1970). The fifth achievement. *Journal of Applied Behavioral Science, 6*(4), 413–426.

leaders will almost exclusively use reward and recognition to encourage the team to accomplish its goals.

Authoritarian

These leaders are characterized by task orientation and a tendency to be tough with their group or team members. Authoritarian leaders will focus their energy on getting the work done at all costs and expect people to do exactly what they are told without questions. If something goes wrong, they are likely to "blame, shame, and train" in order to prevent the issue from occurring again. These types of leaders are intolerant of dissent and perceive it as disloyalty, making it difficult for their group or team members to comfortably contribute their valuable input.

Team Leader

These leaders strive to lead by example, foster a productive team environment, and encourage teams and individuals to achieve their highest potential. They constantly work at strengthening the bonds among team members and colleagues to promote successful outcomes and goal achievement.

The most desirable place to be on the grid is the Team Leader area. However, elements of the other leadership styles may sometimes be useful in specific situations.

▶ Four Framework Approach

In the Four Framework Approach, Bolman and Deal (1991) propose that leaders frequently display leadership styles and behaviors that fit one of four types of frameworks: political, human resources, structural, or symbolic (see **FIGURE 1.3**).

This model suggests that leaders can be matched with one of the following four frameworks of leadership.

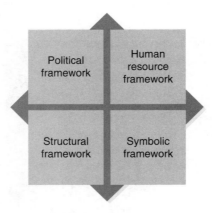

FIGURE 1.3 The Four Framework Approach

Bolman, L., & Deal, T. (1991, Winter). Leadership and management effectiveness: A multi-frame, multi-sector analysis. *Human Resource Management, 30*(4), 509–534.

Political Framework

This leader is an advocate whose approach includes coalition-building. Political leaders are clear and realistic about their goals, build connections with other stakeholders, determine distribution of power and interests, and use influence and persuasion before they resort to negotiation or coercion. This type of leadership orientation can be observed when issues are framed around the use of power, exchange of interests, coalition-building, bargaining, and networking.

Human Resource Framework

This leader is a servant and advocate. Human resource leaders use an approach that is supportive and empowering; believe in people; are visible and accessible; share information widely and encourage participation; and allow decisions to be made by relevant employees at all levels of the organization. This type of leadership orientation can be observed when issues are framed around the use of inclusion, motivation, nurturing, training, empowerment, and emotional intelligence.

Structural Framework

This leader emphasizes analysis and design. Structural leaders serve as social architects to address issues, focusing on structure, strategy, environment, execution, and adaptation. This type of leadership orientation can be observed when issues are framed around the use of rationality, coordination, control, rules, formal authority, and chain of command.

Symbolic Framework

This leader is inspirational and prophetic. Symbolic leaders view the organization as a theater in which they must communicate a vision to their audience. They play specific roles, use symbolism to create a setting or impression, and interpret and dynamically pitch the organization's potential future on behalf of its members. This type of leadership orientation can be observed when issues are framed around the use of culture, ceremony, meaning, storytelling, and inspiration by example.

In the healthcare industry, situations may arise in which one of the above frameworks or approaches may be more effective than another. Successful leaders may be able to adopt aspects of a different framework to achieve a specific outcome.

▶ Understanding Yourself and Others: The Key to Successful Interpersonal Skills

The 6th-century BCE Chinese philosopher Lao Tzu has been quoted as saying, "He who knows others is wise. He who knows himself is enlightened." In no milieu is this adage truer than in the practice of leadership. How can one lead others if one is uninformed about, and unable to lead, oneself? The manner in which leaders engage in professional behaviors such as conversation, planning, problem-solving, decision-making, and other leadership functions has profound effects on other individuals. Our personality and our environment influence our innate behaviors, but when behavior change is valuable in order to enhance leadership effectiveness, we are able to learn new skills and behaviors that will make us more productive and successful.

Before setting out to understand and work effectively with others, we must first strive to understand ourselves. We must become aware of our individual mental maps or models. Peter Senge (1990, p. 8) in his classic book, *The Fifth Discipline*, defined **mental models** as: … deeply ingrained assumptions, generalizations, or even pictures or images that influence how we understand the world and how we take action. Very often, we are not consciously aware of our mental models or the effect it has [*sic*] on our behavior.

Our mental model serves as a window, which frames (and sometimes distorts) the world we see (Osland, Kolb, Rubin, & Turner, 2007). We react in different ways because our "windows" show us different perspectives. One of the best ways to understand our own perspectives, reactions, and behaviors is to identify our maps or models and become aware of our own beliefs, values, and expectations by using self-assessment instruments. These tools of self-discovery include instruments that assess characteristics central to leadership effectiveness such as learning style, personality, motivation, and **ethics**.

▶ The Psychological Contract: Mutual Expectation Setting

When we enter into a personal or professional relationship, we aim for the relationship to have a strong foundation of trust. Trust allows us to develop integrity and credibility in our relationships. Employees joining an organization are establishing a professional relationship with their employer. This relationship starts with an implicit, unwritten **psychological contract**. Psychological contracts are defined as a person's beliefs, formed by the organization, regarding the terms and conditions of a reciprocal agreement between people and their organization (Rousseau, 1995). The development of mutually agreed-upon expectations between the employee and the employer, and stability and reciprocity in the professional relationship, promotes employee and organizational productivity.

Unfortunately, psychological contracts can be violated or broken. Broken contracts occur when one of the parties fails to meet the stated obligations or expectations. The result can be a negative impact on attitudes, behaviors, performance, and productivity.

Setting expectations can be a double-edged sword. Researchers have demonstrated a *Pygmalion Effect*—that is, "people perform in accordance with a rater's expectation of them" (Osland et al., 2007, p. 13). If a rater expects an employee to perform at a high level, the employee is likely to meet that expectation. Leaders may give highly-rated employees more challenging assignments and provide the support and encouragement the individual may need to achieve the assignments successfully. On the other hand, if a rater expects poor performance, poor performance is more likely because the leader may interact negatively with the low-rated employee and not provide the support and direction necessary to succeed. Effective leaders

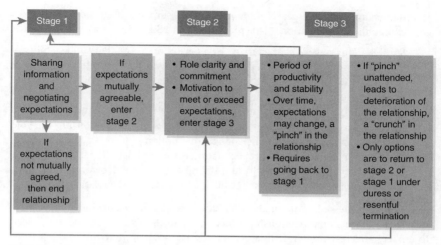

FIGURE 1.4 The Pinch Model

Modified from Sherwood, J. J., & Glidewell, J. C. (1972). Planned negotiation: A norm-setting OD intervention. In W. W. Burke (Ed.), *Contemporary organization development: Orientations and interventions* (pp. 35–46). Washington, DC: NTL Institute.

seek to identify their perceptions, prejudices, and preconceived notions that could negatively influence interactions with their employees and take the necessary corrective actions to minimize potentially negative behaviors.

Understanding one's own theories of management and identifying one's personal leadership style is imperative in this self-development process. Effective leaders make every effort to analyze their skills, perceptions, and values; develop strategies to implement necessary changes; educate themselves in the areas and skills they need to master; practice newly learned skills; and obtain feedback about how well they are performing.

A method of managing psychological contracts is called the *Pinch Model* (see **FIGURE 1.4**), developed by Sherwood and Glidewell in 1972 and still in use today (Osland et al., 2007). This model describes the dynamic nature of these contracts and recommends ways to mitigate the negative consequences of changing expectations.

The Pinch Model

Osland et al. (2007) identify and describe the stages of this model as follows:

> *Stage 1*—The first stage of an employee–employer relationship is characterized by the sharing of information and the subsequent negotiation of expectations of one another. If the individual or organization determines the expectations to be unreasonable, they will deselect themselves from the relationship (i.e., "planned termination"). On the other hand, if both parties accept the mutually agreed-upon expectations, then they enter Stage 2.
>
> *Stage 2*—The second stage allows the relationship to move to role clarity and commitment between the parties. Leaders and their employees accept and

understand the roles each plays and are presumably motivated to meet or exceed those expectations. This process leads to Stage 3.

Stage 3—This stage is characterized by a period of productivity and stability in the relationship and allows for maximum energy to be dedicated to the work at hand. However, as in most relationships, with the passage of time, changes in expectations may occur due to intrinsic or extrinsic reasons. Sherwood and Glidewell (1972) call this a "pinch point" in the relationship and suggest that this is a warning sign to return to the first stages of the relationship to avoid disruption. When expectations change, one option is to renegotiate, meeting agreed-upon expectations. If renegotiation is successful, both parties will move through the stages of role clarity and stability once again. However, if renegotiation fails, one or both parties may decide to terminate the relationship.

Left unaddressed, a dissonance in shared expectations can lead to a deterioration of a professional relationship. Uncertainty or ambiguity can eventually lead to anxiety and resentment. If this occurs, the relationship may respond via three options: (1) a return to Stage 2 by attempting to return expectations to the previous contract, (2) a return to Stage 1 by renegotiating expectations (under duress), or (3) termination of the relationship either administratively or emotionally.

The key to successful leadership is to be clear about mutual expectations and to manage those expectations just as would be done with any other important operational function or process.

▶ Individual and Organizational Learning

A **learning organization** is one that is skilled at acquiring, creating, and transferring knowledge, and modifying its behavior to reflect this new knowledge and insight (Osland et al., 2007). Members of successful learning organizations are themselves active adult learners. Kolb (1999) has postulated that adult learning is a cyclical process composed of four primary modes:

1. *Concrete experience* or learning by experiencing. This is a feeling mode that is characterized by responses to specific experiences, relating to people, and sensitivity to feelings.
2. *Reflective observation* or learning by reflecting. This is a watching mode characterized by observation before making judgments, viewing issues from varying perspectives, and looking for meaning in functions or events.
3. *Abstract conceptualization* or learning by thinking. This mode is characterized by the logical analysis of ideas, systematic planning, and the intellectual-based responses to situations.
4. *Active experimentation* or learning by doing. This mode is characterized by taking risks, demonstrating the ability to get things done, and influencing people through action.

Most adult learners tend to favor one or more of these learning modes. Organizations can benefit by having members with different learning styles involved in problem-solving and decision-making. Leaders who identify their learning modes can better understand how they approach work-related issues and how they can best interface with others who use a different mode or style.

Personality

Personality has been defined as a person's consistent pattern of thought, behavior, and emotions, and the psychological mechanisms that drive and support those patterns (Osland et al., 2007). Effective leaders are aware of their own personality traits and the traits of others and understand the impact these traits may have on professional interpersonal relationships. Instruments such as the Myers-Briggs Type Indicator (MBTI) and Jung Typology are available for leaders to identify and learn about the components of their own personality as well as those of colleagues and employees. Both of these instruments suggest four components to personality:

- Extraversion/Introversion (E/I): how an individual interacts with society
- Sensing/Intuiting (S/N): how an individual collects information
- Thinking/Feeling (T/F): how an individual evaluates information
- Judging/Perceiving (J/P): how an individual prefers to make decisions

Effective leaders try to develop a robust picture of all the individuals with whom they work and attempt to understand their personalities and their "rules of engagement." They strive to analyze the causes of individual's behaviors, remembering to observe specific characteristics such as motivation and skills, to be able to ensure that the "job, group, and organizational characteristics are exerting the intended consequences on behavior" (Osland et al., 2007, p. 90), and not triggering unintended negative outcomes.

Motivation

It is often heard that good leaders "motivate" others. This expression is frequently misunderstood to mean that motivation is something that is done by someone to someone else. Motivation is, in fact, an internal state, something within an individual that directs him or her toward certain goals and objectives. Motivation is facilitated by internal psychological forces that influence behavior, levels of effort, and levels of persistence (Osland et al., 2007).

It has been said that it is much better to light a fire within someone than to light a fire underneath them. The task of an effective leader is to understand, enhance, and guide the motivation employees already possess, and channel the motivation toward activities that further the goals and objectives of the organization. Effective leaders understand that the sources of motivation can be either intrinsic (e.g., the work itself) or extrinsic (e.g., economic rewards). Different people are motivated by different things; there are a variety of tools (i.e., Maslow's hierarchy of needs, McClelland's theory of motivation, Alderfer's ERG theory, etc.) available to determine people's motivators. The leader's role is to create an environment that encourages motivation by setting clear standards of performance and ensuring that there is a good "fit" between the needs of the employee and the position.

Determining what motivates individuals is not always an easy task. In addition to using the tools mentioned previously, leaders can observe individuals in the work setting and discover what type of work or projects they enjoy. Face to face discussion, for example, during the performance appraisal or annual evaluation, can allow employees to provide leaders with feedback about their areas of interest for future assignments.

Ethics and Values

Healthcare leaders are frequently faced with ethical dilemmas that may challenge their decision-making. These issues may include clinical challenges such as end-of-life care, queries regarding experimental research on human subjects, and operational questions about contractual and revenue-generating arrangements. Effective leaders have a responsibility to set the moral tone of an organization, should always strive to behave in an ethical manner, and should set clear expectations for subordinates and others to do the same. Standards or codes of ethical behavior have been clearly identified by professional associations such as ACHE. Members of ACHE are accountable for adhering to codes of conduct that cover responsibilities to

- The profession of healthcare management
- Patients and others served
- The organization
- Employees
- Community and society
- Report violations of the codes

In addition, ACHE has developed ethical policy statements that encompass such areas as leader–vendor relationships, reductions in force (layoffs), and health information confidentiality. The code of ethics and ethical policy statements can be viewed at www.ache.org/ABT_ACHE/code.cfm.

Much of a leader's behavior is rooted in his or her personal values, ethics, and moral reasoning. It is critical for effective leaders to understand their own value system and project their response to issues and situations that may arise. Values are defined as core beliefs that guide attitudes and actions. Terminal values are desired end-states or goals, either social or personal, that people would like to achieve. Instrumental values are preferable modes of behavior or means to achieving terminal values. There are two types of instrumental values: competence and moral. Osland et al. (2007) have identified an instrument titled the *Rokeach Values Survey,* which can identify both instrumental and terminal values for self-exploration. Individuals are placed into one of four value orientation quadrants:

1. Preference for personal competence values
2. Preference for social competence values
3. Preference for personal moral values
4. Preference for social moral values

Ethics, on the other hand, refers to standards of conduct that "indicate how a person should behave based on moral duties and virtues arising from principles about right or wrong" (Osland et al., 2007, p. 146). An ethical framework that successful healthcare leaders adopt includes the following:

- Respect for persons
  - Autonomy (self-governing)
  - Truth-telling
  - Confidentiality
  - Fidelity (duty)
- Beneficence
  - Refraining from actions that worsen a problem or cause negative results

- Non-maleficence
  - First, do no harm
- Justice
  - Consistently apply clear and prospectively determined criteria in decision-making

Effective leaders work at identifying and understanding different perspectives on issues, and then discuss the benefits, risks, and consequences of alternative actions. One way to promote positive ethical practices is through the use of the Josephson Ethical Warning System (Josephson, 2002), which includes the following elements:

- Golden Rule—Are you treating others as you would want to be treated?
- Publicity—Would you be comfortable if your reasoning and decisions were to be publicized?
- Kid on your shoulder—Would you be comfortable if your children were observing you?

Healthcare organizations are launched with mission statements that ideally define their values, beliefs, and vision, which in turn determine the responsibilities of their leaders and stakeholders. After an organization makes a decision or takes action, the consequences are scrutinized by state and federal regulatory agencies, accrediting and licensing agencies, and the public, and frequently address whether the action is ethical and legal. In order to ensure that leaders function with an optimal standard of ethical behavior, codes of conduct should be developed and used as instructions, guidelines, and/or internal organizational regulations.

Healthcare leaders can use resources such as ACHE's *Code of Ethics* for guidance regarding standards of behavior and ethical decision-making. The Code can also be used as a basis for developing the organization's policies and performance metrics, and can serve as a teaching tool for colleagues, employees, and students.

Understanding yourself and others, and respecting and appreciating our differences, is key to effectiveness and success as a healthcare leader and should be a commitment that begins early in your career and continues throughout your professional life. Your efforts in this regard will ensure that your colleagues, clients, and communities will be "gifted" by your leadership.

Summary

Health care in the United States is dynamically ever-changing, due to a combination of legislative and market reform measures. These platforms provide numerous professional challenges and opportunities for healthcare leaders with modern competencies. Use of best practices and development of skilled leaders are needed to assist the healthcare industry in meeting the challenge of improving access and establishing value through higher quality and lower costs. Today's healthcare leaders must seek to continuously improve the quality of their leadership and the quality of the services of their organizations. Critical to this process is active learning and ongoing self-assessment of one's ethics and values, and one's leadership and interpersonal styles and skills.

Discussion Questions

1. Can leadership be taught?
2. How have leadership theories changed over the last century?
3. Which competencies are most important for successful leadership during this era of healthcare reform?
4. Why is it important for leaders to "know themselves"?
5. What is the value of understanding mutual expectations?
6. When faced with an ethical dilemma, which approaches could a leader use to resolve the issue?

Related Websites

American Association for Physician Leadership: https://www.physicianleaders.org/
American College of Health Care Administrators: www.achca.org
American College of Healthcare Executives: www.ache.org
American Organization of Nurse Executives: www.aone.org
CEO Checklist for High Value Health Care: https://nam.edu/wp-content/uploads/2015/06/CEO HighValueChecklist.pdf
Complete Patient Protection and Affordable Care Act: http://docs.house.gov/energycommerce /ppacacon.pdf
Health and Human Services Information about the ACA: https://www.hhs.gov/healthcare/about -the-aca/index.html
Healthcare Financial Management Association: www.hfma.org
Medical Group Management Association: www.mgma.com

References

Abrishami, D. (2018). The need for cultural competency in health care. *Radiologic Technology, 89*(5), 441–448.

American College of Healthcare Executives (ACHE). (2012). *Competencies assessment tool.* Chicago, IL: Healthcare Leadership Alliance and the American College of Healthcare Executives.

Atchison, T. A. (2003). *Followership: A practical guide to aligning leaders and followers.* Chicago, IL: Health Administration Press.

Awo Osei-Anto, H. (2011). Preparing hospital and system leadership for change. *Hospitals and Health Networks, 85*(9), 62.

Bennis, W. (1989). *On becoming a leader.* Reading, MA: Addison-Wesley.

Blake, R. R., & Mouton, J. S. (1985). *The managerial grid III: The key to leadership excellence.* Houston, TX: Gulf.

Bolman, L., & Deal, T. (1991). *Reframing organizations.* San Francisco, CA: Jossey-Bass.

Bolster, C. J., & Larrere, J. B. (2012). The next great explorers. *Trustee, 65*(2), 19–21.

Bowen, D. (2018). Leading the way to organizational resilience. *Healthcare Executive, 33*(1), 8–9.

Buchbinder, S., & Shanks, N. (2012). *Introduction to health care management* (2nd ed.). Burlington, MA: Jones & Bartlett Learning.

Caldararo, K., & Nash, D., (2017). Population health research: Early description of the organizational shift toward population health management and defining a vision for leadership. *Population Health Management, 20*(5), 368–373.

Chatfield, J., Byrd, H., Longenecker, C., Fink, L., & Gold, J. (2017). Ten CEO imperatives for healthcare transformation: Lessons from top-performing academic medical centers. *Journal of Healthcare Management, 62*(6), 371–383.

Cosgrove, D., Fisher, M., Gabow, P., Gottlieb, G., Halvorson, G., James, B., ... Toussaint, J. (2012, June 5). A CEO checklist for high-value health care. *Institute of Medicine of the National Academies.* Retrieved July 19, 2012 from www.iom.edu/CEOChecklist

Gabow, P., Halvorson, G., & Kaplan, G. (2012, June 5). Marshaling leadership for high-value health care: An institute of medicine discussion paper. *Journal of the American Medical Association.* Retrieved from http://jama.jamanetwork.com/article.aspx?articleid=1172505

Japsen, B. (2012, June 22). *Health leaders look to 2032 for opportunities to improve the health of the nation.* Robert Wood Johnson Foundation. Retrieved from www.rwjf.org/pr/product .jsp?id=74533

Josephson, M. S. (2002). *Making ethical decisions* (2nd ed.). Los Angeles, CA: Josephson Institute of Ethics.

Kaissi, A. (2017). How to be a "humbitious" leader. *Healthcare Executive, 32*(6), 54.

Katz, R. L. (1955). Skills of an effective administrator. *Harvard Business Review, 33*(1), 33–42.

Kolb, D. A. (1999). *Learning style inventory.* Boston, MA: McBer and Company.

Manion, J. (2011). *From management to leadership: Strategies for transforming health care* (3rd ed.). San Francisco, CA: Jossey-Bass.

McDonough, J. E. (2012, July 5). The road ahead for the Affordable Care Act. *New England Journal of Medicine.* Retrieved from www.nejm.org/doi/full/10.1056/NEJMp1206845

McLaughlin, D. B. (2011). *Responding to healthcare reform: A strategy guide for healthcare leaders.* Chicago, IL: Health Administration Press.

Northouse, P. (2019). *Leadership: Theory and practice* (8th ed.). Thousand Oaks, CA: Sage Publishing.

Osland, J. S., Kolb, D. A., Rubin, I. M., & Turner, M. E. (2007). *Organizational behavior: An experiential approach* (8th ed.). Upper Saddle River, NJ: Pearson Prentice Hall.

Perlo, J., & Feeley, D. (2018). Why focusing on professional burnout is not enough. *Journal of Healthcare Management, 63*(2), 85–89.

Reinertsen, J. L., Bisognano, M., & Pugh, M. D. (2008). *Seven leadership leverage points for organization-level improvement in health care* (2nd ed.). Cambridge, MA: Institute for Healthcare Improvement.

Rousseau, D. M. (1995). *Psychological contracts in organizations: Understanding written and unwritten agreements.* Newbury Park, CA: Sage.

Rubino, L. (2012). Leadership. In S. Buchbinder & N. Shanks (Eds.), *Introduction to health care management* (2nd ed.). Burlington, MA: Jones & Bartlett Learning.

Senge, P. M. (1990). *The fifth discipline: The art and practice of the learning organization.* New York, NY: Doubleday Currency.

Sherwood, J. J., & Glidewell, J. C. (1972). Planned negotiation: A norm-setting OD intervention. In W. W. Burke (Ed.), *Contemporary organization development: Orientations and interventions* (pp. 35–46). Washington, DC: NTL Institute.

Wachter, R. M. (2012). Why the Supreme Court's decision means a lot… and not so much. *The Governance Institute's E-Briefings, 9*(4), 1–2.

Walker, L., Fineran, C., & Giella, T. (2018). Succession planning: An investment in leadership continuity and success. *Trustee, 71*(1), 23–25.

Wolf, J.A. (2017). Patient experience: The new heart of healthcare leadership. *Frontiers of Health Services Management, 33*(3), 3–16.

CHAPTER 2

Developing Healthcare Leaders

Brenda Freshman and Brian O. Underhill

LEARNING OBJECTIVES

By the end of this chapter, the student will be able to:

- Explain the importance of leadership development in health care.
- Discuss key components of a talent management system.
- Identify competencies critical to leadership success.
- Describe two distinct paths to healthcare leadership positions (clinical and administrative).
- Describe models and development methods used for training healthcare leaders.

KEY TERMS

360-degree evaluation	Leadership pipeline
Accountable Care Organization (ACO)	Shadowing
Bench strength	Stretch assignment
Executive coaching	Succession planning
High potentials	Talent management

▶ Introduction

Healthcare organizations today are facing unprecedented challenges. The rapid evolution of technology; the constant changes in regulations, policies, and laws; and the shifting demographics of the workforce and patients place ever-greater pressures on healthcare leaders to excel. However, there is a notable shortage of outstanding leaders who are qualified to meet and address these challenges. And the healthcare industry is not alone in this dilemma, which is exacerbated by increasing rates of retirement among Baby Boomers and earlier generations. Organizations across industries would benefit from a strategically aligned performance management approach to talent development. In the words of Jennie Sobecki, co-owner of Focused Results, "Talent management puts teeth into a succession plan" (Seitz, 2017).

▶ Development of Business Leaders

The lack of effective leaders with the necessary skills and expertise has become one of the greatest business perils in these early decades of the 21st century. Approximately 70% of the 62 companies surveyed in 2005 reported moderate-to-major leadership shortages (Executive Development Associates, 2005). A prominent study entitled "The War for Talent" (Michaels, Handfield-Jones, & Axelrod, 2001) discovered that the highest-performing companies in a breadth of industries had better **talent management** strategies (i.e., methods to identify, train, and develop leaders) than lower-performing organizations. A disturbing statistic from this report is that "while 72% of all managers surveyed say that winning the war for talent is critical to their company's success, only 9% are confident that their current actions will lead to a stronger talent pool" (p. 3).

▶ Identifying a Gap between Espoused Vision and Strategic Action

In another major study, "Increasing **bench strength**" and "Accelerating development of high-potentials" were listed as the #1 and #2 top workforce development priorities, respectively (Executive Development Associates, 2009). "Increasing bench strength" is a term commonly used in organizations today to refer to the growth of new leaders who can provide backup and eventually replace the current leaders in charge. A company is said to have a "deep bench" if several other leaders within the organization are considered fully capable of assuming the positions of key leaders who vacate their posts. To provide an example, when General Electric's iconic CEO Jack Welch retired, the company had already groomed at least three internal leaders who could immediately take over the reins.

A common way to increase bench strength is to focus on the development of **high potentials**. Often called "HiPos," these are individuals who have been identified as possessing above-average potential (and interest) to take on greater and greater levels of responsibility. Some organizations begin identifying these employees at entry-level positions. After these employees are identified, organizations focus additional development efforts on them early in their careers, giving them **stretch assignments**, coaching and mentoring, and even sending them to graduate school.

▶ Leadership Development in Health Care

A leadership drought is exacerbated in health care under negative economic conditions, changes in government oversight (McAlearney, 2006), and fluctuations in health policy on national and state levels. Furthermore, many healthcare organizations (HCOs) are nonprofit operations and face constant budget pressures. These HCO structures often include professional staff, such as doctors, who are not directly under the authority of the parent company, but instead are contracted from outside organizations. The absence of direct authority increases the challenges for leaders and managers seeking to promote staff development while controlling expenditures and costs.

Compared to other business sectors, the healthcare industry has historically been slow to respond to changing trends (Beinecke, Daniels, Peters, & Silvestri, 2009; McAlearney, 2006). McAlearney (2010) sent surveys to 355 U.S. healthcare executives in July 2007 and collected 104 responses (29% of the sample). Survey results indicated that about half (53) of the respondents' healthcare systems reported having a formal leadership development program in place. The organizations which had developed these programs were driven by their dissatisfaction with the level of preparation of executives promoted to positions of senior leadership. The Mayo Clinic, for example, has been very purposeful about its focus on developing leaders. Priscilla Gill, Director of Workforce Learning at the Mayo Clinic, says, "With the rapid pace of change our industry has experienced over the past several years, we have been very intentional and focused on our investment in talent to ensure we have leadership capability to both manage change and accelerate actions to anticipate and prepare for the future" (P. Gill, personal communication, February 4, 2018).

Charan, Drotter, and Noel (2011) suggest addressing these challenges by developing "a framework shared by all leaders to ensure consistency of judgment and application on the human side of the business so that a cumulative leadership effect results" (p. xvi). These authors propose a structure to codify this framework, which they label the **leadership pipeline**.

This chapter uses the leadership pipeline framework to describe how leaders are selected and groomed within a healthcare organization. First, we will cover guiding principles for building bench strength—the critical components of a talent management system. Second, we will present two professional career paths for healthcare leaders. Third, we will describe competencies and methods used in training and development. The chapter concludes with a sample case study on how coaching can be conducted in a healthcare organization.

▶ Guiding Principles for Developing Leaders

Conger and Fulmer (2003) suggest five guiding principles of best practice for building an organizational leadership pipeline:

1. Actively focus on developing talent
2. Identify key assignments and positions that move talent through the pipeline
3. Maintain transparency
4. Implement assessment on a regular basis
5. Engage in continuous improvement

These five principles will be discussed with a focus on their applications in healthcare settings.

#1: A Development Focus

A focus on developing management talent involves integrating traditional activities such as workshops and seminars closely and directly with an individual's assigned roles and responsibilities. "On-the-job" learning and practice should be promoted and linked to any formal training that is offered. A common missed development opportunity occurs when an employee attends a class session to learn a new management skill but then has no opportunity to apply and practice the new skill in the workplace. The valuable time and cost of the training can be wasted. Monitoring employees for implementation of new skills and demonstration of learned behaviors as they work can show that training has been successful.

Take the case of Jaclyn Smith, a nurse practitioner working at a community clinic. She has demonstrated excellent clinical skills and knowledge, strong interpersonal and communications skills, and is a proactive problem-solver. The clinic director has identified her as a potential leader who might fill his position in the future. However, to be effective in this new arena, Ms. Smith would need to learn additional management skills and develop a systems perspective rather than a one-on-one approach. To achieve this goal, the clinic director decides to send Jaclyn to a strategic planning training session that one of his old college classmates is facilitating. The director believes that he will be rewarding Jaclyn with an educational perk as well as supporting this friend's seminar series. He assumes Ms. Smith will be grateful for the opportunity to learn new skills at the clinic's time and expense.

Unfortunately, the outcome is just the opposite. Jaclyn's current responsibilities do not involve strategic planning, so the seminar content seems unrelated and irrelevant to her duties and responsibilities. In fact, she experiences the training as a distraction from her enjoyable "real work" of patient care and becomes stressed because her day away from the clinic has left her with a pileup of tasks and paperwork. She also worries that her patients will be disappointed that their appointments will be rescheduled and that her overburdened colleagues will need to cover her patient care duties.

The clinic director had not planned strategically for the necessary training to promote Jaclyn's leadership skills, nor had he done the necessary preparation to give her the background to fully understand the relevance of the training to her professional development. As a result, the training decreased Jaclyn's morale and undermined her confidence in the director as an effective leader.

Jaclyn's story is an example of what not to do with respect to employee development.

Supervisors commonly make a variety of mistakes in talent management. Exploring the next principle suggested by Conger and Fulmer (2003), "key assignments," provides positive examples of how to effectively develop leadership talent.

#2: Identify Key Assignments and Positions That Move Talent through the Pipeline (On-the-Job Training)

To avoid unproductive employee development efforts, a wise leader can incorporate best practices such as those proposed by Garman and Dye (2009). They suggest that an individual's ability to learn in the workplace is positively influenced by the following conditions: (1) awareness of learning needs, (2) characteristics of work assignments, and (3) attitudes about learning. In Jaclyn's case, these conditions had not been effectively addressed. Garman and Dye describe the awareness of one's learning needs as a continuum, moving through a series of four phases:

- A complete lack of awareness of need to learn (unconscious development need)
- Understanding and identifying specifics for knowledge or skills that can be addressed with a learning plan (conscious development need)
- Thoughtful practice and application of a new skill, improving performance (conscious proficiency)
- Skill mastery, wherein the skill has become a natural, effective, and consistent behavior across a variety of circumstances (unconscious proficiency)

In the aforementioned example, the clinic director's plan for Jaclyn fell short in Phase 1. Jaclyn did not have awareness of the "need" to learn strategic planning. If the director had discussed her potential career path within the organization and shared his vision for her future development in advance of the seminar, Jaclyn may have had a greater awareness of the need for this training and been better able to appreciate the learning opportunity. Additionally, such a preliminary meeting and discussion would have allowed her to express her professional goals and ambitions to the director, so that they could have created a professional development plan for Jaclyn together. The director's plan also neglected to implement Phase 3, "practice." After taking the seminar, Jaclyn was not given specific on-the-job assignments to use the new skills. Without the aforementioned steps to promote effective learning, Jaclyn understandably perceived the seminar as a waste of her time.

Garman and Dye (2009) attest that characteristics of a job assignment can impact the level of engagement and professional growth of an employee. These authors cite the work of McCauley and Brutus (1998), which lists the following four types of experiences that facilitate on-the-job learning:

1. Assignment of new roles and responsibilities
2. Implementation of necessary changes
3. Granting of expanded responsibility
4. Learning from new and diverse experiences and from success and failure

Giving an employee new duties that embody one or more of these four characteristics is termed a "stretch" assignment. Organizations facilitate leadership development by tasking trainees to perform duties that will challenge, motivate, and enhance their leadership abilities. For example, such stretch assignments are a component of leadership development programs at Gundersen Lutheran Health System in La Crosse, Wisconsin. Gundersen Health is an integrated healthcare delivery system composed of a medical center with 325 beds, 41 affiliated clinics and offices, and a multispecialty medical clinic. Gundersen's successful talent management program consists of five steps (Noelke, 2009):

1. Define leadership competency.
2. Identify high-potential talent.
3. Assess talent.
4. Develop individual plans.
5. Track progress.

In this model, tasking trainees with stretch assignments corresponds with Step 4, developing individual plans. Nancy Noelke, leadership coach at Gundersen, assesses the identified high-potential talent, Step 2, by compiling and analyzing employee evaluations into a summary of strengths and weaknesses. In Step 5, she collaborates with a designated review team to develop strategic interventions that will "close the gap between where the candidates are and where they would like to be from a leadership standpoint" (2009, p. 36). These strategies are then discussed with the candidates' supervisors and fine-tuned as needed. The resulting development plan will focus on meeting the needs of the organization as well as motivating the candidate to learn and grow, and will include stretch assignments and other growth activities such as coaching, mentoring, committee participation, role expansion, cross-functional duties, and job rotation.

This multistep approach to leadership development is widely used and has been shown to increase successful outcomes. Miller, Umble, Frederick, and Dinkin (2007) evaluated a multimethod program aimed at developing leaders in the public health sector. Their study compared the self-reported effectiveness of a variety of interventions such as assessment tools and coaching, learning projects, skill-building seminars, textbooks and reading, and distance-learning conference calls. Then, 6 months after graduating from the program, participants were asked to rate the utility of each of the training methods. The "learning project" received the highest rating, and the "assessment tools and coaching" garnered the top scores. The learning project required participants to tackle a community health challenge or address a public health infrastructure issue. Project components included an assessment of the problem and development of a problem statement and action plan. The assessment tools administered to the public health leaders were the Myers-Briggs Type Indicator (MBTI), Change Style Indicator (Discovery Learning, Inc. in Greensboro, NC), and a 360 (multi-rater) feedback survey. The 360 survey and in-depth personal coaching were facilitated by the Center for Creative Leadership (Greensboro, NC). The results were not surprising: The more specific and focused the learning methodology, the more likely the learner will find value in the activity and succeed in achieving the desired skills and outcomes.

#3: Transparency

Traditionally, succession plans had been developed behind a veil of secrecy. However, Conger and Fulmer's (2003) research on best practices in leadership development showed that transparent talent management systems produce the best results.

Two critical components of transparency are clarity of process and ease of use. The clarity of the process involves employees' ability to assess their own potential for advancement as well as managers' ability to identify a list of potential candidates for the leadership positions. However, the optimum level of information provided to an employee might vary based on operational considerations. For example, at a base level, employees simply know that they have been identified as having a high potential. A higher level of transparency would allow an employee to see exactly where he or she stands in a rank order when compared to others in the company. Whereas in some cases this knowledge could be motivating, in other cases knowing one's ranking among colleagues could have a negative impact on morale and instigate unproductive internal competition.

Another aspect of transparency, from an employee's perspective, is the availability of clear and precise information about how one can progress through the system, what potential professional opportunities can promote advancement, and what skills or expertise are needed to grow as a leader. To implement a transparent talent management system, managers should be able to obtain customizable searches of available opportunities and match them with each employee's past experience, current skill level, ability gaps, and development plans.

Therefore, to support transparency for "high potentials" as well as managers, a system that is easy to access and navigate is critical. The best practice companies in the Conger and Fulmer study (2003) make judicious use of the Internet to provide a user-friendly interface for their talent management systems. They cite Lilly's "1-click model," a web-based application tool on the desktop of employee's computers. With one click, employees can obtain access to information about their personal skills and explore potential compatible job opportunities.

Research studies indicate that a lack of information regarding one's task and responsibilities can inhibit learning (Kyndt, Dochy, Struyven, & Cascallar, 2011) and that role ambiguity and role conflict inhibit on-the-job learning effectiveness (Lin, 2010). Therefore, having a transparent talent management system with the necessary components can promote successful employee development and advancement and prevent unfortunate and demotivating experiences such as the one that Jaclyn and her manager shared.

#4: Assessment of Quantity and Quality of the Pipeline on a Regular Basis

Transparency also requires the presence of a system that can monitor the population and strength of the leadership pipeline and succession plan on an ongoing basis at consistent intervals and in real time; this is a key component of best practices for healthcare organizations (Conger & Fulmer, 2003). For example, succession plan measurements should reveal how many qualified candidates are in the pipeline for each leadership position at any point in time. Automatic triggers should be in place that notify the HR department when the ratio of potentials to incumbents dips below a minimum threshold. Each management position should have an explicit ratio of internal employees that could be ready to step into that position in case of a vacancy. For example, a 2:1 ratio for a mid-level management position would mean that for every incumbent currently in that position, two internal employees should be capable of serving as replacements if needed.

In addition to tracking the number of individuals in the pipeline, other valuable metrics can be used to assess the quality and effectiveness of a talent management system. These include:

- The time taken to fill vacant positions
- Demographic diversity of high potentials
- Satisfaction of coworkers regarding performance of internal hires
- Self-reported satisfaction by promoted employees at 3 and 6 months on the job
- Measures that assess the employee's performance of newly assigned duties
- Employee turnover and high-potential retention rates
- Ratio of internal versus external hires (see further discussion on this issue later in this chapter)

Using technology to quickly and easily access data can promote the success of a talent management system and allows programs to be designed and administered with accuracy, transparency, and flexibility. Ongoing assessment can monitor the effectiveness of the program, suggest revisions for continuous improvement, and encourage flexibility and favorable adaptation in a changing healthcare environment.

#5: Continual Improvement—Flexibility to Adapt to Improve the Strength of the Pipeline

Conger and Fulmer's (2003) best practices underscore that talent management systems can be effective only if they are used, trusted, and flexible. A sociotechnical system, such as a leadership pipeline, must be responsive to forces of constant and rapid change in order to maintain its relevance. Elasticity to adjust to internal pressures for continuous quality improvement (CQI), as well as to external forces such as economic conditions or regulatory changes, allows the effective implementation of the preceding principles.

The focus on talent can be manifested by aligning development opportunities with an individual's needs and career trajectory, as well as with organizational goals. Organizational goals are driven by CQI efforts, personnel changes, and strategic planning to address impending growth or recession. An effective pipeline must adjust accordingly as different competencies become prominent and necessary.

The field of information technology (IT) is a good example of a former support function that has become an integral part of an organization's foundational structure. Health IT is now a critical element in the internal coordination and provision of care among clinician colleagues and administrators (e.g., via practice management systems and electronic health records) as well as across entities such as **Accountable Care Organizations (ACOs)**. The result is an increased need for skilled IT workers, knowledgeable and effective IT managers, and senior leaders with vision who can guide strategic planning and decision-making regarding health IT Leaders and managers will need to stay abreast of emerging health service technologies such as radio frequency identification (RFID), global positioning systems (GPS), and nanotechnology to make informed decisions about capital investments and future service lines (McGrady, Conger, Blanke, Landry, & Zalucki, 2010).

IT also plays an integral role in the internal operations of healthcare organizations as well as for the provision of services and education. Multifunctional, easy-to-use, and secure information systems can manage not only leadership pipelines but also other Human Resource (HR) functions. The new role of IT has mandated adjustments in talent management focus. Key development assignments and job positions must adapt to this new environment; some former assignments will become obsolete and new roles and responsibilities will emerge, requiring different skills and revised training and assessment initiatives. These shifts will aid the organization in responding to the rapid pace of change, successfully guiding strategic planning, staff, and leadership development in effective directions.

▶ Leadership Pathways

Healthcare leaders can move into their positions from a variety of disciplines, including medicine, nursing, business, health administration, and public health. For example, the American College of Healthcare Executives (ACHE, 2018B) reported a membership of over 48,000 in January 2017. The 2017 ACHE demographic profile of Members and Fellows showed that 54% of membership held their highest degree in hospital/health administration services, 22% in business, and 14% in clinical/allied health administration. Approximately 24% of ACHE members either earned a doctorate or two master's degrees, 60% had one master's degree, and 15% had education up to a bachelor's degree.

There are typically two distinct paths through which healthcare leaders can begin their careers: as clinicians trained in a healthcare delivery discipline, and as nonclinicians trained in management or another administrative discipline such as finance, marketing, economics, or IT. Leaders on the first path start off in health care as clinically trained direct service providers (e.g., doctors, nurses, radiologic technologists) and are promoted up the organizational hierarchy into roles with increasing leadership responsibility. The second route is traveled by individuals who begin their careers in an administrative or support area (e.g., accounting, management, law, HR, marketing, or IT) and receive promotions in their original discipline and cross-training in relevant and related fields.

Each pathway to the executive suite provides healthcare leaders with strong skills, but also with potential gaps in expertise and blind spots in perspective. Leaders who emerge from a clinical background are usually adept at understanding patient and clinician needs, but may lack business knowledge in the areas of finance, marketing, operations, systems thinking, collaboration, and management. Leaders who emerge from a business discipline, such as finance, administration, marketing, or operations, often lack the perceptual framework to understand the needs, values, and expectations of clinicians and patients. If we accept the premise that a good leader needs to be able to relate to and engage the attention, loyalty, and motivation of a wide range of followers, a leader in health care must be able to view any given situation from multiple perspectives and listen to and understand the various stakeholders who can provide valuable input with respect to specific issues (Freshman, 2010). Leaders must actively "learn on the job" to fill in the gaps in their training and expertise; for example, clinicians may take courses in business and management, and administrative specialists may rely on mentors, professional allies, and champions in relevant fields as well as immersion in industry professional groups to gain information and knowledge.

The following stories of "Sam Kapur" (clinician) and "Lily Rodriquez" (administrator) provide examples of each path to successful healthcare leadership.

▶ Clinical Path to Leadership

Sam Kapur

Sam Kapur was trained as a family physician in St. Louis, Missouri. At the age of 32, he and his family moved to Massachusetts so that he could accept a primary care position with a large medical group practice in Boston. Dr. Kapur displayed an excellent bedside manner and developed good rapport with his practice's patients. Through referrals, his roster of patients grew rather quickly. Sam consistently demonstrated that he was an active learner; the medical group leadership noted he was proactive in making changes and adopting technology that enhanced the practice's productivity and increased quality of care. The CEO of the group took notice of Sam's outstanding performance and invited him to sit in on key meetings in which important decisions would be made. After 2 years of working in the medical group, Dr. Kapur was asked to join the CQI team, through which he continued to display excellent performance. Dr. Kapur realized that CQI was one of his professional strengths. Therefore, he requested, and was granted, tuition support to attend additional training in this arena. This training allowed him to become a CQI team leader, in addition to his clinical duties.

Dr. Kapur also embraced a high-visibility role as an educator and networker, building his reputation in the local community by attending and speaking at professional association events. The medical group's executives saw him as a "high potential" employee and continued to nurture his professional development with stretch assignments. In time, the HR director offered him the opportunity to get a Master's in Healthcare Administration (MHA) degree to expand his administrative competencies and refine his management and leadership skills. After Dr. Kapur had been working with the medical group for a little more than 8 years, the Chief Medical Executive retired, and Dr. Kapur was offered and accepted the position. With excellent preparation, Dr. Kapur brought a strong skillset to this position and successfully continued to promote high morale and increase quality and profitability for the practice.

▶ Administrative Path to Leadership

Lily Rodriquez

Shortly after graduating with a bachelor's degree in health services, Lily Rodriquez began her career as a receptionist and file clerk at an outpatient surgery center. This facility was part of larger health system that included two hospitals, several medical offices, and two other outpatient surgery centers in Los Angeles County. Ms. Rodriquez was noted for being outgoing, organized, and having a good rapport with the office staff and the center's clients. The office manager appreciated her work ethic and "people skills" and began to enlist Ms. Rodriquez' assistance on various HR projects. As a quick learner and hard worker, Ms. Rodriquez was promoted to assistant office manager and coordinated compensation and benefits administration for several years. The office manager identified Ms. Rodriquez as a high-potential employee and suggested she take advantage of the organization's tuition reimbursement program to obtain a master's degree in HR management. During her graduate studies, Ms. Rodriquez volunteered to intern in the health system's HR department to further develop her skills and expand her professional network. Shortly after graduation, she accepted a position in the system's HR department as a compensation and benefits specialist.

The office manager was sad to have her high-potential employee leave the surgery center, but was very proud of Lily and pleased to see her professionally advance and succeed. Lily herself was grateful to her mentor and continued to stay in touch and provide professional support when needed.

The system's HR director also identified Ms. Rodriquez as a high-potential employee, and, over the next few years, provided her with stretch assignments and cross-training in other HR areas such as recruitment and leadership development and training. Subsequently, she was promoted to vice president (VP) of Organization Development, developed and enhanced new initiatives, and challenged herself and her staff with stretch assignments. Supported by her supervisor, she received and provided formal and informal coaching and mentoring, attended professional seminars and conferences, and lectured to others within and beyond the organization on a regular basis. When the HR director retired, Lily Rodriquez was offered the position. Confident and well prepared, she accepted the senior leadership post.

FIGURE 2.1 illustrates examples of a leadership pipeline and key assignments for both clinical and administrative pathways.

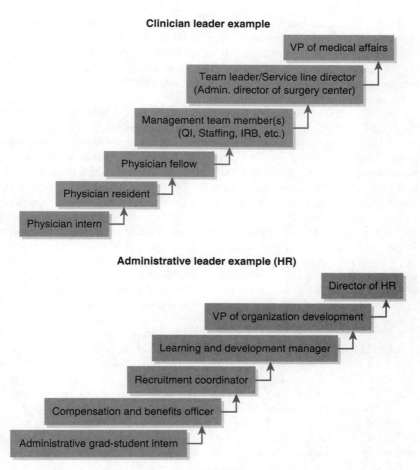

FIGURE 2.1 Clinician and Administrative Leader Pipeline Example

Filling and Maintaining the Leadership Pipeline

An organization's HR department performs many key functions involved in developing and maintaining a leadership pipeline. Data management, performance evaluations, and **succession planning** are all critical components of a talent management system and are typically handled by HR. Optimally, the HR department of an organization will track each employee's work history, performance appraisals, skills strengths, weaknesses, and development plans, and provide critical input to the managers utilizing the pipeline.

Performance appraisals play a critical role in helping to identify high-potential employees, and track their progress and professional development. Many performance evaluations are designed and administered by HR. An employee and his or her supervisor will fill out an annual performance assessment, which will be collected and stored by HR. Broader assessments are also common, wherein other stakeholders such as peers, direct reports, patients, and vendors are asked to rate and comment on an individual employee's performance. The term, "360," as in 360 degrees, is used to describe the collection of feedback from multiple sources regarding an employee's performance and can provide insight to employees as to how others perceive their skills and function in the professional setting. These **360-degree evaluations** are most successful when used in a nonjudgmental fashion by coaches and employees to identify areas of strength and opportunities for improvement. The 360 process and its role in staff development and mentoring are described in more detail in the case study at the end of this chapter.

HR departments can use the collected evaluation data to help managers project the numbers and levels of potential leaders needed in a pipeline. Executives must also decide on whether specific positions can be filled by current employees of an organization (internal strategy) or by recruitment of qualified candidates from outside the organization (external strategy). Each option has its benefits and drawbacks, and both are used in healthcare organizations. The talent management system (leadership pipeline) is an internal structure and process for developing and nurturing leaders within an organization. Kathy Klock, VP of Operations and Human Resources at Gundersen Lutheran Health System, explains the value of an internal development strategy: "It ensures continuity, sends a positive message throughout the organization and provides better odds of a good cultural fit" (Noelke, 2009, p. 35). Increased motivation, higher morale, and improved retention rates are also potential benefits of internal recruitment. However, there are a few potential disadvantages associated with exclusively looking inside the organization for new talent. Internal competition could instigate resentment among those not chosen for advancement, and morale could suffer. Concerns about the influence of office politics, favoritism, and discrimination could undermine morale and productivity, and opportunities to bring fresh perspectives into an organization may be lost. These potential drawbacks to exclusive internal recruitment could damage employee relations and negatively impact quality of care.

Therefore, leadership candidates are also sought from outside the enterprise. External strategies to locate qualified applicants to fill open positions (recruitment) include advertisements in trade journals, job fairs, online job postings, social media, and employee referrals. The search for external talent can also be outsourced to employment agencies and executive search firms. The benefits of external recruitment are an increased potential for fresh perspective/new ideas, reduced training expenses if a new hire comes on board with needed expertise, and fewer risks of dysfunctional and/or politically charged associations within the organization. Disadvantages of external recruitment, however, can include hiring an individual who might not fit with organizational culture. Morale might also decrease among those within the organization who were passed over for the position. Furthermore, orientation training will be needed for new hires, as well as time for them to socialize and adjust. Ultimately, an organization's leaders and HR decision makers will weigh the risks and benefits of internal versus external recruitment, and determine when external recruitment is needed. The more accurate and comprehensive their talent management system, the more informed their decision will be.

▶ Leadership Competencies

What knowledge, skills, and behaviors do "high potentials" need to demonstrate and/or learn to be effective leaders in health care? These skillsets have been well documented thanks to professional associations such as the National Center for Healthcare Leadership (NCHL, 2012), the Healthcare Leadership Alliance (HLA, 2010), and the American College of Healthcare Executives (2018A), which have conducted collaborative research across the industry to develop competency models on which to base evaluation and training. Because the healthcare industry is constantly changing, these organizations continually review and update their models to adapt accordingly. **FIGURE 2.2** depicts the NCHL's version 2.1, which is composed of 3 domains and 26 competencies.

This summary version of the model provides background on the behavioral and technical competencies identified by the research. The full model contains levels for each competency that distinguish outstanding leadership at each career stage (entry-, mid-, and advanced-level) and by the disciplines of administration, nursing, and medicine (National Center for Healthcare Leadership, 2005–2010).

Health management researchers Garman and Dye (2009) reviewed seven distinct competency models developed specifically for application to the healthcare industry. These models range in complexity and scope from the Healthcare Leadership Alliance model, which identifies 300 competencies in five clusters, to Dye and Garman's (2006) "Exceptional Leadership Competency Model," which lists 16 competencies across four clusters (cornerstones). Practitioners working in the field might find a concise model more applicable for their training purposes, whereas researchers and academic institutions might prefer to use a more complex model

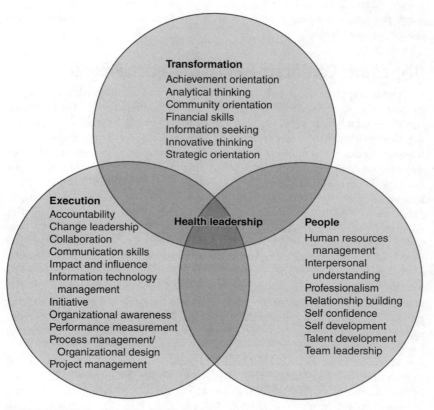

FIGURE 2.2 NCHL Health Leadership Competency Model™ Reprinted with Permission from the National Center for Health Leadership (www.nchl.org), Chicago, IL

that lists a greater number of specific competencies. When selecting a model, the form should fit the function. An organization could also develop its own model for talent management, adding in specific components related to its mission, goals, and demographics. Regardless of the version chosen, the strategic use of a vetted competency model can provide evidence-based direction for recruiting, training, development, and promotion in a healthcare environment.

▶ Development Methods

Leadership skills can be nurtured and honed in a variety of ways: through degree and certificate programs, seminars, on-the-job training, mentoring, modeling, **shadowing**, and coaching. These approaches can be included in an employee's development plan and tracked through a well-designed talent management system. Many organizations will offer tuition reimbursement as a benefit to employees seeking to enhance their professional development. This perk pays off for both the organization and the employee; studies indicate that employees who are offered the opportunity to grow and learn are more satisfied with their work environments and are less likely to leave the facility for a position elsewhere (Campbell, 2001; Nelson, Sassaman, & Phillips, 2008). The organization benefits as well by supporting its rising stars and preparing those individuals to take over for retiring personnel (succession planning).

Degree and Certificate Formal Education Programs

Undergraduate programs in healthcare management and administration can prepare baccalaureate students for entry-level positions in health care. Current healthcare workforce members can also enroll in a university to obtain a bachelor's or master's degree to further their career aspirations. Baccalaureate level programs offer training in the basics of management and leadership, develop skillsets and competencies, and provide students with guidance about potential career paths in the healthcare industry. There are hundreds of schools advertising undergraduate healthcare management degree programs; however, according to the Association of University Programs in Health Administration (AUPHA), only 45 are currently certified by AUPHA (2018). AUPHA certification is a quality assessment similar to an accreditation. Its review committees are composed of program directors and faculty members from undergraduate health administration programs who are familiar with curriculum development, program management, and evaluation. Students completing a bachelor's degree program may not yet be prepared for leadership positions, but do graduate with an understanding of the healthcare industry, and with skillsets that provide a solid foundation for further training and career-building. For upper management positions, several years of field experience in increasingly more responsible roles is typically required.

A master's degree in healthcare management can be the next step needed to move up the career ladder to greater responsibility for professionals already in the healthcare workforce. The Commission on Accreditation of Healthcare Management Education reports 99 accredited master's level programs at 76 colleges or universities in 2017 (CAHME, 2018). Although there are many unaccredited programs in health management and related disciplines, the designation of accreditation indicates that a program has participated in a quality review and formal evaluation of adherence to high standards. Accredited programs are required to engage in continual improvement through self-studies as well as formal reviews by the Commission.

Executive Education Formats

Formal educational institutions such as colleges and universities have embraced the market opportunity to train and retrain working adults. Programs available to suit the executive or the full-time employed are offered by many educational institutions in onsite, hybrid, and online formats. Campus courses are often offered at night or on the weekends to accommodate students with full-time jobs. Several years of work experience in the healthcare industry or related fields are often a prerequisite for these programs; experienced students will bring to the classroom a higher level of knowledge and skills and a greater understanding of healthcare management issues and allow the program to provide a correspondingly increased level of student engagement through discussions, interactions, and networking with seasoned peers.

Seminars, Webinars, and Conferences

Seminars, webinars, and conference retreats can also provide formal training on specific topics and broader industry challenges. Delivery formats include week-long retreats in resort locations, 2–3-hour workshops in a conference facility, or online via webinars. Healthcare professional associations frequently offer seminars, conferences, and webinars on current trends and industry challenges. Training is readily available on topics such as general management skills, including conflict resolution, employee motivation, strategic planning, and time management.

However, these stand-alone outsourced training opportunities offer many benefits as well as a few drawbacks. Many of these programs are led by external subject-matter experts who can bring fresh, up-to-date perspectives and provide greater understanding of current issues and concerns. In a setting away from their daily workplace, attendees might feel more comfortable asking questions and seeking further knowledge, allowing for a deeper "stretch" in the learning activity. Additionally, by bringing together participants from many organizations, these gatherings provide excellent networking opportunities.

However, a drawback of these stand-alone trainings is that they are often "one-shot" experiences. If the skillsets learned are not used on the job, employees may not effectively institutionalize new behaviors and approaches. Another drawback is that the vendor controls the precise content and scheduling of the training; employees will need to attend when sessions are available, not when it is most convenient for them and their organization. To promote maximum effectiveness when external training seminars are recommended as part of an employee's development plan, it is critical that managers and employees have a clear understanding of what the learning objectives are, and how they relate to an individual's current and future work.

TABLE 2.1 provides examples of healthcare professional organizations' training programs.

TABLE 2.1 Healthcare Professional Organization Seminars, Webinars, and Conferences

Name of Organization	Organization Website	Examples of Training Programs Provided
American College of Health Executives	www.ache.org	1. Executive Workshop 2. Strategic Planning That Works: Integrating Strategy with Performance 3. Superior Productivity in Healthcare Organizations
American Association for Physician Leadership	www.physicianleaders.org/	1. Financial Decision Making 2. Science of High Reliability 3. Physician in Management
American Health Information Management Association	www.ahima.org	1. Interventional Cardiovascular Coding
American Society for Healthcare Human Resources Association	www.ashhra.org	1. ASHHRA Wellness Webinar: Use Stress to Your Advantage 2. The Chapter Leadership Workshop
America's Health Insurance Plans	www.ahip.org	1. D109: ICD-10 and Administrative Simplification—Exploring the Dual Impact 2. Enabling Consumerism Through People, Process, and Technology: Best Practices for Healthcare Payers 3. Effective Strategies to Promote Influenza Vaccine Uptake Among Culturally Diverse Populations
Healthcare Financial Management Association	www.hfma.org	1. Constructing Financial Forecasting Models: Modeling for Reform 2. Creating an ICD-10 Transition Plan on the Fast Track 3. Show Me Chapter Medicare Workshops

Health Care Executives of Southern California	http://hce-socal .org	1. Managing Conflict—Avoiding the Pitfalls of Control 2. A Medicare and Medicaid Update
Medical Group Management Association	www.mgma.com	1. Mastering Business Operations and Staffing in Your Medical Practice 2. Train Your Office for Success: Mastering Patient Flow 3. Administrators in Transition: Skills for Administrators During and After Integration
National Association of Health Services Executives	www.nahse.org	1. Board Meeting 2. Educational Meeting 3. Membership Meeting
Southern California Association for Healthcare Risk Management	www.scahrm.org	1. Ostensible Agency: Tag, You're It! 2. The Circle of Innovation
Women in Health Administration of Southern California	http://whasocal .org	1. A.D.D.R.E.S.S.I.N.G. Diversity 2. Early Careerist Panel 3. Accountable Care Organizations

On-the-Job Leadership Training

As mentioned earlier in this chapter, stretch assignments can provide excellent professional development opportunities. These should be on-the-job assignments that are just beyond an employee's current level of confidence in the specific area and include the four types of experiences valuable to facilitating learning (McCauley & Brutus, 1998):

1. New roles and responsibilities
2. Implementing needed change
3. Expanded responsibility
4. Learning from failure
5. Learning from diversity

Upper-level managers should also seek out occasions in which high potentials (HiPos) can exercise skills identified in their personal development plan. Before assigning a stretch goal or task, as part of an individual development plan, the manager and HiPo should review and discuss the HiPo's current and future goals, the benefits the new assignment can offer, and the manager's expectations for achievement. Optimally, all of these elements should be in alignment with the HiPo's individual goals as well as the organization's mission.

Mentoring

Successful people often express gratitude for the assistance they have received along their career path from valued mentors and suggest that they might not have achieved their current level of accomplishment if not for the mentors who were influential in their developing careers. A mentor is an individual who has knowledge, skills, and experience, that, when shared, can be of benefit to another. In addition, a good mentor possesses a genuine desire to be of service to others and strong interpersonal communication skills.

Mentoring relationships can be formal or informal. A formal mentor is intentionally paired with a protégé for the purpose of assisting the mentee in career advancement. In formal mentoring, the objectives, communication methods, frequency, and timeline for the relationship should be clarified, preferably in writing. A written mentor agreement can assist both parties in staying on track with their responsibilities and will allow goal achievement to be more easily assessed.

In an informal mentoring relationship, the parties involved might not even use the terms *mentor* or *mentee*. Instead, a professional relationship develops between two colleagues that includes the sharing of career advice, frank discussions, coaching, and counseling. Informal mentors often share a feeling of kinship and great respect for each other and may acknowledge the existence and quality of the professional relationship in hindsight.

Formal or informal, mentors are a valuable resource for employees, and such professional associations should be encouraged by supervisors and included in development planning discussions.

Modeling and Shadowing

Executives in every industry must remain aware that they are role models for their employees—that is, their behaviors in the workplace may inspire or facilitate the behaviors of their staff. This finding is utilized in training future leaders via two methods: modeling and shadowing.

Constructive modeling occurs when people in positions of authority understand that their behavior provides an example to others and therefore act intentionally and consciously in ways that support and promote the desired organizational culture. For example, many organizations express the values of respect and integrity; their organizational leaders should demonstrate respect and integrity in all actions in the workplace. Unfortunately, destructive modeling (a negative effect) can result if leaders violate espoused values and principles. Not "walking the talk" can be damaging to employee morale and can send the wrong message to future leaders.

Shadowing is a formal technique that invites a high-potential employee to follow (or shadow) a leader for a designated period of time, witnessing and learning about their daily work life. The HiPos might follow the leader around the office, sit in on meetings, listen to phone conversations, meet with clients, and observe negotiations and decision-making. A conversation between the parties should occur in advance of the shadowing activity to clarify goals and expectations. At appropriate points, debriefing discussions should also take place, identifying lessons learned as well as next steps and follow-up that will enhance the HiPo's training.

Coaching

Executive coaching, used regularly in many industries, has gained popularity in the healthcare field in recent years. In the past, coaching was used only for those leaders who were struggling and possibly on their way out the organization's door. Today, coaching is used primarily to aid the growth of leaders in whom the organization wants to invest. Executive coaching is the "one-to-one development of an organizational leader" (Underhill, McAnally, & Koriath, 2007), a confidential set of consultations between a qualified coach and an executive, which focuses on improving the executive's leadership skills.

In an interview with McKinsey's senior partner Mary Meaney, Roberto Pucci, executive vice president for HR at Sanofi, stated "To develop leaders you have to give them feedback on their ability to manage people" (June 2017). Coaching is considered one of the most effective methods of developing leaders, because it provides and integrates accessible and ongoing feedback. Coaching resembles partnering with a personal trainer—not only do individuals learn proper exercise techniques but also they have partners to reinforce the new skills and ensure new exercises are practiced regularly. Areas that are often addressed through coaching for employees include motivating others, treating people with respect, creating and communicating a vision, implementing accountability, and improving time management.

After a coach is selected, the process begins with an assessment of the executive's strengths and weaknesses as well as the personality traits that can impact leadership effectiveness. The coach creates a summary of these findings, and then collaborates with the executive to select an area or two for development. An action plan is created, indicating all the key steps required to improve in the selected area(s). Coaching then proceeds with ongoing meetings aimed at helping to implement the plan. After a period of time, the outcomes of the coaching are assessed, often via a 360 evaluation. Coaching usually continues for 6–9 months, but can extend from a couple of sessions to as long as a year.

Executive coaches are often former business executives themselves or come from backgrounds in business consulting or psychology. Coaches will usually possess an advanced academic degree, such as a master's in business administration or a doctorate in organizational psychology, and some may possess a certification in coaching. Coaches are experienced in the use of skill and personality assessments, such as 360 feedback tools, Myers-Briggs Indicators, Hogan Assessments, or Fundamental Interpersonal Relations Orientation (FIRO-B).

A number of studies have demonstrated the value of executive coaching. In one study, participants who had completed a training program increased their productivity by 22%. However, if coaching was paired with the same training program, productivity increased by 88% (Olivero, Bane, & Kopelman, 1997). Another study reported significant improvement in leadership effectiveness among those being coached who engaged in regular follow-up during the coaching process (Goldsmith & Morgan, 2004). While data linking coaching to actual business results (e.g., increased revenue, higher stock prices) are less reliable, studies have shown that coaching has a demonstrable impact on leadership effectiveness.

▶ Call Out Box: Clogs in the Pipeline

Now that we have described the motivation, methodologies, and frameworks for leadership development, we might ask why some organizations develop internal leaders more effectively than others. Through their experience assisting more than 100 international companies in developing leadership succession plans, Charan et al. (2011) identified four common "deep-seated, development errors" (p. ix):

1. Lack of skills required to select high-potential employees.
2. HR focuses too much on "input" (identifying employees with high potential) and not enough on "output" (identifying what type of work should be done and what position level and how to measure success).
3. Lack of a consistent, integrated system for talent management by executives and/or HR.
4. Leaders are not updating their skills rapidly enough to keep up with industry changes, requiring shifts in leadership roles and responsibilities.

Summary

The Center for Creative Leadership conducted research on how successful leaders develop and report that the bulk of professional learning (70%) takes place on the job through real-world experiences, that is, completing tasks and solving problems while at work. Feedback and observation account for 20% of workplace learning, and formal training accounts for 10% (Lombardo & Eichinger, 2000). The leadership pipeline provides a framework by which organizations can structure and track the effectiveness of these three development opportunities.

With a leadership crisis in the healthcare industry looming, organizations need to implement reliable and effective strategies to train and retain high potentials. Health care has traditionally lagged behind other industries in the area of leadership development. Healthcare organizations that embrace successful talent management strategies will not only increase their chances of survival in a changing and challenging environment, but will also be better equipped to provide cost-effective, high-quality services and products.

This chapter has provided a picture of leadership development within the healthcare environment. First, using the framework provided by Conger and Fulmer (2003), we introduced the five basic principles by which organizations can build their bench strength. The "leadership pipeline" was presented as a logical pathway for employee advancement from frontline manager to enterprise leader. The recruitment of high-potential future leaders was discussed and the key competencies expected of healthcare leaders identified. Finally, we described specific methods through which high-potential employees can be developed into outstanding leaders with training, mentoring, modeling, and coaching.

Discussion Questions

1. What are the key competencies for a successful healthcare leader?
2. What are the two primary career paths to healthcare leadership?
3. Name and discuss various methods for developing leaders.
4. List and describe the five key guiding principles for building a leadership pipeline.

5. How does a leader progress through the pipeline? What are the steps he or she must go through?

6. From the case study that follows, what were Kevin's strengths and areas needing development? What did he do to improve his knowledge and skillsets?

🔍 CASE STUDY: Leadership in Practice

Although fictitious in nature, this is a typical case study for how leadership development looks when 360 feedback and executive coaching is used to develop a healthcare leader.

Kevin is the Chief Operating Officer (COO) of a tertiary-care hospital, one of many in a large chain in the northeastern United States. At 48 years of age, he has moved into this position much more rapidly than anyone (including he himself) expected. An unplanned vacancy had occurred in the COO position only 6 months before, and the CEO and Board of Directors chose not to recruit externally. As the director of administration for the hospital for the previous 4 years, Kevin was considered the only qualified internal candidate and was offered the position.

As COO, Kevin is responsible for all day-to-day operations of the hospital. The directors of nursing, administration, HR, government affairs, and quality now report to him, but the doctors are part of a contracted medical group that is instead coordinated by the Medical Chief of Staff.

The CEO and the Board of Directors of the system view Kevin as a "high potential" leader who could one day become the CEO. They also recognize that Kevin's promotion might have been premature, but believe that with further coaching and training, he could develop the needed skills to be a successful leader. To support and promote Kevin's professional development, they have hired an outside consultant to serve as a leadership coach and mentor.

The executive coach was hired to work with Kevin for 6 months. The coach first began with an assessment of Kevin's strengths and weaknesses through a 360 feedback process. A survey of approximately 75 questions was sent electronically to those who worked most closely with Kevin—his boss, his direct reports, and his peers who also worked for Kevin's boss. These raters completed the survey anonymously, and their scores were combined in the final report and analysis.

Kevin's highest and lowest scores were then identified (see **TABLE 2.2**). The highest score a rater can provide is 5.0, the lowest score is 1.0.

The executive coach also gave Kevin a Myers-Briggs Type Indicator (MBTI) assessment, a survey that Kevin completed himself. The result identified Kevin as fitting into 1 of 16 different personality types and helped him to better understand how he perceives, communicates, and functions in the workplace. The coach also reviewed past performance reviews Kevin received from his supervisors, along with other assessments he may have taken earlier in his career. Finally, the coach interviewed Kevin's boss, the hospital CEO.

Following the assessment, the coach and Kevin met for a feedback debriefing. In this confidential meeting, which lasted for several hours, the coach presented a summary report that highlighted Kevin's key strengths and areas for development. In this meeting, Kevin learned the information laid out in **TABLE 2.3**.

Kevin agreed that he is a person of high integrity and of solid execution, and was pleasantly surprised that people felt he treated them with such respect. Kevin was also very surprised that people felt he did not have much of a vision, and struggled

(continues)

TABLE 2.2 Kevin's Highest and Lowest Scores

	Highest-Rated Items	Average Score (from all raters)
1.	Ensures that the highest standards for ethical behavior are established and maintained throughout the organization	5.0
2.	Genuinely listens to others	4.9
3.	Demonstrates honest, ethical behavior in all personal and business transactions	4.9
4.	Consistently treats people with respect and dignity	4.8
5.	Is a role model for the organization's values (leads by example)	4.8
6.	Appreciates the value of diversity (avoids discrimination based upon race, gender, age, or background)	4.6
7.	Builds people's confidence	4.6
8.	Discourages destructive comments about other people or groups	4.6
9.	Consistently meets or exceeds customer expectations	4.5
10.	Effectively recognizes team members for teamwork and team performance	4.4
Lowest-Rated Items		
75.	Creates and communicates a clear vision for his/her organization	2.4
74.	Is willing to take risks in letting others make decisions	2.5
73.	Effectively anticipates future opportunities	2.5
72.	Communicates a clear strategy on how to achieve the vision	2.7
71.	Gives people the freedom they need to do their work	2.7
70.	Effectively involves coworkers in determining how to achieve the vision	2.9
69.	Looks beyond "the way we do things now" in considering future opportunities	2.9
68.	Trusts people enough to "let go" (avoids over-controlling or micromanagement)	3.2
67.	Clearly identifies priorities (focuses on the "vital few")	3.3
66.	Encourages active participation in strategy development and decision making	3.4

TABLE 2.3 Feedback Debrief Summary Report

Strengths	Supporting Data
Cares for People	360 items 2, 4, 6, 7, 8, 10: MBTI reveals he is more of a "feeler" and an "extrovert"; that is, he is able to tune in to others and empathize with them.
High Integrity	360 items 1, 3, 5: Performance review gives him a perfect score in "Integrity."
Executes—Gets the Job Done	360 item 9: Past performance review data; boss's interview: "It doesn't matter what you give Kevin, he will always get the job done flawlessly."

Areas of Development	Supporting Data
Lack of Vision	360 items 75, 73, 72, 70, 69, 66: MBTI reveals he is more of a "sensing" (works with immediate data, rather than thinking about future options) and "judging" (likes to move to closure, not leave things open for future possibility). Boss's interview: "Kevin has his head down working, he does not seem to have or communicate a vision of where his organization is going."
Micromanagement	360 items 74, 71, 68: Boss's interview: "Kevin's direct reports indicate he is doing their jobs rather than letting them do their jobs. His standards are so high, he feels he is the only one who can do things correctly."
Time Management	360 item 68: Past performance reviews say Kevin is such a nice guy, he never says no to any request. Boss's interview: "Kevin has difficulty figuring out what to work on first. He is so busy doing everyone's jobs, he just can't keep up. He is not working at the level of a COO, but at the level of those working under him."

with the feedback that he was "too nice to say no to anyone." After further discussion with the coach, Kevin eventually came to terms with the less positive feedback, recognizing that this input was influenced by the perceptions of those around him, which may not always match his view of himself.

In the next meeting, Kevin and his coach conducted action planning. In this session, Kevin first selected the area for development in which he planned to improve. After some thought and consideration, Kevin decided he needed to improve his ability *to create and communicate a vision* for his organization.

For his action plan, Kevin and his coach came up with a variety of action steps designed to help him create and communicate a vision. During this brainstorming

(continues)

session, Kevin, inspired by key questions posed by his coach, generated ideas based on his knowledge and experience with his job responsibilities. The coach also offered suggestions based on his experiences working with other leaders with similar areas needing development. A sample action plan is provided for Kevin in **TABLE 2.4**.

TABLE 2.4 Action Plan Worksheet for Kevin			
Area for Development: Create and Communicate a Vision for His Organization			
Action Step	**Support Required**	**Timeline**	**Completed?**
Create a Vision			
Meet with CEO regarding her vision	CEO meeting	Within 2 weeks	
Review industry journals for latest industry trends	Obtain journals	Within 2 weeks	
Attend industry conference for ideas	Funding for conference	April 17–20	
Draft vision statement; share with boss and others	CEO support, review of others	May 1	
Communicate the Vision			
Make sure vision is clear, compelling, easy to remember	Review with coach	May 14	
Host team offsite to unveil the vision	Funds for offsite expenses	May 14/15 (tentative)	
Internal website to promote vision	Marketing/web staff to design	May 21	
Distribute T-shirts with graphic promoting new vision to all staff	Marketing/design team	June 1	

Begin each staff meeting with a review of vision		Each month	
Ensure each staff members' goals directly relate to the organization vision		During June performance reviews	
Survey everyone in 6 months to see if they can remember vision	Survey design team	December	

Preliminary Case Study Discussion Questions

1. What are Kevin's strengths as noted in the evaluation? Can you combine these strengths into a few main "themes"?
2. What are Kevin's areas of development? What themes do you identify?
3. Given your analysis of these test results, would you choose to work for Kevin?

After the action plan was created, Kevin could begin to accomplish his objectives. His first step was to meet with his boss to gain her acceptance of the action plan and to gather her ideas and those of other stakeholders. In the ongoing coaching phase, Kevin and his coach will meet approximately every 1–2 weeks by phone, video chat, or in person. During each meeting, the coach will review the action plan to see which key steps have been accomplished and which steps still remain incomplete. As is often the case, Kevin may find himself falling behind or losing focus in his areas of development. Like a personal trainer, the coach will refocus him toward his objectives and help him stay on task. Barriers and obstacles that arise are also analyzed and addressed through the coaching process.

During ongoing coaching, Kevin will engage personnel who provided input about his plan so that they can be aware and supportive of his upcoming development. He will check in with them every other month to ask them whether they have noticed improvements. Research shows that the more often Kevin follows up with key people, the more likely they are to notice improvement. The coach will also follow up with the involved colleagues independently to ask if they have also noticed any progress. Additionally, the coach checks in with Kevin's supervisor, the CEO, and Kevin's HR representative to gain their input on his improvement.

At the end of the coaching term, a brief follow-up mini survey is sent to all the previous raters to assess development. Each person indicates whether he or she has observed improvement in Kevin's ability to create and communicate a vision for the organization over the past 6 months. Once again, the mini survey is anonymous, with the answers being combined so that individual input cannot be identified. The results are then depicted in **TABLE 2.5**.

A total of 12 raters working with Kevin answered the anonymous survey. In question #1, one rater saw no change in his overall leadership effectiveness, but 11 saw improvement on a +1, +2, +3 level. In question #2, Kevin also showed improvement in his area of development "creates and communicates a clear vision for his/her organization." Of 12 raters, a total of 10 felt that he had improved in this area.

(continues)

TABLE 2.5 Mini Survey for Kevin

1. Did Kevin become more (or less) effective as a leader over the past 6 months?

−3 Less effective	−2	−1	0 No change	+1	+2	+3 More effective
			1	6	4	1

2. Over the past 6 months, did this leader become more (or less) effective in the following area for development: Creates and communicates a clear vision for his/her organization?

−3 Less effective	−2	−1	0 No change	+1	+2	+3 More effective
			2	7	2	1

Following successful improvement as demonstrated by the mini survey, coaching was effectively concluded. However, Kevin continues to check in with his key raters every 6 months to see if they are still clear on his vision. He also continues to practice each of his action steps as he moves forward with his responsibilities. The CEO and Board have noticed great improvement in his leadership capabilities and are now contemplating renewing coaching for an additional 6 months to help him address one of his other two development objectives.

Concluding Case Study Discussion Questions

1. What other action steps would you recommend for Kevin to consider in creating or communicating the vision?
2. If Kevin had not followed up regularly with those working with him regarding his developmental opportunities, do you think he would have improved as much as he did? Why or why not?
3. Would you promote Kevin now to CEO of this hospital? If so, why? If not now, why not?

Related Websites

Assessment +: http://site.assessmentplus.com
Association of University Programs in Health Administration: www.aupha.org
Commission on Accreditation of Healthcare Management Education: www.cahme.org
Healthcare Leadership Alliance: http://healthcareleadershipalliance.org
National Center for Healthcare Leadership: www.nchl.org

References

American College of Healthcare Executives. (2018a). *Healthcare Leadership Competencies.* Retrieved July 18, 2018 from https://www.ache.org/newclub/resource/competencies.cfm

American College of Healthcare Executives. (2018b). *Members and fellows profile.* Retrieved February 18, 2018 from www.ache.org/pubs/research/demographics.cfm

Association of University Programs in Health Administration (AUPHA). (2018). Undergraduate Certification. *Association of University Programs in Health Administration.* Retrieved February 18, 2018 from network.aupha.org/members/findaprogram

Beinecke, R., Daniels, A., Peters, J., & Silvestri, F. (2009). Guest editors' introduction: The International Initiative for Mental Health Leadership (IIMHL): A model for global knowledge exchange. *International Journal of Mental Health, 38*(1), 3–13.

Campbell, D. S. (2001). Training as a retention tool. *The Internal Auditor, 58*(5), 47–51.

Charan, R., Drotter, S., & Noel, J. (2011). *The leadership pipeline: How to build the leadership powered company.* San Francisco, CA: John Wiley & Sons, Jossey-Bass.

Commission on Accreditation of Healthcare Management Education (CAHME). (2018). Retrieved February 18, 2018 from cahme.org/files/aupha/cahme-update-at-aupha-annual-meeting-2017.pdf

Conger, J. A., & Fulmer, R. M. (2003, December). Developing your leadership pipeline. *Harvard Business Review, 81*(12), 76–84.

Dye, C. F., & Garman, A. N. (2006). *Exceptional leadership: 16 critical competencies for healthcare executives.* Chicago, IL: Health Administration Press.

Executive Development Associates. (2005). *The leadership bench strength challenge: Building integrated talent management systems.* Oklahoma City, OK: Executive Development Associates.

Executive Development Associates. (2009). *Trends in executive development.* Oklahoma City, OK: Executive Development Associates.

Freshman, B. (2010). The forest and the trees: An organizational psychologist's perspective on collaborating across the disciplines in health. In B. Freshman, L. Rubino, & Y. Reid Chassaikos (Eds.), *Collaboration across the disciplines in healthcare* (pp. 345–368). Burlington, MA: Jones & Bartlett Learning.

Garman, A. N., & Dye, C. F. (2009). *The healthcare C-suite.* Chicago, IL: Health Administration Press.

Gill, P. (2018, February 4). Personal Communication with Brian Underhill.

Goldsmith, M., & Morgan, H. (2004). Leadership is a contact sport. *Strategy + Business, 36.* Retrieved from https://www.strategy-business.com/article/04307?pg=0

Healthcare Leadership Alliance (HLA). (2010). *HLA competency directory.* Retrieved January 9, 2012 from www.healthcareleadershipalliance.org/directory.htm

Kyndt, E., Dochy, F., Struyven, K., & Cascallar, E. (2011). The perception of workload and task complexity and its influence on students' approaches to learning: A study in higher education. *European Journal of Psychology of Education—EJPE (Springer Science & Business Media B.V.), 26*(3), 393–415. doi:10.1007/s10212-010-0053-2

Lin, C. (2010). Understanding negative impacts of perceived cognitive load on job learning effectiveness: A social capital solution. *Human Factors, 52*(6), 627–642. doi:10.1177/0018720810386606

Lombardo, M., & Eichinger, B. (2000). *Career architect development planner* (3rd ed.). Minneapolis, MN: Lominger Limited.

McAlearney, A. S. (2006). Leadership development in healthcare: A qualitative study. *Journal of Organizational Behavior, 27*(7), 967–967.

McAlearney, A. S. (2010). Executive leadership development in U.S. health systems. *Journal of Healthcare Management, 55*(3), 206–222.

McCauley, C. D., & Brutus, S. (1998). *Management development through job experiences: An annotated bibliography.* Greensboro, NC: Center for Creative Leadership.

McGrady, E., Conger, S., Blanke, S., Landry, B. J. L., & Zalucki, P. M. (2010). Emerging technologies in healthcare: Navigating risks, evaluating rewards/practitioner application. *Journal of Healthcare Management, 55*(5), 353–364; discussion 364–365.

Meaney, M., & Pucci, R. (2017, June). *What talent management can do to shape next-generation pharma leaders*. Retrieved November 30, 2017 from www.mckinsey.com/industries/pharmaceuticals -and-medical-products/our-insights/what-talent-management-can-do-to-shape-next-generation -pharma-leaders

Michaels, E., Handfield-Jones, H., & Axelrod, B. (2001). *The war for talent*. Boston, MA: McKinsey & Company.

Miller, D. L., Umble, K. E., Frederick, S. L., & Dinkin, D. R. (2007). Linking learning methods to outcomes in public health leadership development. *Leadership in Health Services, 20*(2), 97–123. doi:10.1108/17511870710745439

National Center for Healthcare Leadership. (2005–2010). *Health leadership competency model summary*. Retrieved August 31, 2012 from www.nchl.org/Documents/NavLink/Competency _Model-summary_uid31020101024281.pdf

National Center for Healthcare Leadership. (2012). *NCHL health leadership competency model*. Retrieved January 9, 2012 from www.nchl.org/static.asp?path=2852,3238

Nelson, J., Sassaman, B., & Phillips, A. (2008). Career ladder program for registered nurses in ambulatory care. *Nursing Economics, 26*(6), 393–398.

Noelke, N. (2009). Leverage the present to build the future. *HR Magazine, 54*(3), 34–36.

Olivero, G., Bane, K. D., & Kopelman, R. (1997, Winter). Executive coaching as a transfer of training tool: Effects on productivity in a public agency. *Personnel Public Management, 26*(4), 461–469.

Seitz, A. (2017, March 2). *The benefits of bench strength*. Retrieved December 7, 2017 from www .wisbank.com/articles/2017/03/the-benefits-of-bench-strength/

Underhill, B., McAnally, K., & Koriath, J. (2007). *Executive coaching for results: The definitive guide to developing organizational leaders*. San Francisco, CA: Berrett-Koehler.

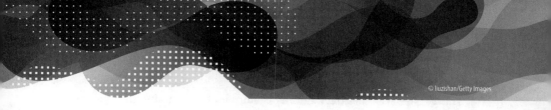

CHAPTER 3

The Culturally Competent and Inclusive Leader

Carol Molinari, Sandra Lundahl, and Laurie Shanderson

LEARNING OBJECTIVES

By the end of this chapter, the student will be able to:

- Define and discuss dimensions of demographic and cultural diversity related to patients and workers in the United States.
- Discuss diversity challenges facing healthcare leaders and managers today.
- Discuss the impact and challenges of a multigenerational workforce.
- Define and distinguish between culturally competent and inclusive leadership.
- Define and discuss unconscious or implicit bias and its effects on individual and organizational behavior.
- Discuss ways that healthcare leaders can address implicit bias at individual and organizational levels.
- Discuss current challenges related to diversity training.
- Discuss implicit bias training and lessons learned from the U.S. Veterans Health Administration's diversity training.

KEY TERMS

Cultural competence
Diversity
Implicit/unconscious bias
Inclusive leadership

Multigenerational workers
Priority populations
Sexual orientation

▶ Introduction

This chapter examines the ways 21st-century leaders of healthcare organizations can better serve their increasingly diverse patients by effectively managing their increasingly diverse workforce. Demographic and cultural **diversity** among patients and workers require that healthcare leaders model culturally competent and inclusive behaviors to create cultures that respect and embrace diversity. Unconscious or implicit bias is examined as an obstacle to applying respectful and inclusive behaviors. The components of effective diversity training are presented, including results from training that address **implicit/unconscious bias** among leaders, managers, and staff working in the largest U.S. integrated health system, the Veterans Health Administration.

▶ Background and Rationale

Over the past three decades, seminal national reports on the status of U.S. health care have identified disparities and inequities related to the delivery of health care to various populations who have been socially and economically disadvantaged and whose health needs that have not been served. In 1999, the Institute of Medicine (IOM) published the report "To Err Is Human," which discussed medical errors such as medication and surgical blunders that resulted in approximately 44,000 deaths each year (Kohn, Corrigan, & Donaldson, 2000). In 2001, the IOM released "Crossing the Quality Chasm," identifying major gaps between expected quality of care and measured quality of care, most significantly for people of color. The IOM followed with another report, "Unequal Treatment: Confronting Racial and Ethnic Disparities in Health Care" in 2002, which identified a set of root causes leading to these racial disparities (Betancourt, Green, Carrillo, & Ananeh-Firempong, 2003; Smedley, Stith, & Nelson, 2003).

By 2045, the United States is projected to become a "majority minority" nation (Vespa, Armstrong, & Medina, 2018). Individuals from mixed ethnic and racial minorities, older adults, and members from the LGBT community are identified by the Agency for Healthcare Research and Quality (AHRQ) as underserved and disadvantaged (AHRQ, 2016).

As the U.S. population becomes more diverse, so does its workforce. While this growing diversity is evident among healthcare workers, the leadership of healthcare organizations often does not reflect these demographics. For example, less than 10% of hospital CEO positions are held by minorities (IFDHRET, 2012).

With a scarcity of racially/ethnically diverse healthcare leaders, the potential for executive blind spots related to bias, intergenerational conflict, and health disparities is greater, underscoring an urgent need for today's health organizations to take action (Dotson, Bonam, & Jagers, 2017). Today's health leaders need to be aware of their own biases, empathize by taking another's perspective, show fairness and respect toward others, and have the courage to engage constructively in difficult conversations to help create and sustain organizational cultures that are inclusive.

The extent to which healthcare leaders create organizational cultures in which workers embrace the benefits of serving diverse patients, the more likely it will be that barriers such as unconscious bias can be minimized, helping to reduce the persistently high level of healthcare disparities among some populations.

▶ Overview of Selected Populations: Key Diversity Definitions

Diversity refers to personal, cultural, and lifestyle attributes among groups of individuals (Molinari & Takagi, 2017). Some common examples include racial and ethnic backgrounds, gender identity, **sexual orientation**, age, income and educational levels, religious affiliations, political views, marital statuses, and physical and mental capacities (Betancourt, 2005). Diverse populations that include race, ethnicity, sexual orientation, and older adults are discussed in relation to differences or disparities in patients' health care and health status. Additionally, demographic differences are reviewed in relation to the multigenerational workforce in the United States.

Diverse Populations

The Agency for Healthcare Research and Quality (AHRQ) has identified "**priority populations**" in the United States to include ethnic and racial minorities, older adults, and LGBT groups (AHRQ, 2016). In fact, the fastest growing groups in the United States are those who identify with from two or more ethnic or racial groups, with 200% growth projections by 2016 (Ibid.). Yet, the health status of many people from multi-racial and multi-ethnic groups is poor; studies have demonstrated shorter life spans and higher incidences of chronic diseases (e.g., diabetes and cardiovascular disease), higher infant mortality, and higher substance abuse (CDC, 2011). In terms of the delivery of health care, these individuals often report poorer physician–patient relationships and communications as compared to white patients (Gonzalez, Kim, & Marantz, 2014).

Another important priority population category is sexual orientation. Gay or lesbian refers to attraction to the same sex; bisexual refers to attraction to both sexes. Sexual orientation is different from gender identity. Transgender individuals identify as a gender different from their gender at birth or as nonbinary. Their sexual orientation can be to the same gender, to a different gender, or to all genders and nonbinary partners—that is, pansexual. The health disparities among gay, bisexual, or transgender (LGBT) individuals have been linked to long-standing social and societal discrimination (Lim, Brown, & Kim, 2014).

Transgender adults have the highest rates of victimization, with high rates of disability, stress, and poor mental and physical health as compared to nontransgender lesbian, gay, and bisexual adults (Fredriksen-Goldsen et al., 2013). There is growing evidence that LGBT adults face greater health risks due to their unwillingness to seek health services, based on their experiences and perceptions of bias and discrimination by providers (Rowan & Giunta, 2016).

Americans are living longer than previous generations and are more racially and ethnically diverse (Molinari & Takagi, 2017). For example, African-American elders have shorter life expectancy as compared to white older adults (Administration on Aging, 2014). Older Latina women have higher mortality from cervical and uterine cancers than older white women (Byrd, Chavez, & Wilson, 2007).

Older adults use healthcare services more than younger adults; therefore, it is important to examine how ageist stereotypes affect older adults' access to health care, healthcare options, and health status.

The first study to link individual beliefs about aging to cause-specific mortality was conducted by Levy and Myers (2005) and found that older individuals' beliefs about their own aging predicted the likelihood of their dying from respiratory causes. Kornadt, Meissner, and Rothermund (2016) conducted a meta-analysis and found clear evidence that negative and positive age stereotypes can result in self-fulfilling prophecies.

Data from the Health and Retirement Study of community-dwelling adults aged 50 and older, who had visited the doctor at least once in the past two years, reported that the individuals were worried or afraid that they were being judged by medical staff because of their age. Previous experiences of age discrimination, poorer self-perceptions of aging, and having less control over one's health were associated with reporting a stereotype threat because of age (Phibbs & Hooker, 2017). Among the older adults participating in this study, a one unit increase in poor self-perception of aging was associated with a 34% increase in the odds of reporting an ageist stereotype threat in the medical setting.

Multigenerational Workforce

Five generations are now working together, creating an incredibly diverse multigenerational workforce. Generation Z, or Gen Z, born 1995 to 2012, is entering the workforce. Millennials, born between 1980 and 1994, are done with college, now own their own homes, and have launched their careers. Generation X, or Gen X, born between 1965 and 1979, are being groomed to take over leadership positions. Boomers, born roughly between the mid-1940s and 1964, are preparing for and entering retirement. Traditionalists, born before 1946, may still be working, but most have retired to follow other pursuits, which include starting their own businesses and nonprofits and serving as volunteers and mentors (**TABLE 3.1**).

Each generation shares a common history that results in a unique "generational personality" that influences how each generation views the world. Too often, when individuals from two generations collide, they focus on who is right or wrong, rather than trying to understand the other's perspective (Stillman & Stillman, 2017).

Multigenerational workers with varying skills and education are enhancing organizations by providing diverse perspectives that invigorate problem-solving and can add value (Guérin-Marion, Manion, & Parsons, 2018). Conversely, perceptions and biases about generational differences often engender unproductive intergenerational conflict (Rudolph & Zacher, 2015).

Leading Diverse Populations: Cultural Competence and Inclusion

Cultural competence can be defined as the ability to successfully adapt to an unfamiliar cultural setting (Moua, 2010), and to apply knowledge from different cultures to become sensitive and responsive to cultural differences (Thomas & Inkson, 2009).

The primary goal of cultural competence for health organizations is to provide high quality, respectful care, while decreasing inequities in health (Watt, Abbott, & Reath, 2015). Being culturally competent requires individuals to have the ability to recognize their own personal bias and to learn and possess the

TABLE 3.1 Multiple Generations in U.S. Workforce

Gen Z	Gen Z is phigital, the first generation born into a world where every physical aspect (people and places) has a digital equivalent; Gen Zs expect to customize. They are realistic, having grown up in an environment of recessions and terrorism. Staying on top of all trends, Gen Zs worry about missing out—on anything. They have only known a world with a shared economy and technical and entrepreneurial innovations such as Uber and Airbnb. They expect to collaborate to fix the wrongs they see in the world. Gen Zs believe they can do just about anything themselves or by watching YouTube videos, and are true do-it-yourselfers. Gen Z is a driven and largely competitive generation.[1]
Millennials	Millennials have been immersed in digital technology from early childhood, which has led them to evolve into a forward-looking, learning-focused, and creative generation of workers.
	They are technologically savvy and tend to value digital modes of communication (e.g., social media outlets, texting) more than previous generations. Research also shows that, much like Gen Xers, Millennials often look for variety and mobility in their early careers. Given today's widespread uptake of higher education, Millennials often find themselves competing for positions against a growing mass of equally-educated peers. This reality, together with the increased tendency for job mobility, is thought to fuel Millennials' drive toward professional development and learning, with a particular focus on the building of marketable skills.
	Millennials are particularly fond of continuous learning opportunities at work. In addition, because they were exposed to more strength-based, child-centered education than previous generations, Millennials tend to come into organizations with high expectations for guidance, recognition, and professional growth. Immediate feedback, recognition, and career advancement were significantly more important to Millennials than to older generations.[2]
Gen X	Gen X was born between 1965 and 1981, which is a period marked by high divorce rates and busy working parents. Often referred to as a generation of latchkey kids, Xers made self-reliance their generational hallmark, entering the workforce with distinctive autonomy, independence, and adaptability. Xers tended to be more self-reliant and independent workers than the Boomers and tend to adopt more individualistic work approaches than their predecessors. It has also been suggested that Xers have a certain dislike for top-down management practices and value opportunities to work free from supervision and feel empowered in their work. Considerable research shows that Xers are more inclined to leave organizations for new job opportunities than Boomers. Perhaps the most evident finding on Xers is that they care to join organizations that allow them to have flexible work hours and maintain a seamless work-life balance.

(continues)

1 Stillman & Stillman (2017).
2 Wiedmer (2015).

TABLE 3.1 Multiple Generations in U.S. Workforce	*(continued)*
Boomers	Boomers grew up in a time brightened with a flourishing world economy. They were later challenged by the cumulative tensions of the Cold War, the Vietnam War, and the oil embargo, among other international challenges. Boomers are known as collectivistic, hard-working, and loyal employees who place value on achieving job security within organizations. Boomers' formative professional years (1970s–1980s) were marked by the increased popularity of participative and team-oriented styles of management. One study suggests that Boomers value personal growth (measured therein as the degree of intellectual stimulation, altruism, creativity, and achievement) more than other generations. Boomers are often depicted as tireless workhorses who live to work often at the expense of leisure time. Research shows that they are indeed more likely than younger generations to view work as central to their lives and identity.[3]
Traditionalists	Traditionalists generally prefer to work in conservative, hierarchical places where there is a clear chain of command (top-down). Historically, Traditionalists lived through Hitler's 1941 Russian invasion, the United States' 1941 World War II entry with the bombing of Pearl Harbor, the 1945 end of World War II in Japan and Europe, and the beginning of the 1950 Korean War. Typically, Traditionalists respect authority and possess family values that keep their work and family lives separate. Generally motivated by money and position, Traditionalists take pride in being self-sacrificing and thrifty. They tend to work hard from a sense of pride and determination, consider debt or obligation to be embarrassing, and acknowledge that change comes slowly. Traditionalists describe themselves with two words—loyal and disciplined—and view education to be a dream. They reportedly learn best through traditional, instructor-led teaching; generally prefer tangible items for recognition or reward, such as certificates, plaques, or trophies; and seek to feel supported and valued by their employers and supervisors.[4]

attitudes, behaviors, and beliefs necessary to interact confidently and with empathy toward others who may be different (Behar-Horenstein, Feng, Isaac, & Lee, 2017). Cultural competence can be learned and developed, and thus provides a way for leadership and management to reduce healthcare disparities, especially among "priority populations."

Cultural competency for healthcare workers and providers has been a priority focus within the U.S. Substance Abuse, Mental Health Services Administration (SAMHSA) because of the diverse populations served. Culturally competent health practitioners are aware of their own culture and values and acknowledge their own assumptions and biases about other cultures. In a 2014 Treatment Improvement Protocol on Improving Cultural Competency, cultural competence referred

---

3 Guérin-Marion (2018).
4 Wiedmer (2015).

to more than a discrete skill set or knowledge base; cultural competence entailed self-evaluation on the part of a health practitioner. Moreover, culturally competent health practitioners should strive to understand how these assumptions affect their ability to provide culturally responsive services to patients/clients from similar or diverse cultures (SAMHSA, 2014).

Inclusion

Inclusion refers to the degree to which all members of the workforce are involved in the structures of their organizations. It is not enough, for example, to have a substantial number of people of color in an organization, if they are still underrepresented in leadership and if the dominant group does not embrace their issues, concerns, and needs. Inclusion is a function of connection and of workers being fully integrated into the cultural dynamics, leadership, and decision-making structures of the organization. The people who work for inclusive leaders believe they are integral to the way their organization functions in decision-making, responsibility, and leadership.

A primary benefit of inclusion is to have individuals feel valued for their unique attributes and strengths (Sugiyama, Cavanagh, van Esch, Bilimoria, & Brown, 2016). Inclusion helps make the work environment a place of meaning, dignity, and community (Weisbord, 2012). Inclusive leaders motivate others by their humility and respect for their experiences and by requesting, sharing, and supporting authentic feedback (Schein, 2013). For today's leaders, achieving organizational goals cannot occur without building these connections with and among workers (Sugiyama et al., 2016).

Bias is an attitude, value, belief, or preference that favors for or against one thing, person, or group as compared with another, usually in a way considered to be unfair. To keep us safe, our brain is structured to remember past events (good and bad) and to respond and react instantaneously when a similar situation arises. Biases may be thought of as misjudgments that can influence individuals subconsciously. The more emotional, confused, uncertain, unsure, excited, distracted, tired, or stressed people are, the easier it is for them to make misjudgments. Well-educated people are no exception. **BOX 3.1** lists the most common misjudgments people make (Bevelin, 2017).

Implicit bias, also called unconscious bias, operates outside one's conscious awareness, and can manifest as overt discrimination or as micro-messages that communicate exclusion. The person at the receiving end of the discriminatory action or exclusionary message feels diminished, overlooked, ignored, discounted, or dismissed—whether or not that was the intent.

Unconscious biases are universal and unescapable; everyone has them. Sometimes, an unconscious bias is helpful. However, more often than not, biases adversely affect one's ability to make objective evaluations and fair decisions that involve those who are different. Unconscious biases are not permanent and can be changed by devoting time to notice thoughts, feelings, and behaviors, especially in tense and conflictual situations. Observing oneself (being mindful) and exploring alternative interpretations and approaches to handle tough situations can help individuals make conscious decisions to treat everyone respectfully and inclusively.

There has been growing attention paid to implicit bias among health professionals especially in preparing and training today's current generation of physicians

---

BOX 3.1 Common Misjudgments Biases

1. Automatically connecting two things, which includes seeing situations as identical because they seem similar.
2. Repeating actions that resulted in previous rewards and avoiding situations where there was a previous negative consequence, even though the present circumstance is different from the past situation.
3. Separating and underestimating bias from own self-interest and incentives.
4. Overly positive view of one's abilities, including over-optimism of the future.
5. Denial—self-deception and distortion of reality to reduce pain.
6. Being consistent with prior commitments and ideas in the presence of disconfirming evidence.
7. Strongly reacting when something we like or have is about to be taken away.
8. Keeping things the way they are, minimizing effort preference for default positions.
9. Judging something not on its own merits but by comparing to something else closely related in time.
10. Over-weighing initial information as a reference point for future decisions.
11. Over-influence by vivid or the most recent information.
12. Repaying in kind what others have done for us, like favors, concessions, information, and attitudes.
13. Believing, trusting, and agreeing with people we know and like.
14. Imitating the behavior of others.
15. Trusting and obeying a perceived authority or expert.

(Sukera & Watling, 2017). Implicit bias interferes with the ability to empathize and to see issues or challenges from different perspectives. It is a significant obstacle to cultural competence.

Micro: Messages, Aggressions, and Inequities

Persistent misjudgments, biases, and conflict unfortunately may continue to exist in society, but leaders can help move the needle forward by focusing on controllable elements: that is, the micro-messages, microaggressions, and micro-inequities communicated in the workplace. Individuals may act out personal biases negatively through overt discrimination or through small, micro behaviors (written or spoken words and body language) that convey messages of inequity or even aggression.

In his book about micro-messaging, Young (2017) explains that micro-messages can help individuals feel valued or dismissed. Positive micro-messages have the ability to uplift and motivate employees to their full potential. Conversely, negative micro-messages accumulate, wear down, and infect an otherwise healthy self-image, negatively affecting the entire organization.

Mary P. Rowe (1990) coined the term micro-inequity in her investigation of the underlying cause of why some felt included while others did not. According to Rowe (1990), micro-inequities can have dual adverse effects: They make those who are different feel left out, and this exclusion erodes one's self-confidence and performance.

Sue (2010) notes that superior–subordinate relationships can have a greater detrimental impact on marginalized groups than peer-to-peer relationships. When negative micro-messages are delivered by supervisors or superiors, minority employees report lower job satisfaction, organizational commitment, morale, motivation, self-esteem, and overall life satisfaction. In other words, microaggressions from superiors can have far-reaching negative effects on the psyche and work productivity of the minority employee, which in turn adversely affect the overall performance of the organization (Ibid.).

Awareness of micro-messages and their effects on workers' sense of value provide leaders with opportunities to craft and control these messages in ways that reduce bias and promote improved morale among workers (Young, 2017).

▶ Becoming Culturally Competent and Inclusive Leaders

Culturally competent and inclusive leaders embrace and leverage the thinking, ideas, and contributions of diverse groups for innovation and decision-making (Bourke & Dillon, 2016). To tap into the benefits of diversity (e.g., talent and new thinking), leaders can cultivate qualities such as cultural intelligence, cognizance, curiosity, courage, collaboration, and commitment (Ibid.). Leaders that develop these inclusive characteristics are those that are most likely to harness the benefits of cultural competence. Additionally, a culturally competent and inclusive leader has the responsibility to be aware of micro messages, aggressions, and inequities, and to address these sooner rather than later.

Inclusive leadership includes the following key elements (Bourke & Dillon, 2016):

1. Treating individuals and teams fairly, based on the unique qualities of individuals and team members, not on stereotypes.
2. Personalizing individuals by valuing and accepting the uniqueness of each person.
3. Leveraging the thinking of diverse individuals and teams for synergistic innovation and decision-making.

Leaders that demonstrate these practices more effectively connect with diverse customers, promote more innovative thinking, and help diverse workers reach their potential (Bourke & Dillon, 2016).

Welcoming the diversity that comes from multiple generations working together can inject energy and provide the creativity, innovation, stability, and perspectives needed to ensure an organization is cognizant and responsive to the needs of their customers and their workforce. Stereotyping and not treating people as individuals endanger the harmony, collaboration, and productivity needed to meet organizational goals. Miranda and Allen (2017) say that opportunities for conflict exist when employees face differing standards, values, and beliefs; lack clear guidance for duties and tasks; observe disparities in responsibilities and in pay; and pursue different goals.

A culturally competent and inclusive leader will strive to address individual differences, note how each generation perceives the others, and coach employees in achieving productive partnerships across generations. Guérin-Marion (2018) presents several strategies to promote a generationally competent and inclusive work environment,[5] including the following examples:

- Long-term career development is very important to the most recent entrants into the workforce, Gen Z. Establish ways for new workers to grow within the organization so that they do not have to leave to learn new skills.
- Address Millennials' concerns about work/life balance and their focus on advancing their careers.
- Create mentorship relationships for Gen Xers with Boomers and Traditionalists.

Communication is intimately tied with relationship-building. Younger generations rely more heavily on the use of technology while older workers may be more comfortable with face-to-face interactions such as hallway conversations and formal meetings. A way to bridge these differences, suggest Guerin, is to have a mix of communication strategies (Guérin-Marion et al., 2018). For example, leaders may initiate organizational top-down messages by email which are written in a conversational tone, but which are transparent about internal and external issues affecting the organization. A monthly newsletter with responsibility for its production shifting among the generations would amplify each generation's perspectives and worldview. Having regular meetings in a variety of ways that allow for bidirectionality between leaders and staff (e.g., strategic planning meetings and town hall-type forums) would allow dynamic and open conversations to occur among all members of the workforce.

Paying attention to individual needs, recognizing the cultural preferences of each generation, and initiating ways to obtain input from each age group, provide a culturally competent and inclusive approach for leading multigenerational workers.

Becoming a culturally competent and inclusive leader requires a willingness to do the following two things to root out personal and organizational bias: (1) deepen one's self-awareness and (2) conduct an objective, clear-eyed analysis of one's organization.

▶ Self-Awareness

"If you want to avoid irrationality, it helps to understand the quirks in your own mental wiring and then you can take appropriate precautions" Charles Munger.[6]

Becoming Aware of Unconscious Bias

Biases presumably originated in response to fears and were evolutionarily helpful for ensuring safety and survival. Humans quickly perceived surroundings and filled in missing information with unconscious cognition to guide behavior. Byyny (2017) argues that people today still use personal characteristics such as race, age, and gender to make quick decisions. As a physician himself, Byyny focuses his

---

5 Guérin-Marion (2018).
6 Bevelin (2017).

comments on physicians. He reveals that when physicians are under time pressures, fatigue, stress, and information overload, their tendency is to reaffirm personal perceptions that people of a certain category are more homogeneous than they are in reality (Ibid.).

Learning what research has discovered is the first step toward uncovering biases that affect your decision-making. Although people prefer to believe that personal decisions are based on conscious deliberations, neuroscience research has shown that individuals often use mental shortcuts by forming impressions of people without any conscious awareness of biases. These biases occur despite the best intentions, and result in potentially destructive effects that favor one group of people over another.

One way of conceptualizing unconscious bias is through fast thinking (intuitive and emotional) and slow thinking (deliberate, logical reasoning), studied by Daniel Kahneman, a psychologist and Nobel Prize winner in economic sciences noted for his work on the psychology of judgment and decision-making. Kahneman (2012) describes the faults of fast thinking and the influence of our intuitive impressions on thoughts and behaviors in his sobering presentation of predictable biases in judgments.

Organizational psychologist and researcher Tasha Eurich found, in her study of nearly 5000 participants, that even though most people believe they are self-aware, self-awareness is a truly rare quality (Eurich, 2018). She estimates that only 10%–15% of the people she studied actually fit the criteria of being self-aware, which included two broad categories. The first, internal self-awareness, represented how clearly we see our own values, passions, reactions (including thoughts, feelings, behaviors, strengths, and weaknesses), and aspirations; and how we perceive our fit in our environment, and our impact on others. The second category, external self-awareness, refers to understanding how people view each other. Eurich's research showed that people who are aware how others see or perceive them are more skilled at showing empathy and understanding others' perspectives.

To build self-awareness, Eurich recommends the following effective tools. Mindfulness, simply registering what one is thinking, feeling, and doing—without judgment or reaction—allows a person to notice what is happening, relinquish preconceived mindsets, and act upon new observations. Some mindfulness practices include 10 minutes of daily mindfulness meditation that involve remaining silent to gain skill in simply observing thoughts, feelings, and physical sensations. Other nonmeditative mindfulness practices include reframing, that is, looking at our circumstances, behaviors, and relationships from a new and different angle; comparing and contrasting, that is, looking for similarities and differences between our experiences, thoughts, feelings, and behaviors over time; and daily check-ins, that is, taking 5 minutes each day to ask yourself: "What went well today? What didn't go well? What did I learn and how will I do better tomorrow?"

One of the most effective ways to mitigate unconscious biases is to actively and intentionally communicate an inclusive, respectful, and welcoming environment (Van Ryn et al., 2011), and to approach every encounter with patients, colleagues, employees, students, and especially those who are members of underprivileged or stereotypical social groups as an opportunity to reinforce and act consistently with a commitment to egalitarian values (Byyny, 2017).

The good news is that individuals can gain awareness of unconscious biases that may be affecting their decisions. Unconscious biases are not permanent and can be changed by devoting intention and attention to developing new associations. Creating new associations requires taking the time to consciously think about potential biases prior to acting or making decisions.

Because biases are fast, reflexive reactions, it is important that individuals move to a more thoughtful conscious state to start engaging the prefrontal neocortex in more productive thinking. Howard Ross, one of the world's foremost experts on identifying and addressing unconscious bias, advises that people need to pause to take time to observe themselves. Taking time to observe ourselves provides the opportunity to evaluate the situation. Ross (2014) uses the word "PAUSE" as an acronym as a reminder to:

> **P**ay attention to what's happening beneath the judgments and assessments. When we slow down and look at what's happening, we have an opportunity to distinguish between an event and our interpretation of that event. For example, say somebody shakes your hand softly. Do you have a visceral reaction and association with weakness as many people in the United States do? ("Limp!" "Cold fish!") What happened is that they used less pressure in the handshake than you are used to from most people. The rest is your interpretation, which leads us to the next step.

> **A**cknowledge your own reactions, interpretations, and judgments. This is where you have an opportunity to identify your interpretation as an interpretation. You might say something to yourself like, "I can see that when he shook my hand softly, I interpreted that as weakness." As soon as you notice an interpretation as an interpretation, you have moved to a higher level of consciousness.

> **U**nderstand the other possible reactions, interpretations, and judgments that may be possible. There may be any number of other reasons for the behavior. In the case of the handshake, the person may come from a different culture (because a significant percentage of people in different parts of the world shake hands more softly than we do in the United States), or may have or be recovering from an injury or illness, such as arthritis. Looking at all the possibilities reinforces our dis-identification from our initial reaction and opens up the possibility to:

> **S**earch for the most constructive, empowering, or productive way to deal with the situation. What makes the most sense? Should I assume that the person is weak because of my initial reaction to his handshake, or should I get to know him a little better before I make a definitive assessment? What should I say? What is the best way to handle the circumstance? Once you have a plan in place, you can:

> **E**xecute your action plan. Act consistently with what makes the most sense, in accordance with your highest values and desired way of behaving.

Ross, Howard J. (2014) *Everyday bias: Identifying and navigating unconscious judgments in our daily lives.* Lanham, MD: Rowman & Littlefield Publishers.

Ross (2011) encourages us to ask the following questions:

- Am I reacting to what is happening now, or is this person or situation currently threatening to me?
- Is there any immediate action that needs to be taken?
- How do people or situations like this affect my behavior on a regular basis?
- Is there somebody with whom I should talk about the circumstances?

▶ Awareness of Organizational Implicit Bias

Healthcare leaders are being exhorted by federal regulatory agencies and accreditation bodies, such as the Joint Commission and American College of Healthcare Executives (ACHE), to address implicit bias, and to treat all patients with cultural competence and sensitivity that promotes a sense of inclusion. By 2009, the Joint Commission, as part of a larger initiative to increase healthcare quality and safety through effective communication and cultural competence, approved a new requirement to improve patient–provider communication for hospitals (Wilson-Stronks & Tschurtz, 2010). New Joint Commission Standards of Practice were established to promote culturally competent inpatient care and to foster quality of care outcome for diverse patients. In 2013, ACHE released a policy statement, *The Healthcare Executive's Role in Fostering Inclusion of LGBT Patients and Employees*.

Part of the process to become a culturally competent and inclusive leader includes analyzing conscious and unconscious bias in one's organization. In Ross's book (2011), *Reinventing Diversity: Transforming Organizational Community to Strengthen People, Purpose, and Performance*, the following checklist provides key questions to start the process of analyzing organization bias:

- Is there a diverse mix of people on the leadership team?
- What kind of organizational practices are in place to support diversity, inclusion, and cultural competency?
- Are there consistent communication structures in place that keep all people informed as to what is going on within the organization?
- How does it feel to work in the organization?
- Do people interact comfortably with people of diverse backgrounds and feel free to discuss diversity issues when they emerge?
- Are there constructive ways to deal with conflict?
- Is there a high level of employee satisfaction across diverse groups?
- Are there consistent standards and behaviors regarding mentoring and career development?
- Are people given clear performance standards and feedback that allow them to know how to be successful and assess whether they are successful?
- How does the organization relate to the marketplace and the community?
- Is client/customer/patient satisfaction high across diverse groups?
- Does the organization capture its share of the multicultural market?
- Does the organization do a good job of representing itself to various communities in its marketing and public relations?
- Are diverse vendors used to provide services to the organization?

▶ Diversity Training: Updates and Challenges

Despite all of the time, effort, and money that have been spent, the reality is that diversity programs have, to a large degree, simply not yet fulfilled their promise (Noon, 2018; Ross, 2011).

Based on a contemporary analysis of the effectiveness of diversity training programs, Bezrukova, Spell, Perry, and Jehn (2016) explained why nonminority participants have reacted defensively to diversity training: because they do not want to be made to feel guilty. Minority participants may resist because they may have underlying resentment or feelings of disempowerment. The following diversity training guidelines take these perspectives into account, and provide a pathway for successful training:

- Support of leadership is critically important for any new quality improvement project, especially when addressing sensitive topics like unconscious bias. Therefore, conduct bias training for organizational leadership.
- Have skilled trainers conduct diversity training. Trainers need to be able to identify learners' readiness to engage in conversations and dialogue regarding unconscious bias and be able to create a safe learning environment in which individuals are willing and able to examine their own biases.
- Stress that unconscious bias can be addressed, and its effect on behavior reduced, by introducing specific techniques to achieve these changes. Dedicate time to educating individuals about bias reduction strategies.
- Design the training to maximize engagement and reduce learner fatigue. Use group activities to engage individuals. Keep sessions short and consider alternative ways to deliver training content, that is flexible and convenient with trainees' busy schedules.

One challenge facing training programs is that their assessment has focused more on process than outcomes. In fact, a study by Kalev, Dobbin, and Kelly in 2007, found that diversity training, particularly *when offered independently of other interventions*, could not be proven to contribute to an increase in diversity.

Subjective standards of success are not useful; objective outcome measures that accurately reflect organizational performance are preferable if leaders are to create organizations that are truly inclusive. Findings from the national center for healthcare leadership diversity demonstration project (Weech-Maldonado et al. 2018) demonstrate that cultural competency interventions can improve implicit bias and diversity attitudes. The result can be effective diversity leadership (in which cultural competency is a part of strategic planning and implementation); strategic human resources management recruitment and retention of diverse workers; greater minority representation in leadership positions; and patient cultural competency that reflect effective communications and delivery of care to diverse patients (Ibid.).

Howard Ross (2011) argues for a concept of organizational community because only creating diversity "programs" will not be effective. Creating a long-term diversity commitment is necessary. The concept of organizational community addresses the interdependence of all people and all areas of the organization: that is, a community approach that includes all levels of leadership (Ibid.).

Ways (Ross, 2011) to enhance the effectiveness of diversity training efforts include:

- Ensuring that all levels of leadership participate in diversity training.
- One-on-one coaching to ensure that leaders model the desired diversity behaviors.
- Regular opportunities to obtain feedback from patients and employees as to the organization's diversity-related performance (e.g., 360 feedback).
- Customizing training to meet an identified training need, for which a gap in knowledge, skill, or attitude has been observed. For example, an organization's needs assessment may reveal issues related to a specific population or

age group (e.g., LGBT), to a specific negative behavior that is occurring (e.g., sexual harassment), or to a lack of opportunity for employees to talk about their concerns or engage in self-reflection.

■ Enhance training in areas that receive concerns and complaints, such as human resources, legal, union, and ombuds departments. Focus on staff awareness of unconscious attitudes and behaviors, and teach and model techniques to respond affirmatively, such as education and counseling, rather than rejection or disciplinary action.

Diversity training can be completed in one session, such as a half-day workshop educating participants about cultural competency and covering legal and compliance issues. Alternatively, diversity training can be part of a comprehensive employee training curriculum and integrated with other diversity-related initiatives. A national study of diversity programs conducted by Bendick, Egan, and Lofhjelm (2001) supported the view that integrated training programs taking an organizational development approach were more effective than isolated, stand-alone training. This approach includes the following nine benchmarks:

1. Training has support from top management.
2. Training is customized to each organization.
3. Training is linked to central operating goals such as increased productivity, reduced costs, easier recruitment, enhanced creativity, improved client service, or expanded markets.
4. Trainers are managerial and development professionals.
5. Training enrolls all levels of employees.
6. Training presents discrimination as a general process of inclusion and exclusion, and discusses stereotyping, in-group bias, social comfort, and groupthink, using a wide range of examples to show how individuals of all backgrounds can be affected.
7. Training explicitly addresses individual behavior and includes opportunities to practice new behaviors that can be carried over to the workplace.
8. Training is accompanied by organizational changes: for example, in human resource practices for recruitment, hiring, assignment, compensation, training, evaluation, promotion, and dismissal.
9. Training positively impacts the corporate culture and leads to organizational self-examination, cultural competence, inclusion, and a more diverse workforce.

Summary

As populations become more diverse, healthcare leaders need to embrace this diversity by implementing initiatives that ensure that cultural beliefs and attitudes are respected and valued (Molinari & Shanderson, 2014). Leaders in helping professions such as health care are increasingly expected to embrace and promote cultural competence that reflects respect and sensitivity to varied groups of employees and clients in their organizations.

Effectively leading a diverse workforce and serving diverse patients requires reshaping leaders' and employees' thoughts and behavior to become more sensitive and responsive to these differences. The ability to communicate successfully, and to build trusting relationships with others who are different, requires an understanding of cultural competence and inclusion among healthcare leaders and their staff.

Personal unconscious or implicit bias often poses a major obstacle that interferes with the ability to empathize and to understand an issue or challenge from a different perspective. These biases can erode trust between individuals and undermine interpersonal interactions and lead to biased behaviors and disparities in healthcare delivery.

Healthcare managers and leaders help shape organizations' missions, values, and culture. Leadership support of diversity training focused on unconscious bias can promote trust and help workers adapt to change. Becoming a culturally competent and inclusive leader is a long-term process that begins with self-awareness of personal bias. Commitment and courage to address uncomfortable feelings and behaviors are key. The understood effects of implicit bias on organizational behaviors and practices mandate that students entering today's healthcare workforce must become aware of their implicit biases. As they lead a diverse workforce and serve a diverse clientele, students must develop competencies in empathy and communications that promote productive interpersonal relationships in their work and in their personal lives. Studying and understanding the effects of implicit bias on individuals and healthcare organizations will deepen the body of knowledge in this critical arena and set a high standard of respect and value needed to equitably and appropriately serve the health needs of diverse patients.

Discussion Questions (With Answers Provided)

1. Discuss two reasons why healthcare managers or leaders need to become culturally competent and inclusive.
2. Define cultural competence and inclusion in health care. Explain how bias affects both.
3. Explain two ways that a culturally competent and inclusive leader can deepen their self-awareness?
4. Discuss two ways that leaders can help develop an organizational culture that embraces differences and promotes inclusion.

🔍 CASE STUDY: Patient Aligned Care Teams

The Veterans Health Administration (VHA) is the largest integrated healthcare system in the United States. Its commitment to addressing unconscious bias in clinical settings parallels its goal to reduce healthcare disparities, and to provide direction to reduce the effects of unconscious bias. The VHA's implemented a quality improvement project to improve patient healthcare experiences through patient aligned care teams (PACTs). This project included a cultural competency training program for PACTs that was focused on raising awareness about the presence and effect of unconscious bias in the healthcare setting (Hausmann et al., 2014).

An interactive and team-based cultural competency training program for patient-aligned care teams raised awareness about the presence and effect of unconscious bias in the healthcare setting. The training educated PACTs about ways to prevent unconscious bias from adversely impacting patient care. This focus set it apart from other cultural competency training programs. Attitudes of PACT members about implicit bias and cultural competency were rigorously assessed, as were the effects of the training program on patient experiences and satisfaction.

As a result, trainees reported that they:

- Had successfully applied the training in their work practice as long as 30 and 90 days after the training occurred.
- Became more mindful about ways in which biases can and do affect patient care, and how biases can affect interactions with vulnerable patient populations (e.g., LBGT).
- Became more empathic toward their patients and better listeners during clinical encounters.

Lessons learned (Hausmann et al., 2014) include:

- Clarify the purpose of diversity training at the start to help reduce defensiveness that can interfere with learning.
- Enlist leadership support and provide necessary leadership training to serve as role models.
- Have skilled trainers conduct the training who can engage participants, reduce learner fatigue, and create a safe learning environment.

Teach skills and strategies that address unconscious bias and promote positive behavior change.

Case Study Discussion Questions

1. Assess the VA's diversity program presented in the Case Study in terms of addressing implicit bias.
2. Explain whether it was effective.

Related Websites

Agency for Healthcare Research and Quality: www.ahrq.gov/topics/disparities.html
Cook Ross: http://cookross.com/
Edutopia: www.edutopia.org/blog/preparing-cultural-diversity-resources-teachers
Gallup Blog: https://news.gallup.com/opinion/gallup/220649/not-supporting-workplace-inclusion .aspx
Project Implicit: https://implicit.harvard.edu/implicit/
Substance Abuse and Mental Health Services Administration: www.samhsa.gov/health-disparities

References

Administration on Aging. (2014). A profile of older Americans: 2014. *PsycEXTRA Dataset*. doi:10.1037/e572582012-001

Agency for Healthcare Research and Quality. (2016). *Priority populations*. Retrieved from www .ahrq.gov/topics/priority-populations/index.html

Behar-Horenstein, L. S., Feng, X., Isaac, C. A., & Lee, B. (2017). Dental students' expression of cultural competence. *Journal of Ethnographic & Qualitative Research, 11*, 171–187.

Bendick, M., Egan, M. L. & Lofhjelm, S. M. (2001). Workforce diversity training: From anti-discrimination compliance to organizational development. *Human Resource Planning, 24*(2), 10–25; United States: Human Resource Planning Society.

Betancourt, J. R. (2005). *Improving quality and achieving equity: The role of cultural competence in reducing racial and ethnic disparities in health care*. New York, NY: Commonwealth Fund.

Betancourt, J., Green, A., Carrillo, J., & Ananeh-Firempong, O. (2003). Defining cultural competence: A practical framework for addressing racial/ethnic disparities in health and health care. *Public Health Reports, 118*, 293–302.

Bevelin, P. (2017). *Seeking wisdom: From Darwin to Munger*. Sweden and Marceline, MO: Post Scriptum AM and Walsworth Publishing Company.

Bezrukova, K., Spell, C. S., Perry, J. L., & Jehn, K. A. (2016, November). A meta-analytical integration of over 40 years of research on diversity training evaluation. *Psychological Bulletin, 142*(11), 1227–1274.

Bourke, J., & Dillon, B. (2016, April). *The six signature traits of inclusive leadership*. Retrieved from www2.deloitte.com/insights/us/en/topics/talent/six-signature-traits-of-inclusive-leadership.html

Byrd, T., Chavez, R., & Wilson, K. (2007, Winter). Barriers and facilitators of cervical cancer screening. *Ethnicity and Disease, 17*, 129–134.

Byyny, R. (2017, Winter). Cognitive bias: Recognizing and managing our unconscious biases. *The Pharos, Alpha Omega Alpha's Quarterly Journal, 80*(1), 2–7.

Center for Disease Control (CDC). (2011). *Fact sheet-CEC health disparities and inequalities report*. Retrieved from www.cc.gov/minorityhealth/chdir/2011/factsheet.pdf

Dotson, E., Bonam, C., & Jagers, J. (2017, Spring). Redefining race as a process: Implication for healthcare leadership. *Journal of Health Administration Education, 34*(2), 295–318.

Eurich, T. (2018, April 23). *What self-awareness really is (and how to cultivate it)*. Retrieved from https://hbr.org/2018/01/what-self-awareness-really-is-and-how-to-cultivate-it

Fredriksen-Goldsen, K. I., Cook-Daniels, L., Kim, H. J., Erosheva, E. A., Emlet, C. A., Hoy-Ellis, C. P., Muraco, A. 2013. Health disparities among lesbian, gay, and bisexual older adults: Results from a population-based study. *American Journal of Public Health, 103*(10), 1802–1809.

Gonzalez, C. M., Kim, M. Y., & Marantz, P. R. (2014). Implicit bias and its relation to health disparities: A teaching program and survey of medical students. *Teaching and Learning in Medicine, 26*(1), 64–71.

Guérin-Marion, C., Manion, I., & Parsons, H. (2018). Leading an intergenerational workforce: An integrative conceptual framework. *International Journal of Public Leadership, 14*(1), 48–58.

Hausmann, L., Burgess, D., Frankenfield, L., Long, J., Mor, M., Obrosky, D., ... Saha, S., (2014). *Evaluation of a pilot program to improve patient health care experiences through PACT cultural competency training about unconscious bias*. Office of Health Equity, Center for Health Equity Research and Promotion VA Pittsburgh Healthcare System. U.S. Department of Veterans Affairs (p. 66). Retrieved from www.researchgate.net/publication/301625572

IFDHRET. (2012). *Diversity and disparities: A benchmark study of U.S. hospitals*. Chicago, IL; Institute for Diversity in Health Management and Health Research & Educational Trust.

Improving Cultural Competence. (2014). Retrieved from https://store.samhsa.gov/shin/content /SMA14–4849/SMA14–4849.pdf

Kahneman, D. (2012). Two systems in the mind. *Bulletin of the American Academy of Arts and Sciences, 65*(2), 55–59.

Kalev, A., Dobbin, F., & Kelly, E., (2007). *Best practices or best guesses? Diversity management and the remediation of inequality*. Berkeley, CA: University of California Press.

Kohn, L., Corrigan, J., & Donaldson, M. (2000). *To err is human: Building a safer health system*. Washington, DC: Institute of Medicine.

Kornadt, A., Meissner, F., & Rothermund, F. (2016). Implicit and explicit age stereotypes for specific life domains across the life span: Distinct patterns and age group differences. *Experimental Aging Research, 42*(2), 195–211. doi:10.1080/0361073X.2016.1132899

Levy, B. R., & Myers, L. M. (2005). Relationship between respiratory mortality and self-perceptions of aging. *Psychology & Health, 20*, 553–564. doi:10.1080/14768320500066381

Lim, F., Brown, D., & Kim, S., (2014). Addressing health care disparities in the lesbian, gay, bisexual, and transgender population. *American Journal of Nursing, 14*(6), 24–34.

Miranda, G., & Allen, P., (2017, September–November). Strategies for leading a multi-generational organization. *I-managers' Journal on Management, 12*(2), 14–25.

Molinari, C., & Shanderson, L. (2014). The culturally competent leader. In L. G. Rubino & S. J. Esparza (Eds.), *New leadership for today's health professionals: Concepts and cases* (pp. 57–75). Sudbury, MA: Jones and Bartlett Learning.

Molinari, C., & Takagi, E. (2017). Diversity and the delivery of long term care services. In M. H. McSweeney-Feld, C. Molinari, & R. Oetgen (Eds.), *Dimensions of long term care management: An introduction* (2nd ed., pp. 171–198). Chicago, IL: Health Administration Press.

Moua, M. (2010). *Culturally intelligent leadership*. New York, NY: Business Expert.

Noon, M. (2018). Pointless diversity training: Unconscious bias, new racism and agency Mike Noon. *Work, Employment and Society, 32*(1), 198–209.

Phibbs, S., & Hooker, K. (2017). An exploration of factors associated with ageist stereotype threat in a medical setting. *Journals of Gerontology Series B: Psychological Sciences and Social Sciences.* doi:10.1093/geronb/gbx034

Ross, H. J. (2011). *Reinventing diversity: Transforming organizational community to strengthen people, purpose, and performance* (p. 172). Lanham, MD: Rowman & Littlefield Publishers.

Ross, H. J. (2014). *Everyday bias: Identifying and navigating unconscious judgments in Our Daily Lives.* Lanham, MD: Rowman & Littlefield Publishers.

Rowan, N. L., & Giunta, N. (2016). Lessons on social and health disparities from older lesbians with alcoholism and the role of interventions to promote culturally competent interventions. *Journal of Human Behavior in the Social Environment, 26*(2), 210–216.

Rowe, M. (1990, June). Barriers to equality. *Employee Responsibilities and Rights Journal, 3*(2), 153–163.

Rudolph, C. W., & Zacher, H. (2015). Intergenerational perceptions and conflicts in multi-age and multigenerational work environments. In L. Finkelstein, D. Truxillo, F. Fraccaroli, & R. Kanfer, (Eds.). *Facing the challenges of a multi-age workforce: A use-inspired approach* (pp. 253–282). New York, NY: Routledge.

SAMHSA. (2014). *Improving cultural competency.* Publication No. (SMA) 14–4849 First Printed 2014. Retrieved from https://store.samhsa.gov/shin/content/SMA14-4849/SMA14-4849.pdf

Schein, E. H. (2013). *Humble inquiry: The gentle art of asking instead of telling.* Oakland, CA: Berrett-Koehler Publishers.

Smedley, B., Stith, A., & Nelson, A. (2003). *Unequal treatment: Confronting racial and ethnic disparities in health care.* Washington, DC: National Academies Press.

Stillman, D., & Stillman, J., (2017). *GenZ@Work: How the next generation is transforming the workplace.* New York, NY: Harper Collins.

Sue, D. W. (2010). *Microaggressions in everyday life: Race, gender, and sexual orientation.* Hoboken, NJ: John Wiley & Sons.

Sugiyama, K., Cavanagh, K. V., van Esch, C., Bilimoria, D., & Brown, C. (2016). Inclusive leadership development: Drawing from pedagogies of women's and general leadership development programs. *Journal of Management Education, 40*(3), 253–292.

Sukhera, J., & Waitling, C. (2017). A Framework for integrating implicit bias recognition into health professions education. *Academic Medicine, 20*(10). doi:10.1097/ACM.0000000000001819

Thomas, D., & Inkson, K. (2009). *Cultural intelligence living and working globally* (2nd ed.). San Francisco, CA: Berrett Koehler.

Van Ryn, M., Burgess, D. J., Dovidio, J. F., Phelan, S. M., Saha, S., Malat, J., & Perry, S. (2011). The impact of racism on clinician cognition, behavior, and clinical decision making. *Du Bois Review: Social Science Research on Race, 8*(1), 199–218.

Vespa, J., Armstrong, D., & Medina, L. (2018, March). Demographic turning points for the United States: Population projections for 2020 to 2060. *U.S. Department of Commerce Economics and Statistics Administration U.S. Census Bureau* (pp. 25–1144).

Watt, K., Abbott, P., & Reath, J. (2015). Cultural competency training of GP registrars-exploring the views of GP supervisors. *International Journal for Equity in Health, 14*(89), 1–10.

Weech-Maldonado, R., Dreachslin, J., Epane, J., Gail, J., Gupta, S., & Wainio, J. (2018). Hospital cultural competency as a systematic organization intervention: Key findings from the national centers for healthcare leadership diversity demonstration project. *Health Care Management Review, 43*(1), 30–41.

Weisbord, M. R. (2012). *Productive workplaces: Dignity, meaning, and community in the 21st century.* Hoboken, NJ: John Wiley & Sons.

Wiedmer, T. (2015). Generations do differ: Best practices in leading traditionalists, boomers, and generations X, Y, and Z. *Delta Kappa Gamma Bulletin, 82*(1), 51.

Wilson-Stronks, A., & Tschurtz, B., (2010, August). *Advancing effective communication, cultural competence, and patient and family centered care: A roadmap for hospitals.* Oakbrook Terrace, IL: The Joint Commission.

Young, Stephen. (2017). *Micromessaging: Why great leadership is beyond words* (p. 12). New York, NY: McGraw-Hill Education.

CHAPTER 4

Creating a Culture of Professionalism

Keith Benson and Chris Hummer

LEARNING OBJECTIVES

By the end of this chapter, the student will be able to:

- Define professional behaviors.
- Describe how leaders can create and promote a culture of professionalism within an organization.
- Compare and contrast professionalism as a healthcare leader with professionalism as a staff clinician/physician.
- Discuss the role of professional/organizational ethics or codes of conduct in building and promoting professionalism.
- Describe the leader's role in sustaining a culture of professionalism.

KEY TERMS

Character	Obligation
Competency	PIE²
Conduct	Professionalism
Leadership	Relationships

▶ Introduction

What Is Professionalism?

Healthcare executives have many different skill sets they can use in managing healthcare organizations. A key component in their management toolbox is **professionalism**. A strong professionalism skill set facilitates successful **leadership**.

What is professionalism and why is it so critical to executives' success? The Oxford English Dictionary defines professionalism as "Professional quality, character, or conduct; a professional system or method" (http:// www.oed.com/view /Entry/152054?redirectedFrom=professionalism#eid). Why is professionalism so important in the healthcare industry? The simple reason is that professionalism benefits all stakeholders. Brennan and Monson aptly state "Professionalism: Good for Patients and Health Care Organizations" (2014).

Professionals best serve their chosen profession by adopting a broad approach to meeting **obligations**. These obligations are to clients (customers), to the community, the profession, and to societal needs (Medical Professionalism Project, 2002; Shapiro, Whittenmore, & Tsen, 2014; Swick, 2000; Wyatt, 2004). Medical professionalism is a set of behaviors, attitudes, and values that serves the interests of patients and society before one's own interests (Egener et al., 2017; Reynolds, 1994, Wynia, Latham, Kao, & Emmanuel, 1999). We posit that managerial professionalism parallels medical professionalism, but with the inclusion of the employee/staff interests in the equation. All healthcare providers and managers have both an ethical and professional duty to practice professionalism (medical/clinical and managerial) to promote high-quality patient care and a desirable workplace environment.

▶ The Components of Professionalism

Achieving this standard can be facilitated by understanding the three basic components of professionalism: (1) **character**, (2) **conduct**, and (3) quality (**FIGURE 4.1**).

For example, one of the first lessons students learn in school is not to cheat. By not cheating, students are exhibiting a desired professional behavior that directly

FIGURE 4.1 Components of Professionalism
© Yuri Arcurs/Shutterstock.

relates to both character and conduct. Many academic institutions have institutionalized this expected professional behavior through the creation and adoption of honor codes or pledges. The University of Texas Medical Branch at Galveston uses the honor pledge "On my honor, as a member of the UTMB community, I pledge to act with integrity, compassion, and respect in all my academic and professional endeavors," as a statement of professionalism (Smith, Saavedra, Raeke, & O'Donell, 2007). At Johns Hopkins University, all medical students must sign that they have read and understand the honor code, which can be found at https://www.hopkins medicine.org/som/students/policies/HonorCode.pdf. This honor code binds all to a higher level of expectations and professionalism. Honor codes and pledges clearly outline expected professional behavior. These standards are explicit examples that academic leaders should demonstrate, model, and promote. Some healthcare organizations use honor codes as well to standardize and summarize behavior expectations for all members of the organization.

Examples of professionalism can be considered from two perspectives, as in the model **PIE**[2]—that is, Personal (Internal and External) and Professional (Internal and External) Professionalism. This model was created as a guide to professional behaviors and conduct. The Internal perspective of professionalism relates to behaviors/actions that are not always visible to others. In this perspective, an individual might be the only one who knows their actions or behaviors are professional. The external perspective is clearly visible to others and can be judged by them. Others rate the level of professionalism by these behaviors. **TABLE 4.1** lists items included in each perspective.

▶ The Value of Professionalism

All healthcare professionals should practice medical professionalism. Healthcare leaders have the additional responsibility of practicing leadership/managerial professionalism. Modeling medical professionalism is also critical for healthcare leaders as they interface with physicians and other clinical staff to create and sustain a culture of professionalism and respect. Healthcare leaders are responsible for the professional behavior of employees, many of whom work with little or no direct supervision. Ingrained medical professionalism usually requires less direct supervision and results in better patient care and improved organizational outcomes (Cruess & Cruess, 2016; Sergiovanni, 1992; Wojciech et al., 2006).

Healthcare organizations practicing lower levels of professional behavior (higher levels of unprofessional behavior) tend to demonstrate poor adherence to policies and procedures; lower staff morale and increased turnover; drops in patient volume; and a greater number of medical errors, adverse outcomes, and malpractice suits (Hickson, Pichert, Webb, & Gabbe, 2007; Webb et al., 2016). A study by the Studer Group and the Center for Patient and Professional Advocacy (CPPA) at Vanderbilt University Medical Center found that, when policies, processes, and training to prevent disruptive behaviors do not exist in an organization, workplace satisfaction is jeopardized. For example, 66% of survey respondents considered leaving their job as a result of unprofessional behavior of leaders or peers. Unprofessional behavior negatively impacts job satisfaction, workplace safety, and clinical outcomes. It is imperative for healthcare leaders to expect and promote medical and

TABLE 4.1 PIE² or Personal and Professional Professionalism

Personal Professionalism

Internal	External
Being honest	Demonstrating integrity
Striving to be reliable and dependable	Being on time, meeting deadlines, keeping promises
Caring about others	Treating all people with respect
Respecting oneself	Dressing appropriately for the dress code

Professional Professionalism

Internal	External
Respecting others	Dealing with sensitive issues privately
Being an active learner	Accepting criticism in a positive manner
Maintaining integrity	Ensuring honesty and accuracy in communications and other administrative tasks, avoiding real or perceived conflicts of interest
Aiming for self-control	Engaging in respectful and considerate communications
Doing your job to the best of your ability	Demonstrating that you value the privilege of caring for patients and respect others who engage in this role as well

Courtesy of Keith J. Benson, PhD.

managerial professionalism, and to intervene and take corrective action in cases where unprofessional or disruptive behaviors are reported or observed (Studer Group 2011, http://www.studergroup.com/DB.)

▶ Implementing Professionalism

Successful medical professionalism requires: (1) professional expertise and **competency** as a manager and/or clinician; (2) the ability to communicate and connect effectively with others, such as patients and colleagues, in a professional capacity; and (3) the ability and commitment to achieve organizational goals through development of strong fiduciary **relationships**, trust, and morality (ABIM, 2002).

TABLE 4.2 The CHS-Pineville Way
■ Set the best example of the desired behavior.   ■ Listen to everyone—patients, patient families, employees, physicians, providers.   ■ Get to know your employees so they can see you as a role model. A great way to do this is to frequently take walks throughout the facility.   ■ Hold people accountable—congratulate them on a job well done. Coach them if they need to improve to meet a standard.   ■ Smile—it makes others feel better and inspires them to act professionally.   ■ Finally, and perhaps the most important—CARE! Care for your patients, care for your employees, care your providers, care for your organization, and care for your community.

Courtesy of Carolinas Medical Center–Pineville.

Mueller (2009) shares the renowned Mayo Clinic's foundation of professionalism: clinical knowledge and skills, communication skills, ethics, accountability, altruism, excellence, and humanism. The Mayo Clinic, whose primary value is "the needs of the patient come first," uses PLEASE CARE (Present, Listen, Empathize, Action, Summarize, Excite, Confidentiality, Attitude, Respect, and Emotional intelligence) to advance medical professionalism within its organization.

Reynolds (1991) stated that, in healthcare organizations, professional behaviors include a nonjudgmental and respectful approach to patients, a commitment to excellence and lifelong competency, and a collegial and cooperative approach to working with members of the healthcare team. Even though this guide for behaviors is somewhat dated, it still serves as a recipe for healthcare professionals seeking to practice a high standard of medical professionalism.

Healthcare leaders play a critical role in inspiring and promoting a culture of medical professionalism. An example of this process can be witnessed in the Carolinas HealthCare System Pineville (CHS-Pineville) initiatives. CHS-P's motto, which drives the organization, is "Uncompromising Excellence. Commitment to Care." In the spring of 2011, Dr. Benson worked as a faculty intern for Chris Hummer, CEO Carolinas HealthCare System Pineville. During this time, Benson observed firsthand how Hummer and the CHS-Pineville leadership team promoted professionalism by modeling these guidelines and mentoring staff. Every day, the "A-Team," as Hummer called them, demonstrated a commitment to care by practicing uncompromising excellence. **TABLE 4.2** demonstrates the CHS-Pineville Way, that is, the professional behaviors the senior leadership team exhibited.

▶ Sources of Professionalism

Leaders of healthcare organizations should develop resources and tools to help promote professionalism from internal (within the organization) or external (outside the organization) sources. A source of professionalism can be an organization's mission, vision, and value statements. These statements prescribe why the organization exists, what the organization believes in, and what is important to the organization.

© Comstock Images/Thinkstock.

Codes of Conduct, Professional Oaths, and Codes of Ethics

Most occupations embrace a definition of professionalism that is often embedded in their codes of conduct. The code of conduct dictates duties and responsibilities and typically shares the following common elements:

1. An expectation of selflessness
2. An expectation of skill
3. An expectation of trust-worthiness
4. An expectation of discipline (Gawande, 2009)

The American College of Healthcare Executives (ACHE) is an international professional society of more than 35,000 healthcare executives. ACHE developed a code of ethics to guide healthcare executives in their professional duties and obligations. This code of ethics and conduct includes:

I.   The healthcare executive's responsibilities to the profession of healthcare management.
II. The healthcare executive's responsibilities to patients or others served.

III. The healthcare executive's responsibilities to the organization.

IV. The healthcare executive's responsibilities to employees.

V. The healthcare executive's responsibilities to community and society.

VI. The healthcare executive's responsibility to report violations of the ACHE code.

The complete ACHE code of ethics is available at http://www.ache.org/abt _ache/code.cfm. Other professional associations for healthcare executives such as the Medical Group Management Association (MGMA), http://www.mgma.com/; the American Health Information Management Association (AHIMA), http:// www.ahima.org/; and the American Health Care Association (AHCA), http://www .ahcancal.org/Pages/Default.aspx, also have codes of ethics to help guide their members' professional behavior.

Professional oaths reflect a binding promise. One of the earliest professional oaths was authored by Hippocrates, a 5th-century BC physician, who prescribed that physicians should treat the sick to the best of their ability, preserve patient privacy, teach the secrets of medicine to the next generation, and, above all, "abstain from doing harm." Physician professionalism emerged directly from the Hippocratic Oath (Harms, 2004). Clinical professionals must not only care for and about the patient but also deliver necessary medical care in a high-quality, cost-effective, compassionate manner. Each member of a clinical care team is guided by the professional oath related to their clinical profession. Understanding the elements of each profession's oath and the promises that each clinical professional has made can help healthcare leaders use common elements to advance medical professionalism in the organization as a whole.

Chris Hummer came to CHS-Pineville in 2006 as its CEO. When Hummer arrived, there was growing friction between the physician staff and the administrative team. In just two years, Hummer and his leadership team forged strong relationships with the physicians. Together they joined to build a medical center practicing professionalism and delivering high-quality care. During this engagement process, physician satisfaction scores with CHS-Pineville increased dramatically. The following case study describes Hummer's experience maintaining and sustaining professionalism (both medical and managerial) in a healthcare organization during a period of growth and change.

▶ Leadership in Practice

Working with Physicians to Create a Culture of Professionalism: A CEO's Perspective

Carolinas HealthCare System Pineville (CHS-Pineville) is a 120-bed community hospital located in Pineville, a town in the south end of Charlotte, North Carolina.

The hospital was built in 1987 as a satellite of Mercy Hospital. Mercy Hospital was acquired by Carolinas HealthCare System (CHS) in 1995 and was renamed CHS-Pineville in 2016.

In 2007, CHS-Pineville launched an ambitious multiphase expansion to transform the facility from a community hospital to a tertiary medical center. The expansion cost was more than $300 million and was completed in 2013. A new energy plant, a parking deck, a medical office building, 86 additional inpatient beds (25 of which are intensive care), four operating rooms, 10 emergency department bays, and 10 private neonatal intensive care rooms went into operation. The CHS-Pineville facility grew from 175,000 square feet to 515,000 square feet. New tertiary services included inpatient dialysis, medical and surgical intensive care, interventional and vascular cardiology, cardiothoracic surgery, and surgical oncology, with emphases on breast and lung cancer. This growth occurred in a time when many facilities were experiencing a contraction of services.

CHS-Pineville's reputation continues to be strong and positive in all operational areas, resulting in patient selection gains. For example, for the past several years, CHS-Pineville has excelled in quality (e.g., top 10% in mortality, multiple Joint Commission disease specific certifications), patient satisfaction (e.g., top quartile or higher as rated by the Professional Research Corporation, multiple JD Power awards), physician satisfaction (top 10% as rated by Healthstream), and employee satisfaction (top 15% as rated by Press Ganey). These positive results can be directly correlated to the culture of professionalism cultivated and sustained by the CHS-Pineville leadership team.

CHS-Pineville medical staff today are highly engaged in working with the administration team to deliver high quality care. The medical staff includes veteran physicians who were affiliated with Mercy, along with physicians hired more recently by Atrium Health, its parent organization. CHS-Pineville physicians are generally accepting of technology, collaborative and reasonable in their approach to problem-solving; value the contributions and professionalism of their colleagues, and hold them accountable for their actions both clinically and behaviorally. Most importantly, the physicians understand that the medical staff's role and contributions as a whole are more significant than those of its individual practitioners alone.

Since the launch of the first expansion, CHS-Pineville's medical staff has grown by more than 200 physicians. Though the physical and programmatic growth at CHS-Pineville and the improvement of facilities increased access for patients, there were concerns that an influx of new physicians could erode the positive and collegial culture of CHS-Pineville's medical staff. Efforts over the past few years to promote and sustain a culture of professionalism indeed proved worthwhile. The professionalism of CHS-Pineville's medical staff not only weathered the transformation but also excelled in this new environment.[1]

---

1 Since the time of construction, the hospital has increased its full-time equivalents (FTEs) from 535 to 940 in 2011, adding another 191 in 2012. In 2017, Pineville employs 1,700 FTEs. Several efforts are underway to ensure that the support for CHS employee professional development (via, for example, enhanced peer interviewing, more robust orientation, expanded training and education, increased reward and recognition, etc.) continues to strengthen the culture.

▶ Rebuilding Engagement

Efforts to maintain the atmosphere of professionalism have been guided by CHS-Pineville's history. In 2005, the relationship between administration and CHS-Pineville's medical staff was strained. In its first physician satisfaction survey, the Carolinas HealthCare System's Metro Group, Healthstream, ranked CHS-Pineville last in Overall Satisfaction—at the 23rd percentile nationally.[2]

In 2006, the leadership change at CHS-Pineville, along with the renewed Carolina HealthCare System focus on physician satisfaction, led to changes that reversed the hospital's position from last to first, with a 3.32 mean score, equal to the 83rd percentile nationally. This level of engagement continues today. The overall physician score has moved from 23% before Hummer was hired, to averaging about 90% satisfaction since 2008.

CHS-Pineville administrative leadership used a variety of tactics to promote physician engagement by inviting input and participation in strategic planning and decision-making. Supporting the medical staff's professionalism resulted in improved physician satisfaction as well as productivity.

For example, CHS-Pineville's administrative leadership team worked closely with the medical staff leadership in two areas. The first is to develop methods to obtain internal and external input about the organizational culture via an annual event. The second is to address the growing separation between physicians who were based at the hospital, such as emergency physicians, hospitalists, anesthesiologists, radiologists, proceduralists and surgeons, and the growing number of primary care physicians who did not practice with the hospital or admit patients.

After the addition of hospitalists at CHS-Pineville in 2003, family practice and internal medicine doctors in the local community began using the hospital less and less, if at all. The results: (1) Medical staff responsibilities fell on fewer individuals. (2) The medical staff developed a high and disproportionate concentration of specialty and hospital-based physicians. (3) The interaction and communication between referring primary care physicians and specialists was sharply reduced.

To bridge this separation, CHS-Pineville leaders launched an event in October 2006, the "State of the Hospital," to bring together community and hospital. The invitation list included physicians who had previously had privileges but were no longer active medical staff. After welcoming the guests and allowing a period for networking and fellowship among the attendees, the leaders offered a formal program that included medical staff business (e.g., election of officers), departmental updates, awards and recognitions, and even a humorous video that offered a parody of modern medicine. This event helped to rebuild CHS-Pineville connections with community physicians and has been continued at the annual medical staff meetings.

Additionally, the economics of health care placed a premium on productivity, which drove physicians to try to save time as they cared for their patients. When orders were placed or questions about a referred patient arose, busy doctors would opt to communicate with available office personnel, nurses, or mid-level providers,

---

2　Carolinas HealthCare System's Metro Group includes the following facilities: CMC, CHS-Mercy, CHS-Pineville, CHS-University, CHS-Randolph, CHS-Northeast, CHS-Lincoln, CHS-Rehabilitation, CHS-Union, CHS-Anson, Levine Children's Hospital, Jeff Gordon Children's Hospital, and CHS Stanly.

and bypass physician-to-physician communication. This practice eroded collegiality and risked increasing conflict and negative patient outcomes. Failure to communicate directly with physician colleagues became an important issue that needed to be addressed by the CHS-Pineville's Medical Executive Committee (MEC). The MEC was comprised of physician leaders selected by the physicians with staff privileges. As a result, in 2007, the bylaws were revised requiring doctor-to-doctor communication regarding hospitalized patients.

Finally, the recognition of practice and time demands on physicians, which limited physician participation in committee activities, led the MEC to reorganize committee structure and function so that committee service became a meaningful use of physicians' time. Departmental Committees instituted operational subcommittees to deal with routine items, allowing a more substantive agenda for the large-group meetings that addressed quality of care. One tool to improve use of physician time was the implantation of consent agendas. A consent agenda allows routine matters that do not need much explanation or discussion to be bundled and voted one as one package. Consent agendas addressed less critical matters and allowed time at meetings for meaningful debate about hospital-wide issues of concern to the medical staff. To encourage retention of physician leaders and recruitment of new champions, the organizational structure of the medical staff was updated and revised, and an annual MEC orientation and retreat was scheduled at the beginning of each year to prepare new and existing leaders for the year ahead.

▶ Physician Oath

CHS-Pineville's medical staff has long valued and promoted both clinical competence and professionalism among its members. To underscore this commitment in an atmosphere of rapid growth and expansion, the MEC developed a physician oath in late 2010 with two objectives in mind: (1) to remind current medical staff of its professional culture and its responsibility to foster it for the next generation, and (2) to provide an explicit description of the CHS-Pineville professional culture and its expectations for the newest members. The complete oath is:

Health care has undergone a seismic evolution in recent years that has changed physician practice from independent autonomy to team function. CHS-Pineville recognized that the ground-breaking changes in its institution, as well as the healthcare industry as a whole, have had a significant impact on physicians and could negatively impact professionalism. By acknowledging that physicians, just like other professionals, value being respected, empowered, recognized and rewarded, and included in strategic planning and decision-making that affects their practice, CHS-Pineville enlisted and enhanced physician engagement and support, and promoted and encouraged ongoing physician professionalism.

At CHS-Pineville, the professionalism of the medical staff has not only been affected by the changes in the industry, but also the growth of the campus. In 2006, CHS-Pineville managed about 6,000 discharges, 10,000 adjusted discharges, 45,000 ED visits, and 5,800 surgeries. By 2017, volumes had increased significantly to more than 19,000 discharges, 36,000 adjusted patient days, 100,000 emergency department visits, and 9,000 surgeries.

In order to address the increased volume, the medical staff has grown from about 75 physicians who practiced full-time at CHS-Pineville in 2006 to 350 in 2017. Employees of the hospital, who numbered 535 in 2006, have reached 1,700 today. If not managed appropriately, the professionalism of CHS-Pineville's medical staff and employees could erode during this period of high growth, resulting in poor engagement, suboptimal quality, and a less than stellar patient experience.

However, throughout this period of time, Pineville sustained or improved its Patient Experience scores and physician and employee engagement results. Most importantly, the quality of care provided at Pineville improved as well. In 2017, CHS-Pineville was ranked by *Business North Carolina* magazine as the 7th best hospital in the state, and the Centers for Medicare and Medicaid Services (CMS) awarded Pineville 5 Stars—the only Charlotte hospital to receive such a distinction. Pineville was also named a Truven Healthcare Top 100 hospital from 2013–2015, and remains a Leapfrog Grade A hospital.

▶ Leadership in Practice Case Discussion Questions

1. From your perspective, what are the skills that the CHS-Pineville's CEO used to create a culture of professionalism?
2. Why is physician and employee satisfaction a marker of a professional organizational culture?
3. If you had to create an organizational oath similar to the CHS-Pineville physician oath, what concepts and components would you ensure were included?
4. What lessons from the Leadership in Practice case are applicable to long-term care facilities, physician practices, and other healthcare organizations?

▶ Developing and Promoting Professionalism Throughout an Organization

Healthcare leaders have many tools at their disposal that can help develop professionalism throughout an organization. One of the most effective methods for leaders to mentor employees is to serve as exemplary role models and demonstrate the desired professional behaviors themselves. The tools below afford opportunities for executives to lead by example.

Meetings

When leading a meeting, run it in a professional manner. Have an agenda and follow it. Keep people focused on the meeting topics and limit tangential discussions. And most importantly, respect people's time. Time is a valuable commodity and needs to be guarded and not wasted. One sign of an effective leader is his/her ability to run a professional/productive meeting.

Communications

Effective communications facilitate professionalism. Leaders should use clear, precise, and concise statements; avoid jargon and acronyms whenever possible; listen with empathy; read and interpret nonverbal communications such as body language and gestures; and ask pertinent questions. Managers also need to focus beyond just the words of a conversation. In addition to demonstrating clarity and articulateness with the written word, leaders in today's media-rich environments need to be effective communicators and display professionalism in presentations, documents, and when using email and social media.

Organizational Culture

Leaders must monitor and evaluate the organization's culture on an ongoing basis, to ensure the promotion of professionalism. Fortunately, there are leadership models available for leaders to help create, shape, and influence professionalism within an organization.

There are several sources for executives that can help guide leader efforts in this regard. One source that addresses creating and maintaining an organizational culture that promotes professionalism is *The Leadership Challenge* by Kouzes and Posner (2004). Its First Five Practices are outlined in **BOX 4.1**.

Another leadership expert in health care, Quint Studer, discusses Straight-A Leadership (2009) based on his teams' work with organizations. Studer notes: "If everyone in the organization doesn't truly understand the behavior that's needed to be successful, the organization won't achieve its goals," pg. XVI. This statement demonstrates that leaders must not only understand and model necessary professional behaviors themselves: They must also educate, train, and mentor staff in understanding and practicing these behaviors.

To help leaders realize this objective, Studer developed the Straight-A Leadership model for delivering consistency in a professional organization. Straight A

BOX 4.1 First Five Practices

Model the Way "Leaders establish principles concerning the way people (constituents, peers, colleagues, and customers alike) should be treated and the way goals should be pursued. They create standards of excellence and then set an example for others to follow. Because the prospect of complex change can overwhelm people and stifle action, they set interim goals so that people can achieve small wins as they work toward larger objectives. They unravel bureaucracy when it impedes action; they put up signposts when people are unsure of where to go or how to get there; and they create opportunities for victory."

   Inspire a Shared Vision "Leaders passionately believe that they can make a difference. They envision the future, creating an ideal and unique image of what the organization can become. Through their magnetism and quiet persuasion, leaders enlist others in their dreams. They breathe life into their visions and get people to see exciting possibilities for the future."

   Challenge the Process "Leaders search for opportunities to change the status quo. They look for innovative ways to improve the organization. In doing so, they experiment and take risks. And because leaders know that risk taking involves mistakes and failures, they accept the inevitable disappointments as learning opportunities."

   Enable Others to Act "Leaders foster collaboration and build spirited teams. They actively involve others. Leaders understand that mutual respect is what sustains extraordinary efforts; they strive to create an atmosphere of trust and human dignity. They strengthen others, making each person feel capable and powerful."

   Encourage the Heart "Accomplishing extraordinary things in organizations is hard work. To keep hope and determination alive, leaders recognize contributions that individuals make. In every winning team, the members need to share in the rewards of their efforts, so leaders celebrate accomplishments. They make people feel like heroes," http://www.leadershipchallenge.com/WileyCDA/Section/id-131055.html

http://www.leadershipchallenge.com/WileyCDA/Section/id-131055.html

stands for Alignment, Action, and Accountability. Studer states that all senior leaders need to be aligned—that is, on the same page—and should expect accountability from employees. Leaders should assess employee professionalism and performance, and reward high performers, help advance mid-range performers, and intervene to assist those not performing up to standards (Studer, 2009).

▶ Hiring/Performance Management

One of the best ways to support professionalism within an organization is to begin with its hiring process. Mueller (2009) and Reynolds (1991) recommend a team approach to evaluating interviewing, and hiring applicants who are able to practice the expected behaviors and conduct. Professionalism should be included in the job description and addressed in employee performance evaluations. After employees are hired, ongoing staff assessment and development can help underperformers meet the organization standards and expectations. Methods for assessing compliance include:

- Direct observation
- Tests that measure specific skills, for example, communication skills, conflict resolution, ethical judgment

- 360-degree reviews
- Clinical evaluations and peer reviews
- Patient feedback
- Critical incident reports (Mueller, 2009)

▶ Coaching/Mentoring

Developing a culture of professionalism does not happen overnight. A critical step in developing and maintaining a culture of professionalism within an organization is implementing a viable and active coaching/mentoring program, strongly and openly supported by the senior management. Mentors, including senior leaders, can serve as role models for employees and provide advice, guidance, and coaching when needed (Webb et al., 2016; Wells, 2002). Sadly, failure of senior management to uphold the organization's standards of professionalism can have a profound negative impact on employees and must be avoided at all cost.

▶ Organizational Support and Commitment

To sustain a culture of professionalism, the senior leaders of the organization must be committed and more importantly demonstrate support for professionalism. A key finding in studying the positive transformation at CHS-Pineville was that the organization's success was not due to one person. It took a dedicated senior leadership team that valued professionalism and committed valuable resources to sustain professionalism to increase both patient and physician satisfaction.

Other organizations have also institutionalized support to maintain professionalism. A healthy and mutually respectful relationship between the medical staff and organizational leadership has been a critical factor in success (Swensen et al., 2016). For example, the Mayo Clinic created the Office of Staff Services (OSS) to provide peer support to physicians, scientists, and senior administrators (Shanafelt et al., 2017). The Mayo Clinic acknowledged that staff are their most valuable resource and have made a commitment through OSS to encourage and improve the well-being of organizational leaders. The Mayo OSS even offers personal services, such as financial planning, which help leaders spend less time on personal issues and distractions, and allow them to focus on improving the organizational culture. Brigham and Women's Hospital has created a similar Center for Professional and Peer Support (Shapiro, Whittemore, & Tsen 2014).

▶ Conclusion

Healthcare leadership best serves its organization, mission, employees, and clients by promoting professionalism. An organization practicing a high level of professionalism delivers better care, encourages improved employee satisfaction and productivity, and sees greater achievement of organizational goals. It is up to healthcare managers to lead by example and set the expectations for professionalism to flourish and thrive within our healthcare organizations. The senior leadership team at CHS-Pineville was aware of this fundamental relationship and made the necessary commitment and investment. The return on their investment was increased growth and engagement from the physicians and other employees, leading to higher and sustained patient satisfaction.

Summary

This chapter discusses the relationship between professionalism and leadership. The concept of professionalism spans the entire range of interactions between a health-care manager and patients, physicians, nurses, allied health professionals, payers, employees, and other stakeholders. To help managers better understand the concept of professionalism and the relations between leadership and professionalism, we present the PIE² model. This model provides guidance and gives example of professional behaviors.

Discussion Questions

1. What is professionalism?
2. Relate your academic training to the three basic components of professionalism?
3. How can professionalism help improve patient care?
4. How can professionalism improve relationships with physicians, nurses, and other medical staff professionals?
5. What are examples of "good" professional behavior you have encountered in your life? Examples of "bad" professional behavior you have encountered in your life? What leadership lessons can be learned from these examples?
6. How can developing your professionalism help develop the professionalism in others?

🔍 CASE STUDY: A Violation of Professional Standards

Ms. Smith, the newly hired vice president for support services at a 250-bed, not-for-profit hospital, was faced with a dilemma. After starting her position, she discovered that some long-time members of the governing board (GB) were having services provided at their homes by employed staff of the hospital. Specifically, the director of Plant Maintenance was sending staff once a week to the two longest-serving GB members' homes to maintain their yards while the staff were on the clock. She also discovered this practice had been going on for years. Upon this discovery, Ms. Smith asked the director if the CEO was aware of this practice and he said, "Yes, and in fact the CEO approved it." Both Ms. Smith and the CEO are members in good standing of the American College of Healthcare Executives (ACHE) and both are bound by the code of conduct of the College. Ms. Smith then asked the director to provide her with information about the annual fixed and variable cost of providing this service and for how many years it had been going on. The director refused to provide the information, stating that he did not want to incur the wrath of the CEO or the long-time GB members, who were prominent members of the community. Ms. Smith pondered what to do.

(continues)

Case Discussion Questions

1. Does the provision of these services violate any professional standards of conduct by the GB members? If so, what standards are being violated?
2. If there are violations, is the CEO complicit in these violations? How?
3. What are Ms. Smith's obligations as a member of ACHE?
4. What options does Ms. Smith have or what actions can or should she take?

Related Websites

American College of Healthcare Executives: http://www.ache.org/abt_ache/code.cfm
American Healthcare Association: https://www.ahcancal.org/Pages/Default.aspx
American Health Information Management Association: http://www.ahima.org/
Atrium Health: https://www.carolinashealthcare.org/
Hopkins Medicine: www.hopkinsmedicine.org/som/students/policies/HonorCode.pdf
The Leadership Challenge: http://www.leadershipchallenge.com/about-section-our-approach.aspx
Medical Group Management Association: https://www.mgma.com/
Student Group: https://www.studergroup.com/resources/articles-and-industry-updates

References

ABIM Foundation. American Board of Internal Medicine; ACP–ASIM Foundation. American College of Physicians–American Society of Internal Medicine; European Federation of Internal Medicine. (2002). Medical professionalism in the new millennium: A physician charter. *Annuals of Internal Medicine, 136*, 243–246.

Carolinas HealthCare System, Mission and Value Statement. Retrieved from https://www.carolinashealthcare.org/about-us/mission-vision

Cruess, S. R., & Cruess, R. L. (2016, May 1). Professionalism as a social construct: The evolution of a concept. *Journal of Graduate Medical Education, 8*, 265–267.

Egener, B. E., Mason, D. J., McDonald, W. J., Okun, S., Gaines, M. E., Fleming, D. A., … Andresen, M-L. (2017). The charter on professionalism for healthcare organizations. *Academic Medicine, 92*, 1091–1099.

Gawande, A. (2009). *The checklist manifesto*. New York, NY: McMillian.

Harms, R. (2004). Physicians, professionalism, and organizational efforts to improve quality—A systems perspective. *Wisconsin Medical Journal, 103*(3), 63–64.

Hickson, G. B., Pichert, J. W., Webb, L. E., & Gabbe, S. G. (2007). A complementary approach to promoting professionalism: Identifying, measuring, and addressing unprofessional behaviors. *Academic Medicine, 82*, 1040–1048. Retrieved from http://www.leadershipchallenge.com/WileyCDA/Section/id-131055.html

Kouzes, J. M., & Posner, B. Z. (2004). *The leadership challenge*. Hoboken, NJ: Jossey-Bass.

Medical Professionalism Project. (2002). Medical professionalism in the new millennium: A physician charter. *Lancet, 359*, 520–522.

Mueller, P. (2009, September). Incorporating professionalism into medical education: The Mayo Clinic experience. Keio Journal of Medicine, 58(3), 133–143.

Oxford English Dictionary, web-based version. Retrieved from www.oed.com

Reynolds, P. P. (1991). Professionalism in residency. (editorial). *Annual Internal Medicine, 91*, 91–92.

Reynolds, P. P. (1994). Reaffirming professionalism through the education community. *Annual Internal Medicine, 20*(10), 609–614.

Sergiovanni, T. J. (1992). Why we should seek substitutes for leadership. *Educational Leadership, 49*(5), 41–45.

Shapiro, J., Whittemore, A., & Tsen, L. C. (2014). Instituting a culture of professionalism: The establishment of a center for professionalism and peer support. *The Joint Commission Journal on Quality and Patient Safety, 40*, 168–177, AP1.

Shanafelt, T. D., Lightner, D. J., Conley, C. R., Petrou, S. P., Richardson, J. W., Schroeder, P. J., & Brown, W. A. (2017). An organizational to assist individual physicians, scientists, and senior administrators with personal and professional needs. *Mayo Clinic Proceedings, 92*(11), 1688–1696.

Smith, K. L., Saavedra, R., Raeke, J. L., & O'Donell, A. A. (2007). The journey to creating a campus-wide culture of professionalism. *Academic Medicine, 82*, 1015–1021.

Studer, Q. (2009). *Straight A leadership.* Gulf Breeze, FL: Fire Starter Publishing.

Studer Group. (2011). *Disruptive behaviors in healthcare.* Retrieved from http://www.studergroup.com/DB

Swick, H. M. (2000). Toward a normative definition of medical professionalism. *Academic Medicine, 75*, 612–616.

Webb, L. E., Dmochowski, R. R., Moore, I. N., Pichert, J. W., Catron, T. F., Troyer, M., … Hickson, G. B. (2016). Using coworker observations to promote accountability for disrespectful and unsafe behaviors by physicians and advanced practice professionals. *The Joint Commission Journal on Quality and Patient Safety, 42*(4), 149, 161, AP1, AP2, AP3.

Wells, B. G. (2002). Leadership for reaffirmation of professionalism. *American Journal of Pharmaceutical Education, 66*, 334–335.

Wojciech, P., Hromanik, M. J., Milanese, T. R., Dierkhising, R., Viggiano, T. R., & Carmichael, S. W. (2006). Leadership and professionalism curriculum in the gross anatomy course. *Annuals Academic Medicine Singapore, 35*, 609–614.

Wyatt, A. R. (2004). Accounting professionalism—They just don't get it! *Accounting Horizons, 18*(1), 45–53.

Wynia, M. K., Latham, S. R., Kao, A. C., & Emmanuel, L. L. (1999). Medical professionalism in society. *New England Journal of Medicine, 341*, 1612–1616.

CHAPTER 5

Human Resource Considerations at the Top

Mary Helen McSweeney-Feld and Nancy Rubin

LEARNING OBJECTIVES

By the end of this chapter, the student will be able to:

- Define the functions and responsibilities of human resources in a healthcare organization.
- Describe the concept of strategic management of healthcare human resources and its importance in delivering cost-effective healthcare services with quality outcomes using a diverse workforce.
- Identify key human resources metrics that are indicators of successful human resources management in a healthcare organization.
- Define and describe talent management, retention, and succession planning strategies for healthcare organizations.
- Describe the role of change management and its connection to strategic human resources management in health care.
- Identify opportunities for improvement of healthcare human resources management in light of demographic trends and a changing regulatory environment for healthcare organizations.

KEY TERMS

Diversity	Recruitment
Human resources metrics	Retention
Interdisciplinary care teams	Selection
Mentoring	Succession planning
Multicultural workforce	Total rewards model
Multigenerational workforce	Training and development
Paid time off	Workforce planning
Performance evaluation	Work-life balance

▶ Introduction

People are key components in the provision of services and care for any health-care organization. Healthcare organizations would not exist without a well-trained, highly motivated workforce that works together to produce the best quality care for its patients or residents. However, the healthcare world is complex and requires extensive amounts of specialized training for its professionals who utilize evolving amounts of technology in the provision of these services. Demographic changes have also become important, as the U.S. healthcare industry faces **recruitment** and retention challenges with a workforce of immigrants and others from different cultures, as well as a multigenerational workforce of Boomers (born 1946–1964) to Millennials (born 1982–2004) (Bump, 2014). Consequently, it is important to look at the concept of strategic human resources management, or the comprehensive set of managerial activities and tasks related to developing and maintaining a qualified workforce that can contribute to an organization's effectiveness as defined by their strategic goals (Fottler, 2008).

In this chapter, we will outline the components of human resources management, their application to healthcare organizations, and how these concepts translate to the strategic management of any healthcare workforce. We will also introduce the concept of **human resources metrics**, or how a healthcare organization can measure how effective it is in the management of its highly skilled workers. An overview of new developments in the management of human resources will be discussed, as well as future directions for healthcare providers in light of demographic trends and an evolving regulatory environment.

▶ Human Resources Management in Health Care: The Basics

Human Resources Activities

Human resources management is typically defined as the process of planning, recruitment, **selection**, rewarding, training, and development of an organization's workforce. It is a system of activities and strategies that focus on successfully managing employees at all levels of an organization to achieve organizational goals (Byars & Rue, 2007). To be a high-performing healthcare entity, its overall strategic plan should be matched with its workforce plan. A strategic plan will include a mission and vision statement, performance objectives, a plan for achieving these objectives, and a method for evaluating and correcting the actions of the organization based on its evaluation of outcomes from its performance. Departments, in turn, may create their own mission, vision, and performance goals in light of the organization's overall objectives to guide their activities, and a Human Resources department can create its strategic workforce plan as part of this process. This process is somewhat different from standard human resources planning in that it emphasizes the need to have employees whose knowledge, skills, and abilities help the healthcare organization achieve its specific mission, vision, and goals. An example of these activities would be a healthcare facility that recently adopted an enterprise-wide electronic health record system (EHR). Employees within this facility must be willing to understand the knowledge and skills required to use the EHR, thus acquiring and utilizing these skills effectively so patient services and outcomes can benefit from use of the EHR.

Legal and Regulatory Environment

Surrounding all human resources functions is a complex system of laws and regulations that guide the implementation of these activities. Federal, state, and local laws determine the outcomes of hiring processes, compensation and benefits, training, **performance evaluation**, and work conditions for virtually all individuals in the healthcare field. **TABLE 5.1** provides a summary of key federal legislation that every healthcare manager should know if he or she engages in any aspect of strategic management of the healthcare workforce. These laws guide the employment of individuals, including regulations for specific groups of individuals, the provision of compensation and employee benefits programs, the ability of workers to join unions and collectively bargain for pay, benefits or work conditions, and workplace environment and safety.

Employment regulations include the landmark Title VII of the Civil Rights Act of 1964, prohibiting discrimination in employment on the grounds of gender, race, color, religion, and national origin, which is enforced by the Equal Employment Opportunity Commission (EEOC). This Act laid the groundwork for legislation covering specific groups, such as individuals over the age of 40, people with disabilities, pregnant women, and individuals performing military duty. In 2015, the Supreme Court decision of *Obergefell v. Hodges* ruled that same-sex marriage was legal in all 50 states, allowing dignity and equal status to all same-sex couples, in addition to permitting spousal benefits under Social Security and employer-sponsored employee benefit plans. Other important legislation pending in 2018 and beyond pertains to the repeal of the Deferred Action for Childhood Arrivals (DACA) program, which allows nearly 800,000 immigrants to work and go to school in the US without fear of deportation.

The Employee Retirement Income Security Act of 1974 was the seminal piece of legislation creating regulations for pensions and employee benefits such as life and health insurance, and the Patient Protection and Affordable Care Act of 2010 (also known as the ACA) sought to extend these provisions through the establishment of an individual mandate to purchase health insurance, the creation of state health insurance exchanges, mandated benefits in health insurance policies, and an extension of the time that children may stay as dependents on their parents' health insurance. The Tax Cut and Jobs Act of 2017 made further changes in the provisions of the ACA by eliminating the individual mandate to purchase health insurance in 2019, in addition to simplification of personal tax rates through an increase in the standard deduction.

The Clayton Act of 1914 gave employees the right to form unions, and the National Labor Relations Act of 1935 (also known as the Wagner Act) expanded these rights by allowing employees to organize without detriment through unfair labor practices. Concerns with a safe and healthy work environment led to the passage of the Occupational Safety and Health Act of 1970, which provides guidelines for maintaining a safe workplace, including provisions on training workers to maintain safe work conditions. With respect to workplace regulations, the Worker Adjustment and Retraining Notification (WARN) Act of 1989 made notification of major layoffs or plant closings mandatory for work places with 100 or more employees.

TABLE 5.1 Major Federal Government Human Resources Legislation

Employment Laws	Fair Labor Standards Act of 1935	Established minimum wages, overtime pay, and standard work hours
	Equal Pay Act of 1963	Amended the Fair Labor Standards Act to prohibit wage disparities based on sex
	Title VII, Civil Rights Act of 1964	Prohibits discrimination based on gender, race, color, religion, and national origin
	Age Discrimination in Employment Act of 1967 (ADEA)	Protects employees and job applicants 40 years and older from discrimination in hiring, firing, promotion, layoffs, training, benefits, and assignments
	Pregnancy Discrimination Act of 1978	Protects employees who are pregnant against discrimination
	Americans with Disabilities Act of 1990	Protects individuals with disabilities from employment discrimination
	Lilly Ledbetter Fair Pay Act of 2009	Amendment to Title VII of 1964 that addresses unlawful employment practices related to compensation discrimination
	Obergefell v. Hodges (2015)	Same sex marriage legalized in all 50 states
Compensation and Benefits Laws	Employee Retirement Income Security Act of 1974 (ERISA)	Regulates pension and benefit plans for employees
	Consolidated Omnibus Budget Reconciliation Act of 1986 (COBRA)	Allows employees who change jobs to obtain health insurance
	Older Workers Benefit Protection Act of 1990	Amended ADEA to provide benefits to younger and older workers
	Family Medical Leave Act of 1993 (FMLA)	Requires employers with 50 or more employees working more than 1250 hours annually to provide up to 12 weeks of unpaid leave to any employee in a 12-month period for care of a family member or themselves

Category	Law	Description
Compensation and Benefits Laws (continued)	Uniformed Services Employment and Reemployment Rights Act of 1994 (USSERA)	Employees serving in the military have job protection and benefits extended during this period
	Health Insurance Portability and Accountability Act of 1996 (HIPAA)	Protects the privacy and confidentiality of patient information
	Pension Protection Act of 2006	Strengthens employer funding requirements for pensions and pension insurance
	National Defense Authorization Act of 2008	Extends FMLA to include the families of employees in military service
	Genetic Information Nondiscrimination Act of 2008	Prohibits insurance companies and employers from discriminating in areas of compensation and benefits based on results from genetic testing
	Patient Protection and Affordable Care Act of 2010 (ACA)	Created health insurance exchanges; mandated insurance benefits; children of employees remain on their parents' health insurance up to age 26
	Tax Cuts and Jobs Act Of 2017	Personal tax simplification through an increased standard deduction; repealed the ACA individual mandate; corporate tax reduction from 35% to 21%
Work Environment, Safety & Training Laws	Clayton Act of 1914	Guarantees the right of people to organize
	National Labor Relations Act of 1935 (Wagner Act)	Permits people to join unions without detriment of unfair labor practices.
	Occupational Safety and Health Act of 1970	Requires employers to provide a safe and healthy work environment for their employees; mandates electronic incident reporting
	Worker Adjustment and Retraining Notification Act of 1989	Employers with 100 or more employees must give their employees 60 days' notice of layoffs and closings
	Presidential Executive Order Creating Apprenticeships in America (2017)	Presidential order provides $200 million to expand apprenticeship programs and address shortages of skilled technical workers in the US

In 2017, President Trump signed an executive order that expands funding for apprenticeship programs in the United States by $200 million, and is predicted to address shortages for specifically trained workers in technical fields such as health care (Kellman, 2017). Strategic management of the healthcare workforce requires administrators to be keenly aware of these laws, as well as any amendments or changes in provisions that impact employees or their families.

Demographics, Recruitment, Selection, and Retention

Most forward-thinking human resources organizations take into consideration the racial and ethnic composition of their candidate pool. It is reported that by 2050, racial and ethnic minorities are projected to make up over half of all Americans, while the number of adults over age 65 will double (U.S. Census Bureau, 2008). The importance of religion, gender, generation and every type of **diversity** will become an ever-important business reality.

A **multicultural, multigenerational workforce** has also become the norm for most healthcare organizations. Hiring managers may see as many as four generations of workers: the Greatest Generation (born in 1945 or earlier), Boomers (born 1946–1964), Generation X (born 1965–1984), and Millennials (born 1982–2004) (Bump, 2014). The needs and wants of each of these generations will vary for each cohort and over time, with Boomers today valuing retirement and health insurance plans, and Millennials valuing **work-life balance** in the workplace through flexible work hours and liberal **paid time off**. Such differences will become even more important as the Millennial generation and post-Millennial generation continue to work and/or join the workforce.

The recruitment and selection processes in a healthcare entity utilizing strategic human resources management principles have a specific purpose and direction. Recruitment activities determine how many employees are needed, what kinds of individuals are needed, how many are new, and how many need to be replaced. The goal of recruitment activities is to address areas in which an organization has skill deficits. Recruitment activities cast a wide net and encompass a process with internal and external elements. For example, one may implement an internal recruitment and referral program to encourage existing employees to recommend individuals who would be a good fit for the organization's culture and help it achieve its strategic goals. At the same time, one may engage in online recruitment activities, use social media to promote open positions, participate in job banks, and offer open houses for recruitment, as well as speed interviewing processes. Another key change in the recruitment process is that one may bank the résumés of candidates for the future and hold them in abeyance in case they may be a good fit for future job needs. The selection process also has a broader objective, given that many healthcare organizations have a growing number of Millennial workers as well as valuable, long-service employees. Human resources managers may look at a candidate's ability to perform certain functions and have specific skills, but they may also be looking at the individual's fit with the organization with an eye to succession planning for more senior members of their workforce. A study by the National Center for Healthcare Leadership (NCHL) identified **succession planning**—establishing a process for identifying and training individuals who could perform senior management roles in the future—as an important tool for high-performing healthcare organizations seeking to accomplish their organization's strategy, achieve their projected priorities, and fulfill their staffing needs

(NCHL, 2010, p. 1). The development of a set of leadership competencies for each organization, the ongoing assessment of candidates with strong leadership potential, and the creation of new job opportunities to "stretch" the capabilities of candidates while ensuring their **retention** with the organization were also identified as key components of the succession planning process (NHCL, 2010, p. 2).

After a candidate accepts an offer from a healthcare organization, an orientation period typically occurs, which is referred to as "onboarding." This shift in language is also important, as it goes beyond presenting the new employee with the company's history, an organization chart, and information on health insurance and retirement plan options. It may encompass a multiday process wherein the individual still obtains the standard orientation program information, but starts the process of immersing him- or herself in the culture, vision, and values of the organization.

Retention of employees in healthcare settings has become a major concern in recent years. The natural stressors of the healthcare clinical workplace environment, long work hours, and continual pressures of performance, in light of reduced financial reimbursement for healthcare services, have led many younger workers to leave the field for other career opportunities. Many healthcare organizations have hired retention specialists in their Human Resources departments to create specialized career development and training programs. In a survey conducted by Deloitte, 81% of respondents who participated stated that finding and recruiting the right candidate, as skills and jobs continuously change, is either important or very important (Deloitte University Press, 2017). As organizations redesign how work is done to meet the needs of an ever-changing environment, it will be necessary to assist employees to reinvent themselves many times, obtain mentoring from more experienced employees, improve skills, and be open to working in teams across jobs. Without a solid understanding of race, ethnicity, age, and all diversity issues, it will be very difficult to create a workplace that is nimble and responsive to the changes necessary to operate in a competitive market (Deloitte University Press, 2017).

New ways of configuring human resources work output have also become an outgrowth of strategic human resources management. These developments include a move to **interdisciplinary care teams**—that is, teams of clinical and administrative professionals across healthcare disciplines providing care to patients and residents, which have become the norm. Greater focus on patient and resident outcomes as individuals are transitioned from inpatient or residential settings to home and community-based settings has produced other innovations such as the growth of community-based medical homes, in which a care team continues to provide and monitor patient services through the use of sophisticated technology. All of these developments necessitate a human resources staff that is willing to assist its workforce with implementing and managing these workplace developments, and ensure that outcomes from these new care models result in a high level of reimbursement, as well as continued linkages to the original mission, vision, and goals of the organization.

Workforce Rewards

In healthcare organizations, workers may include the clinical workforce that provides hands-on patient or resident care, and the administrative workforce that ensures the provision of management services such as admission and discharge of patients/residents, housekeeping, and dietary services, as well as marketing the organization and payment for services provided. Determining a process of rewards

FIGURE 5.1 Total Rewards Model
Courtesy of WorldatWork.

for these individuals is a critical component of the processes of recruitment, motivation, retention, and engagement of these workers, due to their specialized education and skills that are high in demand by competing healthcare providers. A **total rewards model** (see **FIGURE 5.1**) addresses these issues, and encompasses six elements: compensation such as salaries and bonuses or incentive payments, benefits such as health and life insurance, retirement plans and wellness programs, work-life effectiveness such as paid time off that allow the worker to balance job responsibilities and family/community obligations, acknowledgment and recognition in the workplace, management of work efforts and performance, and talent development to advance employees' skills (WorldatWork, 2015).

The total rewards model encompasses the monetary and nonmonetary return provided to employees in exchange for their time, talent, efforts, and results (Christofferson & King, 2006). In recent years, this model was revised to reflect the importance of employee engagement as well as talent development through mentoring and intellectual capital development (WorldatWork, 2015). This type of integrated model can help to attract and retain high-performing employees and motivates them to produce results consistent with their organization's strategic plan and the demands of external forces such as changing regulations, cultural norms, economics, and the labor market. Rewarding workers through the provision of competitive salaries, benefits, flexible work hours, time off, and mentoring opportunities can also play a role in retaining workers, as well as providing them with opportunities for continued training and refinement of their clinical and/or managerial skills (Kabene, Orchard, Howard, Soriano, & Leduc, 2006).

Physicians and clinical staff in a healthcare organization are good examples of the need for human resources professionals to develop specialized reward programs. Physicians' performance is controlled by professional norms and culture that arise from outside a healthcare organization, and they expect more autonomy and less managerial oversight than they would receive in a traditional bureaucracy (Olden, 2011, p. 75). However, healthcare organizations need to ensure that the clinical staff is aligned with their strategic plan and goals and are aware of the importance of quality outcomes for their patients. More physicians are moving away from being in independent private practice in the community (with fee-for-service reward relationships), toward institutional ownership of their practice, salaried compensation and benefits, and the use of bundled payments and incentive compensation plans based on quality, production, and utilization metrics (Darves, 2011). These trends may continue to evolve if regulatory reforms continue to emphasize quality and value in patient outcomes.

Performance Evaluation

After employees are hired in a healthcare organization, their performance within their position needs to be evaluated. Performance appraisal is a systematic assessment of how well employees are performing in their jobs in relation to established standards (French, 2007, p. 359). A performance appraisal process typically consists of (1) giving employees feedback about their performance and identifying individual training needs; (2) providing an opportunity to direct employee efforts over the next designated time period; (3) providing line managers with a basis for recommending promotions, raises, and future assignments; (4) clarifying and reinforcing lines of authority; and (5) providing a basis and record for disciplinary action when necessary (McSweeney-Feld, 2010). Appraisals are typically conducted on an annual basis, but in many healthcare organizations, this system of appraisal has been abandoned in favor of more frequent evaluations and spot awards to address workforce diversity and retention issues. Healthcare organizations may also use a 360-degree review feedback evaluation process, in which input from workers at the same level or a grade above and below the worker is obtained. If the individual interacts with entities outside the organization, such as patients, business partners, and community organizations, feedback from these stakeholders may also be solicited as part of the employee's professional development process.

Training and Development

Employees in health care need continual **training and development** to keep their skills consistent with changes in technologies used in the delivery of healthcare services. Training also helps to provide services to an increasingly diverse workforce and patient population, and to keep a workforce engaged and focused on strategic goals. Training may consist of on-the-job programs specific to the needs of the healthcare organization and may be conducted with a facilitator or delivered through self-study or online methods. Programs may include tuition remission for external degree programs, or specialized certificate training. In addition to specialized training programs, many organizations provide employees and managers with ongoing **mentoring** opportunities wherein they can ask questions safely and obtain career advice. Training programs frequently include professional development and leadership programs that cultivate workers for more senior positions by introducing them to new modalities, which in turn help the organization to become resilient in the face of external and internal environmental change. All of these specialized internal training programs can pay off by retaining specialized workers within an organization.

Labor Unions

Unions are membership organizations that can negotiate for workers in healthcare settings on issues of pay, benefits, and work conditions. The right of workers to unionize was created under the Workforce Planning Act (Wagner Act), as was the right of a union to engage in **workforce planning** on behalf of its members with management. Labor unions and their organizing activities have increased in healthcare organizations in recent years, due to the increasing work responsibilities of the healthcare workforce, with greater pressures on employees to improve performance and achieve outcomes. Consequently, workers at entry levels, as well as management professionals, have turned to labor unions.

Unionization continues to be a significant human resource and operational issue for healthcare organizations. Some organizations have adopted a strategy of union avoidance. When a union targets these organizations' employees for unionization, senior management may spend a significant amount of time and resources launching a campaign to maintain a union-free environment. These organizations believe that employees are better served by having a direct relationship with leadership, and that a third party is not necessary to bargain for employees. Other organizations believe that unionization is going to occur despite efforts to avoid union recruitment and choose not to launch a campaign against the union. A benefit of having a collective bargaining agreement with a union is that organizations can predict labor costs for the segment of their employees that are covered by collective bargaining. Most organizations have significant strategies to address interactions with unions, and there are definite pros and cons for both unionization and nonunionization. Human resource professionals are usually tasked with helping to negotiate union contracts and attending to grievances and arbitrations.

▶ The Role of Strategic Human Resources Management

How are these basic human resources management functions transformed by the notion of strategic human resources management? The healthcare industry in the United States has experienced regulatory changes such as the ACA that cause organizations to focus on issues of providing quality care for patients and residents and tying outcomes from healthcare services to payment for these services. In this world, good outcomes are rewarded with high levels of reimbursement for services, and services with medical errors run the risk of zero payment for the organization. In turn, healthcare organizations need to make their workforce keenly aware of their mission and vision, as well as any short-term or long-term organizational goals, which can affect the ability to obtain good clinical outcomes, provide high levels of customer service, and ultimately, receive payment for services at the highest prevailing rates.

Progressive organizations at the CEO level have also made diversity a priority. CEOs no longer judge their progress by how many employees are hired or promoted in different diverse categories. Instead, they hold themselves to the new standards of inclusion: lack of bias in recruitment, pay, and other talent practices. Managers are held accountable for leading inclusively and creating a positive culture for all employees. This culture also includes work-life balance and family and individual wellness (Frey, 2018). This is a profound shift in the notion of healthcare human resources management because it ties employees' performance to levels of service reimbursement and necessitates a new way of thinking about service delivery and work models. It also makes human resources professionals responsible for providing clear linkages between the larger world of the healthcare organization's business strategy and the willingness of workers to be motivated to perform at outstanding levels of service performance.

Human Resources Metrics: How to Gauge Your Workforce Performance

Many healthcare organizations have their doors open for business 24 hours a day, 7 days a week. Consequently, it can become challenging to measure the optimal number of employees that any department needs in order to provide high-quality healthcare services. A typical measure used by healthcare organizations to determine the number of employees needed by any department is called a full-time equivalent, or FTE. This measure provides an organization with their best estimate of the number of full-time employees needed given the number of encounters or services that they typically provide, and it helps them to develop appropriate staffing numbers for departmental budgets. It also allows for development and comparison of workloads across different types of work settings. One FTE is equal to 2080 hours per year (based on an 8 hour day, 40-hour workweek, with 52 weeks in a year), and can be adjusted for days of vacation, sick time, or other measures of leave.

Other important measures of workforce performance critical for healthcare organizations are staff turnover rates and vacancy rates. Turnover can be determined by the number of employees who leave an organization per year divided by the total number of employees; if this number (converted to a percentage) is a double-digit number, we can say that the organization has high turnover of its employees. Similarly, vacancy rates are measured by the ratio of open, unfilled positions divided by the total number of positions within an organization; if vacancy rates are at double-digit levels, this may affect the optimal performance of any healthcare facility.

Healthcare organizations also use a strategic planning process wherein their mission, vision, and goals are translated into measures of financial and operating performance that appear on a "dashboard"—a management tool specific to the needs of that organization. In turn, many healthcare human resources organizations are developing and using specific measures of their contribution to productivity and performance, known as human resources metrics. These measures can be developed for any healthcare organization and compared to industry benchmarks for performance.

The American Society for Healthcare Human Resources Administration (ASHHRA) has developed a human resources metrics tool that provides healthcare organizations with six categories of performance measurement: (1) retention and separations (measures of staff turnover and years of service); (2) workforce productivity and profitability (labor costs and overtime pay); (3) staffing and hiring (cost of hiring and time to accept a job); (4) workforce diversity (diverse personnel headcount); (5) human resources cost and structure (human resources cost and training costs); and (6) compensation and benefits (benefits cost and healthcare costs per employee) (ASHHRA, 2018). A focus on metrics pertaining to key clinical workers, such as nursing staff, have been included in these metrics. Other metrics may include measures of unionization activities and risk management information such as numbers of injuries and numbers of workers' compensation cases (Hospital Association of Southern California, 2011). Specific examples of key metrics that can be applied to a variety of healthcare work settings are (ASHHRA, 2018):

- Staffing and hiring
  - Internal hires percent
  - Cost per hire
  - Time to accept
  - Nurse time to accept
  - Vacancy rate
  - Bedside nurse manager span of control
- Workforce diversity
  - Ethnically diverse headcount/percentage
  - Ethnically diverse external hiring percentage
- Retention and separations
  - Turnover rate
  - Voluntary separation rate
  - First year of service turnover rate
  - Nurse voluntary separation rate

- Nurse first year of service separation rate
- Average tenure
- Compensation and benefits
  - Labor cost per FTE
  - Average benefits per employee
  - Healthcare costs per active employee
- Workforce productivity and profitability
  - Workforce employees operating cost per FTE
  - Labor cost expense percent
  - Nurse overtime pay percent
- Human resource cost and structure
  - HR cost per employee
  - HR headcount ratio
  - Learning and development investment per employee

▶ New Directions in Strategic Human Resources Management

Strategic human resources management can target all types of healthcare workers, as well as specific groups of employees. There is a plethora of research on the best strategies for attracting and retaining clinical employees such as physicians and nurses. However, the issues affecting the healthcare industry in the future go far beyond basic human resources strategies for hiring the right person for an open position. Population dynamics will affect the global healthcare industry in the 21st century, as growth in the Boomer segment of the global population (those born between 1945 and 1960) will create unprecedented demand for healthcare services (Institute of Medicine, 2008). As the demand for healthcare workers increases, the existing healthcare workforce in the United States has become more diverse, with a growing number of millennial workers entering the field along with long-service Generation X and Boomer staff in leadership roles. Increasing focus on quality due to new regulatory and compliance requirements, and evolving approaches to national healthcare reform will also place pressure on healthcare organizations to compete for a smaller number of trained professionals. Consequently, talent management in healthcare organizations—attracting the best members of a trained healthcare workforce while continuing to engage and develop existing employees—is a persistent theme in strategic human resources management.

What types of strategies should healthcare organizations use to effectively manage their talent? Valuing one's workforce and their role in one's organization, allowing them to contribute and providing them with ongoing performance feedback, whether they are a frontline worker or a senior executive, is essential. Healthcare organizations are also facing a variety of forces requiring them to become more nimble players in an increasingly competitive industry. Increasing use of healthcare information technology in the form of electronic health records, new medical devices, and the growing use of simulations and web-based applications require healthcare workers to obtain new skill sets and be open to working in new situations and applications. The use of change management strategies—that is, planned or spontaneous responses to external or internal developments, which require organizations to respond to consumers and/or external stakeholders in new way—demands new and creative uses of an organization's healthcare workforce. Changes in job descriptions and specifications, implementation of specialized interdisciplinary work teams, and creation of work groups that may exist on a temporary or permanent basis are examples of responses to organizational change strategies. Training human resources professionals to act as internal consultants to facilitate change within healthcare organizations, and having a Chief Learning Officer (CLO) to lead the change management and organizational development processes, are new responses taken by healthcare human resources organizations.

Growing attention is being paid to the challenges of providing care for chronically ill individuals by healthcare organizations, especially patient transitions from the hospital to their home or to and from post-acute care settings. These individuals have ongoing needs for care that exist beyond the walls of a hospital or a rehabilitation center. The development of medical homes to improve care after discharge is a new attempt to engage primary care physicians and medical group practices in community-based care services.

Summary

Strategic human resources management in healthcare organizations requires rethinking and redeployment of the healthcare workforce in new ways, with openness to changing strategies based on the evolving needs of the healthcare industry. As the demand for healthcare services increases due to demographic changes, leaders of healthcare organizations need to examine their strategies for managing their frontline, clinical, and administrative talent in light of these changes. These developments also require a system of metrics for evaluating the performance of those workers in new settings. Identification of these management strategies will assist healthcare organizations in maintaining high performance and outcomes, and remaining flexible enough to be proactive if faced with future challenges.

Discussion Questions

1. Define the concept of strategic human resources management and why it is important for healthcare organizations in the 21st century to incorporate this concept into their management of a high-performing workforce.
2. What is the total rewards approach to rewarding employees in the workplace, and how could this be a useful approach to attract and retain key healthcare workers?
3. What are interdisciplinary care teams? What impact do they have on healthcare human resources? Why are healthcare organizations utilizing this model of providing patient or resident healthcare services?
4. Define two human resources metrics that can be used to assess the performance of healthcare professionals and discuss a way in which each metric can be applied in a workforce setting.
5. Define and discuss two types of talent management strategies for a healthcare workforce.
6. How can human resources professionals be used to facilitate organizational change in a healthcare organization?

🔍 CASE STUDY: Registered Apprenticeship Programs and Healthcare Workforce Retention at Agape Senior

Apprenticeship programs have frequently been proposed as a vehicle for improving healthcare workforce skills and improving the quality of care in healthcare settings (Institute of Medicine, 2008). With the passage of the National Apprenticeship Act of 1937, the foundation for developing and expanding the U.S. skilled workforce was created through Registered Apprenticeship Programs (RAPs), a formal employment relationship designed to promote skill training and learning on the job (Kuehn et al., 2011). Since 2003, the U.S. Department of Labor's (USDOL) Office of Apprenticeship (OA) has focused on creating RAPs in the healthcare industry to address both chronic workforce shortages and increasing skill demands for key occupations within the allied health and long-term care industries. RAPs have been developed in health care for 40 occupations, including direct care worker roles such as certified nursing assistants, community health workers, and medical coders in the health information technology field. These programs offer competency-based and time-based models, portable credentials and paid employment, including wage increases with demonstrated proficiency, which respond to the needs for a high-skilled healthcare workforce. Apprenticeship programs have also been shown to pay for themselves and the sponsoring company by reducing turnover, increasing productivity, and lowering the cost of recruitment (National Center for Healthcare Apprenticeships, 2017). Some of the challenges of RAPs include the complex structures by which healthcare providers are reimbursed for their services, limitations of existing licensing systems, and the perception that apprenticeship is primarily for blue-collar workers in construction and manufacturing. The potential for reduced wages while in training may make workers, especially low-wage workers, hesitant to participate (Mauldin, 2011).

Agape Senior, a long-term care service provider in Columbia, South Carolina, experienced dramatic growth in its services since its establishment in 1999, and hired a chief human capital officer in 2007 to oversee the development and implementation of an online, internal learning management system and the development of a comprehensive workforce development solution. At the same time, the State of South Carolina, recognizing the need to further promote RAPs in the state, began to offer employers an annual $1000 tax credit for employees who were registered in a federally approved RAP. Agape began to question why health care had not taken advantage of this opportunity, specifically, for the post-acute and long-term care sector. In consultation with staff (housed at the South Carolina Technical College System), standards and competencies were established for a pilot program at Agape focused on certified nursing assistants (CNAs). CNAs were initially targeted to attempt to thwart an exceptionally high turnover rate among direct care workers. Academic program content was procured through Agape's local Community College and the initial curriculum included an overview of body systems (skeletal, circulatory, nervous, etc.), dementia dialogues, and basic leadership and communication skills. Though content was purchased initially from the local Community College, staff at Agape were charged with developing their own courses which would later form the curricular component of the job-related

(continues)

training in the apprenticeship model. Funding for the initial coursework was acquired using Incumbent Worker Training dollars directly from the South Carolina Regional Workforce Investment Advisory board.

The initial RAP program had 16 CNA participants, all of whom graduated within a 13-month period; subsequent RAP programs at Agape are now 2 years in length. The initial cohort was selected from a regional hospice office. Each of the individuals selected were serving in full-time roles as a certified nursing assistant, an integral part of the interdisciplinary hospice care team. The individuals, realizing the potential to increase their base wage, enthusiastically joined the program. Agape was mindful of demographic mix within the pilot cohort and did not exclude anyone within a geographic radius if they expressed an interest in participating. All employees continued with their normal case load throughout the entire process of completing the job-related education and the on-the-job training. At the graduation, the CEO of Agape was struck with how articulate the graduates were and how knowledgeable they were regarding resident care competencies. A second, larger RAP cohort of 44 CNA participants was then established and utilized distance-learning technology. These initiatives eventually made Agape eligible for $60,000 in workforce tax credits while educating their workforce.

As Agape began to examine their outcomes metrics, they realized that from the initial cohort, 15 of the 16 program participants were retained for 1 year after completion of the program (representing a 94% retention rate), and in the second cohort, 37 stayed for an 83% retention rate. Agape has continued to maintain retention records for certified nursing assistants who complete the program. During a 5 year period, approximately 242 individuals have graduated from the program and the company has consistently shown a retention rate (1 year after graduation) between 74% and 99% (2011 graduate cohort was 74%, 2014 graduate cohort was 99%) (communication with Jimmie Williamson, CLO, LTC Health Solutions, March 29, 2018). The increased retention rates among these certified nursing assistants significantly lowered the costs associated with recruitment and training of their frontline employees. They also began to see patient and family satisfaction levels increase because the CNAs were much more knowledgeable about the body and disease processes, and there was more consistency of care for the patients. One added phenomenon was that Agape began to realize that voluntary participation in the program was a key indicator in whether the individual was suited for work with the company. In other words, those individuals who registered for the program and dropped out early on were likely to leave the employ of the company; those who stayed and took the job-related education seriously were much more likely to remain employed for extended periods.

Agape began to see how this model could be universally applied to all positions within the company. As the company began to expand further and acquire more facilities, the apprenticeship model was applied to mid-level management positions, including their 201 program for department manager employees and their 301 program used to develop their facility administrators. They also began to see that this model could be applied to the clinical component of all business lines as well and, as a result, began to develop apprenticeship programs for nurses.

Due to administrative restructuring in 2016, Agape Senior was restructured into two units, one for hospice and the other for training programs called Long-Term Care Health Solutions (LTCHS). Under the LTCHS umbrella, a Long-Term Care University (LTCU) was formed to support online learning management system for apprenticeships and other internal education requirements. LTCU currently provides some level of service, with one of the remaining business lines, for more than 120 Assisted Living and/or SNF facilities in SC. Since the rebranding of the company, the coursework on the LTCU portal is being revised to be less Agape-specific, but rather more focused on the healthcare industry as a whole. LTCU is currently urging healthcare providers with whom they have a business relationship to consider having their own RAP, and to purchase the instruction from LTCU since it is generic training for the healthcare field and is compliant with South Carolina laws.

Case Study Discussion Questions

1. What are the advantages and disadvantages of RAPs as a tool for addressing healthcare workforce recruitment and retention?
2. How can RAPs become a barometer of employee engagement?
3. What initiatives were taken by the state of South Carolina to help the development of RAPs?
4. How can RAPs help address recruitment and retention issues for other types of healthcare workers, including management employees?

🔍 CASE STUDY: In Search of Optimal FTEs—The Post-Acute Care Unit at Sunnyside Hospital

The question many healthcare leaders grapple with is: "How many staff members (measured as full-time equivalents, or FTEs) do I need to cover my daily census?" This introduces us to a discussion of units of service and what are the determinants of adequate staffing. Consequently, we have developed a case study of a nursing home taking residents for rehabilitation and therapy wherein accurate calculation of FTEs made an enormous difference.

A community hospital, Sunnyside Health Center, provided surgical services on an inpatient and outpatient basis, and was the only surgical center in the city of Sunnyside. The nurse manager of the surgical services department traditionally measured its volume by counting the total number of surgical cases. About 80% of all its rehabilitation cases were transferred to its post-acute care unit, where the manager counted their volume of work in a similar fashion. In February, a new retirement community opened, and its administrator hired a marketing manager who actively recruited rehabilitation cases from Sunnyside, claiming that they could provide the same quality of therapy services at a significantly lower cost. It was estimated that half of all the rehabilitation cases would transfer to the new therapy unit at the nursing home. The staff in the post-acute care unit at Sunnyside was reduced to account for this reduction in outpatient volume. When the nursing home opened, the hospital could not retain sufficient staff to handle the number of cases that remained in the hospital therapy unit, as they did lose rehabilitation cases. However, a different problem arose: the remaining hospital post-acute care staff were working overtime, there was never enough staff for the daytime shift, and existing rehabilitation cases experienced long delays for therapy services. Where had Sunnyside gone wrong?

The majority of the rehabilitation cases that had been transferred to the nursing home were short-stay cases that required minimal therapy services. The cases that remained at Sunnyside were therapy cases that were clinically complex and longer in

(continues)

duration, requiring more rehabilitation services and ongoing nursing care. It became clear that, when it came to measuring the work involved in servicing patients needing rehabilitation care, a case is not a case. A new approach to measuring the workload of the unit had to be devised.

The care team in Sunnyside's post-acute care unit decided to look at each patient's functional assessment and need for rehabilitation care, as these assessments would more accurately reflect the measurement of work. When the team leader did a retrospective review of the 6 months prior to the opening of the nursing home and compared it with the 6 months after the nursing home opening, the department had lost cases and found that, on average, each case kept by the hospital required 30% more services than the average rehabilitation case in the past. This demonstrated the need to measure the units of service that are used for calculating a department's volume to accurately determine workload.

The post-acute care unit team leader also compared the average number of staff needed prior to the nursing home rehabilitation unit opening with the average number of staff needed after the nursing home unit opening. This staff number increased from an average of 4.0 staff per room to 4.5 staff per room. This information was instrumental in helping the unit justify its additional staffing needs.

With its new rehabilitation unit open on the other side of town, the nursing home owners began actively recruiting the best staff from the post-acute care unit at Sunnyside with offers of better shifts, an enhanced benefits package, and onsite childcare. Three key therapists in Sunnyside's unit started to call in sick and take their vacation days earlier than in the past. The unit's team leader asked Human Resources for assistance but was told that Sunnyside had already negotiated union contracts for the next 2 years and that HR had no flexibility in the pay and benefits that could be offered to the therapists.

Case Study Discussion Questions

1. Why is the calculation of FTEs important for Sunnyside's post-acute care unit?
2. How could Sunnyside have better planned for the opening of the nursing home's rehabilitation care unit?
3. What initiatives could be taken by Sunnyside's Human Resources unit to retain their seasoned therapists in the post-acute care unit?

Related Websites

American Hospital Association: http://www.ashhra.org/products/metrics.shtml
National Center for Healthcare Leadership: http://www.nchl.org/
The New England Journal for Medicine: http://www.nejmcareercenter.org/article/92/physician-compensation-models-big-changes-ahead/
Office of The Assistant Secretary for Planning and Evaluation: https://aspe.hhs.gov/report/characteristics-long-term-care-registered-apprenticeship-programs-implications-evaluation-design
World at Work: http://www.worldatwork.org/

References

American Society for Healthcare Human Resources Administration (ASHHRA). (2018). *Human resources metrics tool*. Retrieved from www.ashhra.org/products/metrics.shtml
Bump, P. (2014, March 25). Here is when each generation begins and ends, according to facts. *The Atlantic*. Retrieved from https://www.theatlantic.com/national/archive/2014/03/here-is-when-each-generation-begins-and-ends-according-to-facts/359589/

Byars, L., & Rue, L. (2007). *Human resources management* (9th ed.). New York, NY: McGraw-Hill.

Christofferson, J., & King, B. (2006). The "IT" factor: A new total rewards model leads the way. *Workspan, 49*(4), 2–5.

Communication from Jimmie Williamson, CLO, LTC Health Care Solutions. (2018, March 29). Columbia, SC.

Darves, B. (2011, January). Physician compensation models: Big changes ahead. *NEJM Career Center*. Retrieved from www.nejmcareercenter.org/article/92/physician-compensation-models-big-changes-ahead/

Deloitte University Press. (2017). *Rewriting the rules for the digital age: 2017 Deloitte global human capital trends*. Deloitte University Press is an imprint of Deloitte Development LLC.

Fottler, M. D. (2008). Strategic human resources. In B. Fried & M. D. Fottler (Eds.), *Human resources in healthcare: Managing for success* (3rd ed., pp. 1–26). Chicago, IL: Health Administration Press.

French, W. L. (2007). *Human resources management* (6th ed.). Boston, MA: Houghton Mifflin.

Frey, W. H. (2018). *The millennial generation: A demographic bridge to America's diverse future*. Washington, DC: Metropolitan Policy Program at Brookings.

Hospital Association of Southern California. (2011). *2011 HR metrics report*. Los Angeles, CA: Author.

Institute of Medicine. (2008). *Retooling for an aging America: Building the health care workforce*. Washington, DC: National Academies Press.

Kabene, S. M., Orchard, C., Howard, J. M., Soriano, M. A., & Leduc, R. (2006). The importance of human resources management in health care: A global context. *Human Resources for Health, 4*(20). doi:10.1186/1478-4491-4-20.

Kellman, L. (2017, June 15). Trump orders more cash, industry input, for apprenticeships. *Associated Press*. Retrieved from https://apnews.com/6c006b33b63c4f899e9e8abbbb1a5278

Kuehn, D., Lerman, R., Eyster, L., Anderson, W. L., Khatutsky, G., & Wiener, J. M. (2011). *Characteristics of long-term care registered apprenticeship programs: Implications for evaluation design*. Washington, DC: Urban Institute and RTI International. Retrieved from http://aspe.hhs.gov/daltcp/reports/2011/LTCRAPch.shtml

McSweeney-Feld, M. H. (2010). Human resources. In *NAB nursing home administrators examination study guide* (5th ed.). Washington, DC: National Association of Long-Term Care Administrator Boards.

Mauldin, B. (2011) *Apprenticeships in the health care industry*. Spokane, WA: Washington State University

National Center for Healthcare Apprenticeships. (2017). *Building 21st century labor-management healthcare workforce solutions*. New York, NY: SEIU Healthcare.

National Center for Healthcare Leadership (NCHL). (2010). *Best practices in healthcare talent management and succession planning: Case studies*. Chicago, IL: National Center for Healthcare Leadership.

Olden, P. C. (2011). *Management of healthcare organizations: An introduction*. Chicago, IL: Health Administration Press.

U.S. Census Bureau (2008). Retrieved from https://www.census.gov/data/tables/2008/demo/popproj/2008-summary-tables.html

WorldatWork. (2015, May 15). *WorldatWork introduces revised total rewards model*. Scottsdale, AZ: WorldatWork.

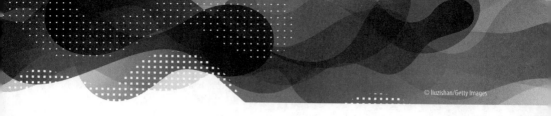

CHAPTER 6

Strategic Thinking Leaders

Thomas F. McIlwain and Michael Ugwueke

LEARNING OBJECTIVES

By the end of this chapter, the student will be able to:

- Explain the importance of strategic management in health care.
- Identify the nature of strategic management and concepts of thinking strategically.
- Describe the characteristics and competencies of strategic thinkers.
- Discuss methods for leading strategically in today's complex healthcare organizations.
- Identify ways to help think creatively.

KEY TERMS

Creative thinking
External environment
Mission, vision, and values
Situation analysis
Strategic management

Strategic planning
Strategic thinking
Strategy formulation
Strategy implementation

▶ Introduction

Leaders of complex healthcare organizations are faced on a daily basis with unique and urgent problems and issues that demand enormous amounts of time and energy. Attention to these immediate problems can leave less time for leaders to think about the future of the organization and the decisions that must be made today to ensure future success. Leaders must carve out time to consider the future and envision a strategy for the organization, and then articulate and communicate it to their staff. Thinking strategically begins as an individual intellectual process, facilitated by experience, perspective, and skills, and utilizes methods of intellectual analysis to provide a pathway for the organization's future success. This chapter focuses on identifying why it is important to think strategically, how one goes about thinking strategically, and how this orientation enables the organization to meet the future needs of its stakeholders.

What Is Strategic Thinking?

Strategic thinking is a mental process of synthesizing and analyzing information to envision the strategies and tactics needed to achieve an ultimate goal. The process can be likened to learning a game in which winning is the objective. Imagine the first time you learned a new board, card, or backyard game. One of the first questions you likely asked yourself was, "How do you win this game?" After you clarified what was considered a victory, you formulated your ideas of what you needed to do to win and then put those strategies into practice. Unfortunately, despite your efforts, you probably did not always succeed. However, many times, the greatest excitement and fun of the game hinged on your "chance" of winning: That is, even though you played by the rules of the game, there was always some part of victory that was left to chance. Strategic thinking very much echoes this process.

Strategic thinking is a prerequisite to **strategic planning** and management. As Mintzberg (1994) pointed out, "Strategic planning is not strategic thinking. One is analysis, the other is synthesis." Strategic planning is used to define the tasks and operationalize activities that must be accomplished to reach an identified or agreed-upon goal. **Strategic management** is how we assign authority and responsibility to implement and monitor the activities that must be accomplished to reach the goal. This entire process begins with strategic thinking. Importantly, as Liedtka (1998a) points out, *individuals* think strategically, not organizations. The following are elements of strategic thinking (Liedtka, 1998a):

1. A systems perspective: Strategic thinking requires analyzing the organization as part of an interdependent and interactive **external environment**, with inputs, processes, outputs, and feedback. This perspective provides the opportunity to see how the world interacts and impacts the internal parts of the organization and the outputs the organization can in turn provide.

2. **Mission-, vision-, and values**-driven: Strategic thinking implies that there is an intention of the organization to accomplish something of value for its clients, customers, and stakeholders. This element provides a unique perspective about the goals of the organization and its relationship with the environment, and at the same time, provides intention. These three drivers—client, staff, and stakeholders—provide a focus and energy that motivate individuals, groups, and the organization to accomplish its goals.

3. Sense of opportunity: Strategic thinking requires being willing to see and take advantage of opportunities. Not only does it require a level of knowledge, experience, and skill to understand when an opportunity presents itself, but it also requires an emotion of willingness to take a risk or advantage of the situation.

4. Sense of time: Strategic thinking requires "seeing" in time, a concept of strategic thinking Mintzberg, Ahlstrand, and Lampel (1998) adapted from Nasi (1991). Mintzberg describes "seeing" as looking ahead in time, but underscores that seeing ahead also means being grounded in the past. Additionally, strategic thinking asks leaders to see the big picture by contemplating issues from above, below, beside, and beyond, and understand that strategies developed, when implemented, will change the future. All of these perspectives are necessary for productive strategic thinking.

5. Connection of cause and effect: Strategic thinking requires the ability to hypothesize that if A happens, it will cause B. Although causation is very hard to prove, strategic thinking requires skills in predicting outcome B from action A. Creative hypothesis testing then becomes critical. Asking "what if" questions is creative, and testing "if... then" is critical assessment. This hypothesis-driven thinking clarifies which actions should be undertaken to take advantage of a possible future. By believing there is a way to affect the future, leaders are motivated to think strategically.

In summary, strategic thinking is an individual intellectual process of considering the organization from a systems perspective, and creatively and critically assessing the future within the context of the past. This intellectual process implies the intent to take advantage of opportunities that sometimes involve risk but may positively change the way the organization competes (how the game is played). To return to the game analogy, one thinks strategically in a new board game when one creatively and critically assesses the game, remembers how it was played the last time, and uses that experience to help predict the future, and monitors and takes advantage of opportunities that might lead to victory. However, if other players observe that your strategy worked, they may attempt it in another cycle of the game, thereby changing the game and triggering the necessity of a new cycle of strategic thinking and action on your part. Heracleous (1998) states that thinking strategically is discovering "novel, imaginative strategies which can re-write the rules of the competitive game; and to envision potential futures significantly different from the present" (p. 485).

It should be noted that strategy literacy is a prerequisite of strategic thinking. This means that the strategic thinking leader must understand the concepts associated with strategic management and the way organizations analyze, formulate, and implement strategies. In later sections, we will discuss the strategy process and the understanding and skills a leader needs in order to think strategically.

▶ Why Focus on Thinking Strategically in Health Care?

Strategic management requires a future orientation that takes into consideration the external and internal environments of the organization. Leaders of healthcare organizations must think and act strategically because the environment around the organization is ever-changing. From customers, competitors, technology, social systems, the economy, and such, significant trends are occurring that will have an impact on the organization. To be successful and remain viable, strategic thinkers and their organizations need to embrace these changes.

Leaders of healthcare organizations make decisions, major and minor, on a daily basis. Major decisions likely carry a great deal of risk and require an investment of significant funding and resources, but may not always provide the returns projected or expected. The organization may keep doing what it is doing, stop doing what it is doing, modify what it is doing, or do new and different things altogether, in addition to choosing to do a combination of these. With so many options, it is important to develop a mission that guides and helps direct the decisions of the leader of the organization. Thinking strategically involves not only deciding the best course of action and weighing its risks and benefits but also making decisions that are consistent, congruent, and in line with the overall mission of the organization.

The Rapidly Changing Healthcare Environment

There is little doubt that rapid changes are occurring in the healthcare industry, many of which are the result of changes in social, regulatory, technology, and political arenas. These changes may seem to be of little consequence to an organization; however, they may have huge implications for the organization.

One of the most active areas of environmental change is the area of healthcare reform. Healthcare reform is both political and social, but has been set in motion through political debate and action. Healthcare reform is the topic of political conversation on a frequent basis in the media, with discussions of what is good and what is bad about the system. Most lay individuals are not aware that what we call a "healthcare" system is really a "sick care" system. Rather than focusing on preventing illness and injury and maximizing individual and public health, our healthcare system is largely reactive, treating diseases and conditions after they appear. Additionally, the variety of healthcare options in place today can be described as an "unsystematic" system of care that includes diverse groups and constituencies of professionals, technicians, organizations, financiers, and patients. Healthcare reform advocates have been challenged to address the needs of the healthcare industry and our population, but continue to use legislative mechanisms to improve service provision. With each change motivated by political agendas and legislation, organizations will need to respond by identifying and acknowledging the change, understanding its impact, and modifying its strategies in order to survive and prosper.

This political issue of reform has an impact on the regulatory environment also. Tendencies to increase or decrease government regulation manifest as tides that ebbs and flow depending on the ruling political party. Healthcare leaders must stay abreast of these trends in the political process and, in some cases, become actively involved in shaping health care's political future.

And finally, there are evolutions in social communications in today's environment that may have a major impact on the organization. The impact of social media on the healthcare system and organizations may be significant, as growing numbers of clients desire to interact with healthcare organizations and their providers through online digital and social media outlets.

All of these changes are drivers for leaders to engage in active strategic thinking to allow their organizations to adapt and survive in an evolving healthcare environment.

The Expected Organizational and System Benefits

Although strategic planning and management are touted as the "be-all and end-all" method of managing in today's volatile business world, they are not panaceas that cure and solve all organizational ills. Studies on the effectiveness of strategic planning have provided mixed results regarding strategic management and financial and organizational performance (Boyd, 1991). Simply because an organization attempts to manage strategically does not mean the organization will be successful. There are many potential obstacles in traveling from point A to point B. Though the road to organizational performance is paved with good intentions, the choice of a particular strategy does not mean the organization will be able to effectively carry out the strategy. On the whole, if an organization understands the business it is in and who its customers are and opts to focus on its best practices, it will more likely be successful. However, the organization must remain responsive in a timely manner to environmental changes in its industry and be able to realign its strategies as needed. Of course, not all changes can be predicted in either type or magnitude; therefore, no matter how well an organization plans and implements its strategic plans, unforeseen factors can negatively influence its ability to reach its intended goals.

We look to strategic management to help the organization be financially successful, but there are many other benefits that accrue from the process. Those benefits include the organizational development of a concept and vision for the future, and an identity (i.e., what the organization is and what it wants [or needs] to become in the future). This process should involve leadership at all levels of the organization, enhancing vertical and horizontal communication, and facilitating buy-in to implement strategies for success. When employees at all levels understand the business they are in, learn about the environmental issues that impact the organization, and provide input regarding solutions to meet identified challenges, they become more innovative and more willing to change themselves. Through this process, the organization may experience greater productivity and profitability.

▶ What Is the Nature of Strategic Management? Why is it Different from Traditional Management? How Does One Think and Manage Strategically?

Strategy Definitions

Strategy can be defined in many different ways. Most authors agree that it is a set of related actions that leadership makes to increase the organization's performance on agreed-upon and significant outcomes and benchmarks. In some industries, these measures of performance may be obvious; but in healthcare organizations, many of which are not-for-profits, the objectives and outcomes may not be initially obvious. Strategic leadership is how leaders guide the organization through the strategy process, including decisions in formulating and implementing a set of strategies that should provide the organization with achievable outcomes and a competitive advantage. The method of developing or selecting a strategy is termed

strategy formulation, and putting those decisions into effect is called **strategy implementation**. Some argue that strategic management follows the 20/80 rule that success is 20% strategy formulation and 80% strategy implementation. Unfortunately, if the strategy formulated is wrong, the implementation is likely to be unsuccessful from the start. Therefore, it behooves the strategic leader to weigh strategic decisions carefully. This chapter is about how leaders can do so.

▶ The Process and Schools of Strategic Management Thought

There is no one "best" definition or approach for strategic management. Henry Mintzberg and his associates, in an effort to shed light on this issue, wrote in *Strategy Safari* (1998) that there are as many as 10 schools of strategic management. These approaches, or schools, are excellent examples of the similarities and dissimilarities in how strategic management can be carried out. But the authors contend that these schools of thought are all part of one overarching process. Though each school and its approaches to strategy differ, they all are important in the overall scheme of strategic formulation and implementation.

As discussed earlier, strategic thinking requires one to be "strategy competent." This competency means that one has an understanding and conceptualization of the strategic development and management process. Based on Mintzberg's discussion, **FIGURE 6.1** serves as an overview of what constitutes a general strategic management process. Mintzberg et al. (1998) provide an extremely well-conceived discussion of the many perspectives of strategic management.

In describing strategic management, the authors use the story of the blind men and the elephant, wherein blind individuals attempt to describe an elephant by

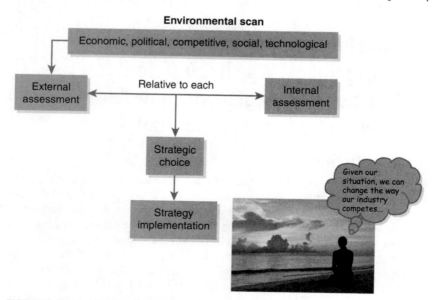

FIGURE 6.1 General Strategic Management Process

touching only one part of the animal. The result is that each individual believed the elephant to be entirely composed in likeness to the part he touched: For example, the man who felt the legs believed it to be round and solid like a tree; the trunk created an image of a snake-like beast; and so forth. None of the participants had a clear picture of the elephant as a whole.

Strategic planning can evolve very similarly. Depending on which element one chooses to focus (or with which one has experience), one may tend to describe the strategic process from only one meaningful but limited viewpoint. So if one sees strategic management as mostly planning, that is not necessarily an incorrect description. If one sees strategic management as putting decisions into action, that too is a component of the process. If one is entrepreneurial and uses insight rather than data analysis to drive decisions, that too is strategic management. Even if an organization rejects planning to avoid being tied to one specific strategy, that omission becomes a method of strategically managing.

The multiple perspectives and schools of thought described by Mintzberg for strategic planning are presented in **TABLE 6.1**. Mintzberg et al. (1998, p. 72) imply that strategy implementation is required to help formulate strategies (strategic thinking), and likewise, formulation of strategies (strategic thinking) is needed for strategy implementation. This idea is noteworthy in that no matter what the approach, strategic thinking is required. Mintzberg and colleagues have critiqued many less successful formal strategic planning approaches, noting that "formal systems could certainly process more information, at least hard information, consolidate it, aggregate it, move it about. But they could never *internalize* it, *comprehend* it, *synthesize* it," (Mintzberg et al., 1998, p. 73).

To internalize, comprehend, and synthesize requires more than just collecting data and information. Information needs to be discussed, analyzed, and mulled over. But most of all it needs to be synthesized—through *thinking*.

TABLE 6.1 Mintzberg's Schools of Strategic Thought

School of Thought	Characteristics: Strategy Formation as a Process of
Design	Conception—seeks to attain a match between internal capabilities and external possibilities
Planning	Formal—strategy can be developed in a structured, formalized process
Positioning	Analytical—matching the right strategy to the conditions at hand; generic strategies match generic conditions; use of analysis to identify the right relationships
Entrepreneurial	Visionary—much of strategic thinking takes place in the mind of the founder or leader; strategy comes from the intuition, judgment, wisdom, and insight of the leader
Cognitive	Mental process—in the mind of the leader, strategies emerge as a map or scheme

(continues)

TABLE 6.1 Mintzberg's Schools of Strategic Thought	(continued)
School of Thought	**Characteristics: Strategy Formation as a Process of**
Learning	Emergent process—strategy comes from lessons learned and involves others in the organization besides the leader
Power	Negotiation—strategy comes from negotiating between leaders (power holders) in the organization
Cultural	Collective—strategies are decided through a collective and cooperative process and reflect the culture of the organization
Environmental	Reactive—strategy is the result of responding to the challenges of the external environment
Configuration	Transformation—strategies are stable but eventually changes in the environment and business require transforming the organization through changing its decision-making structure

Modified from Mintzberg, H., Ahlstrand, B., & Lampel, J. (1998). *Strategy Safari: A guided tour through the wilds of strategic management*. New York, NY: Free Press.

▶ Strategic Decisions

The strategic management process is only a starting point for understanding how organizations decide and then act on their strategic initiatives.

It is also necessary to recognize the typology of strategic choices (see Swayne, Duncan, & Ginter, 2008, for a useful hierarchy of strategic decisions and alternatives). Having a vocabulary of strategies is very helpful when formulating, evaluating, and choosing the best strategies for an organization.

At the most basic level, an organization can choose to grow, stay the same, or get smaller. These strategies can be classified as growth, maintenance, or contraction. In most cases, organizations are driven to grow. Growth can be measured in many ways, including sales and profits. Growth strategies include mergers, acquisitions, and product and market development strategies. Organizations can vertically (both upstream and downstream) and horizontally integrate or diversify (both related and unrelated).

Most individuals want to be part of a vibrant, growing organization; however, in times of economic and environmental uncertainty, an organization may be forced to maintain its size or even contract. Contraction means the divesting of assets, both capital and labor, in an effort to survive. Strategies such as liquidation and harvesting are contraction strategies. In order to determine the best strategy, leaders must be aware of what potential actions are possible. There are numerous sources or texts available describing organizational strategic choices.

There is also much written about financial performance of organizations that the reader is encouraged to study. Many strategy evaluation methods use market share and market growth as dimensions of the market that help guide strategic choices of the organization.

▶ What Are the Characteristics and Competencies of a Strategic Thinking Leader?

A useful way to develop both creative and critical thinking abilities is to study the characteristics and competencies of strategic thinking leaders. A list of important characteristics mentioned throughout the literature when discussing successful leaders includes:

- *Having a vision*—As discussed earlier in the definition of strategic thinking, a successful leader must develop and champion the vision of the organization. Although the leader may involve individuals from all levels in the organization in the strategy process, the top leadership is responsible for carrying forward the vision of the future. Visioning is both a thinking process and a communication process. The vision must be articulated in understandable terms and be shared with the entire organization.

- *Understanding the business and its clients*—Leaders must have a complete understanding of the business of the organization in all its facets. The mission, also known as a directional strategy, defines the business one is in and the customers that one serves, and should manifest the uniqueness of one's organization. Examples of mission statements are found on websites and annual reports of organizations. A typical mission statement articulates the following: target customers, principal services delivered, geographical area served, the organization's philosophy and values, the distinctive services provided, and other items that express the uniqueness of the organization (Swayne et al., 2008).

- *External orientation*—As discussed throughout this chapter, strategic thinking requires systems thinking: that is, envisioning an open system that interacts with its environment. The environment writes the script of change, so its issues and trends must be monitored and analyzed to predict the impact they will have on the organization.

- *Penchant for analyzing data*—Strategic thinkers need data to review and analyze to provide the foundation for creative generation. Little synthesis can occur without data or information to analyze. The strategic thinker's formidable task is to sift through today's enormous amounts of data, convert the data to meaningful information, and synthesize or bring meaning to bear from this synthesis to the organization's decision-making processes.

- *Creatively generating new ideas*—A leader is responsible for keeping an organization on course while generating new ways of meeting the challenges ahead. Much is gained from embracing an entrepreneurial spirit to creatively identify new ways to compete in the marketplace. In addition to helping to generate new ideas, strategic leaders need to develop creative approaches to recruit and engage others.

- *Propensity for questioning assumptions*—Leaders have to develop skills that provide guidance on when and how to question traditions and assumptions. The creative process requires thinking "outside the box"; concurrently, the critical assessment process requires logical assessment of assumptions. Both creative and critical thinking are required of leaders.

- *Understanding the score of the game*—Strategic thinkers should be well aware of how the game they are "playing" is "scored." For most organizations, the scoring occurs through the reporting of market share. Market share can sometimes be difficult to measure and assess, but it is an essential benchmark within and among organizations that measures whether implemented strategies are successful.

- *Knowing that change is inevitable*—Strategic leaders know that change is inevitable and that nothing remains constant. Leaders cannot rest on the laurels of recent successes, but must embrace such evolution. Leaders should track major trends or issues that could have a negative impact on the organization and utilize strategic thinking to develop innovative strategies to address potential challenges and prepare for the future. The strategic leader's mantra is that "change means opportunity."

- *Knowing that strategic choices require focus and force*—Leaders must be very aware that their organization cannot be all things to all people and that there are trade-offs among various choices. For example, in health care, most community hospitals serve as "general acute care" hospitals; they cannot all be on the top-100 hospitals list. A community hospital may aim to develop an open heart or a regional cancer treatment center, but may not be able to do both at a level of excellence. The leader must therefore choose which project to focus on and guide the hospital's implementation team toward the goal that will most likely ensure success.

- *Understanding the business they are in*—Leaders have the responsibility to know the breadth and the nuances of how their business works—to have "business sense." They should be knowledgeable about the firm's operations, market, staff, and clients. Leaders should be aware of the stage of the life cycle of each of their services and how their business is categorized in a portfolio of services and markets. Each stage of the life cycle or each category of the portfolio represents a given phase of sales and profit.

- *Knowing the competition*—Strategic thinking leaders are fully aware of their competition. This awareness is paired with an understanding that the competition is also searching for a way to provide improved services to the marketplace. This reality should motivate leaders to continuously improve their strategic thinking and development to "stay one step ahead." This motivational driver is what Liedtka (1998b) describes as "intent focused."

- *Knowing their customers*—Strategic thinking leaders typically consider the customer the number one priority for the organization. Even so, healthcare leaders must serve a multitude of other stakeholders such as staff, stockholders, trustees, etc. It is necessary to effectively and diplomatically manage all these stakeholder relationships, while acknowledging that customer preferences should be the primary driver of the strategic decisions of the organization.

From a review of the literature and studies of strategic leaders, Nuntamanop, Kauranen, and Igel (2013) proposed that there is a set of strategic thinking competencies. These abilities and skills are conceptual thinking ability, visionary thinking, creativity, analytical thinking ability, synthesizing ability, and objectivity. These competencies are not new to the field of management. It has long been the focus of management and leadership education to admit students with at least some of these characteristics and include these educational objectives in design of curricula and courses. What may be unique to these competencies are visionary and creative thinking competencies. In the next section, we use these and other elements to discuss tools to help stimulate visionary and creative strategic thinking.

▶ What Are Some Tools for Thinking Strategically?

As Liedtka (1998b) noted, strategic thinking involves five elements. These elements are:

- Having a systems perspective.
- Being intent-focused.
- Having a propensity for intelligent opportunism.
- Thinking in time.
- Being hypothesis-driven.

So how do strategic leaders invoke these five elements in the thinking process? The literature is replete with examples of how one can analyze the environment and evaluate, formulate, and implement strategic choices. As discussed by Allio (2006), every day a consultant comes up with a new method or technique designed to be the "latest and greatest." Many of these are helpful, but others are only a repackaging of approaches that have proven to be useful over time (i.e., the tried and true). These include:

- *Scenario writing*: Seeing the big picture and the major trends in a changing environment and envisioning and documenting possible scenarios for the future.
- *Situation or SWOT analysis*: Analyzing a current situation by evaluating the Strengths and Weaknesses internal to the organization and the Opportunities and Threats from the external environment.
- *Competitor analysis*: Learning about the competition and its impact on the marketplace to promote survival and growth of the organization.
- *Evaluation of strategic alternatives*: Using techniques such as the Boston Consulting Group (BCG) portfolio matrix approach, product life cycle (PLC), or strategic position and action evaluation (SPACE) analysis to encourage strategic thinking by providing an understanding and evaluation of strategic options.

▶ Scenario Writing

Scenario writing is a process of describing the likely future of the environment with regard to one or more variables or issues. These environmental issues are usually organized within broad categories: economic, political, technological, social, and regulatory. A scenario is a short story that describes the future as projected through the analysis and judgment of the management and leadership team. Scenarios based on only one issue may be easier to write, but may not provide the richness and depth needed to stimulate successful strategic thinking. Scenarios containing too many variables may be more realistic, but may not continue to accurately reflect risks with the passing of time.

For example, consider the following scenario and variables:

- The healthcare environment will witness rapid change, including political pressures demanding free-market reform and decreased regulation; advances in IT and pharmaceuticals for the treatment of major illnesses; expectations by a growing population of older patients for increased decision-making influence and authority in determining services and treatments; and a robust, booming economy fueled by decreasing unemployment and low interest rates. It is possible, perhaps even likely, that the team has "guessed wrong" on one or more issues in this projection. Strategies based on wrong assumptions of the future can lead to operational and financial challenges for an organization and its leaders. Therefore, it is important to continue to monitor the variables incorporated into a scenario, and to "rewrite the story" if the initial projections are no longer accurate or valid.

▶ Situation Analysis

In the television series *Star Trek*, after the Starship Enterprise had been hit with a photon torpedo from an unfriendly Romulan Bird of Prey, Captain Kirk would invariably ask his chief engineer, Scotty, a question: "What's the situation, Scotty?" Scotty would report to the bridge an assessment of the structural integrity of the ship and its ability to ward off the next attack. In other words, Scotty conducted a **situation analysis**. In strategy analysis, leadership must evaluate the organization's current and expected future situation, and be able to incorporate that assessment into the strategic planning. A SWOT analysis can be very valuable in this regard.

SWOT is an acronym for Strengths, Weaknesses, Opportunities, and Threats. Strengths and weaknesses are factors that are internal to the organization, and opportunities and threats are factors and issues that are external (i.e., from the outside environment). For example, finances, human resources, organizational structures, and information systems are internal to the organization and can manifest both strengths and weaknesses. Factors in the external environment can include the local and national economy, technological advances, consumer needs and advocacies, and the presence and effectiveness of competitors, and can represent either opportunities or threats to the organization.

TABLE 6.2 Example TOWS (Applied SWOT) Analysis for a Typical Healthcare Organization

	Opportunities 1. Growing number of young married professionals 2. Increase in insured population 3. Growing economy	Threats 1. Increased competition 2. Alternative treatments 3. Decrease in population 65+
Strengths 1. Financials 2. New data systems 3. Good employee morale	Develop new labor and delivery services. Develop a new app for patients to access their own information.	Use financial strength to establish physical presence in areas that are threatened with increased competition.
Weaknesses 1. Location 2. Aging facility 3. Increasing physician retirements	Assess the viability of building a replacement facility. Increase physician recruitment in areas of projected market growth.	Develop services that cater to young professionals such as orthopedics, labor and delivery, plastic surgery.

SWOT analyses can be presented in a TOWS matrix, wherein each environmental factor is matched with each internal factor (Weihrich, 1982). This process helps the leader think through how to:

- Use strengths to take advantage of matched opportunities.
- Utilize strengths to address challenges and threats in the environment.
- Overcome weaknesses that make the organization vulnerable to threats.
- Overcome weaknesses that inhibit the organization from taking advantage of opportunities as they arise.

TABLE 6.2 presents an example of a typical TOWS analysis. Note that each quadrant in the matrix provides options for how the organization might react.

▶ Competitor Analysis

Many strategic leaders admit to being concerned that there may be better ways to meet their customers' needs, which "the competition" might develop first. The anxiety that the competition is "on our heels" spurs strategic leaders to communicate the urgency of continuous improvement, so that their organizations can "stay ahead of the game."

To realistically assess the threat from competitors, a thorough competitor analysis should be conducted. Most competitor analyses include these basic steps:

1. Define the services to be assessed.
   - For example, a family medicine physician begins a competitor analysis. She defines her services as "ambulatory primary care services" and will compare her services to competitors in this arena.
2. Define the service area—primary and secondary.
   - Our physician's family practice walk-in clinic sees most of its patients from a particular geographical area. She studies her patient population and identifies that 80% of her patients come mainly from the surrounding county. The rest come from other outlying counties.
3. Identify the competition in all its forms.
   - She investigates not only family care practices but also retail clinics, pharmacies, alternative care providers, internal medicine and OB/GYN specialists, and other providers who provide primary care services.
4. Analyze the strengths, weaknesses, opportunities, and threats of each competitor.
   - The information gained from a thorough analysis of each competitor gives the family physician insight and direction on how best to compete in the marketplace.
5. Synthesize the information from the analysis.
   - Questions she asks include the following: How are the competitors similar to my practice? How are they different? How does the competition threaten my clinic? Are there any needs in my market that are not being fully met? If I implement initiatives to address these needs, such as adding after-hours and weekend appointments, how will my competitors react?

Leaders engaging in competitor analyses should avoid the pitfalls of misjudging the service area, or of too narrowly defining the competition and thereby missing important competitors. Careful attention to the preceding steps will allow for a more accurate and helpful analysis.

▶ Evaluation of Strategic Alternatives

With so many potential strategic choices available, it is sometimes difficult to identify and select the best options. The TOWS matrix in Table 6.2 helps to organize and clarify the strategic choices. Additional frequently used methods for evaluation of strategic alternatives are the Product Life Cycle (PLC), Boston Consulting Group (BCG) Portfolio Matrix (Barksdale & Harris, 1982), and the Strategic Position and Action Evaluation (SPACE) (Rowe, Mason, Dickel, & Snyder, 1989). The following example demonstrates how a BCG Portfolio analysis can help stimulate strategic thinking.

The Boston Consulting Group Portfolio Matrix has its supporters and detractors; however, it is a good example of an analysis technique that generates information to spark creative strategic thinking. A strategic business unit is defined as a unit of an organization that produces a product or service—that is, an individual

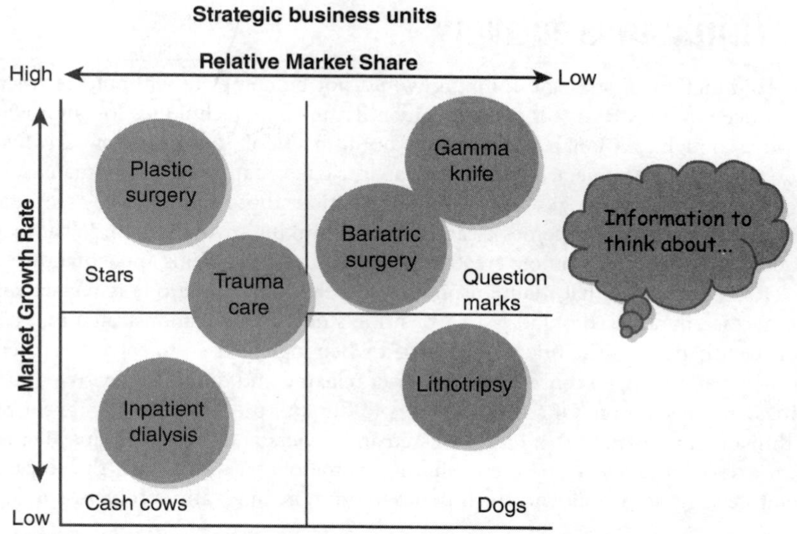

Strategic business units

FIGURE 6.2 Boston Consulting Group Portfolio Analysis

Modified from "The Product Portfolio" (1970) by Bruce D. Henderson, in The Boston Consulting Group on Strategy, edited by Carl W. Stern and Michael S. Deimler. Copyright © 2006 by The Boston Consulting Group, Inc.

operating unit of business within the larger organization. For strategic business units, BCG Portfolio analyses compare the relative growth of the market and the share of the market for each of their products or services. **FIGURE 6.2** illustrates an example of BCG Portfolio Analysis.

The first step in this method is to decide which services within an organization may be considered strategic business units (SBUs). SBUs are in most cases easy to identify because they generate revenue and often have identified competitors. After the SBUs have been designated, the next step is to identify each unit's market share (i.e., the score of the competitive game). In addition to accessing internal organizational data for this purpose, leaders may need to access sources of data from state agencies, hospital alliances, or Medicare or Medicaid for an accurate assessment. Sometimes, the market data have to be assumed, based on the expected disease rates and available services in the service area. The basic formula for market share is:

$$\text{Market Share} = \frac{\text{Units Delivered by SBU}}{\text{Total Units Delivered in Service Area}} \times 100$$

The result is usually reported as a percentage of total market. Data from the same time frame and service area should be used for the denominator and the numerator.

The strategic choice for each SBU depends on the market share and the market growth rate. The BCG matrix provides a picture of how well each service or product is competing in its relative market. Organizations that structure their costs competitively and capture a large share of a growing market will be successful. Services or products that occupy a small share in a slow-growing or contracting market should, depending on the mission of the organization, be downsized or restructured (i.e., divested, liquidated, or closed).

▶ Thinking Creatively

An examination of strategic thinking would not be complete without discussing the process of **creative thinking** and identifying some techniques for improving creative thought. As Jonah Lehrer points out in his book, *Imagine: How Creativity Works* (2012), the subject of creativity has intrigued man for ages. Humans solve problems not only by logic, but also by inspiration, those sudden "aha" moments when a vision or idea becomes clear. Strategic thinking involves both. What techniques can be used to promote creative solutions to our problems and situations?

Research shows that many inspirational ideas come when one is relaxed and not necessarily focused on an issue. Scientific studies have demonstrated that certain specific parts of the brain are involved when logic is used to solve a problem, but when an impasse is encountered, a brief relaxing and distracting activity often brings on the solution. Of course, answers to difficult problems do not appear out of thin air, but the mind that has addressed and understands a problem may benefit from a spell of relaxed, unforced thinking. Some observations from the research literature suggest the following techniques to promote innovative problem-solving:

- Be inspired and guided by the work of others. Strategic thinking involves choosing the right strategy for the right situation, and usually your situation is not totally new to the universe. It is perfectly acceptable to borrow a successful idea or best practice to develop a new strategy and give it your own twist.
- Create a culture of innovation by encouraging collaboration. The best ideas for complicated solutions will most likely emerge from a group effort. People can bring diverse skills and expertise to the table to collaborate and create synergy. Design buildings to encourage and push employees to mingle.
- The strategic team should develop a strong working relationship to promote successful exchange of ideas. Be careful to avoid the pitfall of overfamiliarity, however, in which a group may become less receptive to the generation of new ideas and to the examination of issues in new and different ways.
- Collect and analyze useful and meaningful data. Analyze the data and use the data as the foundation of your strategic thinking. Make assumptions when necessary, but periodically question those assumptions. Then put your planning efforts aside and do something else; if you generate additional creative strategies, jot them down on your tablet or notepad for your next meeting.
- The strategic solutions that develop will not be perfect, so rely on the planning group to help develop and improve them. Encourage constructive criticism in the thinking and planning meetings and be receptive to it as a strategic leader yourself.

▶ What Are Some Final Thoughts for the Strategic Thinking Leader?

Strategic thinking is a key to successful leadership in healthcare organizations, especially in the current environment of regulatory changes and economic challenges. The process can aid healthcare leaders in developing a mission, vision, goals, and objectives, and in developing strategies and initiatives that will promote successful and high-quality operation of their organizations in today's competitive marketplace.

Strategic management promotes the implementation of the leader's creative vision through (Goldman, Cahill, & Filho, 2009):

- Developing and effectively communicating the vision.
- Defining goals and objectives.
- Assigning and delegating tasks and responsibilities.
- Expecting accountability (practice makes perfect).
- Assessing, evaluating, and revising the strategic process.

Mintzberg (1994) noted that the process of strategic management requires interactive participation by both formulators and implementers. He argues that the term *strategic planning* should be dropped altogether, and we should "talk instead about strategic thinking connected to acting" (p. 72). The corporation 3M is famous for requiring all scientists to devote a portion of their time to pursuing new projects of personal interest (Lehrer, 2012; Liedtke, 1998). Organizations that wish to promote innovative strategic thinking at all levels may need to provide "slack" time for leaders and managers, during which they can think creatively and proactively about their businesses (Liedtke, 1998).

Summary

This chapter discussed the definition of strategic thinking and how it is a critical part of the strategic management process of an organization. Leaders of healthcare organizations can be extremely busy handling day-to-day operational challenges, often leaving little time to consider the future of the organization and to make the necessary decisions to ensure ongoing success. Time has to be scheduled to think about the organization's future, envision and develop effective strategies, and articulate and communicate these strategies to managers and employees. Thinking strategically begins as an individual intellectual process but should evolve into a group activity, facilitated by group members' diverse expertise, perspective, and skills. This chapter focuses on identifying why strategic thinking is important, the skills necessary for successful strategic thinking, and how a strategic thinking orientation enables a healthcare organization to meet the future needs of its stakeholders and succeed in an ever-changing healthcare environment.

Discussion Questions

1. Define the difference between strategic management, strategic planning, strategy, and strategic thinking. How are they similar and how are they different?
2. Why is knowing one's market share important? How is market share determined?
3. Define an SBU. How is it used in the Boston Consulting Group Matrix?
4. List the characteristics of strategic thinkers and describe why these characteristics are important to successful strategic management.
5. What are some major categories of external environmental issues? Which issues do you think are more important in this healthcare environment and why?

🔍 CASE STUDY: Strategic Planning Retreat Agenda

"I can't believe the time it's taking to handle all these petty issues," Anne said to Jacob, her administrative assistant. "We've got bigger issues that need addressing than who gets the best parking spots. Don't our employees know they need 10,000 steps a day to live longer?" she added with a hint of cynicism.

"You know that parking space is at a premium in our small employee parking lot, and it's also a status symbol who gets the best spots. So you shouldn't be surprised," Jacob responded sympathetically. "Now, you need to take a look at these financials before the strategic planning retreat next Tuesday. And we need to finalize the agenda."

Anne opened the file with the financials.

"Things are improving, and even though we have 55% of the inpatient market share, we've got to be thinking about the future. I'm not sure what is the best way to get our leadership team to see the importance of thinking about change. Most of the team think we can just continue what we've been doing, and they don't seem to understand or care that things can change very rapidly. We've just been lucky we are in an opportune location. Who would have ever imagined that the most-watched series on television would start filming in our town, and the film industry would draw both employees and fans to live here? Not to mention we had a major auto manufacturer open an assembly plant down the road. It's been difficult for the city leaders to keep up with the demand for city services, and we have seen a significant increase in patient visits; however, I'm really worried about how our competition is opening primary and specialty clinics in our service area."

St. Michael's Memorial Health System, a 325-bed community not-for-profit general acute care hospital with related businesses, recently built a replacement facility in a growing suburban area 50 miles from the center of a major metropolitan area in the southeastern United States. The area used to be a sleepy bedroom community, but the growth has come its way. The growth has brought competition, and three other health systems have opened primary and some specialty clinics in the community. Anne was hired to manage the construction of the new hospital and successfully rose to the challenge. Her challenge now is to provide the vision for the future and communicate it to the organization.

A knock on the CEO's suite interrupted their conversation.

"Hi, Anne, we've got a problem in dietary. Maintenance is on it, but it could delay meals to the patients. What should we do?" Sally, the head of dietary, inquired.

Anne took a deep breath and bit her lip.

"Be sure Maintenance knows we've got 250 patients who expect their meals on time. I'll send a text to Bill if you need some help lighting a fire under him."

"Thanks, I may need the help. Bill acts like he doesn't hear a word I say when I tell him the situation," Sally grumbled as she turned to leave.

Anne shook her head and returned to her computer screen.

"Now, where were we? Right, we need an agenda for the planning retreat. Jacob, you'll graduate this year from the best healthcare management program in the state. Develop a draft agenda for the retreat. Plan a day-long retreat and remember: We need to get everyone involved in thinking strategically about the future of this hospital."

Jacob sat down at his desk knowing if he does a good job, Anne has promised him an analyst's position in the planning and marketing department when he graduates. He begins to identify what needs to be included in the agenda, and first of all, he knows how significant it is to revisit the mission, vision, and values of the organization before anything else.

Case Study Discussion Questions

1. What items should be included on the agenda for the day-long retreat?
2. Who should be invited and be involved in the retreat? Where should the retreat take place?
3. Why is it important to revisit the organization's mission, vision, and values?
4. What type of data should be presented regarding the hospital's situation?
5. What techniques should Jacob most likely suggest for the group? How much time should be allocated for each activity? Is one day long enough to accomplish what needs to be done?
6. What should be the final item on the agenda?
7. How can Anne encourage a sense of urgency in embracing change in the organization?

Related Websites

Boston Consulting Group: www.bcg.com
Harvard Business Review: https://hbr.org/
How to Perform a SWOT Analysis: https://www.youtube.com/watch?v=I_6AVRGLXGA
Strategic Management: https://www.managementstudyguide.com/strategic-management.htm

References

Allio, R. J. (2006). Strategic thinking: The ten big ideas. *Strategy & Leadership, 34*(4), 4–13.

Barksdale, H. C., & Harris, C. E., Jr. (1982). Portfolio analysis and the product life cycle. *Long Range Planning, 15*(6), 74–83.

Boyd, B. K. (1991). Strategic planning and financial performance: A meta-analytic review. *Journal of Management Studies, 28*(4), 353–374.

Goldman, E., Cahill, T., & Filho, R. P. (2009). Experiences that develop the ability to think strategically. *Journal of Healthcare Management, 54*(6), 403–417.

Heracleous, L. (1998). Strategic thinking or strategic planning? *Long Range Planning, 31*(3), 481–487.

Lehrer, J. (2012). *Imagine: How creativity works.* New York, NY: Houghton Mifflin Harcourt.

Liedtka, J. M. (1998a). Linking strategic thinking with strategic planning. *Strategy and Leadership, 26*(4), 30–35.

Liedtka, J. M. (1998b). Strategic thinking: Can it be taught? *Long Range Planning, 31*(1), 120–129.

Mintzberg, H. (1994). Fall and rise of strategic planning. *Harvard Business Review, 72*(1), 107–114.

Mintzberg, H., Ahlstrand, B., & Lampel, J. (1998). *Strategy safari: A guided tour through the wilds of strategic management.* New York, NY: Free Press.

Nasi, J. (1991). *Arenas of strategic thinking.* Helsinki: Foundation for Economic Education.

Nuntamanop, P., Kauranen, I., & Igel, B., (2013). A new model of strategic thinking competency. *Journal of Strategy and Management, 6*(3), 242–264.

Rowe, A. J., Mason, R. O., Dickel, K. E., & Snyder, N. H. (1989). *Strategic management: A methodological approach* (3rd ed.). Reading, MA: Addison Wesley.

Swayne, L., Duncan, J., & Ginter, P. (2008). *Strategic management of healthcare organizations.* Hoboken, NJ: John Wiley & Sons.

Weihrich, H. (1982). The TOWS matrix—A tool for situational analysis. *Long Range Planning, 15*(2), 54–66.

CHAPTER 7

Building a Successful Leadership Team

John Shiver and Craig Nesta

LEARNING OBJECTIVES

By the end of this chapter, the student will be able to:

- Explain the importance of team composition.
- Demonstrate the rationale and importance of having effective teams in health care.
- Identify models and methods of team member selection.
- Describe the characteristics of successful teams in health care.
- Discuss the traits of effective team management.

KEY TERMS

Agendas
Consensus
Groupthink
Healthcare teams

Multidisciplinary team
Process improvement
Team charter
Virtual teams

▶ Introduction

The healthcare industry in the United States is undergoing a revolutionary transformation that will likely continue and accelerate in the foreseeable future. The demand for healthcare services is increasing as life expectancy has extended and the Boomer cohort continues to age. These demographic trends, coupled with the economic impact of shifting health payment plans from traditional employer sponsorship to government payers, and the ongoing shifting of costs from third parties to patients, require a new system of coordinated health-care delivery. Both clinical and administrative teams are essential for the successful delivery of health care in a high-quality, cost-effective, accountable, and transparent manner.

▶ Teams in Health Care

In this era of growing client demands and shrinking human and financial resources, healthcare leaders have turned to collaboration and teamwork as possible sources for solutions to the multiple challenges arising in our changing healthcare landscape. Collaboration, within and among departments and institutions, promotes synergy and can increase the cost-effectiveness and quality of healthcare services delivered.

Teams in health care are essential for the successful management of a healthcare organization and for the delivery of high-quality, safe, and effective care. Teams may be large and complex, or composed of only a few relevant members. For example, a team performing a surgical procedure is composed of individuals with varying but equally important clinical skills. The surgeon is typically considered the team leader, but must work closely with the anesthesiologist and the nurses who coordinate operating-room function. Other members of the surgical team include the orderlies who transport the patients in and out of the operating room suite, the housekeeping staff who disinfect the operating theaters, and the nurses in the recovery rooms where patients awaken from surgery. Each individual brings a unique skillset to the team. Each knows their role and how it relates to the others' roles. Without the invaluable contributions of each and every one of these team members, patients would suffer. In a similar manner, the management of a large healthcare organization such as a hospital, large physician group, or ambulatory care facility requires teams in order to function successfully. In this chapter, you will learn how teams are created and utilized to promote the successful operation of a healthcare organization.

Healthcare entities may develop several teams, perhaps even hundreds of teams; it is important that each team have an organizational purpose. Examples of organizational purposes that can spur the formation of teams or task forces include reducing infection rates, reducing days in accounts receivable (DAR), reducing costs, and improving patient satisfaction. Each of these team purposes aligns with organizational goals that are beneficial to the operating entity and to patients/customers.

Teams are integral to the management structure of a healthcare organization. Two teams commonly found in hospitals are an executive team, which typically consists of a senior executive and his or her direct reports (see **BOX 7.1**); and the executive committee of the medical staff, with the president of the medical staff at the helm, and key officers making up the rest of the team (see **BOX 7.2**).

The terms *committee* and *team* are sometimes used interchangeably, but they have distinct definitions. Committees are typically permanent and integrated into an organizational structure. Membership is defined by the participants' positions within the organization rather than by their skillsets or expertise. Teams are often created with a defined lifespan to address a specific goal or organizational purpose, and enlist members who have the skills and expertise to contribute to the solution or resolution of the specific issue at hand.

BOX 7.1 Executive Team

Executive Team
Chief executive
Chief operating officer
Chief nursing officer
Chief information officer
Chief financial officer

BOX 7.2 Executive Committee of Medical Staff

Executive Committee of Medical Staff
President
Vice president
Department chairs
Chief executive
Secretary of medical staff

▶ Why Teams?

No single individual can possess all the skills necessary to manage a complex health-care organization such as a hospital. Hospitals employ people who have diverse degrees, varied training and expertise, and many specialized skills. Walking through a hospital's halls, one would encounter a breadth of employees: those who clean the facility, build and repair it, perform surgery, prepare food for the patients, diagnose diseases, treat maladies, manage finances, operate sophisticated and dangerous equipment, maintain security, and many other interesting and exciting professions. Healthcare employees reflect many, if not most, of the professions found in any community. In fact, a hospital is not dissimilar to a local community, which provides a source of employment for many diverse individuals who reside in nearby neighborhoods.

To best utilize these varied skills and specialties, hospitals develop interdisciplinary teams that allow for smoother collaboration and synergy. In a team setting, employees can work together to create strategies, guide an organization and its leaders, serve as coordinators and communicators, address unusual situations, solve problems, and contribute to the successful management of a complex organization.

However, teams do not routinely form of their own volition. Teams are created by leaders and managers for a specific organizational purpose. In fact, one of the most important tasks of management is the successful creation and management of teams. Leaders must determine which functions of the organization are best handled by teams, create the teams, develop team charters and guidelines, facilitate team performance, and supervise the process and outcomes.

There is no single rule relative to creating teams, and no formula for developing the correct mix of skills, stakeholders, interpersonal skills, or other characteristics. Every team is, in the end, situation-specific (Shuffler, DiazGranados, & Salas, 2011).

▶ Defining Team Functions

A role for management is to articulate those functions of the organization that are best served by creating teams. These functions can include general managerial duties, clinical care delivery, problem-solving, **process improvement**, and organizational governance. After an organizational purpose has been clearly articulated, the function(s) of the team can be determined.

Charter

Teams must exist for a purpose. The purpose and function of the team may be delineated in the group or **team charter**. The team charter may include:

- *The team name or title.* The team should have a name that broadly represents the team's goals and functions. The name provides an identity for the team and its members and informs the greater organization about the team's mission and role.
- *The team purpose.* Team purpose should be delineated in a clear and concise manner to express why the group was convened. The mission statement of the team, often aligned with the organization's mission, defines the team's purpose and guides the team members to work together to achieve the defined outcomes. Teams may also express a vision that is linked to the group mission, which serves to communicate the team's aspirations and goals and inspire its members.
- *The goals and objectives of a team address the purpose of why the team is necessary.* It is important when convening a group to identify specific goals and objectives for the group as well as to define the scope of the team's activity. Whenever possible, goals should be objective and measurable. Goals that have clear and measurable outcomes can provide a team with the direction necessary to achieve the intended success, and with benchmarks to measure progress.
- For example, one goal in a healthcare delivery setting may be to reduce a hospital's acquired-infection rate from a specified baseline level. In this case, it would be clearer and more measurable to state how much of a reduction in the infection rate is desired. Therefore, the goal may be stated as "reduce the hospital acquired infection rate by 50% from the baseline within 6 months." This goal is clear and concise and can be assessed to determine improvement and ultimate success.
- It may also be helpful to state two goals for a desired outcome. In this particular scenario, the 50% reduction from baseline would be the "base" goal, and a second goal, known as a "stretch" goal, is set for a 75% reduction from the baseline. This provides the group with additional opportunity and incentive not only to meet the stated goal but also to strive to achieve an even better outcome.

▶ Team Membership

A team is a group of individuals who act collectively to offer a contribution or promote an outcome that could not be achieved individually. Team members may have to defer their personal goals to focus on the larger mission of the group.

Team membership should be determined based on the ability of each team member to contribute to the overall purpose of the team. Membership on a team may be guided by the position of a member within the organization (as is seen in executive teams in which senior administrators are appointed to a team by virtue of their position). Other teams might be composed of members selected because of factors such as their professional expertise or education, their professional interests, their diligence, or their collaboration and communications skills. Qualities or attributes to be considered when recruiting team members include the ability to work within a group, knowledge of a relevant subject, specific skillsets and expertise, professional stature and credibility, and formal and informal roles within the organization. In the present rapidly evolving healthcare environment, the ability of team members to think creatively is also a desirable quality.

▶ Deliverables/Milestones

Each team member should know and understand what is expected of the team. The team deliverables (the measurable outcomes of the team's work) should be quantified, documented, and accompanied by anticipated milestones. Although the eventual outcomes may not be specifically predictable, the general deliverables/milestones should be clarified so that the membership can understand the expected goals and the time frame for their achievement. Recent research suggests that, just as there is no formula for creating the right team, there is no specific set of metrics for measuring the effectiveness of a team (Mathieu, Maynard, Rapp, & Gilson, 2008).

It is often difficult to differentiate between goals/objectives and deliverables. For example, a key goal may be to implement a new electronic health record (EHR) system in a physician group practice within the next 9 months. The ultimate goal is the implementation of the system, but the process of implementation may include several key deliverables such as purchasing the necessary hardware to meet software specifications, transferring patient medical records from the legacy system to the new system, and training all medical and administrative staff in the new system's operation and function. The goal is the "big picture," and the deliverables are the steps and processes that must take place to achieve the goal.

▶ Scope

It is important for team leaders to define the scope (the boundaries and limits) of the team's efforts, to help the group stay focused on the designated tasks, and to minimize unnecessary distractions. However, in more formal or official settings, or for committees required by law or regulation, voting is generally expected. If a vote is taken, the results should be recorded in the appropriate team meeting minutes.

▶ Meeting Schedule and Agenda

Team leaders should outline the meeting schedule for the group and define how meetings will be conducted (e.g., in person or remotely by conference call). Clear and concise **agendas** should be crafted and provided to group members in advance of each meeting for review. Some teams also solicit agenda items from members to include in the meeting agenda.

Duration/Time Commitment

Different groups have different purposes and expectations, depending on the tasks at hand. Team members should be informed in advance as to the anticipated duration of the assignment, as well as the time commitment necessary to complete the given task(s). Alternate team members can be considered if time commitments exceed the original estimates.

Decision-Making

Teams, especially those with larger memberships, need to define how decision-making and group **consensus** will be achieved. Team leaders should outline the procedures in advance and ensure the group understands whether there will be formal votes or tallies versus informal consensus building. For most teams, an informal consensus is a good option. Team communications and function in and between meetings should also be reviewed, as should privacy and confidentiality guidelines if necessary or relevant.

Group Progress Reports

Teams should determine and implement a reporting "schedule" of their progress and report their findings regularly to the larger organization. Depending upon the purpose of the group and the issue(s), reporting may be performed daily, weekly, monthly, or quarterly. In order to avoid confusion, the timing of these reports should be specified in the team charter. Every meeting of the team should be documented in the form of minutes, which are distributed to the members after the meeting for review and revision if necessary.

▶ Types of Teams

The healthcare industry is heavily reliant on teams to fulfill its mission. Several types of teams are common in healthcare settings; some are permanent in nature and others are temporary, depending on the mission and the targeted goals and objectives. Teams of varying functionality, purpose, and duration can be developed to accomplish specific tasks. Some examples of common **healthcare teams** include the following:

Executive Leadership Team

The executive leadership team is critical for a healthcare organization. The executive leadership of both for-profit and not-for-profit healthcare organizations includes the chief executive officer (CEO), the vice presidents, and other senior executives who take direction and execute strategic plans on behalf of the governing board. The members of the executive leadership team serve as fiduciaries for the organization and are held to the highest standards of ethical behavior and personal conduct. A fiduciary must act in the best interests of the organization, not solely in his or her personal interest. Executive decisions should be made with unimpeachable integrity and ethics and should reflect the goals, mission, values, and priorities of the organization.

The executive leadership team is tasked with the day-to-day management responsibilities of an organization, directs and drives the performance of the organization and its employees, and ultimately is accountable for that performance. The executive leadership is responsible for implementing strategies and tactics in pursuit of goals and objectives set by the organization's governing body. The leadership team's performance is measured by the achievement of specific targets and anticipated outcomes.

Problem-Solving Team

A problem-solving team is assembled to address a specific problem or a set of related problems. Organizations rely on problem-solving teams to tackle organizational issues and concerns. Employees selected for these teams should have the background and experience to work collaboratively to address issues and propose resolutions. Depending on the breadth of the problem, employees might be recruited for a departmental team to work on an important micro-issue or could be summoned from across an organization to address a macro-issue. Problem-solving teams of all sizes and types function collaboratively in healthcare organizations and also contribute to strategic planning and decision-making efforts.

Self-Managed Work Team

Self-managed work teams function without direct management supervision and are responsible for specific deliverable(s). This delegation of responsibility by management to self-management teams empowers the team and provides its members with a sense of ownership. Affording employees the ability to work in self-managed teams can also serve to improve morale, create a stronger sense of participation, and positively impact organizational performance.

Cross-Functional Team

Cross-functional teams are another important organizational tool to address a relevant task by bringing together employees from diverse work areas to collaborate. The task at hand will help determine the configuration of the team among individuals from across the organization. Each member adds different but complementary values to the team by contributing specific expertise that may be based on education, experience, and/or work history. Members of cross-functional teams are often called upon to think creatively and beyond their own professional expertise. For this reason, the best team members will be able to "think outside the box" of their own current role and be sufficiently flexible to accept new and creative roles.

Virtual Team

With the proliferation of technology, especially in the area of communications, virtual teams are increasingly becoming an option for organizations. **Virtual teams** are especially prevalent and helpful in healthcare organizations that have employees working non-overlapping shifts. Virtual teams are also valuable for healthcare organizations that have multiple points of service/geographic locations and allow additional interaction and communication that may not be possible through traditional face-to-face meetings. Virtual teams may be physically separated in diverse locations but communicate electronically via modern technology.

If circumstances allow, virtual teams benefit from an initial face-to-face kickoff meeting to introduce team members to one another, to discuss the team charter, and to review and train the members in using the technology needed to complete the team's work. Technological tools to communicate and complete given tasks include email, video conferencing, and social media. The virtual team should select tools that work best for their members and most effectively facilitate the achievement of goals and objectives.

▶ The Importance of Team Composition

- *Team formation:* A key factor for a team's success is team formation (i.e., team composition). Regardless of its type and mission, each team needs to be carefully crafted with team members who will add value to the team. Merely establishing a team and providing a task does not translate into success. Leaders should be able to analyze what will be needed to accomplish the task and use that understanding to guide the selection process of the team members. The assessment of candidates' skillsets, technical competencies, and professional behaviors and styles will help leaders determine the makeup of a team (Buchbinder & Shanks, 2012).
- *Skillset evaluation:* The first step is to determine the various skillsets that will be necessary for the team to achieve its goals. Depending on the task, these skillsets may vary substantially. Leaders should match the needed skillsets with the expertise of potential team members and consider the candidates' strengths and weaknesses. The skillset should be the baseline for participation and can then be supplemented by the consideration of professional styles of communications and function that would benefit the group.
- *Technical competence:* The purpose of the team may dictate that team members have technical competence in a particular area. For example, a healthcare organization is seeking to purchase and install a new electronic health records system and develops a team to address this objective. The determination of which system/vendor to choose will require substantial analysis of available information systems and their compatibility with legacy systems from other vendors in the organization. To perform this analysis, team members will not only need to have expertise in health information management, but also technical competence in electronic practice management systems to evaluate how well the software options being considered would serve the needs of the organization.
- *Interpersonal skills:* A critical component of team formation and composition is the assembly of a group that will be able to work together as a team. Beyond the basic skillsets and necessary technical competence, team members should have the skills and expertise to collaborate with others smoothly and to work efficiently toward a common goal. Although disagreements may occur, the ability to transition and gain consensus from respectful and productive dialogue allows the team to proceed with its mission. Team members should be able to be receptive to new and changing professional roles, and to openly discuss and adapt to new professional skillsets beyond their traditional duties.

Understanding and valuing individual roles and contributions helps facilitate an environment that is positive and productive, and creates an *esprit de corps* that promotes achievement of team goals and objectives.

- *Ability to be flexible:* In today's volatile and changing environment, the ability to think "outside the box" has become very important. In order to create new and creative ways to meet market demands, committee members will be called upon to create plans, and revise plans, on a timely basis. The design of new positions, job requirements, and protocols and procedures may be necessary. Technology may assist with these changes, but, at the end of the day, employees will be required to adapt to new duties and work processes. New protocols and procedures will need to be tested and assessed, with revisions made if indicated. New procedures may also necessitate the elimination of specific processes or components of processes that have been in place for some time; therefore, flexibility is critical. Change is rarely easy, but is facilitated by supportive leaders and mentors. Changing processes will require time, education, and training. Committee members may be called upon to implement changes and mentor their colleagues who are impacted by change.

▶ Team Evolution

Team development has been observed to follow a predictable path from formation to full functionality and productivity. When first created, many teams may consist of members who are unfamiliar with each other or have not worked together in the past. In other cases, the selected team members must assume new or different roles within the context of the team. Therefore, team leaders should introduce team members to each other within the framework of the purpose and objective of the team, outlining individual roles, but creating a common understanding of the team's overall goals and mission. For a team to be most effective, its team members will need to begin "singing from the same sheet of music."

Teams generally evolve through a cycle of development toward a more mature stage through the following four phases (Tuckman, 1965):

1. Forming
2. Storming
3. Norming
4. Performing

A **multidisciplinary team** is displayed in **FIGURE 7.1**, and **FIGURE 7.2** features a work team in the storming phase.

The time it takes a team to advance through each phase varies with the group; not every member progresses at the same speed. However, the team as a whole cannot move forward until all members are "in sync."

- *Forming:* During the initial stage of creation, a team is said to be forming. This phase is generally dominated by the team leader and includes the introduction of members as well as of the team's purpose/charter, timelines, and anticipated meeting dates. During this phase, it is not unusual to have nonmembers speak to the team or distribute reading material relevant to the issues the team will need to address.

FIGURE 7.1 Multidisciplinary Team
© Blaj Gabriel/ShutterStock.

FIGURE 7.2 Phase Two of Teaming—Storming
© Andresr/ShutterStock.

- *Storming:* During the initial phase of team creation, forming, and controversy is unusual. Members are learning about their mission and roles and not sufficiently informed to create conflict. However, once a team is established and informed, it enters the storming phase, characterized by questions and disagreement as members begin to internalize the information provided and take on the mantle of their roles. Information is interpreted differently by each individual and filtered through personal beliefs, background, perspectives, and biases. The storming phase is a period of adjustment during which team members ask questions, present opinions, and work toward a group understanding and balance or stasis. The role of the team leader during this phase of team growth is quite different than it was during formation. During the storming period, the leader needs to give the members as much freedom as possible to ask questions and debate within an atmosphere of decorum. The leader may also become the servant to the team by providing answers to questions and supplying additional research material for review.

- *Norming:* As team members better understand themselves, each other, and their roles on the team, they approach a normalized state of understanding and tolerance of each other's personalities and perspectives, and will no longer need to question each other or the team mission in the manner observed during storming. Relationships will begin to normalize. During the norming phase, a committee or team may not produce discernible results, but will be actively learning. During this phase, members discuss matters in more detail and with a productive focus, and team leaders may assume a more proactive role in steering the agenda and conversations.

- *Performing.* Finally, the team enters its mature phase, sufficiently developed to begin producing definitive results. Teams can remain in this phase for very long periods. Every time a new member is introduced to the team or a new task is provided, however, the team regresses to a prior stage to absorb the changes, and then returns to the mature phase more quickly.

A recent addition to the phases of a team's life span has been discovered: "Adjourning." Science fiction writer Robert Heinlein is credited with saying, "A motion to adjourn is always in order." (Heinlein, 1973). Every team should have a defined objective. When this objective is achieved, the team should be permanently adjourned. Allowing a team to continue to function after it has outlived its original charter or after its stated objective has been met can be a disservice to an organization.

▶ Team Dynamics

Teams can be considered "living beings." They are born, learn, evolve, and develop personalities. Successful teams are complex organisms. They may act like 2-year-olds or mature and sensible adults. As with rearing children, nurture and nature both play a role in a team's success or failure. How teams behave and perform speaks more about their leadership and development than their structural constitutional makeup.

Successful team function is a product of a mix of factors, including effective leadership, capable management, productive communications, mentoring and guidance, a clearly defined pathway, facilitated decision-making, and successful closure. The following components are critical to team success.

Leadership

Team leadership is critical to the ultimate success or failure of a team; therefore, selection of leaders must be approached seriously. Depending on the team's purpose and structure, its leader may be appointed or may be elected by the membership. An executive committee consisting of an organization's top leadership, for example, will be led by the most senior executive on the committee, who is, in essence, appointed by virtue of position. An ad hoc committee, on the other hand, may be asked to select its leader from among the members. Each member then carries responsibility for choosing the best leader who will set the tone for the group and serve as an effective guide and mentor. In the latter scenario, team members must delicately balance their personal desires and the good of the group.

▶ Management of a Committee Is a Serious Business

Good management will support the team leader and the members by keeping the process organized, moving forward, informed, and disciplined. The responsibilities of the management function include duties such as developing a schedule of meetings, keeping members advised of meeting dates and times, developing and sharing agendas, documenting attendance, maintaining timely and accurate minutes, ensuring the minutes are distributed and reviewed, reminding members of assignments, and other administrative functions. Without proper and effective management, a committee may stall and not achieve its purpose.

Research has shown that the interaction among team members can play a very significant role in the success or failure of a meeting. Teams that showed more functional interaction, such as problem-solving interaction and action planning, were significantly more satisfied with their meetings. Better meetings were associated with higher team productivity. Moreover, constructive meeting interaction processes have been related to organizational success 2.5 years after the meeting. Dysfunctional communication, such as criticizing others or complaining, resulted in significant negative relationships and outcomes. These negative effects were even more pronounced than the positive effects of functional team meeting interaction. The results suggest that team meeting processes shape both team and organizational outcomes. The critical meeting behaviors identified here provide hints for group researchers and practitioners alike who aim to improve meeting success (Kauffield & Lehmann-Willenbrock, 2012).

▶ Protocols

Most people function best when there is a sense of purpose and order in their lives. So do committees and teams. Knowing the purpose of bringing the group together and focusing on that purpose during the team's lifespan contribute to the success of the initiative. Some components of team rules and guidelines are presented as follows.

Participation

Participation in team activities is the first responsibility of every member. Attendance at meetings is the only way a member can actively participate and interact with the other members and engage fully in the business of the team. Each individual has been assigned to the team for a reason. Members are responsible for contributing their relevant expertise, experience, knowledge, and energy to the activities of the team. Members do not need to have an opinion or voice their thoughts on every topic, but they should consider all agenda items seriously and participate when they can make a positive contribution. The progress of a team is hindered if members do not attend meetings or activities, do not contribute actively to assigned work, or act in ways that are detrimental to the achievement of the team purpose and goals. If such a situation does occur, the team leader should intervene to correct negative behavior via counseling or by replacing the team member.

Respect

As in all aspects of life, including teams, respect for others is the socially acceptable norm. Respectful behavior among team members is necessary in building a cohesive team, whereas lack of respect can destroy a team very quickly. Respect includes understanding and tolerance of the professional, ethnic, and cultural differences among diverse groups of people. At its core, respect demands that all team members treat others with consideration, show common courtesy, listen, avoid open conflict, and maintain focus on the goals and objectives of the team.

Meeting Schedule

Team leaders need to create a schedule for team meetings and abide by it. As the saying goes, "time is money." Time is limited and should not be wasted. Wasting time is disrespectful and unprofessional and hampers progress toward the team's ultimate goals.

Meeting Agenda

A meeting without an agenda often turns into a gathering for chitchat. Routine meetings or briefings held to update staff or other attendees may not require a written agenda, but a meeting that is not routine needs an agenda to wisely utilize the attendees' time and produce valuable results. Creating an agenda gives the team leader an opportunity to think through the purpose and objectives of the meeting and the important issues to be addressed and gives the participants a chance to prepare for the meeting and "hit the ground running." Without an agenda, there should not be a meeting.

Minutes

Every worthy meeting should be documented by accurate records. Minutes of meetings record the important issues addressed, the discussions held, the findings discovered, the decisions reached, and the action plans designed. A specific individual should be assigned responsibility for recording meeting proceedings and producing minutes for the committee to review and revise if necessary. These minutes should be distributed to the meeting attendees within a reasonable time after the meeting so that the participants' memory of the proceedings is still fresh. Meeting minutes should include the following information:

- Attendees
- Date and location of the meeting
- A copy of the agenda
- Summary of key issues addressed, relevant facts or data presented, and the essence of the team discussions at the meeting
- The results of any votes and, if appropriate, how each member voted
- Decisions, recommendations, and conclusions from the meeting
- Action plans developed and assigned responsibility for tasks to be performed

Communication

Throughout history, *great* thinkers and great leaders have been observed to be great communicators. Outstanding leaders must be adept at the sophisticated art of communication to be able to inspire and motivate others. Effective team leadership demands that communications be very well thought out, simple, clear, succinct, and directed toward the team's mandate or purpose. Communications that are not focused on the goal of the team are distracting at best and may misdirect team members and harm the committee's efforts.

Decision-Making

One value of teams is that they can positively impact the quality of decision-making, either by providing reasoned input and feedback to decision makers or by developing a consensus of recommendations based on team members' expertise, research, and discussions. Sometimes, however, teams are unable to reach a conclusion, decision, or recommendation. This lack of closure can be harmful to the team and the organization and indicates the need for leadership to intervene and facilitate resolution of the team's function. Some reasons for the stalling of teams' progress include:

- *Lack of diverse opinions, or "group think":* **Groupthink** occurs when a team's participants find themselves agreeing on almost everything but do not move forward. In these cases, the team leader should intervene and redirect the members back onto the path toward the team's goal. Warning: Commonality of opinion can sometimes be due to a leader dominating the team with his or her agenda and opinions. Teams and their leaders should be on guard to recognize this trait and change tactics if needed.
- *Open hostility/open attacks:* Common courtesy is a bulwark of civilization and is mandatory for team members. Open hostility or personal attacks are to be avoided at all costs and if they occur, should be addressed immediately by the team leader.
- *Change aversion:* One of the most common roles of a team is to evaluate and suggest change. Humankind is well known for an aversion to change;

facilitating change is not easy and must be handled well. Anytime change is recommended it should include consideration of the impact upon others and upon the overall organization. How will people respond to the recommendations for change and the change itself? Whom will it impact? How can the change be implemented, and what must be done to assure the most success? Are there alternatives to this process? What is the exit strategy if the change does not accomplish its intended objective? If all these questions can be answered, yet the team members are still averse to the change, the leader must explore the reasons for the aversion. Why are members not in favor of the changes? Can the issue be looked at differently? Might there be influences outside the purview of the committee, team, or organization that are not being considered? Understanding the reasons for aversion to change can help leaders and teams develop tactics to help ease transitions through the change process.

■ *Intractable issues*: It is not uncommon for a team to find itself in a stalemate with no obvious solutions. If time and other constraints allow, the following steps may help resolve the impasse.

I. Table the issue for future consideration to give the team members time to gather additional information, think through their opinions, and "sleep on it."

II. Assign the issue to a subgroup to further research or analyze it and report back to the team at a future meeting. Some issues can be better addressed by small groups tasked with returning specific recommendations to the larger committee.

III. Sidebar. Have the team leader take the conflicting parties aside and discuss the issue privately "in chambers." In, particularly, sensitive situations, it may be best for the team leader to exercise executive authority and take personal ownership for finding a resolution. This tactic, however, runs the risk of the team leader taking over the team process and alienating team members; therefore, it should be used rarely.

IV. Remove the issue from team responsibility. This tactic is more heavy-handed and, if implemented without the consent of the team members, may be perceived as a rebuke of the team participants.

V. Disband the team. This tactic is the most serious and should be used only as a last resort. Not only will the team purpose remain unfulfilled but also the action may negatively impact the morale, enthusiasm, and reputation of the team members and leadership.

Summary

Teams are an important and integral component of health care. Healthcare systems are among the most complex organizational entities in existence, multidisciplinary and multilayered. No individual or professional is capable of delivering health care alone; teams help healthcare organizations more effectively provide both clinical and administrative functions. Healthcare managers must become adept at successfully creating, managing, and utilizing teams to ensure cost-effective, high-quality services and operations in today's challenging healthcare marketplace.

Discussion Questions

1. Discuss whether health care is unique as an industry in its use of teams.
2. What are the benefits associated with working in teams? What are the detriments?
3. How should a leader manage a team without controlling it?
4. Will healthcare reform change the way we use teams in the healthcare industry?

🔍 CASE STUDY: The Quality Improvement (QI) Team Kick-Off

Jeff looked at his watch again, sighed, and glanced around the room. It was already 5 minutes past the hour. His first quality improvement (QI) project at Suburban Hospital, and only 3 of the 15 people he had invited to the kick-off team meeting had appeared.

Disappointed, Jeff proceeded to talk through the slide presentation he had carefully prepared, which outlined the targeted problems and the structured quality improvement methods that would be used to tackle the concerns. The three people in attendance asked few questions and seemed eager for the meeting to end. After a short and awkward discussion, Jeff watched them hurry out of the room.

Back at his desk in the QI department, Jeff struggled to sort through the mixture of anger, embarrassment, and frustration that he was feeling about his effort to launch this QI team. As the quality director had suggested, Jeff had invited stakeholders from all the clinical and administrative areas involved in these issues to join this team. Using the hospital's email system, he had created and sent an electronic meeting invitation, and at least 10 of the 15 stakeholders recruited had accepted the invitation. Jeff had not wanted to make the e-vite message too long; the invitation had stated that each recipient had been named to a "new QI team." Yet, only three had bothered to show up! And even those who attended did not seem very interested or engaged in what Jeff had to say.

Prior to the meeting, Jeff had been anxious to implement all of the great ideas about self-managing teams and group facilitation that he had learned in his healthcare management courses at State University. Now, based on today's attendance, he found himself feeling desperate about how he would even get the project off the ground, never mind make it self-managing. As a quality analyst, Jeff realized that he had no formal authority over any of the people he had invited. How could his director expect him to get them actively involved?

Case Study Discussion Questions

1. What factors related to team formation do you think contributed to the poor attendance at Jeff's kick-off meeting?
2. Based on what you've learned, what advice would you give Jeff about how to manage the formation of a new team?
3. Assuming the team does get started, are there any steps Jeff can take to keep members engaged and involved in its efforts?
4. What do you think Jeff should do next in his effort to get this team underway?

(Courtesy of Victoria Parker, Program Director Department of Health Policy and Management Boston University School of Public Health)

🔍 *CASE STUDY: Equal Workload*

With a huge sigh, Marianna deleted the latest email from one of the members of her fellow clinic reorganization committee. Picking up her phone and dialing her fiancé, she mulled over the events of the last 2 months with a growing sense of unease.

"Hey," she started, "you won't believe what that clinic reorganization committee is doing now. I've told them over and over again that our wedding and honeymoon fall in the last 3 weeks before the report is due, and I've repeatedly offered to get started on different parts of the report, but they just keep telling me to 'chill out,' and that there's still plenty of time to get our work done. In fact, I just got an email suggesting that we go back and rerun a whole bunch of the predicted patient volume analyses that I know are already complete. Sure, maybe the rest of them have plenty of time, but not me! I'm worried that I'm going to end up having to work all night the whole week before the wedding and walk down the aisle with giant bags under my eyes. It's just not fair. I've been trying to plan ahead, and they are just not working with me on this." After venting a while longer, she hung up and returned to working on other clinic projects needing attention before her planned 3-week absence for the nuptials.

Four Weeks Later

"Marianna! What do you mean 'today's your last day in the office until 3 weeks from now'? We have a ton left to do on this clinic reorganization report, and you're supposed to be part of this committee! I hope you're not expecting us to put your name on this report, given how little you've contributed!" shouted Kyle, the committee chair.

"Kyle, I really don't know what to say. I've been telling you all since the first few committee meetings that I had plans for this time off! I've been offering to work ahead on anything that could be done ahead of time, and you just kept telling me not to get worked up about it. Did you think I was going to reschedule my wedding and honeymoon because the rest of you were determined to wait until the last minute?"

"Well, excuse me for not keeping track of the details of your life. I assumed that if you wanted to be on this committee, you were committed to getting its work done, no matter what it takes. Clearly, I was mistaken about your commitment to organizing the clinic in a better way."

Marianna walked away, muttering, and wondering if she'd still have a job after her "big day." She decided then and there that signing up for an important cross-departmental committee was something she was not going to do again.

Case Study Discussion Questions

1. Do you think this committee could have prevented this conflict over getting its work done by the deadline? If so, how? If not, why not?
2. What could the committee chair have done early in the committee's life to ensure that its members were in agreement about its workplan?
3. Should the team include Marianna's name on its report? Why or why not?
4. If you were coaching the committee chair, what advice would you give Kyle about dealing with this situation?

(Courtesy of Victoria Parker, Program Director Department of Health Policy and Management Boston University School of Public Health)

Related Websites

Agency for Healthcare Research and Quality, TeamSTEPPS: http://teamstepps.ahrq.gov/
Institute for Healthcare Improvement: www.ihi.org/knowledge/Pages/HowtoImprove/ScienceofIm
provementFormingtheTeam.aspx
Learning Center: www.learningcenter.net/library/health.shtml
Mind Tools: www.mindtools.com/pages/article/newTMM_30.htm

Other Suggested Reading

Kovner, A., & Neuhauser, D. (2004). *Health services management, readings, cases and commentary.* Chicago, IL: Health Administration Press.

Liebler, J. G., & McConnell, C. R. (2008). *Management principles for health professionals* (5th ed.). Sudbury, MA: Jones and Bartlett Publishers.

White, K. R., & Griffith, J. R. (2010). *The well-managed healthcare organization* (7th ed.). Chicago: IL: Health Administration Press.

Wolper, L. F. (2011). *Health care administration* (5th ed.). Sudbury, MA: Jones & Bartlett Learning.

References

Buchbinder, S. B., & Shanks, N. H. (2012). *Introduction to health care management* (2nd ed.). Burlington, MA: Jones & Bartlett Learning.

Heinlein, R. (1973). *Time enough for love.* New York, NY: Putnam Publishing Group.

Kauffeld, S., & Lehmann-Willenbrock, N. (2012, April). Meetings matter: Effects of team meetings on team and organizational success. *Small Group Research, 43*(2), 130–158.

Mathieu, J., Maynard, M. T., Rapp, T., & Gilson, L. (2008). Team effectiveness 1997–2007: A review of recent advancements and a glimpse into the future. *Journal of Management, 34,* 410–476.

Shuffler, M. L., DiazGranados, D., & Salas, E. (2011, December). There's a science for that: Team development interventions in organizations. *Current Directions in Psychological Science, 20*(6), 365–372.

Tuckman, B. (1965). Developmental sequence in small groups. *Psychological Bulletin, 63*(6), 384–399.

© liuzishan/Getty Images

CHAPTER 8

Leading Quality Initiatives

Marsha Chan and Louis Rubino

LEARNING OBJECTIVES

By the end of this chapter, the student will be able to:

- Describe the role of leadership in creating a quality-driven organizational culture.
- Identify the key stakeholders and drivers of quality and patient safety.
- Explain the strategies a leader can use to achieve and sustain high-performance levels.
- Understand the influence of public and private agencies in setting the national quality agenda.

KEY TERMS

Aims for improvement
ANCC Nursing Magnet Recognition
    Program
Balanced scorecard
Culture of safety
High reliability organization

Lean
Malcolm Baldrige National Quality Award
Organizational culture
Six Sigma
Transparency
Value-based purchasing

▶ Introduction

Quality initiatives have become essential in today's healthcare industry to promote high standards of care and protect patient safety. In the past, administrators often relied upon a healthcare organization's internal clinical staff to oversee and ensure the quality of the services provided. This self-monitoring is no longer sufficient. Quality of care must now be evaluated by healthcare leaders through quantitative, objective, and reproducible assessments that address external requirements and standards. The Affordable Care Act and the transition to **value-based purchasing** and payment models link payment (and penalties) to quality outcomes. Healthcare entities designated as Accountable Care Organizations are rewarded for meeting specific standards of performance related to quality of care. These measures of success are linked directly to an Accountable Care Organization's rates of reimbursement, and, in many cases, to that healthcare organization's executive compensation. For example, the Center for Medicare and Medicaid Services' value-based purchasing is providing reimbursement incentives to accountable providers who produce high-quality outcomes, and disincentives for the provision of poor-quality outcomes. Other third-party payers are following suit; healthcare leaders will need to focus on demonstrating achievement of high-quality standards to ensure not only the operational excellence but also the fiscal stability of their organizations.

▶ Setting the Quality Agenda

At the turn of the 21st century, new campaigns were led by respected government and voluntary agencies to identify and address the significant and widespread deficiencies identified in U.S. healthcare quality. Research revealed that, over a decade later, some progress (but not nearly enough) had been made in improving quality of care (Chassin & Loeb, 2011). Today, innovative approaches are needed to increase our improvement efforts (Lynch, 2017).

The Institute of Medicine (IOM) has defined high-quality care as being Safe, Timely, Effective, Efficient, Equitable, and Patient centered (STEEEP). The IOM has recommended that quality improvements be addressed on four levels: that of the patient, of health-delivery microsystems (teams or units), of organizations that house such systems (hospitals, clinics, health systems, etc.), and of the regulatory and financial environment in which those systems operate (IOM, 2001). Effective leadership is needed on all four levels to meet these aims and support a quality-driven healthcare system (see **FIGURE 8.1**).

▶ Quality-Driven Leadership

High-performing organizations require effective leadership. Executives must establish and communicate vision to deliver high-quality, patient-centered care while leading efforts to create and foster a **culture of safety**. Leaders must also identify areas in which quality improvement is indicated and establish the strategic directions the organization must follow to achieve positive outcomes. They must be able to facilitate the development and implementation of approaches to promote and ensure quality of care, and to serve as role models and influence others to strive for quality improvements throughout the delivery system.

Through their research, Taylor and Rutherford (2010) have identified challenges and opportunities for executive leaders to establish patient- and family-centeredness in the healthcare setting; their advice also applies to leaders' efforts to improve quality of health care in general. Leaders must inspire a vision for a healthcare organization's future and advocate for the goal that the entity becomes a

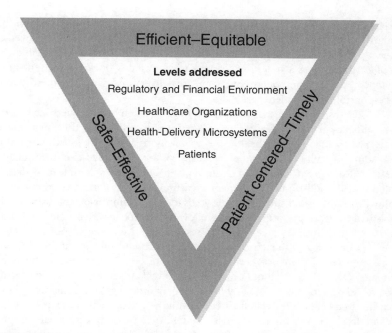

FIGURE 8.1 IOM's Six Aims and Four Levels Addressed

quality-driven organization. Leaders must lead by example and speak openly about quality and patient safety. Leaders must show that they are dissatisfied with "resting on their laurels," and are continuously challenging the organization's processes and procedures to improve patient care. They must enable and empower an organization's employees to work collaboratively to address quality improvement. Finally, leaders must "encourage the heart"—as passion fuels achievement. A leader should inspire and bolster the enthusiasm of an organization's employees and partners, and celebrate the positive contributions individuals and teams make to the organization's quality-enhancement efforts.

Quality and patient safety is driven by and the responsibility of many stakeholders, as we review in this chapter. There should not be any sole reliance or accountability on any one group or individual. A leader who can drive efforts of integrating quality aims with an organization's strategic and financial goals is becoming crucial in healthcare settings. Titles for leaders holding these positions include chief quality officer, chief experience officer, and vice president of quality and patient safety, to name a few.

▶ Governing Boards

Governing boards of healthcare organizations have traditionally been legally accountable for identifying the organizational mission and goals, promoting fiscal viability, monitoring, executive performance, and ensuring the quality of care their individual facilities provide. In the modern healthcare environment, boards in a variety of sectors, such as hospitals, clinics, and long-term care facilities, are tasked with the responsibility of prioritizing patient and worker safety, establishing a culture of safety, and monitoring the organization's progress toward improvement (Agency for Healthcare Research and Quality PSNet, 2017). The Affordable Care Act of 2010 promotes a system-wide emphasis for quality of care, which integrates previously separate components of healthcare delivery and demands interdisciplinary responsibility for patient care.

A proactive, comprehensive approach must be taken by the governing board to guide and support senior leadership in promoting excellence in this environment. For hospitals and other large healthcare organizations, a commissioned subcommittee to address quality of care and patient safety is recommended to ensure adequate oversight (Rubino & Chan, 2008). A survey of hospital and system leaders demonstrated that the following engagement measures were also effective in enhancing quality oversight: establishing strategic goals for quality improvement, using quality dashboards to track performance, and following up on corrective actions related to adverse events (Jiang, Lockee, Bass, & Fraser, 2008). More recent research reveals better performance on benchmarks of quality care and on mortality rates when organizations implement practices such as soliciting both their governing board and their medical staff to collaborate with management in setting the agenda for discussion and development of quality improvement initiatives; requiring new clinical programs to meet quality-related criteria; setting selected quality outcome targets at ideal levels; and requiring the issuance of public quality/safety performance reports (Jiang, Lockee, & Fraser, 2012). Hospitals with boards that pay greater attention to clinical quality were found to have management that more effectively monitors quality performance. Furthermore, hospitals with boards that used clinical quality metrics more effectively demonstrated better performance by hospital management staff with target setting and operations (Tsai et al., 2015). Unfortunately, some studies show that hospital governing boards may have an over-inflated perception of how their organization is engaged in quality and patient safety efforts, and need to perform objective assessments of evidence-based activities and outcomes (McGaffigan, Ullem, & Gandhi, 2017).

▶ Executive and Senior Leaders

Quality and patient safety impact every area of a healthcare leader's responsibility; including patient morbidity; patient, family, and staff satisfaction; and financial metrics. Leaders must be able to measure and evaluate the quality of services and care that their units or divisions provide, and to compare their performance with other units within the organization. They must also be able to assess and understand how their units' quality outcomes affect the performance of the organization as a whole.

Successful leaders develop formal bylaws, policies, and procedures that address quality issues critical to daily operation. For example, medical staff bylaws and nursing policies should include policies and procedures on the performance of credentialing, privileging, peer evaluation, continuing education, skills assessment, and quality improvement studies and audits. Procedures for identifying areas for quality improvement, implementing positive changes, and reassessing performance should be outlined. Creating alignment between individual performance expectations (staff, leaders, physicians), vendor service expectations, and department-based and organizational strategic goals may further support and drive improvements.

Leaders must establish a safety culture in which healthcare professionals and leaders are held accountable for unprofessional conduct, but do not fear admitting to unintended mistakes. All staff should be formally encouraged to report errors, with vital feedback loops that include analysis of the causes of untoward events and implementation of new procedures and training to enable staff to learn from errors and change processes to prevent a recurrence (NPSF, 2015). Additionally, staff should be encouraged to speak up or intervene if they become aware of work-related activities that may endanger patient safety and quality of care. Leaders and staff should be educated in the value of and best practice strategies and tools to create a safety culture change.

Both clinical and nonclinical areas require guidelines for maintaining and improving quality and patient safety. For example, Health Information Management departments and other leaders must ensure the accuracy of documentation as the foundation for the appropriate coding of medical records to mitigate the risk impact on subsequent care, organizational metrics, and reimbursement.

Healthcare leaders' efforts to improve quality not only profoundly improve patient outcomes and satisfaction, but can also result in additional benefits for their organizations, such as increased profits and reduced costs (e.g., via increased efficiencies, prevention of patient harm from hospital acquired conditions). These benefits have encouraged leaders in a broad range of healthcare sectors to identify quality of care and patient safety as their top priority (HealthLeaders Media Industry Survey, 2011a), and to model and facilitate culture shifts promoting quality of care for their organizations.

In a more recent survey, which asked healthcare leaders what will be the top three positive influences on your organization's efforts to reach financial targets over the next 3 years, care improvement strategies (care redesign, care standardization, and new care models) were ranked just beneath cost control. This points out the continuing importance placed on quality and patient safety by today's healthcare leaders (HealthLeaders Media, 2018) (see **TABLE 8.1**).

TABLE 8.1 Healthcare Leaders Ranking of the Top Three Positive Influences to Reach Financial Targets over the Next 3 Years

Influence on Organization's Efforts	Rank Order
Cost control	1
Care redesign	2
Care standardization	3
Care models (e.g., population health, medical home)	4
Expansion of ambulatory/outpatient care	5

Data from HealthLeadersMedia. Jan/Feb 2018, *Intelligence Report*, 1-20. Retrieved April 1, 2018 from http://promos.hcpro.com/pdf/janFeb2018Intel_Final.pdf

▶ Quality and Patient Safety Initiatives

Professional associations from a breadth of healthcare sectors are also promoting the importance of dynamic leadership for successful quality management (AHA & HRET, 2011). These professional associations provide resources and guidance about successful research and evidence-based processes that can inform leaders' strategic planning and initiative development in this arena. The associations promote new best practices and recommendations through their written and online communications with members as well as through meetings, educational programs, seminars, and conferences. The Joint Commission, for example, began annual reporting on high-quality performers and their successful initiatives in their *Improving America's Hospitals Report* (The Joint Commission, 2011).

Several other organizations have launched outreach initiatives to disseminate best practices to their stakeholders. Some recent examples are:

- CMS' Partnership for Patients initiative to make hospital care safer, more reliable, and cost-effective through the Hospital Engagement Networks (HEN), Community-Based Care Transitions, Hospital Improvement Innovation Networks (HIIN), and Patient and Family Engagement.
- The Comprehensive Unit-Based Safety Program, which aims to reduce central-line associated bloodstream infections (CLABSI).
- TeamSTEPPS – an evidence-based set of teamwork tools, aimed at optimizing patient outcomes by improving communication and teamwork skills among healthcare professionals.

▶ Stakeholders and Drivers

The healthcare industry is not monolithic and can include and involve many parties with divergent agendas and interests. Each party, or stakeholder, shares the common goals of supporting the mission of a healthcare organization or system, but also brings its individual objectives to the partnership or collaboration. Stakeholders will seek to assess not only how well the system or organization is performing, but also whether their individual objectives are being met. Executive healthcare leaders need to identify leaders and champions within each stakeholder unit who can ensure that the units' initiatives are not only achieving the individual units' specific objectives but also advancing system improvement as a whole. Selection of effective leaders of stakeholder groups is especially critical for Accountable Care Organizations, for which the success of quality initiatives depends on achieving stakeholder collaboration and alignment (Kocher & Sahni, 2010). An organization's stakeholders, both internal and external, can be effective drivers of quality initiatives. Internal drivers of quality can include an organization's Board of Directors, its executive and senior leaders, the medical staff, the employees, and the patients/clients and their families. Externally, the quality agenda can be driven by payers, purchasers, regulators, accrediting and certifying bodies, professional organizations, public–private agencies, as well as nonprofit agencies whose mission is to improve health care (see **FIGURE 8.2**).

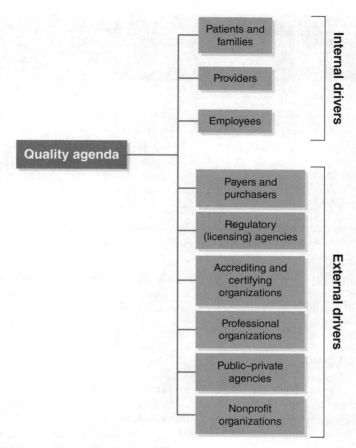

FIGURE 8.2 Stakeholders and Drivers of Quality

▶ Physicians and Other Providers

The selection and retention of engaged, excellent, and cost-effective providers is a key to success in quality improvement; enlisting and empowering providers to embrace quality-improvement initiatives is equally critical for healthcare organizations and systems. For example, physicians have traditionally aimed for high quality in the individual services they provide to each patient, but have come to realize that quality improvement on a broader scale is vital for their practices and for their affiliated healthcare organizations to be successful in today's healthcare environment. Success can be measured in many ways, including client outcomes, patient safety, revenue generation, and most importantly, customer satisfaction. A physician anticipates that not only will her patients be satisfied by her efforts and care, but also by the care provided by her affiliated healthcare organization and the colleagues to whom she refers. Doctors surveyed stated that quality improvement initiatives and enhancement of the patient-care experience will have the greatest positive impact, surpassing other expected advances such as expanded healthcare insurance for the population and the widespread adoption of electronic health records (HealthLeaders

TABLE 8.2 Physician Survey on Important Issues

Issue	Strongly Positive/Positive (%)
Patient experience, patient-centered care	80
Quality-improvement initiatives	76
Electronic health record adoption	67
Increase insured patients	60
Accountable Care Organizations	49

Data from Health Leaders Media Industry Survey. (2011). Physician Leaders Report. Retrieved November 29, 2012 from www .healthleadersmedia.com/pdf/survey_project/2011/Physician_press.pdf

Media Industry Survey, 2011b) (see **TABLE 8.2**). In a more recent survey that examined which continuing education topics are most needed by physicians, practice/ systems improvement competencies were rated higher than research, teaching, and professionalism (Cook et al., 2017).

▶ Payers

In 2015, the U.S. National Health Expenditure (NHE) reached $3.2 trillion and accounted for 17.8% of Gross Domestic Product (GDP), with Medicare accounting for $646.2 billion (20% of NHE), Medicaid, $545.1 billion (17% of NHE), and private health insurers, $1,072.1 billion (33% of NHE). The agencies that pay for health care exert a significant influence on the oversight of care provided with their dollars. For example, the Center for Medicare and Medicaid Services (CMS) has launched a number of quality initiatives aimed at improving the quality of care provided through its programs. These quality initiatives and measures are aligned with the IOM **Aims for Improvement** and are disseminated publicly to promote **transparency** and accountability. They affect a breadth of stakeholders in the healthcare system, including nursing homes, home health agencies, hospitals, kidney dialysis facilities, physicians and mid-level providers, and Accountable Care Organizations. The initiatives have evolved since 2001: Among the changes are moving from voluntary to mandatory reporting, from payment for simple reporting to payment based on the outcomes in reported results (i.e., pay for performance), and to utilizing the collected data to determine value for CMS in purchasing healthcare services. The CMS programs are summarized in **TABLE 8.3**.

Other significant healthcare payers, such as commercial and nonprofit insurance companies, have followed the lead set by CMS in establishing incentives for performance and disincentives for undesired outcomes, such as hospital-acquired conditions and readmissions. Contracts are negotiated by the insurance companies' contract managers, who seek out healthcare providers and organizations in the areas needed by their clientele and negotiate the best quality and price for these purchased or contracted services.

TABLE 8.3 Transition of CMS Quality-Focused Programs

CMS Program	Approach	Participants	Description
Home Health Quality Initiatives (1999-OASIS; 2010-OASIS-C)	Mandatory reporting	Home health agencies	Outcome and Assessment Information Set (OASIS) intended to guide quality improvement; modified dataset launched in 2010 supports evidence-based care (OASIS-C). Results publicly reported on Medicare.gov/homehealthcompare.
Nursing Home Quality Initiative (2002)	Mandatory reporting (informational)	Nursing homes, skilled nursing facilities/centers	Minimum Dataset (MDS) Some MDS measures and certification survey findings are publicly reported data for consumers on Medicare.gov /nursinghomecompare
Reporting Hospital Quality Data for Annual Payment Update (RHQDAPU) (2003–2011 name changed to Hospital Inpatient Quality Reporting Program)	Pay for reporting	Any hospital	Through an increase in the annual market basket for reporting (or a reduction for not reporting). Initially a 0.4% reduction, 2% by 2005.
CMS-Premier Hospital Quality Improvement Demonstration (HQID) Project (2003–2009)	Pay for performance	Premier member hospitals	Financial incentives based on threshold attainment; top performance, and significant improvement. Over the 6 years of the HQID, CMS awarded $60 million to the top performers.
Hospital Outpatient Quality Reporting (Hospital OQR) Program (2006–ongoing)	Pay for reporting	Hospitals—outpatient services	Two-percentage-point reduction in their annual payment update (APU) under the outpatient prospective payment system (OPPS). Includes radiology and emergency department measures.

(continues)

TABLE 8.3 Transition of CMS Quality-Focused Programs *(continued)*

CMS Program	Approach	Participants	Description
Physician Quality Reporting Initiative (2006) (2011: name changed to Physician Quality Reporting System)	Pay for reporting	Physicians	Data on quality measures for covered professional services furnished to Medicare beneficiaries.
Hospital Consumer Assessment of Healthcare Providers and Systems (HCAHPS) (2006)	Mandatory reporting	Patients discharged from a hospital (not restricted to Medicare patients)	Hospital–patient experience survey. Results are publicly reported on Medicare.gov/hospitalcompare.
Hospital Acquired Conditions (HACs) (2008)	Disincentive for hospital-acquired conditions	All hospitals	Beginning in 2007, conditions present on admission (POA) must be identified. Beginning in 2008, specific conditions no longer resulted in higher reimbursement for Medicare patients if acquired during hospitalization.
Electronic Prescribing (e-Rx) Incentive Project (2009)	Incentive program	Physicians	A 2% incentive payment; an individual eligible professional must report the e-Rx measure in at least 50% of the cases in which the measure is reportable.
Nursing Home Value-Based Purchasing (NHVBP) demonstration project (2009)	Pay for performance	Nursing homes in New York, Wisconsin, and Arizona	Domains: staffing, appropriate hospitalizations, outcome measures from the minimum dataset (MDS), and inspection survey deficiencies.
Medicare and Medicaid Electronic Health Records (EHR) Incentive Programs (2011)	Meaningful use incentive program	Eligible professionals, eligible hospitals, critical access hospitals	Incentive for those eligible providers that adopt, implement, upgrade, or demonstrate meaningful use of certified EHR technology, followed by Medicare payment adjustments for failure to meet meaningful use.

End-Stage Renal Disease Quality Incentive Program (ESRD QIP, 2012)	Pay for performance	Dialysis facilities	To enhance the quality of care received by End-Stage Renal Disease patients. Quality measures are publicly available on Medicare.gov/dialysisfacilitycompare.
Hospital Value-Based Purchasing (HVBP, 2012)	Purchaser of value (value = quality/cost)	All hospitals	No longer payment for reporting. Quality incentive payment program based upon performance in quality (70%) and patient experience (30%) measures (HCAHPS). 2012: Hospital 1% contribution "at risk," 0.25% increase each year until 2% in 2017. Leftover funds are redistributed to hospitals based on their Total Performance Scores (TPS).
Accountable Care Organizations (ACO) Quality Measures (2012)	Pay for reporting and pay for performance	Accountable care organizations	Requires reporting of 33 individual measures of quality performance that will be used to determine if an ACO qualifies for shared savings. These 33 measures span four quality domains: patient experience of care, care coordination/patient safety, preventive health, and at-risk population.
Readmissions Reduction Program (HRRP) (2013)	IPPS payment reduction (penalty)	Hospitals	Readmissions within 30 days of hospital discharge.
LTCH-IRF-Hospice Quality Reporting (2014)	Mandatory reporting	Long-term care hospitals (LTCHs), inpatient rehabilitation facilities (IRFs), and hospice programs	CMS required measures published by October 2012; failure to report results in a 2% reduction in the annual payment.
Hospital Star Rating (2016)	Overall rating of 1–5 stars	Hospitals	The overall rating summarizes up to 57 quality measures on Medicare.gov/hospitalcompare.

▶ Purchasers

Purchasers of health care include employers who purchase or subsidize healthcare benefits for their employees. In the past, business leaders focused on finding the lowest-cost services for their employee health insurance plans. Today, employers seek high-value services. There is an added emphasis on creating healthcare benefit plans that engage employees in healthy lifestyle choices, such as smoking cessation, healthy diet choices, and exercise. Healthcare performance data are more transparent, allowing business leaders to consider performance and quality measures, and select the providers and affiliated institutions that can most effectively keep the business' employees healthy and productive.

One heralded approach was developed by the Leapfrog Group, a national nonprofit organization founded in 2000 by large employers and other purchasers. With a mission to "trigger a giant leap forward in quality, customer service, and affordability of healthcare," the Leapfrog Group developed its Leapfrog Hospital Survey to collect and transparently report hospital performance, with the intent to allow purchasers to find the highest-value care and to provide consumers with information to support informed decision-making. Leapfrog has expanded to provide a Hospital Safety Grade based upon their patient safety data, which are released annually to the public at www.leapfroggroup. org. By recognizing and rewarding top performers in its survey, Leapfrog aims to leverage its purchasing influence and motivate lower performers and nonparticipants to meet the Leapfrog safety standards. The overall impact of Leapfrog, however, has been attenuated by limited survey participation and adoption of its standards by healthcare organizations; however, the Leapfrog approach is credited with serving as an early catalyst for transparency of quality and safety measures (Galvin, Delbanco, Milstein, & Belden, 2005; Pronovost, Thompson, Holzmueller, Domran, & Morlock, 2007).

▶ Patients and Families

Before 2008, the end users of health care had not been empowered to advance quality improvement efforts. Spurred by the onset of mandatory performance reporting and public dissemination of patient-experience survey results in the *Hospital Consumer Assessment of Healthcare Providers and Systems* (HCAHPS), healthcare leaders are increasingly implementing patient- and family-centered care, developing patient–family advisory councils, and integrating patient and/or family representatives into key committees.

Former and current patients and their family members are becoming involved in leadership positions on such councils and committees to ensure their voices are heard. The Institute for Patient- and Family-Centered Care (2010) has recommended that their constituents (i.e., patients and families) act as co-leaders on quality improvement teams in healthcare organizations. Depending on their experience, skills, and expertise, these representatives can serve as facilitators of meetings, content experts, evaluators, faculty on educational seminars, and authors of disseminated work that supports the movement. Even sharing the customer experience provided by having been a patient in its facilities can be of great value to a healthcare organization seeking to improve its quality of care and services. Evidence that patients are key stakeholders in improving quality of medical care is beginning to be demonstrated (Greene, Farley, Amy, & Hutcheson, 2018).

▶ Regulators, Accrediting, and Certifying Organizations

Regulatory agencies and accrediting and certifying organizations play a very important role in ensuring high-quality and safe patient care by periodically inspecting and reviewing healthcare organizations and facilities for compliance with designated standards and requirements for licensure, accreditation, and certification. Failure to comply with standards and regulations could lead to significant negative consequences for an organization, such as loss of accreditation, loss of licensure, and criminal or civil liability.

CMS has driven the accreditation process through its development and oversight of the Federal Conditions of Participation. Accreditation organizations such as The Joint Commission, the Accreditation Association for Ambulatory Health Care (AAAHC), Det Norske Veritas (DNV), and the American Osteopathic Association have been granted "deeming" authority (i.e., the authority to appraise and judge that a healthcare organization meets the Medicare and Medicaid certification requirements). The Conditions of Participation, as well as the accreditation organizations' standards, establish the requirements that healthcare organizations must meet in order to become accredited and thus be eligible to treat Medicare and Medicaid patients and to receive federal reimbursement for the care provided. Achieving accredited status serves a dual purpose for healthcare organizations: It allows them to care for and be reimbursed for treating Medicare and Medicaid patients, and it establishes that the organization has met the various performance improvement, quality, and patient safety standards of the accrediting body.

Though certification status may not be a requirement for the provision of specialized services such as stroke care, palliative care, or other disease-specific care, many healthcare organizations seek additional certification for such services as a sign of distinction and excellence. Disease-specific care certification can serve to differentiate an organization from its competitors and may assist in providing leverage in recruiting outstanding physicians and other healthcare professionals, in negotiating favorable or enhanced contracts and in promoting business development. **TABLE 8.4** identifies some of the most commonly utilized certification organizations.

Federal and state regulators, licensing agencies, and accreditation organizations also maintain and enforce requirements regarding significant adverse and sentinel events to which organizations must adhere. In many states, hospitals are required to notify the state department of public health within a specific time frame of discovery if certain types of negative events occur. As of 2014, a total of 26 states (and District of Columbia) have some form of mandatory reporting requirements. For example, since 2007, California hospitals have been required to report certain serious or sentinel "never events" that are considered preventable. Some examples of "never events" are surgery performed on the wrong body part, an infant discharged to the wrong person, a patient death or serious disability associated with a medication error, and a sexual assault on a patient (California Department of Public Health, 2007). The Joint Commission (TJC) does not mandate (but encourages) reporting by its accredited organizations. TJC will require a report and a follow-up action plan should it become aware of an organization's sentinel event or adverse outcomes as a result of a regulatory agency report, media reports, and/or complaints from patients, families, or other individuals. Failure to demonstrate an effective improvement plan may jeopardize an organization's accreditation status.

TABLE 8.4   Examples of Accreditation and Certification Organizations

Accreditation Organization	Accreditation Services (Deemed Status)	Certification(s) Offered

The Joint Commission (TJC) www.joint commission.org /certification/dsc _home.aspx	Ambulatory health care
	    Behavioral health care
	    Critical access hospital
	    Home care
	    Hospitals
	    Laboratory services
	    Nursing care center
		Disease-Specific Care
		    (Behavioral health, cardiovascular, endocrine, hematology–oncology, neonatal/perinatal, neurological, orthopedic joint replacement, pediatric, pulmonary, rheumatology, stroke rehabilitation, acute myocardial infarction, wound care, women's health)
		    Advanced Disease-Specific Care
		    (Chronic kidney disease, chronic obstructive pulmonary disease, heart failure, inpatient diabetes, lung volume reduction, palliative care, ventricular assist device)
		    Healthcare Staffing Services
		    Comprehensive Cardiac Care
		    Integrated Care
		    Medication Compounding
		    Perinatal Care
		    Primary Care Medical Home
		    Patient Blood Management

Accreditation Association for Ambulatory Health Care www.aaahc.org/	Ambulatory health care
	    Ambulatory surgical centers
	    Community health centers
	    Federally Qualified Health Centers
	    Managed care organizations
	    Medical home
		Medicare-deemed status for ASCs

Det Norske Veritas Offers national integrated accreditation for healthcare organizations (NIAHO) http:// dnvaccreditation .com/pr/dnv/default .aspx	Hospitals Critical access hospitals	Primary stroke certification
American Osteopathic Association's Healthcare Facilities Accreditation Program (HFAP) www.hfap.org/	Acute care Critical access hospitals Ambulatory surgical centers Clinical laboratory Behavioral/mental health Ambulatory care/ office-based surgery	Primary stroke center

▶ Professional Organizations/Public–Private Agencies/Nonprofit Organizations

A number of other entities help to drive the quality agenda. For example, the American Nurses Association (ANA) has established the National Database for Nursing Quality Indicators (NDNQI). The NDNQI collects and reports data that assess and reflect nursing-focused processes of care and outcome measures. These metrics allow hospitals to compare patients-per-nurse staffing ratios and other factors that may correlate with quality outcomes, as well as to identify benchmarks for performance improvement.

The Agency for Healthcare Research and Quality (AHRQ), an agency in the U.S. Department of Health and Human Services, supports health services research aimed at improving the quality, safety, efficiency, effectiveness, and cost-effectiveness of health care. The results of research funded through the AHRQ are used by policymakers, providers, payers, consumers, health systems, and health plans to evaluate and improve services, as well as to enhance informed decisions regarding health care. The (AHRQ) encourages utilization of reports to spur quality improvement via root cause analysis (https://psnet.ahrq.gov/primers/primer/13 /reporting-patient-safety-events).

The National Quality Forum (NQF) is a not-for-profit entity that contributes to establishing national healthcare priorities and improvement goals by reporting on the quality and efficiency of health services as measured against NQF-endorsed standards. For additional examples of public and private organizations that influence quality and patient safety policy, see **TABLE 8.5**.

TABLE 8.5 Public/Private Organizations That Influence Quality and Patient Safety Policy

Organization	Type	Mission/Focus
Agency for Healthcare Research and Quality (AHRQ)	One of three human services agencies in the U.S. Department of Health and Human Services	Awards funds to support research to improve the quality, safety, efficiency, and effectiveness of health care for all Americans.
Institute for Healthcare Improvement (IHI)	Independent, not-for-profit organization; Merged with the National Patient Safety Foundation (NPSF) (2017)	Motivating and "building the will for change"; identifying and testing new models of care in partnership with both patients and healthcare professionals, and ensuring the broadest possible adoption of best practices and effective innovations.
Institute for Safe Medication Practices (ISMP)	Independent nonprofit, established in 1975	Devoted entirely to medication error prevention and safe medication use.
Institute of Medicine (IOM)	Independent nonprofit, established in 1970	Works outside of government to provide unbiased and authoritative advice to improve health to decision makers and the public.
Medicare Quality Improvement Organizations (QIOs)	Two types of QIOs: Beneficiary and Family-Centered Care (BFCC) QIOs and Quality Innovation Network (QIN-QIOs)	Work with consumers, physicians, hospitals, and other caregivers to refine care delivery systems to ensure patients, particularly from underserved populations, receive "the right care at the right time." Working to increase patient safety, make communities healthier, better coordinate post-hospital care and improve clinical quality.
National Quality Forum (NQF)	Created in 1999 by a coalition of public and private sector leaders	Works to improve the safety of care provided to patients by building consensus and partnering to promote and achieve national priorities and goals for performance improvement, endorsing national consensus standards for performance to be assessed and publicly reported, and promoting the attainment of national goals through education and outreach programs.

▶ Employees

A quality agenda may be launched from the executive offices of a healthcare organization, but its successful implementation depends on the contributions and commitment of employees at all the organization's levels. To develop and promote a culture of quality and safety, leaders need to provide opportunities for employee education and training in professionally relevant regulations and standards, and to encourage employees to actively participate in planning and implementation of quality initiatives. Healthcare professionals and support staff serving within an organization are likely to be positively motivated by enhancement of the organization's reputation. Leaders can embrace their employees' enthusiasm for excellence and leverage the diligence and expertise of their workforce to build morale and engagement and to drive the quality agenda.

▶ Patient Safety

Patient safety is an essential component of a comprehensive quality program in all healthcare organizations; administrative and clinical alignment is necessary for performance improvement in this arena. As research provides new findings about the causes for procedural errors and policy breakdowns, senior leaders' responsibilities to promote patient safety will continue to increase. Successful healthcare executives embrace their roles as safety change agents who are leading an organization's dynamic patient safety team (Birk, 2011). Among the groundbreaking initiatives to enhance patient safety recently advanced by healthcare leaders are improving infection control practices, focusing on identifying and preventing medical errors, sharing knowledge about patient safety best-practices with staff, implementing programs to reduce falls and injuries, and introducing information-technology-based safety checks (Cantlupe, 2011).

An excellent resource has been developed through a partnership between American College of Healthcare Executives and the IHI/NPSF Lucian Leape Institute. *Leading a Culture of Safety: A Blueprint for Success* provides evidenced-based research, tools, and applicable strategies to assist leaders in this quest (ACHE & NPSF LLI, 2017). Six safety culture domains are identified for leaders to address for the organizations (see **FIGURE 8.3**).

- Domain 1: Establish a Compelling Vision for Safety
- Domain 2: Trust, Respect, and Inclusion
- Domain 3: Select, Develop, and Engage your Board
- Domain 4: Prioritize Safety in Selection and Development of Leaders
- Domain 5: Lead and Reward a Just Culture
- Domain 6: Establish Organizational Behavior Expectations

▶ Organizational Culture

Organizational culture is defined by Hill and Jones (2012), as "the specific collection of values and norms that are shared by people and groups in an organization, and that control the way they interact with each other and with stakeholders outside the organization." Organizational cultures evolve over time, reflect the organization's

FIGURE 8.3 Leading for Safety. © ACHE & IHI/NPSF 2017
Courtesy of American College of Healthcare Executives.

mission, vision, and values, and inform ways of communicating and behaving in the workplace. Quality is a critical value, as well as a goal, that should urgently infuse all aspects of an organization's culture. Successful leaders take dynamic action to promote quality as a key driver in their organizational cultures and to inspire a commitment to quality among their organizations' stakeholders.

The Joint Commission requires that healthcare leaders create and maintain a culture of safety and quality throughout their accredited hospitals (The Joint Commission, 2012). The accreditation agency understands that quality-focused leadership provides the foundation for effective performance and has identified specific standards associated with this expected leadership role.

- Leaders regularly evaluate the culture of safety and quality using valid and reliable tools.
- Leaders prioritize and implement necessary changes identified and indicated by these evaluations.
- Leaders provide opportunities for all individuals who work in the hospital to participate in safety and quality initiatives.

- Leaders develop a code of conduct that defines acceptable, disruptive, and inappropriate behaviors.
- Leaders create and implement a process for managing disruptive and inappropriate behaviors.
- Leaders provide education that focuses on safety and quality for all individuals.
- Leaders establish a team approach among all staff at all levels.
- All individuals who work in the hospital are able to openly discuss issues of safety and quality.
- Literature and advisories relevant to patient safety are available to all individuals who work in the hospital.
- Leaders define how members of the population served can help identify and manage issues of safety and quality within the hospital.

▶ Organizational Framework

Competencies are a set of professional and personal skills, knowledge, values, and traits that guide a leader's performance, behavior, interaction, and decisions (Dye & Garman, 2006). They can be utilized to give developing leaders a means to identify the critical elements of effective leadership and to adopt the necessary skills and practices to achieve success. The National Association for Healthcare Quality (NAHQ) has developed a model to provide healthcare leaders with the knowledge and skills to lead successful quality improvement initiatives in their healthcare organizations (Garman & Scribner, 2011). This Quality Leadership Developmental Competency Model has analyzed and distinguished the skillsets and processes necessary at each level of leadership within an organization.

Leaders at all levels are tasked with maintaining *professionalism* and demonstrating outstanding *values, integrity,* and *performance.* Among the additional competencies necessary for entry-level leaders in the healthcare setting are vision, a focus on the future, engagement in lifelong learning, and effective consumer advocacy. When leaders move into mid-level roles, three other domains emerge as crucial for quality leadership. The first is *performance improvement,* which includes collecting and managing data, implementing analytical thinking and evidence-based decision-making, and developing and promoting a knowledge-rich environment. The second is *communication and education,* which includes demonstrating excellent verbal, written, listening, and educating skills. The third is *self-management,* which includes maintaining a high standard of professional ethics, managing personal limits, and demonstrating resilience and self-restraint. Finally, for leaders who move to the senior levels of the organization, two additional domains are recommended. The first is *organizational awareness,* which includes utilizing and demonstrating systems thinking, strategic thinking and planning, and financial acumen. The second domain, *fostering positive change,* includes competencies such as advocating for and adapting to change, partnering for change, cultivating a quality-supportive climate, and driving results.

These six domains and their associated competencies can guide healthcare leaders to be more effective in their roles and develop capacity in the area of quality leadership (see **FIGURE 8.4**). The Quality Leadership Developmental Competency Model provides a basic framework for successful quality leadership, but additional factors such as a collaborative culture also contribute to quality leadership success.

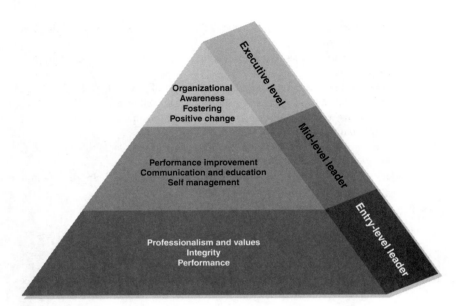

FIGURE 8.4 Quality Leadership Developmental Competency Model

Modified from National Association for Healthcare Quality Leadership Development Model. Retrieved November 30, 2012 from www.nahq.org/membership/leadership/devmodel.html.

In addition, NAHQ provides certification for quality professionals through their affiliated Healthcare Quality Certification Commission. Four areas are addressed in the examination provided in order to become a certified Professional in Healthcare Quality: Organizational Leadership, Health Data Analytics, Performance and Process Improvement, and Patient Safety. Under Organizational Leadership, the content areas addressed in the examination are A, Structure and integration; B, Regulatory, accreditation, and external recognition; and C, Education, training and communication. Retrieved March 31, 2018 from https://bit.ly/2NrFUvP.

▶ Move to Reliability

The industry is challenged by the frequent inability of organizations to reliably maintain performance excellence and high reliability over time. Some doubt that 100% reliability can be achieved, and others suggest its eventual attainment would be dependent on a combination of leadership commitment, fully implemented culture change, and adoption of robust process-improvement tools and methods (Chassin & Loeb, 2011). Health care is moving in the right direction, however, with its increased focus on developing new, improved, and more reliable quality improvement practices, and promoting high reliability organizations. Some examples taken from other industries that have better safety records are removing impediments generated by hierarchical authority; utilizing standardized protocols and checklists; pre- and post-procedural briefings; incident reporting; and huddles. (For a best practice huddle, see Brass, Olney, Glimp, Lemaire, & Kingston, 2018.) Leadership's role in this evolution will be critical to a successful outcome (see **TABLE 8.6**).

TABLE 8.6 Leadership's Evolving Role in a Healthcare Organization's Path to Reliability

Early Minimal Stage	Developing Stage	Approaching Stage
Focus is on regulations and laws	CEO leads proactive quality agenda	Full organizational commitment
Strategic importance not recognized	Board reviews adverse events	Aim toward near zero failure rates
Quality metrics not utilized properly	Few measurable quality aims	Reward system for staff
Little support from information technology (IT)	IT supports some initiatives	IT integral to sustain initiatives
Physicians not actively engaged	Some physician champions	Physicians routinely lead efforts

Modified from Chassin, M. R., & Loeb, J. M. (2011). The ongoing quality improvement journey: Next stop, high reliability. *Health Affairs, 30*(4), 566. Exhibit 1.

▶ Barriers

Experts believe **high reliability organizations** in health care remains elusive and attempt to offer an explanation (Sutcliffe, Paine, & Pronovost, 2017). One explanation is that healthcare organizations have failed to widely institutionalize high-reliability habits of thought and action. Low reliability may persist as well because health care lacks a solid understanding of how to build and maintain fundamental foundational support for highly reliable performance.

As healthcare organizations strive to improve their performance and quality outcomes, they often encounter other barriers that may impair progress or derail the effort altogether. One of the key responsibilities of healthcare leaders in driving performance improvement is to identify and then remove these barriers (see **TABLE 8.7**). One recent survey showed that difficulty changing organizational culture and an abundance of other priorities were the two barriers most identified as affecting patient experience (HealthLeaders Media *Intelligence Report*, 2017).

▶ Strategies and Methods

The IOM publications *To Err Is Human* and *Crossing the Quality Chasm* (2000) advanced the emphasis on quality and patient safety to the top of the healthcare agenda more than a decade ago. The promotion of transparency through the public reporting of clinical performance metrics and significant patient harm events are

TABLE 8.7 Barriers to Quality Improvement

Barriers	Description
Organizational culture	Organization resists change; not a learning-focused culture
Conflicting priorities	Lack of alignment of goals across the organization
Lack of expertise, skepticism	Team composition issues and dysfunctionality; respected, persuasive leadership needed
Lack of commitment, complacency	Lack of urgency, motivation, engagement; rationale not compelling; lack of understanding
Physician buy-in and support	Lack of agreement with the need and/or plan; insufficient evidence to warrant action
Resistance to change	Perception that the costs of change outweigh the benefits; lack of organizational readiness or change-management skills
Resource constraints	Real or perceived limitations in: Time to devote to the project Quantity or quality of human resources Funds and other resources to support the project Access to required information or materials
Technology	Lack of technology to support the changes

additional factors that are providing motivation for providers and healthcare organizations to demonstrate outstanding results. As the champions of quality and patient safety, healthcare leaders must determine which strategies may be most effective in creating sustainable high performance. Some of the most frequently used strategies are summarized as follows.

Collaborative Learning and Improvement

In 1995, the IHI created a model for breakthrough improvement supported through collaborative learning. The model relies upon a short-term (usually 6–18 months) collaboration among a number of teams from various organizations seeking to improve care or services within a specific, focused area. Together, the teams learn key principles of performance improvement as well as best practices, and have the opportunity to brainstorm and create innovative solutions for quality concerns. As the teams work on improvements at their organizations, they share their strategies, performance, progress, and results across the collaborative (IHI, 2003). Regional and state trade associations, nonprofit disease-focused associations, quality and patient safety foundations/groups, and healthcare systems regularly conduct collaborative efforts modeled after the IHI's breakthrough series.

Lean and Six Sigma

Lean methodology is based upon the Toyota Production System (TPS). It focuses on efficiency, removing waste/*muda* (*Muda* (無駄) is a Japanese word meaning "futility; uselessness; wastefulness"), and creating value. The seven types of waste identified are (1) overproduction, (2) waiting, time in queue, (3) transportation, (4) non-value-adding processes, (5) inventory, (6) motion, and (7) costs of quality: scrap, rework, and inspection.

Lean promotes "the customer first" by recommending the following steps: (1) define value as determined by the customer, (2) identify the value stream (the set of actions required to bring a specific product or service from concept to completion), (3) make value-added steps flow from beginning to end, (4) let the customer want and pull the product/service from the supplier rather than push products/services, and (5) pursue perfection of the process (Ransom, Joshi, Nash, & Ransom, 2008).

Motorola is largely credited with successfully developing and launching Sigma, which stemmed from the recognition that producing a high-quality product resulted in fewer repairs and improved customer satisfaction. After implementing **Six Sigma** in 1988, Motorola was among the first recipients of the **Malcolm Baldrige National Quality Award**. Six Sigma uses DMAIC (Define, Measure, Analyze, Improve, Control) as a framework for improvement, and is supported by analytical and statistical tools (Kubiak & Benbow, 2009). Traditionally, Six Sigma focuses on eliminating defects, measured as defects per million opportunities (DPMO), in key business processes. Six Sigma is implemented by an infrastructure of trained leaders: "champions," "master black belts," "black belts," and "green belts," who attain certification after demonstrating expertise in the program methodology and completing black-belt projects.

In a recent survey of healthcare leaders, nearly two-thirds (64%) of respondents say that their organizations use process improvement methodologies such as Lean or Six Sigma to improve patient experience (HealthLeaders Media *Intelligence Report*, 2017).

Baldrige Performance Excellence

The Malcolm Baldrige National Quality Award was developed in 1987 by the U.S. government to encourage American companies to adopt best practices and to make the changes necessary to become high-performing and more competitive in the global market. In 1999, Congress passed an amendment that allowed additional sectors to apply for the award, such as nonprofits and healthcare industries. In 2002, the first healthcare organization received the Baldrige Award; today, the number of healthcare applicants for the Award exceeds all other sectors combined. Many healthcare organizations striving to achieve high performance have applied the Baldrige Framework and Criteria to their quality-improvement programs. The Baldrige Criteria for Performance Excellence include a set of questions within seven categories: (1) Leadership; (2) Strategic Planning; (3) Customer Focus; (4) Measurement, Analysis, and Knowledge Management; (5) Workforce Focus; (6) Operations Focus; and (7) Results (NIST, 2011). One of the most respected academics in health administration, Dr. John Griffith, has called on the healthcare industry to adopt the Baldrige organizational model for improvement. He believes that its comprehensive program emphasizing a shared focus on excellence, systematically responsive management, practice of evidence-based medicine, utilization of multidimensional measures and negotiated goals, improvement of work processes, thorough training, and extensive rewards, could substantially improve the quality and cost of health care (Griffith, 2017).

Nursing Magnet Recognition Program

The **ANCC Nursing Magnet Recognition Program** is a credentialing program of the American Nurses Credentialing Center, which recognizes healthcare organizations that provide outstanding nursing care. The Magnet Recognition Program is considered to be the highest recognition for nursing excellence; fewer than 7% of hospitals have attained Magnet status (AHA Resource Center Blog, 2011). Obtaining this recognition is a strategy by which hospitals can position themselves more competitively, particularly in the areas of nursing recruitment and retention; improved patient care, safety, satisfaction, and experience; and physician recruitment.

▶ Tools for Alignment and Sustainability

To support their quality journey, healthcare leaders can draw on a number of tools. Most valuable are tools to collect and analyze data and information to be used to assess performance of the organization's key processes, systems, and services. These tools allow leaders to evaluate their organizations' progress toward quality goals and to create effective strategic decisions and action plans. Leaders can align goals and objectives throughout an organization and promote common understanding and complementary efforts by multiple units by building a cascade of strategic goals and key processes that begins at the organization-wide level and flows to the department level, and then to the team and individual levels (see **FIGURE 8.5**).

Balanced Scorecard

One approach utilized by businesses and healthcare organizations to draw organizational focus toward its strategic objectives is a **balanced scorecard**, which depicts the organization's key metrics as they relate to the organization's strategic goals. The origins of the balanced scorecard approach are attributed to Kaplan and Norton, authors of "The Balanced Scorecard—Measures that Drive Performance," in the January/February 1992 issue of the *Harvard Business Review*. The balanced scorecard management system aligns unit goals and metrics with organizational goals, and provides an organizational and unit "dashboard" through which managers and leaders can monitor and evaluate progress toward quality goals.

Four key categories of balanced scorecard indicators have been identified: financial measures, customer measures, internal business (process) measures, and innovation and learning measures. Leaders can identify operational objectives within each of the four key categories for their units, which provide "balance" to the organization. This management system creates awareness and directionality throughout the organization toward common goals via a balanced, linked set of performance metrics, and allows leaders to supervise the linkages and maintain organizational focus on achieving the desired results.

Many healthcare organizations have adopted a modified balanced scorecard approach, which identifies key result categories (also referred to as "pillars") such as

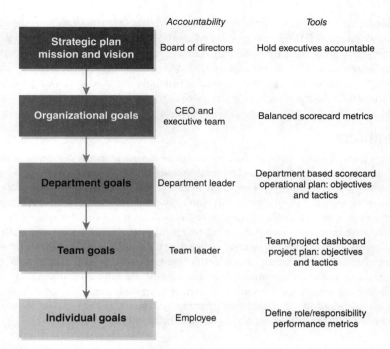

FIGURE 8.5 Cascading Organizational Goals

finance, quality, service, people, and growth (Studer, 2003). As described previously, objectives can be established within each pillar category at all levels of the organization, then through a cascade, objectives at the organizational level, the departmental level, the team level, and the individual employee level can be linked. Employees are able to see how their contributions "fit into the big picture," and managers are able to supervise performance through metrics at each level and determine progress toward the organization's strategic aims.

Operational Plans

Operational plans are used as a roadmap of the various strategies and tactics a leader will deploy and implement in order to achieve his/her operational targets. By establishing operational targets at the department or unit level that support and link to the organization's strategic goals and objectives, the leaders create the "cascading" effect that communicates and demonstrates alignment across the organization. Designed and implemented effectively, these operational plans can assist employees at all levels of an organization in understanding their specific roles and duties that support the institutional goals and mission.

Performance Management Plan

Today's healthcare leaders are expected to facilitate an organizational culture of accountability. An effective performance management plan should be developed to establish a mechanism for ongoing formal and informal feedback between employees and their supervisors, and to guide and support managers and employees in developing and setting career goals and creating an individual development plan. Employees who achieve their individual developmental goals may then be further incentivized to achieve department/unit-based goals. These opportunities create an employee–employer win–win situation, which, if designed correctly, promotes departmental and organizational goals as well as those of the unit and the individual.

Summary

The national quality strategy focuses on three broad aims: better care, healthy people/healthy communities, and affordable care (AHRQ, About the National Quality Strategy, 2017). Improvements to the healthcare system will not be fully successful without skilled, knowledgeable, dynamic, and creative healthcare leadership to set the course and steer the healthcare industry. This type of leader will likely use appreciative inquiry to lead quality improvement initiatives (Ramage et al., 2017). This approach examines the positive rather than the negative, that is, what went well rather than what went wrong, and identifies best practices to disseminate throughout the organization. The evolving healthcare landscape will also demand that leaders lead both within and beyond their own organizations, and will take an active role in collaborating with healthcare partners, customers, and other stakeholders to promote quality improvement across the healthcare system.

Discussion Questions

1. How is healthcare reform influencing the creation of a quality-driven culture in organizations?
2. What style of leadership might be best suited for advancing a quality agenda?
3. How can leaders move their organizations to a state of continual performance reliability?
4. Would different healthcare sectors (e.g., acute, ambulatory, long-term care, etc.) have the same or different challenges associated with leading quality initiatives?
5. What can we learn from other industries to improve healthcare quality and patient safety?

🔍 CASE STUDY: A Leadership Approach to Quality and Patient Safety

In response to the IHI's campaign to protect five million patients from harm, and to a recommendation from the Daughters of Charity Health System's Task Force on Quality, the St. Francis Medical Center's Board of Directors created the Quality and Patient Safety Committee (QPS). The QPS launched its efforts to enhance the Board's accountability for quality and patient safety, by calling for improved performance in clinical quality, as reflected in the core measures; by aiming to reduce mortality (its "Big Dot," or overarching goal) through the adoption of best practices; by improving accountability across the organization and its units; by improving the comprehensiveness and timeliness of the peer review process; and by improving patient satisfaction and fostering a culture of patient safety.

One of the first steps taken by the Board's QPS Committee was to educate itself about key quality and patient-safety initiatives and metrics, about the medical staff credentialing and reappointment process, and about patient satisfaction. To enhance Board and QPS member competency, the QPS Committee made a commitment to continuous learning, and sought knowledge about best practices and the principles of quality improvement and patient safety. Several Board members, physicians, and executive leaders made a site visit to a best-practice facility and met with the facility's leaders to learn about their hospital's keys to achieving top performing results. Additionally, Board members attended IHI and Leapfrog Group conferences, which focused on the role of governing boards in driving quality outcomes. For example, an ongoing commitment to education is demonstrated not only through conference attendance but also through the regular provision and discussion of pertinent literature at each committee meeting.

The QPS explored and supported the adoption of several innovative strategies to foster a culture of quality and safety. These included crew resource management, QPS rounds, and the "Just Culture" approach[1] to errors. The crew resource management model was adapted from the techniques used by aerospace cockpit crews to promote effective teamwork and structured communication for enhanced patient safety. The QPS also began conducting rounds throughout the medical center prior to its monthly meetings. The rounds were used to create greater visibility for leadership's commitment to quality and safety and provide an opportunity for QPS members to assess and validate the deployment of effective, patient/family-centered and evidence-based care practices at the bedside. Rounds were made to various St. Francis units and clinics to interact with frontline staff, physicians, and managers, and evaluate progress using tracer methodology.[2] Some areas assessed during rounds were core measure processes, pressure ulcer prevention, emergency department and hospital throughput, the case management process, and spiritual care. At its monthly meetings, the QPS reviewed a dashboard of metrics that reflect clinical quality, patient safety, and patient satisfaction/experience. The dashboard included data to identify trends over time, actual performance as compared to organization targets, as well as benchmarks with top-performing healthcare institutions. The committee received reports about significant untoward events, performance improvement initiatives, and patient complaints, as well as about medical staff peer review, credentialing, appointments, and reappointments.

In the years since its inception, the QPS has led efforts to engage physicians by creating aligned incentives, such as the incorporation of performance goals in physician administrative contracts and the referral of core measure fall-outs for peer review. The QPS has supported physician leadership in their oversight of medical staff credentialing, proctoring, and tracking of medical staff performance data, as part of their ongoing professional practice evaluation process. To ensure a continued focus on the patient and family experience, a family member representative was added to the committee as a voting member. To reinforce leadership accountability across the organization, the QPS invited department managers and directors to the QPS meetings to communicate their plans for improving their area's performance if their results were falling short of target.

As a result of these efforts, the St. Francis Medical Center has demonstrated significant improvements, including a 25% reduction in mortality, improved core-measure perfect-care scores, emergency department and hospital throughput improvement, a shift to performance-based medical staff reappointment, and the

(continues)

sharing of their best practices with others through publications in peer-reviewed journals. As a founding member of the Premier QUEST program (focused on QUality, patient Experience, Safety, and **Transparency**), the St. Francis Medical Center achieved top performer status in mortality, core-measure perfect care, and cost per case.

Case Study Discussion Questions

1. Identify the stakeholders and drivers discussed in this case study who are involved with the improvement in quality and safety. Are there others who should be mentioned?
2. Which of the key strategies adopted by the St. Francis Quality and Patient Safety Committee do you think are the most effective for ongoing quality improvement?
3. What additional rounds can you suggest for the QPS team besides the ones already mentioned?
4. What other measures can be used to assess the quality and patient safety at St. Francis Medical Center?

---

1 "Just Culture" is a model used to analyze errors, which allows healthcare leaders to consider the contributions of both human behavioral choices along with system design in determining the appropriate follow-up. The Just Culture approach emphasizes individual accountability as part of the duty to prevent harm, to follow procedural rules, and to produce an outcome. For more information, go to www.justculture.org/
2 Patient "tracers" are a technique developed by The Joint Commission that is used to evaluate a patient's care across a continuum of care in order to evaluate compliance to the standards. Surveyors and others use this approach to follow a care scenario to determine if appropriate steps such as patient assessment, care, intervention, and education are provided at the various points of care for a particular patient. For more information, go to www.jointcommission.org/facts_about_the_tracer_methodology/

Related Websites

Agency for Healthcare Research and Quality (AHRQ): www.ahrq.gov
American Nurses Credentialing Center (ANCC): www.nursingworld.org/ancc
American Society for Quality (ASQ): http://asq.org
Baldrige Performance Excellence Program: www.nist.gov/baldrige/enter/health_care.cfm
Center for Medicare & Medicaid Services (CMS): www.cms.gov
Det Norske Veritas Healthcare (DNV): www.dnvglhealthcare.com
Institute for Healthcare Improvement (IHI): www.ihi.org/about/pages/default.aspx
Institute of Medicine (IOM): iom.nationalacademies.org
Institute for Patient- and Family-Centered Care (IPFCC): www.ipfcc.org
The Joint Commission: www.jointcommission.org/
The Leapfrog Group: www.leapfroggroup.org/home
National Association for Healthcare Quality (NAHQ): www.nahq.org
National Database of Nursing Quality Indicators (NDNQI): www.nursingquality.org/
National Quality Forum (NQF): www.qualityforum.org/Home.aspx
Partnership for Patients: https://innovation.cms.gov/initiatives/partnership-for-patients/
Premier Safety Institute: www.premiersafetyinstitute.org

References

Agency for Healthcare Research and Quality (AHRQ) About the National Quality Strategy. (2017). *Agency for healthcare research and quality*, Rockville, MD. Retrieved July 20, 2018 from http://www.ahrq.gov/workingforquality/about/index.html
Agency for Healthcare Research and Quality (AHRQ) Patient Safety Network (PSNet). (2017). *Leadership role in improving safety.* Retrieved November 25, 2017 from https://psnet.ahrq.gov/primers/primer/32/leadership-role-in-improving-safety

Agency for Healthcare Research and Quality (AHRQ) Team STEPPS. Retrieved November 25, 2017 from www.ahrq.gov/teamstepps/index.html

American College of Healthcare Executives (ACHE) & National Patient Safety Foundation's Lucian Leape Institute (NPS LLI). (2017). *Leading a culture of safety: A blueprint for success.* American College of Healthcare Executives: Chicago, IL.

American Hospital Association (AHA) and Health Research & Educational Trust (HRET). (2011, July). *Allied hospital association leadership for quality—2011.* Chicago, IL: Author.

American Hospital Association (AHA) Resource Center Blog. (2011, March). Retrieved from http://aharesourcecenter.wordpress.com/2011/03/22/magnet-status-is-it-worth-it

Birk, S. (2011). The patient safety team: Healthcare executives embrace their role. *Healthcare Executive, 26*(5), 13–22.

Brass, S. D., Olney, G., Glimp, R., Lemaire, A., & Kingston, M. (2018). Using the patient safety huddle as a tool for high reliability. *The Joint Commission Journal on Quality and Patient Safety, 44,* 219–226.

California Department of Public Health. (2007). *Reporting of adverse events AFL 07–10.* Retrieved from www.cdph.ca.gov/certlic/facilities/Documents/LNC-AFL-07–10.pdf

Cantlupe, J. (2011). Who "owns" patient safety? *HealthLeaders, 14*(5), 3–40.

Centers for Medicare & Medicaid Services (CMS). (2017). *Partnership for patients.* Retrieved from https://partnershipforpatients.cms.gov

Chassin, M. R., & Loeb, J. M. (2011). The ongoing quality improvement journey: Next stop, high reliability. *Health Affairs, 30*(4), 559–568.

Cook, D. A., Blachman, M. J., Price, D. W., West, C. P., Berger, R. A., & Wittich, C. M. (2017). Professional development perceptions and practices among U.S. physicians: A cross-specialty national survey. *Academic Medicine, 92*(9), 1335–1345.

Dye, C. F., & Garman, A. N. (2006). *Exceptional leadership: 16 critical competencies for healthcare executives.* Chicago, IL: Health Administration Press.

Galvin, R. S., Delbanco, S., Milstein, A., & Belden, G. (2005). Has the Leapfrog Group had an impact on the health care market? *Health Affairs, 24*(1), 228–233.

Garman, A., & Scribner, L. (2011). Leading for quality in healthcare: Development and validation of a competency model. *Journal of Healthcare Management, 56*(6), 373–382.

Greene, J., Farley, D., Amy, C., & Hutcheson, K. (2018). How patient partners influence quality improvement efforts. *The Joint Commission Journal on Quality and Patient Safety, 44*(4). 186–195.

Griffith, J. (2017). An organizational model for excellence in healthcare delivery: Evidence from winners of the Baldrige Quality Award. *Journal of Healthcare Management, 62*(5), 328–341.

HealthLeaders Media. (2017, July/August). *Intelligence report,* 1–29. Retrieved from http://promos.hcpro.com/pdf/AugustIntel_Change.pdf

HealthLeaders Media. (2018, Jan/Feb). *Intelligence report,* 1–20. Retrieved from http://promos.hcpro.com/pdf/janFeb2018Intel_Final.pdf

HealthLeaders Media Industry Survey. (2011a). *Overall cross-sector survey.* Retrieved from www.healthleadersmedia.com/pdf/survey_project/2011/Overall_Cross_Sector_press.pdf

HealthLeaders Media Industry Survey. (2011b). *Physicians leaders.* Retrieved from www.healthleadersmedia.com/pdf/survey_project/2011/Physician_press.pdf

Hill, C. W., & Jones, G. R. (2012). *Strategic management theory* (10th ed.). Boston, MA: South-Western College Publishing.

Institute for Healthcare Improvement (IHI). (2003). *The breakthrough series: IHI's collaborative model for achieving breakthrough improvement.* IHI Innovation Series white paper. Boston, MA: Institute for Healthcare Improvement. Retrieved from www.doh.wa.gov/Portals/1/Documents/1000/PMC-IHI-BreakthoughSeries2003.pdf

Institute for Patient- and Family-Centered Care. (2010, October). *Framework for patient and family involvement in quality improvement.* Bethesda, MD: Institute for Patient- and Family-Centered Care.

Institute of Medicine (IOM). (2000). In L. T. Kohn, J. M. Corrigan, & M. S. Donaldson (Eds.), *To err is human: Building a safer health system.* Washington, DC: National Academies Press.

Institute of Medicine (IOM). (2001). *Crossing the quality chasm: A new health system for the 21st century.* Washington, DC: National Academies Press.

Jiang, H., Lockee, C., Bass, K., & Fraser, I. (2008). Board engagement in quality: Findings of a survey of hospital and system leaders. *Journal of Healthcare Management, 53*(2), 121–133.

Jiang, H., Lockee, C., & Fraser, I. (2012). Enhancing board oversight on quality of hospital care: An agency theory perspective. *Health Care Management Review, 37*(2), 144–153.

The Joint Commission. (2011). *Improving America's hospitals: The joint commission's annual report on quality and safety 2011.* Retrieved from www.jointcommission.org/2011_annual_report/

The Joint Commission. (2012). *Hospital accreditation standards.* Oakbrook Terrace, IL: Joint Commission Resources.

Kaplan, R. S., & Norton, D. P. (1992, January/February). The balanced scorecard—Measures that drive performance. *Harvard Business Review, 70*(1), 71–79.

Kocher, R., & Sahni, N. R. (2010). Physicians versus hospitals as leaders of accountable care organizations. *New England Journal of Medicine, 363*(26), 2579–2582.

Kubiak, T. M., & Benbow, D. (2009). *The certified Six Sigma black belt handbook* (2nd ed.). Milwaukee, WI: American Society for Quality, Quality Press.

Lynch, J. (2017). The three-legged stool: Why safety, quality, and equity depend on each other. *Journal of Healthcare Management, 62*(5), 298–301.

McGaffigan, P. A., Ullem, B. D., & Gandhi, T. K. (2017). Closing the gap and raising the bar: Assessing board competency in quality and safety. *The Joint Commission Journal on Quality and Patient Safety, 43,* 267–274.

National Academy for State Health Policy. *2014 Guide to state adverse event reporting systems.* Retrieved from https://nashp.org/2014-guide-state-adverse-event-reporting-systems/

National Institute of Standards and Technology (NIST). (2011). *Baldrige 2020: An executive's guide to the criteria for performance excellence.* Retrieved from www.nist.gov/baldrige/publications /upload/Baldrige_20_20.pdf

National Patient Safety Foundation (NPSF). (2015). *Free from harm: Accelerating patient safety improvement fifteen years after To Err Is Human.* Boston, MA: National Patient Safety Foundation.

NHE Fact Sheet. Retrieved from www.cms.gov/research-statistics-data-and-systems/statistics -trends-and-reports/nationalhealthexpenddata/nhe-fact-sheet.html

Pronovost, P., Thompson, D. A., Holzmueller, C. G., Domran, T., & Morlock, L. L. (2007). Impact of the leapfrog group's intensive care unit physician staffing standard. *Journal of Critical Care, 22*(2), 89–96.

Ramage, C., Curtis, K., Glynn, A., Montgomery, J., Hoover, E., Leng, J., … Gallagher, A. (2017). Developing and using a toolkit for cultivating compassion in healthcare: An appreciative inquiry approach. *International Journal of Practice-Based Learning in Health and Social Care, 5*(1), 42–64.

Ransom, E. R., Joshi, M. S., Nash, D. B., & Ransom, S. B. (2008). *The healthcare quality book: Vision, strategy, and tools* (2nd ed.). Chicago, IL: Health Administration Press.

Rubino, L., & Chan, M. (2008). Quality and patient safety from the top: A case study of St. Francis Medical Center governing board's call to action. *Patient Safety and Health Care Management Advances in Health Care Management, 7,* 99–122.

Studer, Q. (2003). *Hardwiring excellence.* Gulf Breeze, FL: Fire Starter.

Sutcliffe, K. M., Paine, L., & Pronovost, P. J. (2017). Re-examining high reliability: Actively organizing for safety. *BMJ Quality & Safety, 26*(3), 248–251.

Taylor, J., & Rutherford, P. (2010). The pursuit of genuine partnerships with patients and family members: The challenge and opportunity for executive leaders. *Frontiers, 26*(4), 3–14.

Tsai, T. C., Jha, A. K., Gawande, A. A., Huckman, R. S., Bloom, N., & Sadun, R. (2015). Hospital board and management practices are strongly related to hospital performance on clinical quality metrics. *Health Affairs, 34*(8), 1304–1311.

U.S. Department of Health and Human Services. (2011). *Report to congress: National strategy for quality improvement in health care.* Retrieved from www.ahrq.gov/workingforquality/nqs /nqsplans.pdf

CHAPTER 9

Collaborative Leadership

Nancy Borkowski and Barbara Perez Deppman

▶ Introduction

After the publication of Rosabeth Moss Kanter's 1994 article on the advantages of collaboration, the term **collaborative leadership** was coined to describe the leadership skills and attributes needed to successfully develop and manage interorganizational strategic alliances and other forms of partnership. Ibarra and Hansen (2011, p. 73) define collaborative leadership as the "capacity to engage people and groups outside one's formal control and inspire them to work toward common goals—despite differences in convictions, cultural values, and operating norms." More simply stated, Archer and Cameron (2008) describe that the basic task of a collaborative leader is to achieve positive outcomes for common objectives among different organizations. For example, a collaborative manager of a county's department of disaster/emergency management must effectively lead and coordinate the emergency responses of multiple organizations, government agencies, and community resources before, during, and after an emergency or disaster. Given the different cultures and goals among organizations, promoting effective collaboration can be a challenging task!

Traditionally, leadership is described as one's ability to move an organization toward its strategic goals by influencing other organizational members to participate in a collaborative effort to achieve corporate success and economic sustainability (Borkowski, 2016). Collaborative leadership is more complex because it requires a leader to achieve success by motivating individuals in multiple organizations, in addition to bringing together and aligning the goals of many stakeholders. However, in many circumstances, these stakeholders may be engaged in adversarial relationships because they hold different perspectives of their missions, visions, objectives, and concerns. As such, leaders need to overcome these challenges when facilitating collaborative endeavors. These challenges include disagreement among stakeholders regarding the definition of the problem; varying interests, resources, and knowledge bases; and past histories of unsuccessful collaborative attempts (see **TABLE 9.1**).

In today's complex and competitive healthcare environment, collaborative relationships allow organizations to achieve better outcomes by obtaining knowledge, skills, technology, or other essential resources that a single organization cannot provide on its own (Kanter, 1994). For example, in Louisville, Kentucky, community leaders developed a cross-sector, collaborative partnership that engaged local government agencies, a nonprofit organization, and a technology company to address the complex public health issue of asthma by developing a self-management asthma program. Individual participants in the asthma program reported better personal health outcomes. In addition, the private–public collaborative cited that they benefitted by "leveraging ideas, resources, and expertise from

TABLE 9.1 Common Challenges Encountered by Collaborative Leaders

Conflict	Disagreement among stakeholders about how the problems/issues should be defined. For example, issues may be multifaceted, technically complex, or under scientific debate.
Lack of coordination	Lack of systematic organization among stakeholders with common, vested interests in specific issues/problems.
Varying resources among stakeholders	Stakeholders have different skills, tools, and resources to deal with issues and problems. For example, differences in levels of authority and influence, different knowledge bases, and disparities in human and financial resources.
Prior relationships	A history of unsuccessful efforts by stakeholders to address these problems/issues, perhaps due to insufficient processes or resources available independently.

Courtesy of London, S. (1995). *Collaboration and community*. A report prepared for the Pew Partnership for Civic Change. Retrieved November 9, 2012 from www.scottlondon.com/reports/collaboration.pdf

a wide range of partners" that contributed to a larger community effort against chronic respiratory disease (Barrett et al., 2018). As noted, collaborative partnerships bring together individuals and organizations with very different knowledge bases, attitudes, and assumptions. Each partner possesses unique knowledge and skills that can benefit the others. As partners organize, plan strategies, and move forward, they create learning opportunities for themselves and each other (North Central Regional Educational Laboratory, n.d.).

Rubin (2009, p. 2) states that a "collaboration is a purposeful relationship in which all parties strategically choose to cooperate in order to accomplish a shared outcome." The New York Genome Center (NYGC, 2012) is an example of how, under highly effective collaborative leadership, an ecosystem from previously fragmented and competitive healthcare sectors can be formed with the goals of improved patient outcomes and the delivery of personalized medicine. NYGC, a public–private coalition of competitors—universities, medical centers, technology firms, and pharmaceutical companies—joined together in a cooperative effort to transform medical research and clinical care. Under NYGC's efforts, stakeholders such as healthcare managers, scientists, clinicians, policymakers, payers, and patients are engaged in information-enabled common projects for therapeutic and diagnostic product development.

Collaborative leadership was first identified with the growth of strategic alliances among private corporations as well as with the formation of social partnerships (i.e., alliances between independent organizations in the public and private sectors). As healthcare reform moved the industry from segment-based delivery models to integrated systems such as Accountable Care Organizations (ACOs), collaborative leadership became critical to organizational success. The leader of an ACO is expected to integrate and coordinate the various component parts of health care, such as primary care, specialty services, hospitals, and home health care, and to ensure that all "parts function well together" to deliver efficient, high quality, and cost-effective patient-centered care. Managers and clinical leaders of 21st-century healthcare organizations must be able to lead diverse groups of people and facilitate their professional efforts and problem-solving both within an organization as well as across formal organizational boundaries. For example, the new bundle payment reimbursement approach seeks to align the financial interests of all providers—hospital, physicians, rehabilitation, long-term care, etc.—for services provided in a single episode of care. This is very different than traditional fee-for-service reimbursement in which each provider is paid separately for services provided—even if all the services related to a single episode of care (Shih, Chen, & Nallamothu, 2015). Under this new reimbursement method, collaborative leaders need to align the incentives of the two or more groups (payers, hospitals, physicians, ancillary services, etc.) for effective cost containment, revenue generation, and quality improvement activities (Burns & Mueller, 2008). (See "Case Study: Collaborative Leadership in Action between a Physician Group and Health System," later in this chapter.)

▶ Characteristics of a Collaborative Leader

In today's complex and ever-changing healthcare environment, **collaborative alliances** are emerging as the preferred model for complex problem-solving, or "getting the job done," especially when diverse stakeholders address issues that affect broad segments of an organization or community. To promote collaborative problem-solving among stakeholders, the healthcare manager should demonstrate specific behaviors, including:

1. Confidence that the goals and objectives are achievable.
2. The skills to clearly communicate with the stakeholders regarding the issues needing to be addressed and the potential approaches to problem-solving.
3. The ability to serve as an active listener.
4. The ability to share knowledge and authority with the collaborators.
5. The ability to assess and handle varying levels of risk in decision-making and implementation (Carter, 2006).

Through their extensive research, Chrislip and Larson (1994, pp. 138–146) discovered that certain principles were displayed by leaders who excelled as **community collaborators**. For example, these leaders influence diverse groups to work together, assist with the group's problem-solving process, and provide the necessary resources for the group to achieve its goals (see **TABLE 9.2**).

Building on Chrislip and Larson's (1994) work, as well as Van Wart's (2005) research in public administrators' competencies, Morse (2008) developed a

TABLE 9.2 Principles Displayed by Community Collaborative Leaders

Inspire commitment and action	Collaborative leaders bring people together when incremental or unilateral efforts are not working. They are action-oriented, but much of the action they drive involves influencing others to work together to achieve a specific goal rather than telling others what needs to be done or doing the work themselves.
Lead as peer problem-solvers	Collaborative leaders guide others so that the entire group can work as a team to problem solve. They avoid engaging in autocratic management behaviors.
Build broad-based involvement	Collaborative leaders make a conscious and disciplined effort to identify and bring together all relevant stakeholders.
Sustain hope and participation	Collaborative leaders communicate that each participant brings value and strengths to the group effort, assist in developing short-term and long-term goals, and celebrate the group's achievements throughout the problem-solving process.
Lead as "servants"	Collaborative leaders serve the group members by providing the resources necessary to meet the participants' internal and external needs.
View leadership as a process	Collaborative leaders safeguard the collaborative process that facilitates productive and rewarding working relationships among the participants and stakeholders.

Reproduced from Chrislip, D. D., & Larson, C. E. (1994). *Collaborative leadership: How citizens and civic leaders can make a difference.* San Francisco, CA: Jossey-Bass.

comprehensive set of traits and skills necessary for successful collaborative leadership (see **TABLE 9.3**).

There are many similarities among the behaviors, traits, and skills observed in various organizational leadership styles. Many equate collaborative leadership with transformational and **servant leadership** styles because of the various

TABLE 9.3 Traits and Skills of Collaborative Leaders

Traits	Skills
Self-confidence	Communication
Decisiveness	Social
Resilience	Influence
Energy	Analytic
Need for achievement	Technical
Willingness to assume responsibility	Continual learning
Flexibility	Self-management
Service mentality	Strategic thinking
Personal integrity	Facilitation
Emotional maturity	
Collaborative mindset	
Passion toward outcomes	
Systems thinking	
Openness	
Risk-taking	
Sense of mutuality and connectedness	
Humility	

Data from Morse, R. S. (2007). *Developing public leaders in an age of collaborative governance.* University of Delaware, Institute for Public Administration. Retrieved November 9, 2012 from www.ipa.udel.edu/3tad/papers/workshop4/Morse.pdf

characteristics displayed by these leaders. **Transformational leaders** provide participants with a vision and motivate them to move beyond self-interest for the good of the organization (Osland, Kolb, & Rubin, 2001). Transformational-style leadership is about value-driven change, innovation, improvement, and entrepreneurship through vision and inspiration. Transformational leadership incorporates both direct and indirect influence through a variety of mechanisms that affect the intellectual, emotional, and behavioral processes of the participants. Servant leadership is an approach to managing people that "begins with a clear and compelling vision that excites passion in the leader and commitment in those who follow" (Blanchard & Hodges, 2003). A servant leader values others' strengths and talents and encourages the use of these strengths and talents to achieve the organization's mission and goals.

Although collaborative leadership has much in common with both transformational and servant leadership theories, there are also many differences. One of the main differences is that collaborative leaders must be able to achieve success through alliances with people and resources beyond their direct reporting control. As Lindon (2003, p. 42) points out, "By definition, collaborative leaders have no formal authority over their peers. They must use persuasion, technical competence, relationship skills, and political smarts to get and keep the coalition together and produce the desired goal." As an example, in 1961, President Kennedy announced his famous goal to place a "man on the moon" by the end of the decade. He motivated and unified the public, inspiring Americans to set aside their own agendas and ideologies to achieve a successful moon landing in 1969 (Hansen, 2009).

Emotional Intelligence

Emotional intelligence (EI) is a leadership attribute that is viewed as increasingly critical to an individual's social effectiveness. When an individual is more socially effective, he or she is more adept at achieving successful collaborative outcomes (Cox, 2011).

Emotional intelligence involves the self-assessment of one's own feelings and the interpretation of others' feelings, which help to guide one's thinking and action. EI has five distinct competencies:

1. Self-awareness
2. Self-management or regulation
3. Self-motivation
4. Empathy or social awareness
5. Social skills

Goleman (1998, p. 318) identified that *self-awareness* involves having knowledge and understanding of one's true feelings at any given moment. *Self-management* requires that managers control their emotions so they can focus on problem-solving and assist with necessary processes and tasks. *Self-motivation* allows the manager to stay focused on the specified goals and desired outcomes and to overcome negative emotional stimuli and accept delayed gratification. *Empathy* is the ability to perceive what others feel and want, expressing sensitivity to their needs and perspectives. Finally, *social skills* relate to one's ability to "read" others and interact effectively in social situations, guiding and influencing others' perspectives and behaviors.

Using the Myers-Briggs personality preference profile, Goldman and Kahnweiler (2000) discovered that successful collaborative leaders are more likely to have high scores on the "feeling" index rather than the "thinking" index. The researchers noted that "the essential ingredients for collaborative leaders' success were flexibility, patience, understanding of others' viewpoints, sensitivity to diversity, and a cooperative spirit" (p. 449).

▶ Strategies for a Collaborative Leader

The Turning Point Leadership Development National Excellence Collaborative (2006) identified six key practices or strategies that are unique to leading a collaborative process:

1. Assess the environment for collaboration
2. Create clarity
3. Build trust and create safety
4. Share power and influence
5. Develop people
6. Self-reflection

Each of the six strategies is a key element in the collaborative process, but the strategies are also interrelated and provide a comprehensive overview of the necessary steps for leaders to guide successful collaborations (see **TABLE 9.4**).

TABLE 9.4 Necessary Steps for Leaders to Guide Successful Collaborations

Strategies	Action
Assess the Environment	A collaborative leader should be able to recognize common interests and understand others' perspectives. Collaboration promotes goal attainment around shared visions, purposes, and value. When different points of view regarding an issue or problem are addressed, a collaborative leader facilitates connections and encourages group thinking to identify clear, positive change for all participants. The first priority is to set common goals. The second priority is to identify the barriers and obstacles to achieving the common goals.
Create Clarity	Having and communicating the "clarity of purpose" (i.e., shared vision) is a quality that characterizes collaborative leaders. Clarity allows the group members to focus so that their energy can be directed toward problem-solving. Visioning in relation to clarity involves making a commitment to an effective process or a way of doing things. Mobilizing refers to helping people develop the confidence to take action and sustain their energies through difficult times.

(continues)

TABLE 9.4 Necessary Steps for Leaders to Guide Successful Collaborations *(continued)*

Build Trust	The collaborative leader must have the ability to promote and sustain trust between and among the participants for the sharing of innovative approaches. If a collaborative leader fails to engender trust and openness among participants, the best ideas and innovative approaches for problem-solving will not be developed or shared by the group.
Share Power and Influence	The collaborative leader must allow the participants to be empowered to fully contribute in the decision-making process. Rather than being concerned about losing power by collaborating, the leader needs to recognize that sharing power actually generates strength.
Develop People	The collaborative leader needs to bring out the best in others, maximize the use of other people's talents and resources, build power through sharing power, and cede authoritarian ownership or control. By doing so, the leader increases others' leadership capacities by encouraging experimentation, goal-setting, empowerment, and performance feedback.
Self-Reflection	Successful collaborative leaders demonstrate high levels of EI or maturity. Through self-reflection, leaders can examine and understand their values and assess whether their behaviors are congruent with their values. In addition, successful leaders critically consider the impact their actions and words have on the group's progress toward achieving its goals, and adjust their behaviors if necessary.

From Turning Point, a national program of the Robert Wood Johnson Foundation from 1996 to 2006. Used with permission from the Robert Wood Johnson Foundation in Princeton, New Jersey.

▶ Building Collaborative Leader Skills

With the value of collaborative leadership having been demonstrated, the good news is that collaborative leadership skills can be learned by dedicated leaders who commit to spending the necessary time and effort. Leadership skill development for healthcare managers has been widely implemented over the past decade. Beginning in 2003, the **Healthcare Leadership Alliance** (HLA), a consortium of six major professional membership organizations, identified competencies that support excellence in healthcare management across diverse professional roles. Through job analyses and research, HLA identified 300 competencies (skills or areas of knowledge) within five major categories:

1. Leadership
2. Communications and relationship management
3. Professionalism, structure, and functions

　　4.　　Business knowledge and skills
　　5.　　Knowledge of the healthcare environment

Drawing upon this HLA framework, the American College of Healthcare Executives (ACHE) developed a **Healthcare Executive Competencies Assessment Tool** to assist managers in identifying areas of strength, as well as areas in which they may wish to improve their performance.

To begin the process of leadership skill development, managers need to identify personal developmental needs, gain a better understanding of how their own and others' behavioral styles influence leadership style, and develop their own leadership philosophy.

To identify personal developmental needs, leaders can engage in a self-reflection process by completing a personal SWOT matrix. In the SWOT matrix, leaders list their:

　　1.　**Strengths** and positive characteristics
　　2.　**Weaknesses** and negative characteristics
　　3.　Dreams, wishes, or goals (**Opportunities**)
　　4.　Barriers preventing the advancement toward personal goals (**Threats**); see **FIGURE 9.1**

In this self-assessment process, there are no right or wrong answers, but honest answers are necessary in order to guide leadership development.

To complete the SWOT Matrix and to obtain a better understanding of how behavioral patterns influence one's leadership style, leaders are encouraged to obtain

Your strengths and positive characteristics	Your areas needing development
1.	1.
2.	2.
3.	3.
4.	4.
5.	5.
Dreams, wishes or goals you have for yourself (growth opportunities)	The barriers that are preventing you from reaching your dreams or achieving your goals (e.g., threats or factors that cause a resistance to change)
1.	1.
2.	2.
3.	3.
4.	4.
5.	5.

FIGURE 9.1 Personal SWOT Matrix

anonymous multi-rater feedback from peers and colleagues, subordinates, and supervisors from current and previous positions. Multi-rater feedback is a valuable method for individuals to gain insight into their strengths and weaknesses as perceived by others.

Additional leadership development tools include self-assessments of one's professional relationships and interactions with others, which provide awareness of how one's own behavioral patterns influence one's leadership style. Many instruments are used in the workplace to assess behavioral patterns that can impact leadership styles. For example, the Myers-Briggs Type Indicator (MBTI) is an instrument that assesses personality types and identifies individual preferences across the spectrums of four dimensions (extraversion/introversion, sensate/intuitive, thinking/feeling, and judging/perceiving). These self-reported preferences and characteristics are useful in assessing leadership strengths and styles and can be utilized to support and enhance managers' training and skills development (Borkowski, 2016).

Through self-assessments and self-reflection, individuals develop their own leadership philosophy. A leadership philosophy is a guiding set of principles that incorporate an individual's values and vision as to personal and professional development. Their philosophy helps individuals "stay on track" as they grow as professionals and provides the framework to guide their actions when interacting with others and making decisions throughout their career.

▶ Potential Pitfalls in Collaborative Leadership

The Work Group for Community Health and Development at the University of Kansas notes that despite the many advantages of collaborative leadership, disadvantages also exist. Some of the challenges associated with collaborative leadership are:

1. Collaboration may be a slow and time-consuming process.
2. There may be a high degree of conflict requiring management and mediation.
3. Collaborative leaders may need to cede some of their power and authority to the partnership and credit the group rather than themselves for the positive outcomes achieved.

Collaborative decision-making may take longer because large groups of participants and stakeholders may proceed slowly and bring multiple "private" agendas to the table, which can lead to significant conflicts. Collaborative leaders can help to mediate when conflicts arise and refocus the group toward achieving the agreed-upon objectives. Of course, collaborative leaders must always remain alert to not force their own biases and demands onto the problem-solving process, but instead promote an open and inclusive process that guides the group to achieve its goals, strategies, and implementation plans (see **TABLE 9.5**).

These simple stretch collaboration tools can help you make progress when trust is low and consensus seems out of reach.

TABLE 9.5 How Do You Solve a Problem You Cannot Agree On?	
Accept the plurality of the situation	You do not have to agree on what the solution is—or even what the problem is—to make progress. Different actors may support the same outcome for different reasons.
Experiment to find a way forward	Keep trying things with the understanding that you cannot control the future, but you can influence it. Success is not coming up with a solution—it is working toward one.
See yourself as part of the problem, not outside of it	You cannot make progress until you realize that you have a role in the situation. If you are not part of the problem, you cannot be part of the solution.

Reproduced from Kahane, A. (2018). How To Collaborate When You Don't Have Consensus. Strategy+Business, online April 5, 2018. Available at: https://www.strategy-business.com/article/How-to-Collaborate-When-You-Dont-Have-Consensus?gko=90356&utm_source=itw&utm_medium=20180405&utm_campaign=resp

Summary

Collaborative leadership is a valuable tool to promote synergy and successful outcomes in today's complex healthcare environment. Though collaboration can be challenging, the advantages of collaborative management within an organization and across entities can outweigh the potential difficulties. The implementation of accountable care organizations requires that leaders add managing collaboration to their skill set for the benefit of their organizations, patients, and communities. As such, tomorrow's healthcare collaborative leaders will need to demonstrate a vision-based, systems-thinking, power-sharing leadership style.

Discussion Questions

1. Explain the increasing importance of collaborative leadership in today's complex and changing healthcare industry.
2. Discuss the interrelatedness of the six key practices/strategies for guiding a successful collaboration. Is one practice/strategy more important than another? If yes, why? If no, why not?
3. Which segment of the health industry do you think would benefit most from using a collaborative leadership style? Why? Explain by using examples.
4. Why is a high degree of EI essential for an individual to be a successful collaborative leader?
5. Why does self-assessment play such an important role in the practice of collaborative leadership?

🔍 *CASE STUDY: Collaborative Leadership in Action Between a Physician Group and Health System*

A large radiology physician group led a collaboration initiative with a large health system's administration, clinicians, and IT leadership to implement the new Centers for Medicare & Medicaid Access and CHIP Reauthorization Act (MACRA) quality-based measures. MACRA requires the reporting of quality-based measures under the Merit-Based Incentive Payment System (MIPS), which incentivizes providers who are part of the patient care continuum to work together to increase quality of care and reduce waste. This collaboration was important to all parties because radiology is an expensive service, and is viewed as a cost center as opposed to a revenue center by hospital administrators.

The collaborative integration was performed in a multi-step process by the radiology physician practice, which began by coordinating a series of strategic sessions with the payer to select the most relevant core measures. Core measures are quality- and outcome-based metrics that must be achieved to be reimbursed by CMS. After the relevant core measures were selected (based on preselected criteria), the physician leaders presented them at the system-wide Imaging Leadership Council meetings. After achieving buy-in from all stakeholders (clinicians, administration, and IT) the final step was to align the communications (to ensure that the same message was heard by all), and to manage the change needed for successful implementation of the core measures by the system's technical teams. This was no small feat considering this was a six-hospital health system with more than 20 radiological imaging centers. Effective collaboration and communication were critical to the success of this implementation to improve quality of care, reduce waste, and increase financial performance by all parties.

Discussion Questions

1. What challenges and barriers could have impacted the collaboration and communication between the parties involved (payers, physicians and other clinical providers, hospital administration, information technology technicians, etc.)?
2. What are some methods to gauge if and when collaborative efforts will be successful?

🔍 *CASE STUDY: Barnabas Medical Center*

Barnabas Medical Center (BMC) is a tertiary-care academic medical center with a Level One trauma center. BMC serves not only as the community's safety net but also as a training center for the U.S. Armed Forces. BMC is renowned for its excellence in care for acutely ill or injured patients. The organization's emergency department (ED) treats more than 120,000 adults and children annually, but has the reputation within the local community of imposing very long wait times.

Dr. Antonio "Tony" Mornan, BMC's new Associate Chief Medical Officer, was challenged to reduce the time a patient is in the ED from 24 hours to 6 hours, calculated from initial intake to either admission or discharge. Dr. Tony was aware that patients' ED experiences included services from many different departments and stakeholders, such as registration, radiology, laboratory, the hospitalist service, and the university medical teams. These services were being delivered through a fragmented system; that is, each service was providing health care to patients independently. Despite hearing his staff report that "that's the way it's always been," Dr. Tony knew that systemic change was necessary to deliver more efficient and effective care to the patient. However, as none of these departments directly reported to him, Dr. Tony did not have the authority to mandate such changes.

Dr. Tony opted to use collaborative leadership to address the challenge. Initially, he set up several workshops in which individuals from the relevant departments could discuss their issues and difficulties with regard to achieving the shared goal—efficient patient-centered care. This sharing of information resulted in the development of a workflow chart identifying inefficiencies, slow communication channels, underutilization of the system's technology, and other problems contributing to the patient care delays. Participants were encouraged to contribute suggested solutions to these concerns.

Dr. Tony's next step was to lead a series of meetings in which the various department managers were brought together to discuss how each department's services impacted other departments, as well as how each department might provide its services more efficiently. For example, the radiology department was tasked with reducing the time from a clinician's order to the start of an imaging study. However, the workflow analysis showed that there were a number of intermediate steps out of the radiology department's control that slowed the process, such as nurse staffing and availability, as well as insurance authorization. Under Dr. Tony's guidance, discussions and workshops continued among the clinicians and the managers of the relevant departments with the shared goal of reducing the span between when a radiology procedure was ordered and the imaging began.

Within 2 months, through this collaborative problem-solving effort, patients' ED times were significantly reduced and patient satisfaction scores improved.

Case Study Discussion Questions

1. What were the driving forces behind the success of this collaborative effort?
2. What were the "boundaries" that posed challenges to this collaborative effort?
3. Who were/are the leaders? What characteristics do you think were displayed by the leader(s) of this collaborative effort that led to its success?
4. Discuss the factors that contributed to the success of this collaborative effort.

🔍 *CASE STUDY: Willow Springs Memorial Hospital*[1]

Dr. Solomon Till has just recently been appointed the new president of Willow Springs Memorial, the only hospital in Willow Springs. Dr. Till has lived in Willow Springs for the past 5 years and has been an active member of the community. Prior to being appointed hospital president, he served as the director of development. Dr. Till is excited about his new appointment and has come to think of Willow Springs as home. He is eager for the opportunity to help his residents achieve the best health possible.

(continues)

During his first week as president, the state announced a budget shortfall and a plan to reduce Medicaid expenditures by 22%. Because almost one-third of the revenue at Willow Springs Memorial is from Medicaid, this change could result in a significant "setback" for the hospital.

Additionally, Dr. Till is aware that the hospital board and many physicians on staff are concerned that Willow Springs Memorial does not have the ability to perform some of the latest procedures in medicine. They want Willow Springs Memorial to be as "technologically advanced" as any hospital in the state. Dr. Till was hired to "fix these problems" quickly.

Dr. Till has decided that one of the first things on his agenda as the new president of Willow Springs Memorial is to reach out and listen to the residents of Willow Springs about what they need and want from a hospital. He has arranged to attend a series of six events in town, such as church meetings, Rotary Club meetings, and senior center lunches, at which he can engage directly with the residents. He has invited a hospital board member and a medical staff member to join him at each of these meetings to listen to the community input. Dr. Till has also asked the county health department director to collaborate on this project by providing additional assessment information, participating in the outreach events, implementing community assessment and documentation, and analyzing study findings.

Through this broad collaborative process, Dr. Till is optimistic that he can facilitate the development of a shared vision of health in Willow Springs and promote Willow Springs Memorial's role in maintaining a healthy community.

Case Study Discussion Questions

1. What were the "boundaries" that posed challenges to this collaborative effort?
2. Who were/are the leaders? What characteristics do you think were displayed by the leader(s) of this collaborative effort that led to its success?
3. Discuss the various stakeholders who can contribute to or create barriers for the success of this collaborative effort.

---

1   From Turning Point, a national program of the Robert Wood Johnson Foundation from 1996 to 2006. Used with permission from the Robert Wood Johnson Foundation in Princeton, New Jersey.

Related Websites

American College of Healthcare Executives: www.ache.org
Healthcare Leadership Alliance: www.healthcareleadershipalliance.org
New York Genome Center: http://nygenome.org/
Turning Point Leadership Development National Excellence Collaborative: www.rwjf.org/content /dam/farm/reports/program_results_reports/2008/rwjf69892
Work Group for Community Health and Development: www.communityhealth.ku.edu/

Other Suggested Readings

Ferren, A. S., & Stanton, W. W. (2004). *Leadership through collaboration*. Westport, CT: Praeger.
Freshman, B., Rubino, L., & Chassiakos, Y. R. (2010). *Collaboration across the disciplines in healthcare care*. Sudbury, MA: Jones & Bartlett Learning.
Goleman, D. (1995). *Emotional intelligence: Why it can matter more than IQ*. New York, NY: Bantam.
Hambrick, D. C., Nadler, D. A., & Tushamn, M. L. (1998). *Navigating change*. Boston, MA: Harvard Business School Press.

Hesselbein, F., Goldsmith, M., & Beckhard, R. (1997). *The organization of the future.* San Francisco, CA: Jossey-Bass.

Lank, E. (2006). *Collaborative advantage.* New York, NY: Palgrave MacMillan.

Lyman, L. L., Ashby, D. E., & Tripses, J. S. (2005). *Leaders who dare: Pushing the boundaries.* Lanham, MD: Rowman & Littlefield Education.

Maccoby, M. (2007). *The leaders we need and what makes us follow.* Boston, MA: Harvard Business School Press.

Marshall, E. (1995). *Transforming the way we work: The power of the collaborative workplace.* New York, NY: AMACOM.

Seifter, H., & Economy, P. (2001). *Leadership ensemble: Lessons in collaborative management from the world's only conductorless orchestra.* New York, NY: Henry Holt.

References

Archer, D., & Cameron, A. (2008). *Collaborative leadership: How to succeed in an interconnected world.* Maryland Heights, MO: Butterworth Heinemann.

Barrett, M., Combs, V., Su, J. G., Henderson, K., Tuffli, M., & The AIR Louisville Collaborative. (2018). AIR Louisville: Addressing asthma with technology, crowdsourcing, cross-sector collaboration, and policy. *Health Affairs, 37*(4), 525–534.

Blanchard, K., & Hodges, P. (2003, May 12). The journey to servant leadership in work, life. *San Diego Business Journal, 24*(19), A2–A3.

Borkowski, N. (2016). *Organizational behavior in healthcare* (3rd ed.). Burlington, MA: Jones & Bartlett Learning.

Burns, L. R., & Muller, R. W. (2008). Hospital-physician collaboration: Landscape of economic integration and impact on clinical integration. *Milbank Quarterly, 86*(3), 375–434.

Carter, M. (2006). The importance of collaborative leadership in achieving effective criminal justice outcomes. *Center for Effective Public Policy.* Retrieved from http://nicic.gov/Library/021201

Chrislip, D. D., & Larson, C. E. (1994). *Collaborative leadership: How citizens and civic leaders can make a difference.* San Francisco, CA: Jossey-Bass.

Cox, J. D. (2011, February). Emotional intelligence and its role in collaboration. *Proceedings of the American Society of Business and Behavioral Sciences (ASBBS) Annual Meeting, 18*(1), Las Vegas, NV. Retrieved from http://asbbs.org/files/2011/ASBBS2011v1/PDF/C/CoxJ.pdf

Goldman, S., & Kahnweiler, W. (2000). A collaborator profile for executives of nonprofit organizations. *Nonprofit Management & Leadership, 10*, 435–450.

Goleman, D. (1998). *Working with emotional intelligence.* New York, NY: Bantam.

Hansen, M. T. (2009). *Collaboration: How leaders avoid the traps, create unity, and reap big results.* Boston, MA: Harvard Business School Press.

Ibarra, H., & Hansen, M. T. (2011). Are you a collaborative leader? *Harvard Business Review, 89*(7/8), 69–74.

Kanter, R. M. (1994, July/August). Collaborative advantage: Successful partnerships manage the relationship, not just the deal. *Harvard Business Review, 72*(4), 96–108.

Lindon, R. (2003). The discipline of collaboration. *Leader to Leader Journal, 29*, 41–47.

London, S. (1995). *Collaboration and community.* Retrieved from www.scottlondon.com/reports/collaboration.pdf

Morse, R. S. (2008). Developing public leaders in an age of collaborative governance. In R. S. Morse & T. F. Buss (Eds.), *Innovations in public leadership development* (pp. 79–100). Armonk, NY: M.E. Sharpe, Inc.

New York Genome Center. (2012). *Making the technology work: A collaborative ecosystem for improved patient outcomes.* Retrieved from http://nygenome.org/

North Central Regional Educational Laboratory. (n.d.). *Putting the pieces together: Comprehensive school-linked strategies for children and families.* Retrieved from www.ncrel.org/sdrs/areas/issues/envrnmnt/css/ppt/putting.htm

Osland, J., Kolb, D., & Rubin, I. (2001). *Organizational behavior: An experiential approach* (7th ed.). Upper Saddle River, NJ: Prentice Hall.

Rubin, H. (2009). *Collaborative leadership: Developing effective partnerships for communities and schools.* Thousand Oaks, CA: Corwin.

Shih, T., Chen, L. M., & Nallamothu, B. K. (2015). Will bundled payments change health care? Examining the evidence thus far in cardiovascular care. *Circulation, 131*(24), 2151–2158.

Turning Point Leadership Development National Excellence Collaborative. (2006). Retrieved from www.turningpointprogram.org and www.collaborativeleadership.org

Van Wart, M. (2005). *Dynamics of leadership in public service: Theory and practice.* Armonk, NY: M.E. Sharpe.

CHAPTER 10

Transformational Leadership

Ethel Elkins, Anne Rogers, and Mellisa Hall

LEARNING OBJECTIVES

By the end of this chapter, the student will be able to:

- Explain the differences between a transactional and transformational leader.
- Discuss the history of leadership theories and the movement toward transformational leadership.
- Identify and explain strategies for transformational leadership.
- Understand personal strategies that can be used for change in the workplace.

KEY TERMS

Core values
Empowerment
Rounding
Theory X

Theory Y
Transactional leader
Transformational
   leader

▶ Introduction

Changing political climates are driving constant changes in our healthcare system. Strategic leadership is critical to address the many challenges facing U.S. healthcare today. A large body of research has attempted to identify and define the principles of effective leadership in today's evolving healthcare arena. However, what "good leadership" means, and how it is best practiced, has significantly changed over time.

The relationship between a leader and his or her employees has been thought of as a *quid pro quo* arrangement. *Quid pro quo* means that something is given with the expectation that something will be received in return. For example, some people give their work in exchange for an anticipated paycheck. Others offer their experience and expertise in anticipation of a promotion or new title. Still others give their talents in order to feel valued and to gain a sense of worth from doing their jobs well. Viewed from this perspective, the relationship between leader and employee is a transaction.

In his book, *The Human Side of Enterprise* (1960), Douglas McGregor introduced the **Theory X** and **Theory Y** concept of motivation, based on the views and preconceptions of leaders (see **FIGURE 10.1**). Those who subscribe to Theory X hold the fundamental belief that people do not really enjoy work and would not engage in it if they did not have to in order to make a living. Because they lack a sense of loyalty or other motivation to perform, they have to be carefully supervised, controlled, and rewarded.

This approach to management was common in the past. For example, in the early years of the American industrial period, the economy was newly forming and work was scarce. People (many of whom were immigrants) were desperate for jobs and would do virtually anything to provide for themselves and their families. For many jobs, few if any skills were required, and workers were replaced with relative ease. There was no need for managers to be concerned about motivating workers who willingly would work incredibly long hours in unsafe conditions for minimal pay.

As the American economy improved, there grew a mandate for managers to adopt alternative approaches for motivating employees. As the workforce became better educated and organized, and as skilled workers became more essential and valuable, new strategies were developed to motivate employees to be productive and

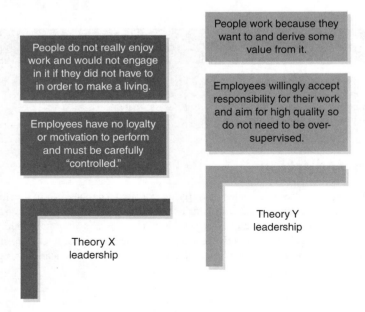

FIGURE 10.1 Theory X Versus Theory Y Leadership

loyal. (This discussion leaves aside the issue of the relative moral values that were ignored under previous leadership models.)

Leaders who operated according to Theory Y believed differently from those who thought that employees were not personally invested in their work and would abstain from working if they could. Theory Y leaders lead out of the conviction that people work because they want to, believing employees derive satisfaction and joy from doing a job and doing it well. As a result, according to Theory Y, employees do not require a significant amount of direction and, if supported by their leaders, willingly accept responsibility for their work, as well as its quality.

This chapter provides an overview of the ways in which effective leaders can provide the motivation necessary to engage employees and encourage their dedication to the work at hand. This is especially important to consider in health care because the workforce is so diverse, change is constant, and the cost of error can be devastating.

Leaders who transform the nature of patient care, and the culture in which it is accomplished, improve employee commitment and motivation. The differences between transactional leadership and transformational leadership will be discussed, from both the perspective of the leader and the clinician.

▶ The Path to Transformational Leadership

Early management models were generally based on the previously mentioned foundational elements of McGregor's (1960) Theory X. Leaders assumed that employees were driven by the singular motivation of making money or receiving something else of value in exchange for their work. This concept provided the basis for the development of James MacGregor Burns' theories of transactional and transformational leadership. In his book, *Leadership* (1978), Burns proposed that exchanges are made by the **transactional leader** to further his or her personal interests. At the same time, followers comply because they realize that their own interests will be best served if they do what the leader wants. The transactional leader is a dealmaker of sorts in which promises and paychecks are offered in exchange for certain work being completed. These leaders make broad generalizations that ignore the differences between individual workers and apply strategies that do not address potential differences that make employees more invested in their jobs (Kuhnert & Lewis, 1987). For example, using transactional leadership theory, pay raises would be an effective way to motivate employees to come to work on time, do their jobs efficiently and effectively, work harder, and increase productivity. Is this a realistic way to view today's healthcare workforce?

Many people who work in health care have advanced degrees and have invested a great deal of time and money in order to be able to do the work they do. They are professionals who are passionate about providing the best possible care, giving accurate diagnoses, maximizing patient comfort and functioning, and assuring the safety of their patients. While healthcare employees are interested in making a living, their motivations go far beyond that. The transactional leader, with her assumption that all workers are motivated by the same thing, misses a tremendous opportunity to capitalize on the dedication and loyalty of these employees to their patients and ultimately to the organization in which they practice. While transactional leadership might be effective in other industries such as sales or marketing, it has less relevance in the healthcare workplace. Employees are intensely driven to practice in their profession by factors that are personal and can be motivated by leaders who allow them to feel valued and to find fulfillment in their work.

▶ Transformational Leadership Defined

Burns expounded on transactional and transformational leadership in his 2003 book *Transforming Leadership*. In this work, he examined the ways in which world leaders and other lesser known but no less important people influenced history with their transforming leadership styles. Yet, it is important to note that all leaders at all levels have an impact, either in a positive or a negative manner.

Most of us can point to a person (or several people) who provided support, mentoring, and motivation that transformed our lives. It might have been a family member, a coach, or a teacher. There are people whom we naturally wanted to please because we valued their opinion of us. We were not driven to do things out of a desire to "get something" from them other than their respect and approval. These are our personal **transformational leaders**.

Randy Dobbs is an acknowledged business leader who is the former CEO of General Electric and a champion of transformational leadership. He suggests that without it, good workers are often worried about their futures, frightened of their supervisors, and simply "punch the clock." Effective leaders transform the work and the workplace so that people feel energized about what they do and where they do it. The exchange for their work is a sense of self-worth and a realization that they are contributing to an organization they value (Dobbs, 2010).

Bernard Bass (1985) expanded on Burns' work by shifting the focus from the behaviors and beliefs of leaders to the importance of the needs and expectations of followers. In his model of transformational leadership, the focus is not on an exchange or transaction between leaders and employees, but on ways to develop and invest in workers in order to motivate them to perform. As a result, these employees develop a sense of loyalty to their work and their organizations. Again, the healthcare leader might have an advantage given the nature of his workforce. People enter the field of health care typically out of a sense of caring about the welfare of others. They tend to be passionate about their work and genuinely want to continue doing it. This offers leaders many opportunities to make the most of the investment that workers provide through their altruistic commitment—an investment that extends beyond financial gain.

Davis Taylor wrote an interesting and engaging book about transformational leadership called *The Imperfect Leader* (2007). Taylor spent 23 years working in leadership positions in small companies as well as Fortune 500 corporations prior to his work with TAI (see http://taiinc.com), a consulting firm focused on values-based leadership. In his book, Taylor looks at lessons learned from both effective leaders and leaders who were not as transformational. He summarizes several "truths" for transformational leaders. Among them, he proposes that transformational leadership must focus on employees and their mission, and it must be driven by a leader who possesses vision, character, humility, and **core values**.

The National Park Service (2018), for example, defines core values not as the description of the work they do or the processes they use to do it, but rather the underlying foundation of their relationships with one another and which strategies they use to accomplish what needs to be done: "They are the practices we use (or should be using) every day in everything we do." Our core values define who we are and what we stand for. They guide us in the practice of our profession and explain why we do what we do. This is especially true in health care.

The importance of core values in the development of a transformational leadership style is noted throughout the literature. Not only is it essential that leaders and employees have a well-developed and defined set of core values, but also that these values are shared. Jo Manion, whose background is in nursing, has become a recognized expert on effective leadership in health care. She proposes that these values lead to a shared sense of mission and vision that create the foundation for organizational commitment (Manion, 2011). By uniting everyone in the organization, there is greater opportunity for improving patient services at all levels.

Unlike the transactional leader, the transformational leader does just that; he transforms people and the work culture so that motivation is based on the individual needs and aspirations of employees. His or her own personal and professional aspirations must be secondary to those of employees. This type of leader understands that different people need different things out of their work, yet recognizes that there are common themes. Among these themes are a sense of being valued and treated as an individual and not just a cog in the production wheel. Transformational leaders understand the importance of relationships and personal interaction. As described by Theory Y, they have a good grasp of the internal motivations that drive employees to maintain high personal standards and dedication to their work.

Another important distinction between the transactional and transformational leader was made by Peter Northouse (2017). He suggests that the traditional notion of the leader as the driver of change is short-sighted and incorrect. While the role of the leader is indeed important, transformational leadership can be incorporated only when employees and leaders work closely together to drive change. In this model, the traditional notions of power and hierarchy are challenged, and the essential involvement of workers in decision-making and acclimation to change is acknowledged. Northouse (2018, p. 178) suggests that leaders function as "social architects" who "build trust and foster collaboration" with those in their organizations.

▶ Transformational Leadership and Motivation

A recent study of the factors that motivate workers to stay in their jobs and increase their productivity was conducted—with surprising findings. Respondents indicated that pay and benefits were much less important to them than personal fulfillment. It was far more important to have a sense of being valued and to be included in workplace decisions that impacted them (Atchinson, 2003). This is good news for healthcare administrators who work for organizations that generally have very low profit margins. Yet, it also presents a challenge to these leaders: How do we identify the specific things that individual employees value and how do we enhance those experiences and opportunities?

How do we learn about employee values? We return to a discussion on the importance of developing relationships. For example, it is relatively safe to assume that asking employees to take on additional tasks outside of those in their job description would have a demotivating effect. However, given the limited resources available to many healthcare organizations, working across departments and cross-training are becoming increasingly common. For example, John in Human Resources is already having a hard time balancing his job and his family obligations. Such a request would hardly serve as a motivation. But Jane in Accounting might value the opportunity to gain skills that are outside of her expertise. She might have hopes of advancing to a position that requires supervising staff, so the experience would be valuable to her.

Clearly, becoming familiar with the interests, priorities, and aspirations of all of the people in a department would be tremendously time-consuming in a larger organization. Benefits have been found by some who have invested the time and effort. Quint Studer was an administrator in a number of different industries, with the majority of his leadership roles having been in healthcare organizations. Studer practices "**rounding**"—which simply means getting to know one's employees—what they need to stay motivated and passionate about their jobs. As an administrator, he rounds on staff in the same manner that doctors round on patients, by spending several minutes each day visiting various departments and talking to those who work there. He reports that the activity more than pays off as staff come to realize that he has a personal interest in what matters to them. In that way, he is able to assist them in their professional development (Studer, 2004).

This approach has the added benefit of lending an air of humility to leaders. It communicates the notion that "I am not better than you; we are peers." By taking the time to understand what motivates employees, the leader acknowledges staff members as "whole persons," who are much more than just their job title. An additional payoff is that as leaders identify the values and aspirations of their staff members, they can devise ways to help them actualize and achieve their goals. The result is an employee who has an increased sense of loyalty along with additional skills that will benefit the organization and culture (see **FIGURE 10.2**).

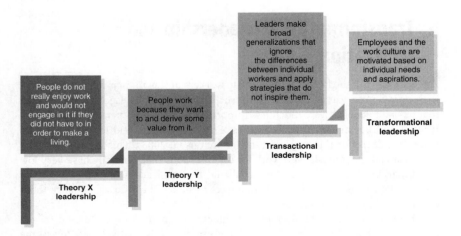

FIGURE 10.2 The Path to Transformational Leadership

▶ Transformational Leadership Strategies

There are many suggested models for transformational leadership that focus on specific and different characteristics of a leader. All of these are important and informative. The following strategies are suggested for the transformational leader:

1. *Integrity above all else.* While it was noted that different things motivate different people, it is clear that dishonesty and inconsistency on the part of a leader will destroy the trust and confidence that followers need in order to invest themselves in their work and the organization. Transformational leaders are always true to their values and honest in their interactions.

2. *Get down in "the trenches."* Transformational leaders will not ask a follower to do anything that they would not do themselves (if they have the training and expertise). They will put in more hours than they ask of followers. They are the first to pitch in when necessary. They "get their hands dirty."

3. *Communicate, communicate, and communicate.* Clear communication is one of the major keys to good leadership. Healthcare leaders in particular must learn to listen to and clarify what others are saying, while honing their own skills so that others understand what is being communicated (Ledlow & Stephens, 2018). Good communication contributes to the good health of an organization. Know how your employees need to hear. Are they visual or verbal communicators? Communicate with them on their level of understanding. Some organizations are even wearing their communications/personality "type" on their badges so that others can easily see what kind of communication works best for them. Do they need to hear a message or do they need to see it in a "picture"? Pay attention to each employee's learning style.

Transformational leaders will maintain a clear and open line of communication. Gone are the days of "the boss" who maintains a "closed door" policy. A lack of transparency with information undermines a sense of community, commonality, and shared goals. Granted, there might be times when it is not in the best interest of the organization to share all information immediately, but such occasions must occur only after serious consideration, and information should be withheld only when it is absolutely necessary.

Lastly, communicate messages repeatedly and often. If someone misses a meeting or did not get the email, they miss the message. It pays for a leader to ensure that everyone who needs a message gets the message—and clearly understands the message.

4. *Have a meeting.* Involving followers in all matters and decisions relative to their work is essential to collaboration and relationship or trust-building. This is especially important given the constantly changing nature of health care. Authoritarian leaders, who feel as though their followers are not equipped or qualified to provide input, forfeit valuable information and perspectives. Everybody can potentially "bring something to the table"; the sharing of new ideas initiates brainstorming and "outside the box" thinking. Staff members who believe that their

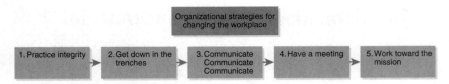

FIGURE 10.3 Organizational Strategies for Changing the Workplace

perspectives were communicated and seriously considered feel more valued and are more likely to accept changes that are made, even if they do not necessarily agree with them.

5. *Keep the mission of the organization in mind.* When discussing business and potential change with employees, keep the mission of the organization and its core values in mind. Reinforcing your core values at every level of the organization can only serve to increase high-quality and safe patient care. Every employee in the organization—from the receptionist who greets visitors to the neurosurgeon who removes a brain tumor—makes an important contribution to the achievement of mission and goals. Everyone in an organization is valuable and deserves respect.

FIGURE 10.3 lays out the steps toward making positive changes in the workplace.

▶ Leading Through Change

Change can be threatening to all of us, especially in situations in which we do not feel we have the power or authority to respond to or prepare for it. Yet, arguably, the healthcare industry is subject to more change than any other, particularly in today's politically charged climate. These changes very often come from external sources and impose regulations and requirements for implementation over which leaders have little control.

Some examples of such changes can be drawn from the not-so-distant past. In 1965, Congress amended the Social Security Act of 1935 and established the Medicare and Medicaid programs to subsidize health care for the poor, elderly, and disabled (Banaszak-Holl, Levitsky, & Zald, 2010). The repercussions for the healthcare industry were significant. Droves of new patients acquired access to care. Limits on reimbursement were put in place. Significant regulatory and legal requirements were enacted (Banaszak-Holl et al., 2010). As a result of the passage of the legislation, 20 million Americans enrolled in these programs in the 3 years following enactment. Basic hospitalization coverage and some assistance paying for the costs of physicians became available, greatly increasing access to care.

In 1996, the Health Insurance Portability and Accountability Act (HIPAA) was enacted. Among other things, HIPAA contained extensive provisions for the protection of personal health information and regulations governing the continuation of some employer-sponsored insurance when patients changed jobs. In addition, it mandated national standards for the electronic transfer of patient information. (Centers for Medicare and Medicaid Services, 2012). See **TABLE 10.1** for a summary of changes in the U.S. healthcare system over the past 150 years.

TABLE 10.1 Significant Changes in the U.S. Healthcare System

1847	American Medical Association founded; largest medical lobby in the United States
1930s	Birth of health insurance plans (Blue Cross/Blue Shield)
1935	Social Security Act: Federal aid to states for public health assistance, maternal and child health, and children with disabilities
1960	Development of biomedical equipment; surge of advanced life-supporting equipment into market
1963	Health Professions Educational Assistance Act: Direct federal aid to students in medical, dental, nursing, and other healthcare professions
1965	Public Health Service Act: Regional medical programs to address leading causes of death
1965	Medicare and Medicaid legislation expanded from original Social Security Act
1966	Comprehensive Health Planning Act: Regional medical resources to improve clinical and educational health services
1970s	Growth of medical specialties
1973	Health Maintenance Organization Act: Health services for prepaid fees
1974	National Health Planning and Resources Development Act (combination of the 1965 and 1966 programs)
1982	Diagnosis-Related Groups (DRGs): Limits to federal reimbursement (Medicare) to health organizations based on patient diagnoses
1994	Death with Dignity Act: Oregon first state to enact a physician-assisted dying statute
2001	Growth of Preferred Provider Organizations
2010	Patient Protection and Affordable Care Act

Data from Sultz, H. A., & Young, K. M. (2011). *Health care USA: Understanding its-organization and delivery* (7th ed.). Burlington, MA: Jones & Bartlett Learning.

The Medicare Part D Prescription Drug Program was enacted in 2003 and implemented in 2006. It represented the largest change to and expansion of the original Medicare program since its inception. By providing subsidies to the elderly and disabled for the purchase of prescription medications, it had the effect of forcing providers to accept reimbursement at federally mandated or negotiated levels.

With the passage of the Patient Protection and Affordable Care Act in 2010, America's healthcare system once again faced change. These changes affected our healthcare facilities and the individuals who work or seek treatment within their walls. More than 20 million people were able to obtain health insurance and access to health care. But, healthcare organizations also faced new challenges regarding capacity and human and financial resources. With legislative efforts to amend or repeal the Affordable Care Act, changes in parameters such as healthcare costs, accessibility, and public health will be expected, providing opportunities for leaders to step forward and embrace what lies ahead.

Additional new challenges face healthcare leaders. These include the aging of the population, the aging of the healthcare workforce, shortages of healthcare providers and pharmaceuticals, and continuing rapid technological advances. All of these will have a direct impact on healthcare services: some of them positive, some negative. Leaders will be tasked to positively transform workplaces and support employees during these necessary transitions.

▶ Become a Game-Changer

A transformational healthcare leader should promote positive dynamics in the workplace and be ahead of change mandated by healthcare legislation. To implement positive change, consider what has been tried in the past and is known to be successful. Develop a personal and organizational action plan (see **FIGURE 10.4**). Try:

1. *Continuously working to motivate employees to higher levels of personal achievement.* This means the leader knows employees well enough to make suggestions for their professional growth and recognize a job well done. The employees should feel enough comfort with their leaders to discuss disagreements with organizational decisions. Leaders should demonstrate respect for employee conversations and feedback, display humble confidence, act as a mentor and a teacher, and help to promote a shared sense of mission for the organization (Grant, Gino, & Hofmann, 2011; Swartz, Spencer, Wilson, & Wood, 2011).

2. *Staying happy!* Emotions are contagious and boost employee and team performance. Significant improvements have been shown in team-helping behaviors, team goal commitment, and team satisfaction when leaders maintain positive moods (Chi, Chung, & Tsai, 2011).

3. *Considering employees' health and wellbeing through* **empowerment**. Northouse (2018) suggests that empowering their employees can be a great challenge for leaders, but that the benefits of doing so are well worth it. Transformational leaders who encourage their employees to be independent, to be a part of the organization's planning process, and to be involved in decision-making nurture employees who are healthier and more engaged in their work. Employees feel empowered to be a part of the organization and consider themselves as more than just a "worker bee." When feeling empowered, employees have been found to have better sleep quality, which is associated with fewer chronic illnesses (Munir & Nielsen, 2009).

4. *Considering safety promotion.* Transformational leaders who specifically work to promote and develop a safe work environment make a difference for their patients as well as their employees. The devastating

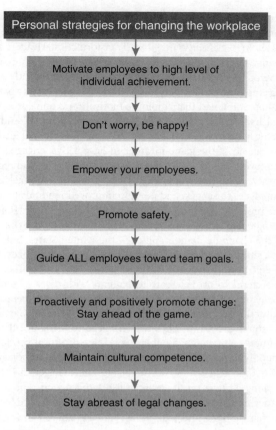

FIGURE 10.4 Personal Strategies for Changing the Workplace

consequences of a patient or employee injury can be prevented by leaders who promote safety awareness through compliance with Occupational Safety and Health Administration (OSHA) requirements, staff education, and reminders posted in the workplace (Mullen & Kelloway, 2009). When productivity suffers, organizations see higher turnover rates, and losses of highly capable talent. It is estimated that between 125 and 190 billion dollars annually is spent on health services for employees due to psychological and physical issues triggered by burn-out (Garton, 2017). The transformational leader can play an integral part in keeping his employees healthy, happy, and motivated (empowered).

5. *Developing the ability to move even the most challenging employee personalities toward team goals.* When dealing with those who might be motivated by self-interest rather than organizational goals, transformational leaders can inspire such individuals to embrace functioning within teams for the betterment of the organization and its customers (Arthur, Woodman, Ong, Hardy, & Ntoumanis, 2011). Kouzes and Posner (2017, p. 129) note that leaders who can demonstrate to others "how their work connects to a larger purpose, and by aligning individual aspirations with organizational ones" present a perspective that allows soloists to see the

benefits of team participation, which include making goals and outcomes more likely to be reached to the satisfaction of all.

6. *Staying a step ahead of the game.* Transformational leaders should embrace change and new policy, greeting it with a positive approach. Looking to develop ways to do things differently and more efficiently is key to improving employee productivity and providing higher quality patient services. A Gallup poll noted that employee motivation is a major issue. It suggested that half of all employees are not "engaged at work" and 20% more are "actively disengaged" (Hood, 2015). Transformational leaders must stay a step ahead of the game in order to have active, engaged, and motivated employees. Helping employees to accept new rules and regulations with a positive, transparent approach is vital. Transformational leaders encourage employees to suggest and develop improved methods that are innovative and promote organizational quality and sustainability (Botting, 2011).

7. *Recognizing the importance of a culturally competent organization.* Because of the changing demographics of the United States, both the workforce and patients served will need a leader who recognizes the importance of cultural competence. Cultural competency is defined as "the ability of systems to provide care to patients with diverse values, beliefs, and behaviors, including tailoring delivery of care to meet patients' social, cultural, and linguistic needs" (Betancourt, Green, Carrillo, & Ananeh-Firempong, 2003, p. 293). Leaders need to recognize the importance of cultural competency for their workforce. Cultural proficiency increases not only patient and employee satisfaction, but is important in the reduction of medical errors (Gertner, Deitrick, & Geiger, 2010).

8. *Keeping a finger on the pulse of legislative action.* The transformational leader has to remain aware of new legislation in order to stay in front of change. State and federal legislative changes can impact billing and reimbursements, compensation, privacy and security, grant funding opportunities, and human resources. A leader who looks ahead and plans ahead will better be able to maintain a strong, effective organization (Greer & Jacobson, 2010).

Summary

Transformational leadership is essential to the development of employee commitment and the promotion of employee retention, which can lead to successful resolution of the challenges facing healthcare organizations. Leaders must understand that they cannot make serious and long-lasting changes alone. Employees are vital to the change process.

Health care is unique in that it does not sleep nor does it take off weekends or holidays. It is a 24/7 industry. Therefore, while change is occurring in our organizations, we must continue to ensure high-quality care and patient safety. A healthcare workforce that is motivated by inclusion, respectful treatment, and the opportunity to grow and develop, both professionally and personally, is a key to transforming an organization and moving it successfully into the years to come.

There continues to be much uncertainty in America's healthcare system. Health care has moved into the informatics age, with most organizations now using electronic health records. The Affordable Care Act, signed into law in 2010, allowed for many previously uninsured or underinsured citizens to obtain coverage. Even so, there remain many unknowns about its future, from both a logistical and a financial perspective. State and federal governments continue to interpret the Affordable Care Act and its details, even amidst new bids to repeal, revise, or replace it. These revisions may meet some resistance. For example, it will be hard to undo the spending caps or coverage extensions (insurance coverage for student dependents until age 26) that have already been put into place. There are many pieces of the Affordable Care Act (ACA) that will likely not be "undone"; but even if the ACA survives largely intact, there is much work yet to be done if America is to offer the world's best health care to each and every one of its citizens.

What is arguably both the greatest challenge and greatest opportunity for transformational healthcare leaders is effectively managing change in times of chaos and uncertainty. Old-school models of top-down authoritarian management are no longer effective. Today's healthcare professionals are engaged and invested. They will not accept being excluded from the change process, nor should they be. Transformational leaders will treat employees with individual respect and consideration, and will involve them in planning and discussion to help the organization achieve its mission and objectives. Transformational leaders will function as engaged peers instead of as distant superiors. They will have a solid set of values and hold to them consistently, moving the organization forward with a clear mission and vision. With these attributes, transformational leaders will lead the way for the development of a professional environment and culture that does not shrink from change, but embraces it and prospers from it.

Discussion Questions

1. How do environmental conditions influence a healthcare leader's chosen style?
2. What are the barriers that prevent a healthcare leader from being transformational?
3. What were some of the changes to hospitals, clinics, pharmacies, and insurance companies brought on by U.S. healthcare developments since the 1960s? How might these have been perceived as threatening by workers?
4. How might the recent healthcare reform measures influence change over these sectors?

🔍 CASE STUDY: The Honeysuckle Clinic

Honeysuckle Family Health Care Clinic

Family Health Care Clinic

The Honeysuckle Clinic is a community rural health clinic that is open 6 days a week and currently manages nearly 4000 patient visits annually. The staff includes one full-time administrator, one full-time nurse practitioner, two part-time nurse

(continues)

practitioners, one full-time intake specialist, one full-time receptionist, and one part-time medical coder/biller. Mental health services, physical therapy, and some complementary and alternative medicine therapies are done by contract providers. Lab services are available 3 days a week. The dental program costs are covered by a grant that covers the cost of a dentist, hygienist, and dental assistant, all of whom work part-time. The clinic is a Medicare/Medicaid provider and accepts most insurance plans. Patients are encouraged to pay in cash rather than with debit and credit cards due to the fees incurred by both the clinic and the patient with card use. This is just one more attempt by clinic administrators to keep patient costs as low as possible.

Patients receive assistance in accessing pharmaceutical benevolent programs. The practitioners work diligently to prescribe generic medications that can be purchased at low cost through a number of large retailers. The clinic does keep on hand some emergency and sample brand name products to dispense if needed.

Nola Salem is the clinic's director. She has been on the job approximately 3 years, arriving after a period of financial difficulty and declining grant monies nearly closed the clinic. Ms. Salem reports to an independent Board of Directors consisting of 12 area citizens and community leaders. Of the 12 members, four are patients of the clinic as required by state law for facilities receiving state grant monies. The Board meets bimonthly at the clinic.

Since Ms. Salem arrived, Honeysuckle has been awarded numerous grants and is currently financially stable. The annual budget for this thriving clinic runs approximately a half million dollars.

Ms. Salem was asked to describe her leadership style. Some of her self-descriptions include the following:

- "I am not a micromanager. Each clinician or staff member was hired to do a job. If someone is not doing his or her job, that person needs to go."
- "I like to stay organized and insist that employees make an appointment if they need to discuss something in private. It helps us all to stay on track."
- "I want to hear their ideas. None of us is comprehensively trained in all fields. Each employee contributes to the team that makes up Honeysuckle."
- "We brainstorm a lot."
- "There are no big people here, only small puzzle pieces that make up the whole. We each need the other and his or her ideas and skills to complete the picture."
- "Everybody's responsible for a piece of that puzzle."
- "I make it a point to walk through the clinic every day so if any employee needs to talk with me, I'm available."
- "After I make a decision, my employees are expected to 'get on the band wagon' and get it implemented."

Ms. Salem does have a regularly scheduled staff meeting with the full-time employees, with part-time employees attending when possible. Most staff meetings are held with 5 minutes notice, while all employees are on the run. She notes the luxury of having a small practice. "We can move fast," she remarks. "If we need a new form created or need to make a policy decision, we do not need committees. We do not work in a slow, cumbersome process like in a larger healthcare system. We can decide something at 10 a.m. and put it in place at noon."

The clinic's medical director, Dr. Seymor, has the final approval on clinical changes. Nurse practitioners feel that they are routinely ignored when they present requests for more information. They feel like they are given no choice about patient flow and documentation, when they are the ones in actual practice with patients. Per policy, Dr. Seymor reviews 100% of the clinical records, but is not present on-site. While the nurse practitioners were willing to talk candidly about the clinic, other employees were reluctant to discuss their leader. All of them declined, citing the constant fear that they might lose their jobs at a moment's notice.

Case Study Discussion Questions

1. Nola Salem, through her business background, has brought many improvements to the Honeysuckle Clinic in the past 3 years. However, there are no strategic plans yet in place. The Board of Directors is pleased at the influx of grant funding, but the staff members worry when the new budgets are announced. Staff reveal that they cannot anticipate if they will have employment on a long-term basis— and morale plunges. Is Ms. Salem a transformational leader? Justify your position. If not, how might a true transformational leader handle some of these issues?

2. Ms. Salem has just tendered her resignation to take another position. The Board of Directors hired a consultant who has recommended that the clinic seek a transformational leader to lead Honeysuckle into the next decade. Relative to what you know about the clinic's structure, financial status, and patient base, what traits should this new leader embody? What questions might you ask the candidate you are interviewing to determine his or her leadership philosophy?

3. You are a community leader in an area similar to the region served by the Honeysuckle Clinic. One of the area's largest employers has just closed its doors, leaving many of your community's "breadwinners" unemployed and uninsured. Your locality seeks a healthcare provider to offer locally based, reduced-fee medical care to its population and turns to you to coordinate the recruitment of this practice or organization. The medium-sized state university 50 miles away has a large nursing school, and nurse practitioners from its faculty have agreed to staff an outpatient clinic on a volunteer basis until a new practice is fully established. As you begin planning for the new low-cost services you plan to launch, you and your team make a site visit to Honeysuckle to observe and learn from their experiences. You have questions about recruitment and retention of qualified medical staff, about the aging of the healthcare workforce, and about how changing technology and healthcare reform demands for accountability and quality may impact your proposed clinic. Please prepare a list of topics/concerns to be discussed.

🔎 CASE STUDY: Transformational Leadership Model or Just a Nightmare?

The Honeysuckle Clinic 5 Years Later

It has been 5 years since the original look at the Honeysuckle Family Health Care Clinic. The consultant hired by the clinic when Ms. Salem announced her resignation suggested that the clinic look for a transformational leader to take them into the next decade. Marianne Oglesby was hired as the administrative director and has indeed been good for the clinic.

Marianne's background included many years of experience with a health system in which she started and managed a number of physician practices. As such, her managerial skills are excellent and she is not afraid to jump into the middle of any issue, either clinical or non-clinical.

(continues)

Growth has been phenomenal! Over the past year alone, the clinic served approximately 3100 patients, with almost 8000 patient visits, nearly doubling what the clinic was doing 5 years ago. The annual budget is now $1.2 million and the bimonthly payroll runs approximately $38,000. Staff numbers have increased to include a part-time medical doctor, two full-time family nurse practitioners, and one full-time and two part-time dentists. Behavioral health services were added approximately 4 years ago.

Two years ago, in an effort to keep up with the exponential growth of the clinic and the need for more opportunity to write grants and seek funding, Alissa Wells was hired as the administrative director, with Marianne's position being relabeled as the executive director. It was intended that Marianne would use her expertise and experience to look for funding to maintain the clinic. It soon became apparent, however, that two executives in such a small space might not be such a good thing. Alissa's experience included managing a surgery center and her background is more business than clinical.

Marianne could be described not so much as a "micro-manager," but perhaps as a "micro-overseer" paying close attention to the finer details of the clinic. She describes her personal leadership style as "service oriented" and says, "If I'm not giving them what they need, they can't do their job." Marianne notes that she is not a top-down kind of leader, but is only comfortable delegating if she can follow-up to see that it is done. She readily admits to having "trust issues." Her message to employees is "Do your job." In working with Alissa, she feels like she is the one most likely to look at the details of the organization. "If we do this, what's the impact down the road, to employees, to patients, to the community, to the clinic?"

Alissa, on the other hand, is very laid back about the details and instead, is a very "big picture" kind of person. She readily admits that details drive her crazy. As a leader, however, she is always willing to "take the blame or give the credit." She notes that as a leader, she believes it is vital that she take the blame for any problems while giving credit to her staff for any and all successes. She could be described as more of a "loyalty" person, expecting that her staff will be loyal to her because of her position. It could be said of Alissa that her employees are empowered to do their jobs and that she trusts that they will get the job done in a professional manner.

Organizational missions, visions, and values are emphasized as shared by the entire team as well. Alissa describes the clinic staff as a "well-oiled machine."

So how has all this worked out? Initially the two were very antagonistic to one another, but have more recently come to a working arrangement that seems, from the outside, to benefit the organization overall. Marianne was reluctant to give up some of her control and Alissa was bent on finding her position. As a result, employees were often conflicted and even today, some employees are loyal and defensive on Marianne's behalf, whereas others think Alissa is the better leader. There are some conflicts in that employees do not always have a clear picture of who is the "boss" when both leaders are in the clinic or sending emails with directions. Marianne is now working more from home and is not as present in the clinic, which leaves Alissa as the day-to-day management.

Recently, in applying for a major change in designation to make the clinic a Federally Qualified Health Center (FQHC), the two, in conjunction with a consultant, worked cooperatively to complete the massive paperwork and policies required on the application. It is often noted, however, that Marianne is quick to interrupt Alissa when she is reporting to the board of directors or conducting a staff meeting. The astute observer can feel a definite tension when the two are felt to be "competing" with one another for the top spot or the last word.

Discussion Questions

1. What transformational leadership qualities do you see in Marianne and Alissa?
2. Does this organizational structure resemble a transformational approach to leadership or is it just a nightmare for those who work there? Defend your answer and explain what changes you might make and why.
3. List and discuss three barriers a transformational leader might face in dealing with two or more managers with disparate management styles.
4. Explain methods a transformational leader could use to foster employee acceptance of change.
5. How do you see transformational leadership helping a newly formed outpatient center?
6. Discuss one historical example of a positive transformational leadership quality in any organization.
7. How do you see transformational leadership helping an existing healthcare organization going through change?
8. What do you feel is the priority quality of a transformational leader? Explain.

Acknowledgment

With acknowledgment to Jeanne Melton for her contributions to the first edition of *New Leadership for Today's Health Care Professionals*.

Related Websites

American College of Healthcare Executives: www.ache.org/
American Recovery and Reinvestment Act of 2009: www.recovery.org
Healthcare Leadership Alliance: www.healthcareleadershipalliance.org/
Health Reform Information: www.healthcare.gov/
Leadership Health Care: www.healthcarecouncil.com/leadership-health-care
National Association of Community Health Centers: http://nachc.com/
Additionally, every state has its own association
National Center for Healthcare Leadership: http://nchl.org/
Primary Health Care Associations are identified by state; for example:

- Illinois at www.iphca.org
- Mississippi at www.mphca.com
- Wisconsin at www.wphca.org

Studer Group: http://studergroup.com/
U.S. Department of Health and Human Services, Health Resources and Services Administration: www.hrsa.gov/

References

Arthur, C. A., Woodman, T., Ong, C. W., Hardy, L., & Ntoumanis, N. (2011). The role of athlete narcissism in moderating the relationship between coaches' transformational leader behaviors and athlete motivation. *Journal of Sport & Exercise Psychology, 33*(1), 3–19.
Atchinson, T. (2003). Exposing the myth of employee satisfaction. *Healthcare Executive, 17*(3), 20.
Banaszak-Holl, J., Levitsky, S., & Zald, M. N. (2010). *Social movements and the transformation of American health care*. New York, NY: Oxford University Press.
Bass, B. (1985). *Leadership and performance beyond expectations*. New York, NY: Free Press.

Betancourt, J. R., Green, A. R., Carrillo, J. E., & Ananeh-Firenpong, O. (2003). Defining cultural competence: A practical framework for addressing racial/ethnic disparities in health and health care. *National Institute of Health Public Health Report, 118*(4), 293–302.

Botting, L. (2011). Transformational change in action. *Nursing Management, 17*(9), 14–19.

Burns, J. (1978). *Leadership.* New York, NY: Harper & Row.

Burns, J. (2003). *Transforming leadership.* New York, NY: Grove.

Centers for Medicare and Medicaid Services. (2012). *HIPAA general information.* Retrieved from www .cms.gov/Regulations-and-Guidance/HIPAA-Administrative-Simplification/HIPAAGenInfo /index.html

Chi, N., Chung, Y., & Tsai, W. (2011). How do happy leaders enhance team success? The mediating roles of transformational leadership, group affective tone, and team processes. *Journal of Applied Social Psychology, 41*(6), 1421–1454.

Dobbs, R. (2010). *Transformational leadership: A blueprint for real organizational change.* Little Rock, AR: Parkhurst Brothers.

Garton, E. (2017). Employee burnout is a problem with the company, not the person. *Harvard Business Review.* Retrieved from https://hbr.org/2017/04/employee-burnout-is-a -problem-with-the-company-not-the-person

Gertner, E. J., Deitrick, L. M., & Geiger, J. F. (2010). Developing a culturally competent health network: A planning framework and guide. *Journal of Healthcare Management, 55*(3), 190–203.

Grant, A. M., Gino, F., & Hofmann, D. A. (2011). Reversing the extroverted leadership advantage: The role of employee proactivity. *Academy of Management Journal, 54*(3), 528–550.

Greer, S. L., & Jacobson, P. D. (2010). Health care reform and federalism. *Journal of Health Politics, Policy, and Law, 35*(2), 203–226.

Hood, B. M. (2015). *Eat more ice cream! A succinct leadership lesson for each week of the year.* (n.p.): Author.

Kouzes, J. M., & Posner, B. Z. (2017). *The leadership challenge* (6th ed.). Hoboken, NJ: John Wiley & Sons, Inc.

Kuhnert, K., & Lewis, P. (1987). Transactional and transformational leadership: A constructive /developmental analysis. *Academy of Management Review, 12*(4), 648–657.

Ledlow, G. R., & Stephens, J. H. (2018). *Leadership for health professionals* (3rd ed.). Burlington, MA: Jones and Bartlett Learning.

Manion, J. (2011). From management to leadership: Practical strategies for health care leaders (3rd ed.). San Francisco, CA: Jossey-Bass.

McGregor, D. (1960). *The human side of enterprise.* New York, NY: McGraw-Hill.

Mullen, J. E., & Kelloway, E. K. (2009). Safety leadership: A longitudinal study of the effects of transformational leadership on safety outcomes. *Journal of Occupational and Organizational Psychology, 82*, 253–272.

Munir, F., & Nielsen, K. (2009). Does self-efficacy mediate the relationship between transformational leadership behaviours and healthcare workers' sleep quality? A longitudinal study. *Journal of Advanced Nursing, 65*(9), 1833–1843.

National Park Service. (2018). *What are core values?* Retrieved from https://www.nps.gov/training /uc/npscv.htm

Northouse, P. (2017). *Introduction to leadership: Concepts and practice* (4th ed.). Thousand Oaks, CA: Sage Publications.

Northouse, P. (2018). *Leadership: Theory and practice* (8th ed.). Thousand Oaks, CA: Sage Publications.

Studer, Q. (2004). *Hardwiring excellence.* Gulf Breeze, FL: Fire Starter.

Sultz, H. A., & Young, K. M. (2011). *Health care USA: Understanding its organization and delivery* (7th ed.). Burlington, MA: Jones & Bartlett Learning.

Swartz, D. B., Spencer, T., Wilson, B., & Wood, K. (2011). Transformational leadership: Implications for nursing leaders in facilities seeking magnet designation. *American Operating Room Nurses Journal, 93*(6), 737–748.

Taylor, D. (2007). *The imperfect leader: A story about discovering the not-so-secret secrets of transformational leadership.* Bloomington, IN: AuthorHouse.

CHAPTER 11

Person- and Family-Centered Leadership

Beverly Quaye and Mary Lynne Knighten

LEARNING OBJECTIVES

By the end of this chapter, the student will be able to:

- Describe core concepts of person–family-centered care (PFCC) and values-based professional practice.
- Define servant leadership and person–family-centered leadership.
- Differentiate between the roles of person–family-centered leadership and management.
- Articulate how to transform a traditional healthcare organizational culture to one that is person and family centered.
- Describe the role Patient Family Advisors play in hospital leadership, safety, and quality.
- Extrapolate the vision, strategies, and actions of PFCC into ambulatory care and community health.

KEY TERMS

Care delivery model
Co-design
Patient activation
Patient- and family-centered care
Patient and family
  partnerships
Patient engagement
Patient Family Advisors

Patient Family Advisory
  Council
Person-centered care
Person–family-centered
  care
Person–family-centered leadership
Professional practice model
Top box achievement

▶ Introduction

Person–family-centered care (PFCC) can enhance the human experience and improve a healthcare organization's operational performance metrics. Effectiveness of PFCC is demonstrated via two examples: (1) an urban, community, formerly faith-based hospital, which adopted a PFCC delivery model, forming new partnerships with families, physicians, and internal and external stakeholders; and developing an organizational culture based on interdependence, mutual learning, and collaboration; and (2) a community-based model of individual and collective engagement and empowerment to improve health outcomes. Improved service, quality, health outcomes, and cost per adjusted discharge were achieved.

▶ Definitions

There are several approaches to healthcare delivery that center around individuals seeking care specifically for their health and wellness needs. Among them are **Patient- and family-centered care**, *family-centered care*, *person-centered care*, and *patient- and family-engaged care* (PFEC). Though the terms are used interchangeably, each approach contains separate and distinct philosophies and care concepts. To better understand **person–family-centered leadership**, it is important to understand the basics of common person-centric philosophies and care models.

Patient-centered care is providing care that is respectful of and responsive to individual patient preferences, needs, and values, and ensuring that patient values guide all clinical decisions (Feeley, 2017). The *person* is defined as the individual who needs and seeks care. *Family* refers to two or more persons who are related in any way—biologically, legally, or emotionally. *Person-centered care* implies that the focus is only on the individual person. The person *is* central to the delivery of care in a wide range of settings across the full healthcare continuum, including the home, but this approach is not typically a dominant focus in an acute care or emergency care setting. In person-centered care, family members may be, and often are, included; however, the concept of partnership with persons and families is not well developed. Chew, Brewster, Tarrant, Martin, and Armstrong (2017) describe a synthesis of person-centered care that may help clarify the varying definitions. There are four underlying principles of person-centered care: (1) affording people dignity, compassion, and respect; (2) making coordinated care, support, or treatment available; (3) personalizing care, support, and treatment; and (4) supporting individuals to develop their own abilities for an independent and fulfilling life (Chew et al., 2017). This approach utilizes **patient engagement** and **patient activation**, whereby individuals use skills, knowledge, and confidence to manage their health and health care with interventions designed to promote positive health behaviors (Patient Engagement Health Policy Brief, 2013). Engaging people in their own health care also includes mentoring them in health literacy—the ability to obtain, process, communicate, and understand fundamental health information and services (Koh, Brach, Harris, & Parchman, 2013).

PFEC is a care that is planned, delivered, managed, and continuously improved by actively partnering with patients and their families (or care partners as defined by the patient) to ensure that patient health and healthcare goals, preferences, and values are addressed, actionable, and integrated with the needs and expectations of the group members.

Patient- and family-centered care is an approach to the planning, delivery, and assessment of health care grounded in mutually beneficial partnerships among healthcare providers, persons, and families IPFCC, 2010. In the **person–family-centered care** PFCC approach, the definition of family, as well as the degree of the family's involvement in health care, is determined by the patient, provided that he or she is developmentally able and competent to do so. The term *family centered* is in no way intended to remove control from individuals who are competent to make decisions concerning their own health care (IPFCC, 2010).

Co-design is a way to identify both problems and solutions together with patients and thereby improve the quality of care experience (healthcodesign.org. nz, 2018). Experience-based co-design (EBCD), developed in the United Kingdom, brings together narrative-based research with service design methods to improve patient and staff experiences of care. These shared experiences create a generative change process, in which patients and staff partner to design, implement, and test healthcare improvements. EBCD has been used in more than 60 projects in six countries and has led to improvements in patients' experiences as well as transformations in healthcare workforce culture, values, and behaviors (Van Citters, 2017). It is this partnership that best defines person–family-centered leadership.

▶ Core Concepts

Health care is provided in many settings beyond acute hospital care; not all persons in such settings are considered patients. PFCC encompasses persons rather than patients in its definition.

Four core concepts comprise PFCC (**TABLE 11.1**). These concepts provide the foundation for person- and family-centered leaders to transform their organizations' cultures.

TABLE 11.1 Core Concepts of Patient- and Family-Centered Care
Dignity and Respect: Healthcare practitioners listen to and honor both person and family perspectives and choices. Person and family knowledge, values, beliefs, and cultural backgrounds are incorporated into the planning and delivery of care.
Information Sharing: Healthcare practitioners communicate and share complete and unbiased information with persons and families in ways that are affirming and useful. Persons and families receive timely, complete, and accurate information in order to effectively participate in care and decision-making.
Participation: Persons and families are encouraged and supported in participating in care and decision-making at the level they choose.
Collaboration: Persons and families are also included on an institution-wide basis. Healthcare leaders collaborate with persons and families in policy and program development, implementation, and evaluation; in healthcare facility design; and in professional education, as well as in the delivery of care.

Reprinted with permission from the Institute for Patient- and Family-Centered Care: www.ipfcc.org

Rationale

Leaders and providers who are person and family centered recognize the vital role that individuals and families play in ensuring the health and wellness of persons of all ages. They listen to and value the individual and collective voice of persons and families and empower persons and their families to take charge of their own health and welfare. There are numerous examples in the literature showing that improved health outcomes, better allocation of resources, and greater satisfaction with the healthcare experience for the person and family are achieved with PFCC. Person- and family-centered leaders astutely recognize that *person and family partnerships* inform and shape their healthcare organization's operational policies, staff interactions, facilities, services, and programs. Health systems, hospitals, ambulatory services, and other healthcare institutions committed to PFCC proactively collaborate with persons and families, advocate for family presence, and facilitate family participation in individualized care. Person- and family-centered leaders extrapolate the core concepts and partnership beyond organizational walls to shape community health initiatives.

▶ Influences at the Health Policy Level

The term *patient-centered medicine* was introduced in psychiatry by Balint and colleagues in 1969. *Patient-centered care* was coined by the Picker Commonwealth Program for patient-centered care, currently the Picker Institute, in 1988. The Picker Commonwealth Program researched and documented personal needs and preferences in order to understand the personal and family definitions of high-quality care and to explore models of care to better address those needs. This qualitative research ultimately resulted in the production of survey instruments that measured the personal experience in eight dimensions of care (see **TABLE 11.2**). In addition to safe and technically excellent care, these eight dimensions of care had been identified by the person and their families to be the most critical aspects of the care experience (Conway et al., 2006, p. 5).

In the 1980s, women and families helped drive family-centered changes within maternity care. U.S. Surgeon General C. Everett Koop, the Maternal and Child Health Bureau of the U.S. Department of Health and Human Services, the Association for the Care of Children's Health, and other organizations collaborated with

TABLE 11.2 Eight Dimensions of Care Measurement (Picker Institute)
Access
Respect for personal values and preferences
Coordination of care
Information, communication, and education
Physical comfort (including help with activities of daily living)
Emotional support
Involvement of friends and family
Preparation for discharge and transitions in care

Reprinted with permission from the Institute for Patient- and Family-Centered Care: www.ipfcc.org

families in defining and providing leadership to advance the practice of *patient-centered care* (Conway et al., 2006, p. 6).

Today, the Institute for Patient- and Family-Centered Care (formerly the Institute for Family-Centered Care) is one of the foremost authorities on the PFCC concept in the United States. According to the Institute's website, its work in the early 1990s focused primarily on family-centered approaches to pediatric care. Within this framework, it was consistently envisioned that as an individual matured, they should be encouraged to become more involved as decision-makers in their own health care along with their families. In the past decade, the Institute has become more involved in adult and geriatric care, and believes it is important to acknowledge the person's role more explicitly. Thus, the Institute began using the term *patient- and family-centered care.*

Families have been shown to positively influence people's health and wellness; social isolation is a risk factor for poor health in today's society. Most people have families or are affiliated with a support system or network, and benefit when healthcare organizations encourage continuing linkage to these natural supports. Additionally, individuals who are most dependent on hospital care, community care, and the broader healthcare system, such as the very young, the elderly, and those with chronic conditions and disabilities, are typically also dependent on and receive invaluable support from families and social networks. This integration of PFCC reflects our social framework.

The original definition of patient-centered care in the literature of the late 1980s and early 1990s did not include the concept of persons and their families as advisors and essential partners to healthcare professionals in improving care practices and systems of care. Individuals and their families have experience, expertise, insights, and perspectives that provide value to promote transformational healthcare change. Partnering for redesign (co-design) of health care needs to occur in all types of organizations, including hospitals, ambulatory services, community-based organizations; at advocacy and health policy levels; and via educational programs that prepare the next generation of healthcare clinicians and leaders (Johnson et al., 2008).

In 2001, the Institute of Medicine (IOM) released a highly influential report entitled *Crossing the Quality Chasm: A New Health System for the 21st Century,* which analyzed problems facing the U.S. healthcare system and presented recommendations for its improvement. PFCC—partnerships among professionals, the person, and families—offers a framework and strategies to enhance the quality and safety of health care. In its "Six Quality Aims for Improving Care," the IOM report defines patient-centered care as "care that is respectful of and responsive to individual personal preferences, needs and values, and ensuring [sic] that individual values guide all clinical decisions" (IOM, 2001, p. 40).

The *Quality Chasm* report also offers "10 Rules to Redesign and Improve Care." All 10 rules are consistent with person- and family-centered approaches; the five most relevant are listed in **TABLE 11.3**.

Organizations such as The Joint Commission (TJC) (formerly the Joint Commission on Accreditation of Healthcare Organizations, or JCAHO), the National Committee for Quality Assurance (NCQA), the Institute for Healthcare Improvement (IHI), the Centers for Medicare and Medicaid Services (CMS), and the American Hospital Association (AHA) are making PFCC a priority in their long-term strategic agendas, validating the essential role these core concepts play in

TABLE 11.3 Person- and Family-Centered Rules to Co-design and Improve Care

Care based in continuous healing relationships. The person should receive care whenever it is needed and in multiple accessible settings.	The healthcare system should be responsive… 24 hours a day, every day… Access to care should be provided over the Internet, by telephone, portals and by other means in addition to face-to-face visits.
Customization based on personal needs and values.	The system of care should be designed to meet the most common types of needs but have the capability to respond to individual personal choices and preferences. The health system should… accommodate differences in the person's preferences, encourage shared decision-making, and avoid paternalistic approaches.
The person as the source of control. Individuals should be given the necessary information and the opportunity to exercise the degree of control they choose over healthcare decisions.	Clinicians and individuals should communicate effectively and share information for optimal informed decision-making.
Shared knowledge and the free flow of information. The person should have unfettered access to their own medical information and to clinical knowledge.	The healthcare system should make information available to the person and their families that allows them to make informed decisions when selecting a health plan, hospital, or clinical practice or choosing among alternative treatments.
The need for transparency.	This should include information describing the system's performance on safety, evidence-based practice, and personal satisfaction.

Data from Institute of Medicine. (2001). Crossing the quality chasm: A new health system for the 21st Century. Washington, DC: Author.

healthcare design and improvement. For example, Conway et al. (2006) cite the influence of four prominent organizations (AHA, JCAHO, IHI, and NCQA) in this area:

- In 2004, the AHA collaborated with the Institute for Family-Centered Care to produce and disseminate a *Toolkit on Patient- and Family-Centered Care* to the chief executive officer of every hospital in the United States.
- In 2006, the JCAHO convened its first Patient and Family Advisory Committee and published a book, *Patients as Partners: How to Involve Patients and Families in Their Own Care.*
- The IHI, under the guidance of Donald Berwick, MD, made Patient- and family-centered care an area of innovation and research for 2006 and ensured

its inclusion in all the Institute's major programs, including the 100,000 Lives Campaign, Quality Allies, and Transforming Care at the Bedside initiatives.

■ The NCQA created a patient- and family-centered physician practice recognition program that rewards medical groups for developing and implementing patient- and family-centered practice designs and interventions.

Person-centered initiatives have become integral to federal and national standards for high-quality healthcare delivery. For example:

■ In 2005, the Agency for Healthcare Research and Quality (AHRQ) and CMS supported the development of the Consumer Assessment of Healthcare Providers and Systems (CAHPS®) surveys of patient experience to assess quality of care from the patient point of view in various ambulatory and institutional settings. The three most widely used CAHPS surveys are:
  - **The CAHPS Health Plan Survey**, which asks enrollees in commercial plans, Medicaid, Children's Health Insurance Programs (CHIP), and Medicare about their experiences with health plan services and ambulatory care.
  - **The CAHPS Clinician & Group Survey (CG-CAHPS)**, which asks patients to report on their experiences with primary or specialty care received from providers and their staff in ambulatory settings.
  - **The CAHPS Hospital Survey (HCAHPS)**, which asks patients about the care delivered during an inpatient stay at a hospital facility (CAHPS, 2016).

The CMS publicly reports data from many of the CAHPS surveys on its website, www.hospitalcompare.hhs.gov (HCAHPS, 2005).

In 2010, to improve the safety and quality of care provided by hospitals, TJC released *Advancing Effective Communication, Cultural Competence, and Patient- and Family-Centered Care; A Roadmap for Hospitals.* This guidance document encourages healthcare leaders to aspire to meet the unique needs of each individual and address personal demographic and personal characteristics, in addition to the clinical aspect of care.

■ The CMS released the Final Rule on changes to the hospital and critical access hospital Conditions of Participation to ensure visitation rights for all patients, which became effective January 1, 2011 (CMS, 2010).

■ In 2011, Health and Human Services Secretary Kathleen Sebelius announced the Partnership for Patients, which requires collaboration between hospitals, physicians, nurses, patient advocates, and others to reduce hospital-acquired conditions and prevent readmissions (HHS, 2011).

■ The IHI published an innovation series white paper entitled, "Achieving Exceptional Patient and Family Experience of Inpatient Hospital Care," which can serve as a guidance document for hospitals wishing to transform the culture from being provider centric to achieving patient and family centeredness (Balik, Conway, Zipperer, & Watson, 2011).

■ The Robert Wood Johnson Foundation produced a policy paper in August 2011 regarding patient-centered medical homes and predicted their potential to positively transform health care (RWJF, 2010). The Patient-Centered Medical Home (PCMH) is a **care delivery model** whereby patient treatment is coordinated through their primary care physician to ensure they receive the necessary care when and where they need it, in a manner they can understand (American College of Physicians, 2018). Medical homes have since become a prominent health service option for patients of all ages and their families.

- In 2017, Dr. Anthony Digioia and Eve Shapiro published *The Patient Centered Value System: Transforming Healthcare Through Co-Design*, which is a performance improvement technique that consists of (1) Shadowing, (2) Patient-and Family-Centered Care Methodology, and (3) Time-Driven Activity-Based Costing. Shadowing is the essential tool in the methodology that provides the lens for every care experience from the patient and family point of view, and Time-Driven Activity-Based Costing enables the calculation of the true costs of health care over the full cycle of care.

- From 2014 to 2018, 36 states, the U.S. Virgin Islands, and Puerto Rico have passed CARE Act legislation; the remaining states have either introduced or have had it passed by their legislatures. The CARE Act is model state-level legislation, created by the AARP, for action at the state level to improve care transitions from and reduce readmissions to hospitals by appropriately preparing caregivers prior to patient discharge. The CARE Act has three required components: (1) hospital staff must record a family caregiver's name at admission to a hospital or rehabilitation facility; (2) the family caregiver must be notified when a loved one will be discharged to another facility or home; and (3) hospital staff must provide an explanation (and instruction) of the care and medical tasks a patient requires that the family caregiver will likely perform at home, such as medication management, injections, wound care, and transfers (AARP, 2018).

- In 2018, PFCCpartners launched a National IT **Patient Family Advisory Council**, in collaboration with OpenNotes with a goal of increasing the value and access for patients to their own healthcare records. In addition, the National IT PFAC provides a resource to inform any health IT vendor or healthcare organization.

This brief synopsis of organizations, agencies, and individuals influencing the advancement of PFCC is by no means all-inclusive. For more information, the work of patient- and family-centered leaders in the United States, such as Donald Berwick, MD; Beverly Johnson; Jim Conway; Patricia Sodomka; and Polly Arango should be referenced, as well as information from Planetree, Family Voices, the AHRQ, the National Quality Forum (NHQ), the American College of Physicians and the American Board of Medical Specialties (ABMS), the Society of Pediatric Nurses, and the American Nurses Association (SPN/ANA). Internationally, PFCC resources may be accessed from the World Health Organization (WHO), the National Health Service (NHS) in the United Kingdom, the Australian Commission on Safety and Quality in Healthcare and Clinical Excellence Commission, the Australian Institute for PFCC, and the Picker Institute Europe. PFCC is influencing many of the policies included in the ongoing healthcare reform initiatives in the United States and is incentivized with payment for performance (P4P), value based-purchasing, and value-based care by governmental agencies. Healthcare leaders are challenged with designing PFCC models to deliver care that will improve and optimize the person's quality of care, safety, and clinical outcomes, which also results in enhanced operational efficiency, organizational effectiveness, and sustainability.

▶ Leadership and Organizational Culture

Assessment

The transition from traditional provider-centric healthcare models to transformational models that are person- and family-centric is challenging, and demands that leaders adopt a new global and population-based public health perspective on care delivery. Since the advent of the Affordable Care Act (ACA), which went into effect in 2014, there has been a paradigm shift from a disease-driven healthcare response to a health-promotion, disease-prevention approach, along with emphasis on early detection and treatment of disease. The ACA has directed healthcare services to be inclusive of the full continuum of care for each patient (Patient Protection and Affordable Care Act, 2010). Specifically, the ACA has added provisions for programs and funding for long-term care services in the home or in the community. This healthcare policy change has resulted in healthcare organizations ensuring services encompass the individuals' experience beyond the hospital, in all healthcare settings such as community-based organizations and the home.

Implementation of the PFCC approach begins with an organization's assessment of leadership readiness. There are a few excellent assessment tools available from the IPFCC, the American Hospital Association, Family Voices, IHI, and the National Institute for Children's Health Quality (NICHQ) that can be used for this purpose. Healthcare executives and managers aspiring to be person and family centered will then need to research best practices; identify leadership role models; and initiate open, evidence-based dialogue regarding PFCC with employees, colleagues, medical staff, individuals, and their families. Dialogue about PFCC planning and focus, benefits and barriers, and strengths and challenges, can be facilitated via tools such as the World Café, fishbowl exercises, brainstorming, nominal group technique, and swim-lane flow charts. Engaged parties involved in this dialogue frequently transform their perspectives, and many voluntarily agree to assist with PFCC design and implementation.

Along with an assessment of leadership readiness, an assessment of organizational culture receptivity and readiness for embedded person- and family-centered approaches should be conducted. Among key areas to evaluate are the organization's mission, vision, values, and philosophy of care statements; the language in the organization's policies; and the tone of the communications and signage. The *Patient-Family-Centered Care: A Hospital Self-Assessment Inventory* (IPFCC, 2010) is a robust tool which healthcare leaders can use to obtain a comprehensive assessment of an organization's current practices, generate a gap analysis, and develop action plans for transformational change to a PFCC model. A simpler self-assessment tool produced by IHI and NICHQ, in collaboration with IPFCC, *The Patient- and Family-Centered Care Organizational Self-Assessment Tool*, evaluates elements of hospital-based PFCC and examples of current practice with **patient and family partnerships** and facilitates understanding of the range and breadth of PFCC as compared to the leading edge of practice (IHI & NICHQ, 2013). There is a need to formulate a comprehensive PFCC-oriented community needs assessment tool.

Managing Systemic Change

Since change is inherent in moving from a traditional organizational culture to one that is person and family centered, PFCC leaders must be adept at managing change. Change will occur even if it is not managed, but successful culture transformation often depends on how well change was managed. There are several change management and transition models that can be useful at key intervals at macro-, meso-, and microsystem levels, including the improvement model.

According to Donald Nelson, a physician and expert on quality, an organization will transform the culture only when it moves from improvement projects to systems improvement (Nelson, Batalden, & Godfrey, 2007, p. 201). **FIGURE 11.1** depicts the progression from improvement projects to systems improvements.

The first phase of improvement involves improvement projects that focus on areas of high interest and potential impact, with a clear beginning and clear end. An example of a PFCC improvement project was to recruit a Patient Family Advisor to the Quality and Patient Safety Committee of the hospital's governing board.

The second phase of improvement focuses on microsystem change, building the habit for improvement into frontline systems. Individual microsystems (units, departments, teams) are encouraged to plan and make changes as part of their regular work routines (Nelson et al., 2007). Examples of PFCC microsystem changes might include encouraging PFCC practices in the Neonatal Intensive Care Unit (NICU). This could result in family presence guidelines, family participation in multidisciplinary treatment rounds, as well as seeking family advice and embedding PFCC projects in the NICU unit council goals.

The third phase focuses on the mesosystem, in which the best practice that was designed and implemented in one microsystem is spread to other microsystems. For example, when family presence guidelines at a hospital were shared, the Radiology Department implemented family presence guidelines for children undergoing radiologic procedures, a policy revision for family presence in the Intensive Care Unit was facilitated, and family presence during resuscitation efforts was defined.

The fourth phase of improvement focuses on change for the entire system, when all parts of the system become aligned with the goal of organization-wide improvement (Nelson et al., 2007). An example of macrosystem improvement was the design

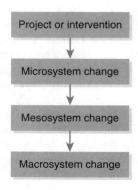

FIGURE 11.1 Improvement Model: Systems Change

Modified from Nelson, E. C., Batalden, P. B., & Godfrey, M. M. (2007). *Quality by design: A clinical microsystems approach.* San Francisco, CA: Jossey-Bass.

TABLE 11.4 Organizational Barriers to Person-Centered Care

Difficulty recruiting and retaining physicians (and other culturally competent professionals) from underrepresented groups/minorities.

Lack of defined "boundaries" for outreach staff, who may be overwhelmed dealing with interrelated health, social, cultural, and economic issues of individuals.

Fatigue and burnout.

Competing priorities.

Strict hiring requirements that pose obstacles to hiring neighborhood residents.

Lack of tools to gauge and reward person- and family-centered performance.

Financial constraints.

Traditional attitudes among staff unwilling to change the "old school" provider/individual relationship, or acknowledge and address cultural and socioeconomic issues.

Data from Silow-Carroll, S., Alteras, T., & Stepnick, L. (2006, January). *Patient-centered care for underserved populations: Definition and best practices* (White Paper, p. 6). Washington, DC: Economic and Social Research Institute.

of a PFCC family and visitor guidelines policy applicable to the entire organization to replace the traditional "restrictive" visitor policy. True culture change about family presence and visitation has occurred when hospital staff inquire who the patient would like to have present, and then make arrangements for family to stay with the patient, as desired.

Organizational culture includes not only the internal policies and functioning of the organization itself, but also the composition and culture of the community the organization serves. Many healthcare institutions, teaching hospitals, and health systems with vast resources have been successful in implementing PFCC, but organizations with limited resources, serving vulnerable and underserved populations, may face significant challenges. A study conducted by the Economic and Social Research Institute for the W. K. Kellogg Foundation found that certain populations, such as low-income individuals, uninsured persons, immigrants, racial and ethnic minorities, and the elderly face greater barriers to PFCC; and organizations that serve these populations face numerous barriers in pursuing PFCC (Silow-Carroll, Alteras, & Stepnick, 2006, p. 4). Some organizational barriers are listed in **TABLE 11.4**.

To help overcome these potential barriers to PFCC, Silow-Carroll et al. (2006) suggested a set of recommendations (outlined in **TABLE 11.5**) for implementing PFCC with underserved populations.

Table 11.5 depicts core components recommended by Silow-Carroll et al. (2006) for a comprehensive person- and family-centered approach, which can serve as a blueprint for leaders to successfully implement PFCC in underserved populations.

Clinician Engagement and Integration

Prior to implementation of PFCC, the clinical staff leadership must be engaged and begin orienting and integrating physicians and other healthcare professionals into the PFCC approach. Alignment between clinicians and hospital leaders is critical to the success of PFCC. Collaboration between providers and administration is essential when engaging in any assessment, planning (short-, long-, or midterm), implementation, or evaluation of the key components of PFCC.

TABLE 11.5 Core Components for PFCC in Underserved Populations

Welcoming environment	Provide physical space and initial interactions that are familiar and not intimidating.
Respect for personal values and expressed needs	■ Inquire about the person's care preferences and priorities. ■ Inform and involve individuals/families/caregivers in decision-making. ■ Individualize care. ■ Promote consistent, mutually respectful person–provider relationships.
Person empowerment or "activation"	Educate and encourage the person to expand health-related behaviors, self-management, and decision-making roles.
Sociocultural competence	■ Understand and consider culture, economic and educational status, health literacy level, family patterns/situation, and traditions (including alternative or folk remedies). ■ Communicate in language and at levels the person understands.
Coordination and integration of care	■ Assess the need for formal/informal services that impact health or treatment. ■ Provide team-based care/care management. ■ Advocate for the persons and their families. ■ Make appropriate referrals. ■ Ensure smooth transitions between providers and phases of care.
Comfort and support	Emphasize physical comfort, privacy, emotional support, and family/friends' involvement.
Access and navigation skills	Provide what the person considers a "medical home." Minimize waiting times. Provide convenient service hours. Promote access and flow for the individual. Help individuals attain better healthcare system navigation skills.
Community outreach	Make demonstrable, proactive efforts to understand and reach out to local communities.

Data from Silow-Carroll, S., Alteras, T., & Stepnick, L. (2006, January). Patient-centered care for underserved populations: Definition and best practices (White Paper, p. 6). Washington, DC: Economic and Social Research Institute.

Among the items that should be included in the orientation is the idea that all aspects of communication and decision-making should include the person and, with the person's approval, the family; be transparent; and be guided by clear expectations informed by mutual goals for improved personal care. PFCC leaders must value and keep open the lines of communication with clinicians' offices and clinics, provide education and knowledge to help clinicians achieve the mutual goal of enhancing the personal and family experience, and reward and recognize clinicians who adopt PFCC practices.

Hospital leadership and providers can also promote PFCC by collaborating with **Patient Family Advisors** (PFA) as they develop policies and procedures, and engage in healthcare organization operational decision-making and planning. PFAs are specially trained former patients and/or family members who, as partners with healthcare leadership, can counsel healthcare leaders on options for equipment, supplies, electronic health records, forms, educational materials, interior design, and signage, policies, and areas of improvement, which will enhance PFCC. Patient Family Advisory Councils (PFAC), with a balanced membership of clinical staff, administrative leadership, patients and their families, reflect partnership in co-design and shared decision-making for organizational improvement. The IPFCC has published a guidance document, *Tips for how to be an effective Patient or Family Advisor: A beginning list to help organizations develop the PFA role* (IPFCC, 2010). It is important for healthcare leaders to recognize that PFAs come to the table as patients and family members with complaints, concerns, problems, and ideas about how health care should be delivered from their perspective. It is critical to help convert patients or family members with complaints to advisors who can provide a catalogue of stories, based on their experiences, that can be used to teach and implement change. There are a number of organizations that provide PFA training to help patients and families move into the role, including IHI and IPFCC. PFCCpartners in Long Beach, CA has several excellent programs designed to provide PFAs with skills, role immersion, and leadership development. One such program, the PFA Core Competencies Training, was designed by PFAs for PFAs through the PFA Network, with input from over 600 PFAs across the nation. Its framework is based on building advisor skills up from the basics and the understanding that not everyone will enter this work with necessary competencies (see **TABLE 11.6**) in place. Learned skills and a clear role description can ease the person's development into the role of PFA.

TABLE 11.6 Core Competencies of PFAs	
Establishing partnerships	Present yourself as a partner; do not wait for the "invitation" but rather establish yourself as a willing, respectful partner in co-designing improvement.
Constructive collaboration	Present challenges and opportunities using strengths-based language. By doing so, you keep the door open to true collaboration. Recognize that true collaboration requires perspectives to differ before coming to a consensus. If you maintain respect during that phase of conflict, progress from consensus will come more quickly and have a greater impact.
Solution-focused	After a challenge or opportunity has been identified, move into co-designing solutions. Avoid getting "stuck" in restating the problem over and over. If you need to add details, make sure the details add information to the discussion.

(continues)

TABLE 11.6 Core Competencies of PFAs	*(continued)*
Representative voice	In the role of advisor, you will share your own experiences in the context of the agenda item; however, it is important to balance that opportunity with your responsibility to represent not only your own perspective, but that of other patients and families in your scope and environment.
Teachable spirit	Acknowledge that health care is hard work; respect the expertise of others and recognize that there is much you and I do not know about one another's experiences. Be open to new understanding.

Reproduced with permission from Libby Hoy. Core Competencies Talking Points: Core Competencies Training for PFAs, PFCCpartners, Long Beach, CA (2018).

PFCC implementation challenges for clinicians may include:

- The shift from provider-centric to person-centric mindset and approach.
- The shift from pay-for-service to pay-for-performance.
- The inability to make necessary changes due to declining reimbursement and dwindling net revenue, with fewer liquid resources available to hire staff, fund marketing, and maintain practice operations.
- Higher reliance on evidence-based care and regulatory and healthcare reform requirements for PFCC, including from the Joint Commission, the Centers for Medicare and Medicaid Services, and the federal government.
- Affirming the value of clinician and hospital leadership interdependence. However, when both stakeholders share common goals and objectives to improve quality and cost-effectiveness of care, it can be a win–win for both clinicians and hospitals. The development of contracts and healthcare frameworks that can address current and future demands of ongoing healthcare reform can be helpful in this process. In a successful PFCC model, hospitals and clinicians are aligned on the approach to the provision of personal care, and the person's perception of care is thereby improved. Successful alignment between clinicians and hospital leaders results in more effective decision-making, less competition, improved personal and family loyalty and satisfaction, and a higher-quality inter-professional experience.

▶ Partnership with the Person, Their Family, and Communities

Atlas, Grant, Ferris, Chang, and Barry (2009) determined that patients' satisfaction with their health care was not tied to the technical quality of their care, but rather to the quality of communication with their provider, a critical component of the PFCC model. A key driver of overall personal (and family) satisfaction is effective physician communication, with 61% of the variability in patient (and family) satisfaction tied to physician behaviors (Resnick et al., 2008). More than any other group, physicians influence the person's perception of care. Information exchange between providers and individuals can be enhanced by partnering with family members to ensure accurate personal interpretation of information and education, obtain customer feedback, and promote patient adherence to treatment recommendations, which are instrumental to the person's healing and recovery.

One of the essential precepts in PFCC is the tenet that the person and their family (as determined by the person) are true partners in care, decision-making, and setting policy at the individual, organizational, and community level. (Refer to the Four Concepts of PFCC featured in Table 11.1.) Healthcare leaders must serve as role models to inspire healthcare professionals to engage each person as an individual as well as to listen to the collective voice of the person and family.

Personal and family partnerships may take the form of:

- Partnership in the processes of the patient's assessment, planning and delivery of their care, treatment, and necessary support.
- Partnership in advisory roles for the healthcare organization.
- Partnership in hiring, training, and evaluating clinicians.
- Partnership in leading local and larger-scale advocacy efforts (see **TABLE 11.7**).

A stellar example of the reach that PFAs have in co-designing and improving healthcare delivery is HealthInsight, a Quality Improvement Organization (QIO) serving four states—Oregon, Utah, Nevada, and New Mexico. The PFACs educated hundreds of people about diabetes self-management, increased flu vaccination in communities, and wrote proposals to promote behavioral health and immunization access and procure resources, to name a few initiatives (HealthInsight, 2018).

Healthcare leaders working with persons and their families have begun to address social determinants of health, integral to improving health outcomes for individuals, families, and the community. The Social Determinants of Health topic area within Healthy People 2020 has been designed to identify ways to create social and physical environments that promote good health for all. All Americans deserve an equal opportunity to make the choices that lead to good health. But to ensure that all Americans have that opportunity, advances are needed not only in health care, but also in fields such as education, childcare, housing, business, law, media, community planning, transportation, and agriculture (Healthy People 2020 [2018]). Strategies include using community health workers to visit patients' homes and identify issues with transportation, nutrition, hunger, and safety; technical innovations and healthcare applications to track disease processes and address symptoms in real time; automated telephone and online supply delivery systems; and mobile health services.

According to Larry Kaiser, M.D., president and CEO of the Temple University Health System in Philadelphia; for care to truly be person centered, it is imperative to know one's patient population. Community-based organizations that understand the value of person-centered care are also improving the health of cities and states. The Church Health Center in Memphis, Tennessee is one such organization. Founded by Dr. G. Scott Morris, a primary care physician and ordained Methodist minister, this community clinic created a health ministry for the working poor. Starting with one doctor and one nurse, they saw 12 patients on the first day; and now provide health care for more than 55,000 people. Their organization offers an integrated network of specialists, support services with hundreds of volunteers,

TABLE 11.7 Form of Partnership and Strategies for Partnership with Person and Families

Form of Partnership	Strategies for Partnership
Partnership in the processes of person assessment and in planning person care and treatment	The family provides input into the individual's assessment and, together with clinicians, plans care collaboratively. The person and family attend care-planning conferences (more commonly seen in long-term care, behavioral health, and rehabilitation programs, but becoming more common in critical care and the medical/surgical areas). Family members participate in physician and multidisciplinary rounds with the person. A family support person (family caregiver and/or family spokesperson) is identified on admission and actively participates throughout the care episode. The person and authorized family members have access to information in their health record and can contribute their own observations verbally or in writing. Sharing medical records through electronic Patient Portals and OpenNotes® online access to medical records. Family members participate with the person during nursing bedside shift report. The family interfaces with all of the person's providers during transitions of care. The family and important community members participate in care at home and community health and wellness initiatives.
Partnership in organizational and advisory roles	The person and family provide feedback on the care experience through a variety of mechanisms (during rounds by executives and other leaders on persons and families, in post-discharge satisfaction surveys, in family feedback sessions, in focus groups, etc.). The person and family members are placed in the formal role of PFAs (paid or unpaid). The person and family members participate on Advisory Councils at the departmental and organizational level. The person and family members serve as designers, editors, and advisors for educational materials in which health literacy and cultural competence is involved. The person and family members participate in creative supportive roles such as compassionate listener, peer advocate, and peer navigator.

	The person and family members provide input on the environment and architectural design of healthcare facilities (e.g., informally, by completing a "noise at night" feedback survey during hospitalization or, formally, by serving on facility design teams).
	The person and family members provide input into the development and revision of policies and processes; policies are written from the perspective that individuals and families are partners.
	The person and family members fully participate as equal members of key organizational committees, teams or councils at the departmental, organizational, and governing board levels (e.g., quality and patient safety committees).
Partnership in hiring, educating, and evaluating clinicians	The person and family members provide input into the design of behavioral interviewing questions and participate in the interview process for recruiting and hiring new clinicians and PFAs, to ensure individuals with person- and family-centered attributes are hired.
	The person and family members act as adjunct faculty to teach physicians and clinical staff about PFCC and participate in curriculum design for hospital-associated nursing and medical schools and other health professions training.
	The person and family members provide feedback on important aspects of care, and leaders actively seek feedback about the effectiveness and person-family-centeredness of the care provided. This feedback informs the criteria for clinician position descriptions, coaching, and performance evaluations.
	Individuals and their families are incorporated into orientation programs for new hires and medical staff.
Partnership in leading advocacy efforts	The person and family members participate on national healthcare advisory councils, Hospital Improvement Innovation Networks (HIIN), Quality Improvement Networks (QIN), and Quality Improvement Organizations (QIO).
	Persons and their families, along with organizational leaders, participate in national efforts, such as PFANetwork, Partnership for Patients (PFP), and Patient Family Engagement Learning events.
	Individuals participate in collective roles, such as members of local governing boards resulting from merger and acquisition (M&A) transactions.
	Persons and families with healthcare leaders contribute to health systems' focus on social determinants of health.

Data from Knighten, M.L. Swimlane Flow Chart: House-wide, Departmental Specfic & Council Driven PFCC Strategies. 2011.

a wellness center with educational modalities, and an industrial kitchen to teach healthy cooking (and sell delicious healthy baked goods, with proceeds cycled back into community services). The Church Health Center is changing Memphis by empowering people to own their health and then contribute to their community to improve the health of their neighbors.

Summary

Transforming an organization from a provider-centric and hospital-convenient care delivery approach to a PFCC model and person-centered focus beyond an organization's walls requires its leaders to form new partnerships with individuals, families, clinicians, and other staff, as well as internal and external stakeholders. Person- and family-centered healthcare leaders create and promote a culture based on collaboration between health professionals, healthcare organizations, and persons with their families to promote mutual learning and shared accountability, co-design healthcare improvements, and achieve key outcomes for quality of care.

Discussion Questions

1. What are the implications of shifting care delivery strategies for the workforce from provider-centric to PFCC?
2. Describe ways to effectively prepare a workforce to operate in a changing care delivery context.
3. What does a partnership between healthcare leaders, providers, individuals, and families look like?
4. In what ways might PFCC introduce additional internal dynamics and support requirements that need to be met?
5. How do we as healthcare leaders model collaboration with the person and family?
6. How does PFCC extrapolate vision, strategies, and actions beyond organizational walls to impact community health?

🔎 CASE STUDY: A Values-Based Approach

As a result of changing local, state, and national economic and societal circumstances, leaders of acute care hospitals face complex concerns. Although financial and quality outcomes are critical benchmarks for successful leaders, leaders must also focus on how to empower individuals and families to make personal healthcare decisions, better prepare them to prevent illness, and manage chronic conditions and diseases. For this reason, St. Francis Medical Center (SFMC), an urban, formerly faith-based (Catholic) organization used as an example in this chapter, elected to use PFCC as its care delivery model in 2010. SFMC's goal is, over time, to improve the health of the general population in its economically depressed and underserved community.

As a component of its healthcare reform strategy, SFMC utilized *Accountable Care Organization (ACO)* structures and incentive-generated healthcare reform programs. An ACO is defined as an entity in which healthcare providers are jointly held accountable for achieving measured quality improvements and reductions in the rate of spending growth for services. While caring for a defined population, the ACO should achieve overall cost and quality improvements per capita. ACOs may involve a variety of provider configurations—that is, integrated delivery systems, primary care medical groups, hospital-based systems, virtual networks such as integrated practice associations and community-based organizations. All ACOs, however, have a strong basis in primary care, and hospitals are encouraged to participate in ACOs to provide a breadth of healthcare options (McClellan, McKethan, Lewis, Roski, & Fisher, 2010). Partnerships with the person, family, and community healthcare providers are essential for a hospital to be able to provide a full range of care to its clients.

SFMC, founded on the values of Saint Vincent de Paul, Saint Louise de Marillac, and Saint Elizabeth Ann Seton, created a **professional practice model** based on the Vincentian values: simplicity, respect, compassionate care, advocacy for the poor, and inventiveness to infinity. This professional practice model (i.e., a practice system that included specific structures, processes, and values) supported registered nurse control over the delivery of nursing care and the environment in which the nursing care was delivered (Hoffart & Woods, 1996). This model was named VVOOM, an acronym for "Vincentian Values Optimizing Our Mission" (**FIGURE 11.2**).

In December 2015, the health system underwent a merger and acquisition (M&A) transaction, which included new sponsors, and became a community hospital with no faith-based affiliation, with new system leadership and with new mission and values statements. This necessitated a change in the values-based professional practice model to depict "Verity" Values Optimizing Our Mission (VVOOM). Verity Health System worked to build upon the rich legacy left by the Daughters of Charity Health System through a transformation of healthcare practices. That work included a focus on more efficient delivery of quality health care and an enhanced alignment with the system's physician partners. The ultimate goal was to position SFMC and the Verity hospitals to serve their communities for generations to come, to engage their workforce in meaningful ways and to align professional staff in those efforts. The current strategic focus is on

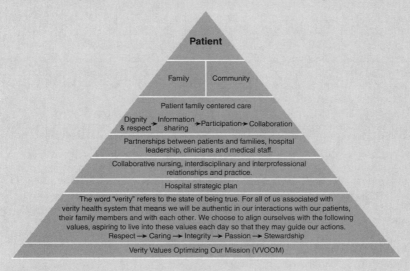

FIGURE 11.2 "VVOOM" Values-Based Professional Practice Model

Reproduced from the St. Francis Medical Center. (2018). Plan for the Provision of Care. Lynwood, CA.

(continues)

implementing sound business practices, while providing compassionate care, building new clinical programs with physician partners, and engaging community supporters.

The word "verity" refers to the state of being true. For all associated with the Verity Health System, their organization's name promotes the expectation of authenticity in interactions with patients, their family members, and with each other. The following values are lived each day by Verity employees and guide their professional practice.

Respect

The hospital demonstrates the value for others and themselves through words and actions.

Caring

The hospital provides patients and their families with compassionate, quality care, treating them and each other with kindness.

Integrity

The hospital and its staff act with honesty and transparency and do the right thing.

Passion

The hospital is dedicated to making a difference in the health of our communities and in the lives of those we serve.

Stewardship

The hospital is committed to being a wise steward of resources, creative in the approach to challenges and opportunities, and accountable for the results achieved as a charitable organization.

Servant Leadership

SFMC for many years had promoted the concept of servant leadership… being a servant for the greater good of the people served, as well being effective stewards of the hospital's resources and relationships. According to the model's founder, Robert K. Greenleaf (1976, p. 9): "Caring for persons, the more able and the less able serving each other, is the rock upon which a good society is built… if a better society is to be built, one that is more just and more loving, that provides greater creative opportunity for its people, then the most open course is to raise both the capacity to serve and the very performance as servant of leaders and existing major institutions."

Servant leadership is a model that is conducive to PFCC and complements the four key components of dignity and respect, information sharing, participation, and collaboration, which are the foundation of the VVOOM model's structure. By serving all clients and customers, the staff of SFMC placed the person and family at the heart of the plan of care and humbly provided support and assistance with the management of their recuperation and healthcare needs. This has been particularly important, in light of the Kellogg Foundation research, since SFMC's primary and secondary service areas have been in the two most economically challenged and underserved Service Planning Areas (SPAs) in Los Angeles County.

Values Congruency

SFMC leaders believed it was important to assess whether the internal/personal values of those entrusted to promote and model Vincentian (and now Verity) culture were congruent with those of the organization. Nursing research was conducted, and congruency of nursing personal values with Vincentian values was evaluated (Quaye, 2009).

Using the concept of managing by values can enhance organizational effectiveness for organizations that face increasing complexity, competitive challenge, and a high rate of change (Blanchard & O'Connor, 1997). However, SFMC needed a professional practice model based on "caring by values" versus "managing by values." According to Covey (1990), one cannot transform an organization into a total quality culture unless and until basic habits of personal character and interpersonal relations based on principles (values) are built within the workforce.

Building the foundation to make a culture change was dependent on first creating VVOOM to support PFCC delivery. Then, leadership and management at all organizational levels, including the governing board, executive leadership, department directors, unit managers, and clinicians, participated in the planning, design, and implementation of both the professional practice model and the care delivery model. Hospital leaders added PFCC to the hospital's strategic plan and the nursing strategic plan. PFCC became the fundamental approach for a key area of the SFMC strategic plan: "Excellence, Consistency & Sustainability," defined as consistent and sustainable top performance, top 10% performance, and **top box achievement** across the areas of personal safety, quality, service (patient and family experience), and financial indicators through a balance of systematic approaches and innovation (SFMC, 2010).

■ Simultaneously with the Patient Care Service Division's defining and designing the professional and care delivery models, SFMC also participated in Premier Healthcare Alliance's national collaborative: "QUEST," a program for quality, evidence-based medicine, cost efficiency, and mortality reduction (May, 2011). SFMC met or exceeded clinical quality and cost benchmarks for mortality, CMS core measures, and cost per adjusted discharge, and was designated a top performer in 2010 among 157 non-profit hospitals. SFMC continued to achieve awards and recognition for top quality performance, including but not limited to:
  • Achieved 100% of ST-Elevation Myocardial Infarction (STEMI) procedures with door-to-needle times in 90 minutes or less, since inception of STEMI program.
  • Achieved quality awards: TJC top performer for core measures, Patient Safety First for reducing *C. difficile*, and decreased risk-adjusted mortality to 0.69, exceeding Premier top performance threshold (2016–2017).
  • Achieved UNICEF/WHO Baby Friendly® certification in October 2014.
  • Achieved American Heart Association/American Stroke Association repeated recognition for Get With the Guidelines®–Stroke Gold Plus Achievement Award and in 2018 Target: Stroke Honor Roll Elite.

Many individual and family approaches became a part of the SFMC initiatives to improve outcomes. Among them were person- and family-initiated rapid-response teams. Specific interventions and standardized bundles of care were implemented, and persons and families were encouraged to partner and participate with SFMC healthcare professionals. As utilization of evidence-based care increased, mortality rates declined. Education and communication were also key drivers among the individuals, families, and multidisciplinary team to ensure an appropriate level of care and length of stay in preparation for the transition to home/community.

The management team identified key departmental/hospital policies and procedures that needed revision in order to support the goals of PFCC as well as to design department-specific tactics that would improve the personal experience. The chief nursing officer (CNO) used the PFCC approach to uphold the mission, identifying leadership and management competencies, defining strategies, and prioritizing tactics (**FIGURE 11.3**).

(continues)

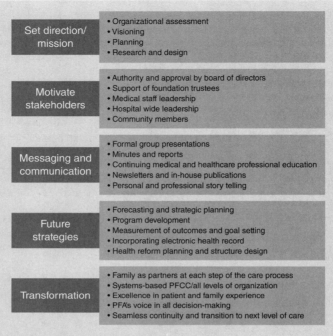

Set direction/ mission
- Organizational assessment
- Visioning
- Planning
- Research and design

Motivate stakeholders
- Authority and approval by board of directors
- Support of foundation trustees
- Medical staff leadership
- Hospital wide leadership
- Community members

Messaging and communication
- Formal group presentations
- Minutes and reports
- Continuing medical and healthcare professional education
- Newsletters and in-house publications
- Personal and professional story telling

Future strategies
- Forecasting and strategic planning
- Program development
- Measurement of outcomes and goal setting
- Incorporating electronic health record
- Health reform planning and structure design

Transformation
- Family as partners at each step of the care process
- Systems-based PFCC/all levels of organization
- Excellence in patient and family experience
- PFA's voice in all decision-making
- Seamless continuity and transition to next level of care

FIGURE 11.3 PFCC Leadership Competencies

The directors and managers at the point of service were charged with specific tasks and actions, such as coordinating staffing, coordinating and supervising internal and patient/family communications, and holding personnel accountable to perform in alignment with leadership's vision and the mission (**FIGURE 11.4**).

Demonstrated outcomes for the SFMC PFCC process during the specified interval included the following:

- The establishment of the role of Patient Family Advisor on high-level quality and safety committees and task groups.
- Input from patients and families on hospital design, signage, and brochures.
- Establishing a Patient Family Advisory Council.
- Revising visitation policies that welcomed family to be present and a part of the patient's care, as defined by the patient.
- Preparing Patient Family Advisors to assume local governing board positions to represent the community and ensure accountability to the attorney general's conditions of the M&A.
- The partnership between hospital leadership and patient/family leaders achieved 75% of the goals set in the original strategic plan.

Case Study Discussion Questions
1. How could SFMC obtain input or feedback from individuals and their families?
2. How could employees at all levels of SFMC be guided and facilitated to engage in constructive, open dialogue regarding necessary capabilities and skills to partner with persons and families in health care?
3. In what ways could a PFCC model help to mitigate the healthcare reform pressures SFMC faced?

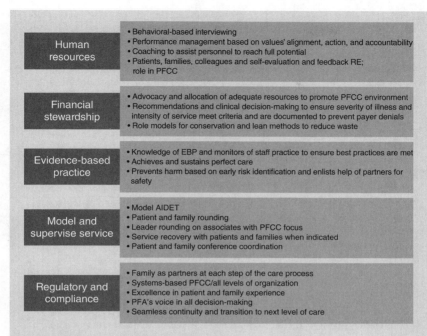

Human resources	• Behavioral-based interviewing • Performance management based on values' alignment, action, and accountability • Coaching to assist personnel to reach full potential • Patients, families, colleagues and self-evaluation and feedback RE; role in PFCC
Financial stewardship	• Advocacy and allocation of adequate resources to promote PFCC environment • Recommendations and clinical decision-making to ensure severity of illness and intensity of service meet criteria and are documented to prevent payer denials • Role models for conservation and lean methods to reduce waste
Evidence-based practice	• Knowledge of EBP and monitors of staff practice to ensure best practices are met • Achieves and sustains perfect care • Prevents harm based on early risk identification and enlists help of partners for safety
Model and supervise service	• Model AIDET • Patient and family rounding • Leader rounding on associates with PFCC focus • Service recovery with patients and families when indicated • Patient and family conference coordination
Regulatory and compliance	• Family as partners at each step of the care process • Systems-based PFCC/all levels of organization • Excellence in patient and family experience • PFA's voice in all decision-making • Seamless continuity and transition to next level of care

FIGURE 11.4 PFCC Management Competencies

4. Given the changing nature of healthcare delivery in hospitals, what are the training and workforce development implications for an organization such as SFMC that have adopted a servant leadership approach?

🔍 CASE STUDY: Home Person- and Family-Centered Assessment

Today in the United States, there is a growing emphasis for healthcare professionals to work along a full continuum of care for individuals and families. In that model, PFCC extends beyond the hospital. From the perspective of Bowen's family system theory, the family is organized as a whole, but composed of individuals whereby one affects the other (1974). By recognizing the family in this context, the family can be instrumental in partnering with the provider and person during the assessment, plan of care, support and treatment process. The concept of family as a system reinforces the value of the family's role in adaptation to internal and external stressors created by change. For example, in the Screening, Brief Intervention, Referral and Treatment (SBIRT), related to alcohol use (Titelman, 2003), the family can play a role in providing support for referral and treatment.

An innovative nursing leader pursued and received a grant from the Substance Abuse Mental Health Administration (SAMHSA) to design and implement a university–community partnership for teaching students, clinicians, and healthcare providers to appropriately assess and refer persons and families for alcohol and substance use. The program was designed to address the need for change at the project (student

(continues)

assignment), micro- (nursing curriculum), and meso-system (university interprofessional courses) levels, and had the potential to disrupt healthcare delivery at the macro-system level in the county by enlisting community front-line providers. (Refer to Figure 11.1.) The interprofessional training grant included human services, nursing, and social work students. SBIRT content was integrated into each discipline's curriculum. The nursing practicum for the training was in the undergraduate community health section.

In the following case study (names were changed to protect privacy), a nursing student and their clinical faculty demonstrate how screening for alcohol and substance use and/or misuse was completed with one individual during a family assessment conducted in the home setting. The interview included obtaining information from the person related to her family history and significant relationships from her past and current status. A genogram, similar to a family tree, was developed to provide a visual depiction of the family history. The overview of a family is typically limited to three generations and often identifies hidden patterns that later can be used by the person to develop strategies for behavioral change (Friedman and Allen, 2011). Genograms are standard tools for clinical social workers, but with more inter-professional collaboration in community-based treatment, they are being adopted by other healthcare disciplines in current PFCC settings. Therefore, it is useful for person- and family-centered leadership to share a common language and understanding of the purpose of evolving skills, tools, and clinical methods.

Additionally, an ecogram that defined the person's current social context was created by depicting circles that represented key factors that affected the person as well as identifying other interfacing systems. The person can then identify the nature and direction of the flow of energy between the identified area and themselves. According to Friedman and Allen (2004), the person can then develop a better understanding of his or her situation and ultimately develop strategies for resolving the issue at hand.

The SBIRT process is a reliable evidence-based practice that employs the Alcohol Use Disorders Identification Test (AUDIT) tool (Saunders et al., 1993). Screening for alcohol/drug abuse is a sensitive subject, but with the help of a self-assessment tool, the nurse can ease into a conversation about how the person's score compares to the general population, and then partner with the individual (and family) to create self-identified goals for behavioral change. The Public Health Nurse (PHN) can also provide additional resources to support the person and the family. Since the PHN has a role in the community, this approach has successfully improved population health to aid in prevention and/or early detection of alcoholism and substance use disorder. Including the person's family and her boyfriend in the assessment increases the likelihood for success of early intervention by incorporating a family systems approach.

A family assessment that is person-family centered is conducted in the home in the community. The individual, Sylvia Sanchez (SS), is a 25-year-old Hispanic female, a full-time student who works part-time providing administrative support to a non-profit organization. She lives with her boyfriend in a one-bedroom apartment located in a middle-class neighborhood. She is Roman Catholic. The family part of this assessment includes her 79-year-old grandmother, deceased grandfather, deceased mother, 60-year-old father, 27-year-old sister, 35-year-old sister, and live-in boyfriend in the genogram shown in **FIGURE 11.5**.

The ecogram shown in **FIGURE 11.6** depicts the nature of the relationships between SS, her family members, and boyfriend.

During the home visits over the past few years, SS showed signs of alcohol dependency. The nurse was able to see beer cans that SS had attempted to hide on the

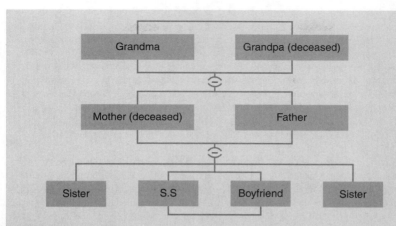

FIGURE 11.5 Genogram

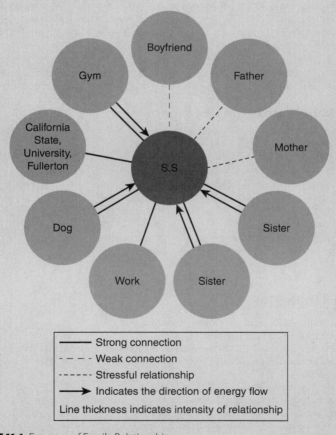

FIGURE 11.6 Ecogram of Family Relationships

side of her bed. SS lost her mother suddenly 6 weeks after she turned 18 years old. The nurse's suspicion was that, as a result of her loss, she had not adequately grieved, and for the past 7 years she had used alcohol as a coping mechanism. SS was willing to fill out an alcohol screening tool that would compare her drinking to that of the general population. In completing the psycho-social part of the interview, it was revealed that SS had fairly good support from her family, friends, and the school. Sylvia reported that her family support needs were met, but were not often utilized. She also emphasized that her finances were in order, and she used the gym to relieve her stress.

Needs she self-identified as unmet included spiritual, health, and social needs. She tended to isolate herself and spent too much time alone. In further discussion, SS was able to share the strengths in her life. She is nearly finished with her business degree, has a reliable and stable place to live and work, and has a great pet who comforts her. She is able to identify social support, but has not always followed through on social interactions.

The areas in which SS needed help were identified via the SBIRT assessment process. SS scored 17, which placed her in the level 3 harmful category. She identified her boyfriend as co-dependent and was aware that he thought it was okay for her to drink to suppress her feelings. She also had a poor diet. When performing the family assessment, the PHN noticed that the major problems in this family were health problems related to drinking. Her father and mother both had a history of alcoholism, which has greatly influenced her past, current, and future life plans. At times, meals were replaced with alcohol. Additionally, SS also shared that recently she had had blood work done and the doctor had ordered a repeat lab panel because her liver enzymes were elevated. Although SS was aware of the abnormal lab results, throughout the interview she continued to make it clear that she believed she did not have a problem, until her scores were reviewed with her by the PHN.

Case Study Discussion Questions

1. What are the primary social determinants of health relevant for this person and her family?
2. Describe how you would inform and educate SS and her family members about the risks of excessive alcohol consumption.
3. What type of healthy behaviors and reinforcement of her personal values would you review with SS that would reduce risky behaviors?
4. What is one physical problem SS will need to follow up on as a measure of continued progress?
5. What, if any, opportunities does SS have to move beyond her personal needs to contribute to the health of her family and/or community?

Related Websites

Agency for Healthcare Research and Quality: www.ahrq.gov
American Hospital Association: www.aha.org
American Institute of Research (AIR) Patient Family Engagement Council: https://pfccpartners.com/american-institute-of-research-air-patient-family-engagement-council/ Family Voices: www.familyvoices.org
HealthInsight: HealthInsight.org
Institute for Healthcare Improvement: www.ihi.org
Institute for Patient-Family-Centered Care: www.ipfcc.org
Partnership for Patients: https://partnershipforpatients.cms.gov/
Patient-Centered Outcomes Research Institute: www.pcori.org/
PFCC Connect: https://pfcc.connect.ipfcc.org/home
PFCC Partners: www.pfccpartners.com

Planetree: www.planetree.org
Picker Institute: www.pickerinstitute.org
Screening, Brief Intervention, Referral and Treatment (SBIRT): www.samhsa.gov/sbirt
Substance Abuse Mental Health Services Administration (SAMHSA): www.samhsa.gov
The Joint Commission: http://jointcommission.org
The Schwartz Center for Compassionate Healthcare: www.theschwartzcenter.org
World Café: http://www.theworldcafe.com/key-concepts-resources/world-cafe-method/

Additional Resources

Advancing Effective Communication, Cultural Competence, and Patient- Family-Centered Care: A Roadmap for Hospitals Advancing the Practice of Patient- and Family-Centered Care: A Road Map for Hospitals: https://www.jointcommission.org/assets/1/6/ARoadmapforHospitals finalversion727.pdf

The Family as Patient Care Partner: Leveraging Family Involvement to Improve Quality, Safety and Satisfaction: www.advisory.com/Research/Nursing-Executive-Center/Studies/2006/The-Family -as-Patient-Care-PartnerGateways to PFAC Learning: https://pfccpartners.com/gateways -program/

National Academy of Medicine Guiding Framework for Person Family Engaged Care: https:// nam.edu/harnessing-evidence-and-experience-to-change-culture-a-guiding-framework-for -patient-and-family-engaged-care/

Open Notes: https://www.opennotes.org/

The Orange County Health Care Community SBIRT Program: http://sbirt.fullerton.edu

Patient-Centered Care Improvement Guide: www.patient-centeredcare.org

SBIRT AUDIT tool: http://pubs.niaaa.nih.gov/publications/Practitioner/pocketguide/pocket _guide2.htm

Strategies for Leadership: Patient- and Family-Centered Care: www.aha.org

References

AARP. (2018). New state law to help family caregivers. Retrieved from https://www.aarp.org /politics-society/advocacy/caregiving-advocacy/info-2014/aarp-creates-model-state-bill.html

About healthcare service co-design. Retrieved from www.healthcodesign.org.nz/about.html

American College of Physicians. (2018). What is the patient-centered medical home? Retrieved from https://www.acponline.org/practice-resources/business/payment/models/pcmh/understanding /what-pcmh

Atlas, S. J., Grant, R. W., Ferris, T. G., Chang, Y., & Barry, M. J. (2009, March 3). Patient-physician connectedness and quality of primary care. *Annals of Internal Medicine, 150*(5), 325–335.

Balik, B., Conway, J., Zipperer, L., & Watson, J. (2011). *Achieving and exceptional patient and family experience of inpatient hospital care* [IHI Innovation Series White Paper]. Retrieved from http://www.ihi.org/resources/Pages/IHIWhitePapers/AchievingExceptional PatientFamilyExperienceInpatientHospitalCareWhitePaper.aspx

Blanchard, K., & O'Connor, M. (1997). *Managing by values*. San Francisco, CA: Berrett-Koehler.

Bowen, M. (1974). Alcoholism as viewed through family systems theory and family psychotherapy. *Annals of the New York Academy of Sciences, 233*(1), 115–122.

CAHPS: Assessing health care quality for the patient's perspective. (2016, March). *Agency for healthcare research and quality*. Rockville, MD. Retrieved from www.ahrq.gov/cahps/about -cahps/cahps-program/cahps_brief.html

Centers for Medicare and Medicaid Services (CMS). (2010, November 19). *Federal register rules and regulations, final rule. Medicare and Medicaid programs: Changes to the hospital and critical access hospital conditions of participation to ensure visitation rights for all patients* (Federal Register/Vol. 75, No. 223). Washington, DC: U.S. Government Printing Office.

Chew, S., Brewster, L., Tarrant, C., Martin, G., & Armstrong, N. (2017). Fidelity of flexibility: An ethnographic study of the implementation and use of the patient activation measure. *Patient Education and Counseling*. Elsevier, Ireland. doi:10.101.pec.2017.12.012

Conway, J., Johnson, B., Edgman-Levitan, S., Schlucter, J., Ford, D., Sodomka, P., & Simmons, L. (2006). *Partnering with patients and families to design a patient- and family-centered health care system: A roadmap for the future: A work in progress.* Retrieved from www.ihi.org/knowledge /pages/publications/partneringwithPatientsandfamilies.aspx

Covey, S. R. (1990). *Principle-centered leadership.* New York, NY: Free Press.

Digioia, A., & Shapiro, E. (2017). *The patient centered value system: Transforming healthcare through co-design.* Boca Raton, FL: Productivity Press. ISBN: 9781138055964.

Feeley, D. (2017). *What health care leaders need to know about patient centered co-design.* Retrieved from www.ihi.org/communities

Friedman, B. D., & Allen, K. N. (2004). Systems theory. In J.B. Brandell (Ed.), *Treatment and practice in clinical social work,* (1st ed.), Los Angeles, CA: SAGE.

Friedman, B. D., & Allen, K. N. (2011). Systems theory. In J.B. Brandell (Ed.), *Treatment and practice in clinical social work,* (2nd ed.), Los Angeles, CA: SAGE.

Greenleaf, R. K. (1976). *The institution as servant.* Indianapolis, IN: Robert K. Greenleaf Center.

HCAHPS. (2005). Retrieved from www.hcahpsonline.org/home.aspx

Health Policy Brief-Patient Engagement. (2013, February 14). Health affairs. doi:10.1377 /hpb2013214.898775

HealthInsight. (2018). *Patient and family advisory councils at HealthInsight.* Retrieved from www .youtube.com/watch?v=C3qLz8M6fe0

Healthy People 2020. (2018, April 13). *Social determinants of health.* Retrieved from www .healthypeople.gov/2020/topics-objectives/topic/social-determinants-of-health

HHS. (2011). *Partnership for patients: Better care, lower costs.* Retrieved from www.healthcare.gov /compare/partnership-for-Persons/

Hoffart, N., & Woods, C. Q. (1996, November/December). Elements of a nursing professional practice model. *Journal of Professional Nursing, 12*(6), 354–384.

Hoy, L. (2018). *Core competencies talking points: Core competencies training for PFAs.* Long Beach, CA: PFCCpartners.

Institute for Patient- and Family-Centered Care (IPFCC). (2010). *Patient- and family-centered care: A hospital self-assessment inventory.* Retrieved from www.aha.org/content/00-10/assessment .pdf

Johnson, B., Abraham, M., Conway, J., Simmons, L., Edgman-Levitan, S., Sodomka, P., … Ford, F. (April 2008). *Partnering with patients and families to design a patient-and-family centered health care system: Recommendations and promising practices.* Bethesda, MD: Institute for Patient-and -Family Centered Care and Institute for Healthcare Improvement.

The Joint Commission (TJC). (2010). *Advancing effective communication, cultural competence and patient- and family-centered care: A roadmap for hospitals.* Retrieved from www.jointcommission. org/assets/1/6/ARoadmapforHospitalsfinalversion727.pdf

Koh, H. K., Brach, C., Harris, L. M., & Parchman, M. L. (2013, February). A proposed 'Health Literate Care Model' would constitute a systems approach to improving patients' engagement in care. *Health Affairs, 32*(2), 357–367. doi:10.137/hlthaff.2012.1205

May, E. L. (2011, March/April). The efficient healthcare organization: Creating a new standard in healthcare. *Healthcare Executive, 26*(2), 14–24.

McClellan, M., McKethan, A. N., Lewis, J. L., Roski, J., & Fisher, E. S. (2010, May). A national strategy to put accountable care into practice. *Health Affairs, 29*(5), 982–990.

National Academies Press. (2001). *Crossing the quality chasm: A new health system for the 21st century.* Washington, DC.

Nelson, E. C., Batalden, P. B., & Godfrey, M. M. (2007). *Quality by design: A clinical microsystems approach.* San Francisco, CA: Jossey-Bass.

Patient- and family-centered care organizational self-assessment tool. (2013). Institute for Healthcare Improvement & National Institute for Children's Health Quality. Retrieved from IHI.org

Patient Protection and Affordable Care Act. (2010). 42 U.S.C δ 18001 et seq.

Quaye, B. (2009). Dissertation: Pepperdine University. An evaluation of congruency of nursing staff values and organizational values.

Resnick, A. S., Disbot, M., Wurster, A., Mullen, J. L., Kaiser, L. R., & Morris, J. B. (2008). Contributions of surgical residents to patient satisfaction: Impact of residents beyond clinical care. *Journal of Surgical Education, 65*(3), 243–252.

Robert Wood Johnson Foundation (RWJF). (2010, September 14). Patient-centered medical homes. *Health Affairs,* 1–6. doi:10.1377/hpb2010.17

Saunders, J. B., Aasland, O. G., Babor, T. F., De La Fuente, & Grant, M. (1993). Development of the alcohol use disorders identification audit: WHO collaborative project on early detection of persons with harmful alcohol consumption. *Addiction, 88,* 791–804.

Silow-Carroll, S., Alteras, T., & Stepnick, L. (2006, January). *Patient-centered care for underserved populations: Definition and best practices* [White paper]. Washington, DC: Economic and Social Research Institute.

St. Francis Medical Center (SFMC). (2010). SFMC strategic plan: "Excellence, Consistency & Sustainability. Lynwood, CA.

Titelman, P. (2003). *Emotional cutoff: Bowen family systems theory perspectives.* New York: Haworth Clinical Practice Press.

Van Citters, A. (2017). Experience-based co-design of health care services. Cambridge, MA: Institute for Healthcare Improvement. Retrieved from ihi.org

CHAPTER 12

Financial Considerations for Healthcare Leaders

Linda J. Gunn and John A. Orsini

LEARNING OBJECTIVES

By the end of this chapter, the student will be able to:

- Explain the importance of financial management in health care.
- Identify the components of effective financial management.
- Describe financial management models utilized in the healthcare industry.
- Discuss the financial implications of healthcare reform initiatives.

KEY TERMS

Benchmarking
Financial management
Healthcare reform

Key drivers
Management models
Performance reporting

▶ Introduction

Healthcare facilities are rapidly growing and expanding. To ensure the sustainability and viability of their healthcare institutions, healthcare leaders must understand how to utilize financial information to make the best decisions regarding their institutions' financial management.

Financial Management Considerations

Financial management is vital to healthcare organizations' success. Financial management combines strategic and operational elements that allow healthcare leaders to develop, invest in, and implement effective and sustainable business models for their organizations. Intuition and professional experiences clearly inspire leadership vision. But by analyzing past and present financial performance and using those data and assessments to inform future projections and scenarios, leaders can reduce risks and maximize opportunities for successful achievement of the mission, goals, and objectives of their organizations.

▶ Measure and Monitor Key Drivers

Key drivers are factors that influence and direct the outcome of a process, mission, program, or strategic plan. Key drivers can be used to identify the steps to be taken toward the organization's goals and objectives and the data to be collected to assess effective performance and progress. Each industry has refined its key drivers, which are available from industry associations or rating agency reports and analyses. From these industry sources, healthcare leaders should select "the vital few" drivers that are most relevant to their operations and monitor those indicators on a regular basis. Following too many indicators, or measuring drivers unrelated to organizational performance, can result in management distraction and delay necessary action. For that reason, it is critical for healthcare leaders to identify and focus on the vital few.

Key drivers in health care include:

- Salary and benefits as a percentage of revenue or per unit of service performance
- Supplies as a percentage of revenue or per unit of service
- Contribution margin by product or service line
- Bad debt and charity as a percentage of revenue
- Market share percentage
- Cash collections as a percentage of net collectable revenue (net revenue less bad debt) Operating margin percentage
- Earnings before interest, taxes, depreciation, and amortization (EBITDA percentage)

Glossary of Key Drivers

- *Salary and benefits as a percentage of revenue or per unit of service performance:* The percentage of the organization's budget allotted for labor, which includes employee salaries and also takes into consideration payroll and unemployment insurance taxes, benefits, reimbursements, overtime, workers' compensation, leave time, and holiday pay (Deeb, 2012).
- *Supplies as a percentage of revenue or per unit of service:* Total supplies divided by net operating revenue.
- *Contribution margin by product or service line:* A cost accounting concept that allows a company to determine the profitability of individual products or service lines. This figure can then be used to determine whether variable costs for that product can be reduced. The contribution margin is the revenue left over after paying variable costs (Investopia, n.d.a).
- *Bad debt and charity as a percentage of revenue:* Bad debt expense plus charity write-offs divided by net operating revenue.

- *Market share percentage*: The percentage of an industry or market's total sales that is earned by a particular company over a specified time period. Market share is calculated by taking the company's sales over the period and dividing it by the total sales of the industry over the same period. This metric is used to give a general idea of the size of a company to its market and its competitors (Investopia, n.d.b).

- *Cash collections as a percentage of net collectable revenue (net revenue less bad debt)*: The total patient cash collections divided by net collectible revenue. Over time, this total should add up to 100%. If it is less than 100%, your net revenue may be overstated or accounts receivable are growing. If it is greater than 100%, accounts receivable should be declining or net revenue is understated.

- *Operating margin percentage*: A measurement of what portion of a company's revenue is left over after paying all costs. A healthy operating margin is required for a company to pay for its fixed costs, such as interest on debt (Investopia, n.d.c).

- *Earnings before interest, taxes, depreciation, and amortization*: These are intended to be an indicator of a company's financial position. EBITDA tells an investor how much money a company would have made if it did not have to pay *interest expense* on its debt or *taxes*, or take *depreciation and amortization charges* (Investopia, n.d.d).

Functional Performance Reports

Financial performance in an organization can be assessed by monitoring its vital few key drivers. For example, a performance report can assess productivity, a key indicator. Because labor costs are one of the top expense categories in healthcare organizations, such a report allows each business unit to identify its underperforming departments on a biweekly basis. This process depersonalizes performance issues and facilitates a culture of transparency and a commitment to rapid cycle improvement. Units and managers can use the data to understand "how we got here," and develop operational plans and specific actions to improve future performance—that is, "where we want to go" (see **TABLE 12.1**).

Performance reporting can also be used as a learning tool that highlights best practices within an organization. A best practice that has been successfully implemented by one unit or department can be shared with or adopted by other similar units to facilitate more rapid process improvement (Laurent, 2010). This process allows for examination of the data, analysis of data, and using good judgment to ensure the appropriate actions are taken for the benefit of the organization (Cranfield Centre for Business Performance, 2017).

Benchmarking and Best Practices

For the vital few key drivers, performance can also be evaluated and compared among internal or external cohorts through the process of **benchmarking**. Comparing performance among units can highlight operational excellence, identify best practices for dissemination, uncover areas for potential growth, and facilitate an environment of continuous quality improvement. Benchmarking allows quantitative

TABLE 12.1 MOR Summary Report

Monthly Operating Review (MOR)

Summary Report

FY 20XX–April 20XX

Part I. Global Measures

Productivity Index*	Current Month					Year-to-Date		
	ACT	BUD	P/YR	P/MO	ACT	BUD	P/YR	
Adjusted Occupied Bed (AOB)	578	549	543	570	551	541	534	
General ALOS	4.2	4.4	4.6	4.2	4.4	4.4	4.5	
FTEs all employee-hours	3947	3718	3716	3902	3842	3688	3573	
FTEs per AOB	6.11	6.06	6.25	6.23	6.30	6.11	6.09	
Salaries and benefits as percentage of net revenue	46.0%	45.3%	48.0%	43.9%	45.0%	45.1%	44.7%	
Average hourly rate	$31.13	$27.82	$28.03	$29.28	$28.65	$27.41	$26.67	

Part II. Challenges

| Department | ACT | BUD | FTE |
	FTEs	FTES	VAR
740000 Labor and Delivery	95.46	82.00	−13.46
856000 Admitting	68.39	55.54	−12.85
615010 Cardiac Telemetry	58.76	48.06	−10.70

Part III. Operational Plan

Please write your action plan below your cost center.

740000 Labor and Delivery			

Continuing to flex labor care staff accordingly, based on census. Antenatal unit being used as a med/surg overflow. Staffing for caregiver hours affecting department's productivity with no credit for midnight census.

*Legend: ACT = Actual; BUD = Budget; P/YR = Prior year; P/MO = Prior month; FTE = Full-time equivalent; VAR = Variance.

assessments that support the well-known adage, "You can successfully manage only what you measure." Examples of benchmarking reports are discussed as follows.

Balanced Scorecard

A balanced scorecard combines performance management and benchmarking. The tool reports the performance of a business unit's individual goals, but also allows the comparison of performance among all the units assessed. These comparisons can promote communication and information sharing, best practice implementation, performance consistency, and collaboration toward the achievement of common goals.

Trending

Benchmarking allows similar cohorts to compare performance on specific indicators, as well as to monitor trends and variation in performance. Organizations often prepare a benchmarking report that groups cohorts together to facilitate performance comparisons and also allows individual units to track their own performance over time. Knowing the relationship between among cohorts allows for an opportunity to focus on strengths and areas for improvement (Zinner & Co., 2018).

Department Specific Performance

TABLE 12.2 offers an example of a more detailed benchmarking tool that reports performance for specific similar departments in like cohorts. Such reports allow performance comparisons and opportunity identification on a micro level.

▶ Levels of Accountability

Accountability at every level of the organization is critical for effective performance and continuous quality improvement. Successful **management models** strive to create and advance accountability not only in the executive suite, but also on the "front lines," where employees are implementing the strategies to achieve the organization's mission and goals. "Lowest common denominator accountability" acknowledges that employees providing the organization's services are likely to have valuable insight about clients, procedures, issues, and such, and can suggest excellent ideas to improve performance. Granting frontline employees the authority to identify concerns and to formulate and implement solutions can promote accountability and enhance successful performance (Office of the Auditor General of Canada, 2008).

Some accountability questions include:

- What is the performance issue we have identified?
- What is the magnitude of the problem?
- What are some of the potential causes of the problem?
- What tools or resources do we need to solve the problem?
- What would be a successful solution to the problem?
- How can we measure success?
- How often will performance be assessed? Hourly? Daily? Weekly? Monthly?

TABLE 12.2 Benchmarking Summary for Transcription

Transcription FTEs	YTD Feb Current Year		FY Last Year		FY 2 Years Ago	
	Per Adjusted Patient Day	Per Adjusted Discharge	Per Adjusted Patient Day	Per Adjusted Discharge	Per Adjusted Patient Day	Per Adjusted Discharge
Our System						
Hosp. A	10.69	51.34	12.38	60.05	10.64	50.14
Hosp. B	10.54	35.70	12.36	43.30	11.73	40.28
Hosp. C	10.61	46.14	15.70	73.03	14.35	71.10
Competitor System						
Hosp. A			7.57	35.57	14.09	63.28
Hosp. B			4.55	19.30	6.51	27.95
Hosp. C			11.38	43.44	14.92	52.42

Team Player and Facilitator

Healthcare leaders play a crucial role in problem solving by facilitating collaboration and teamwork to address issues. A traditional autocratic approach wherein the team leader directs the quest for solutions from the "top down" can result in lost opportunities. Effective leaders approach performance issues with the "beginner's mind"—that is, an openness to new ideas and learning; consider all alternatives suggested (especially from those who work most closely with the issue of concern); and encourage a climate of good will and trust.

Intellectual Curiosity and a Culture of Excellence

Performance management is not a destination, but a journey. Leaders who promote a culture of intellectual curiosity and excellence are most likely to enlist employees in collaborating to identify concerns and to develop and implement creative and effective solutions.

A commitment to excellence can inspire units and departments to aim for a higher level of performance. Benchmarking results demonstrate performance in a particular quartile, for example, median or top. Whereas median performance may be adequate in some settings, most units strive to provide services of superior quality. Setting performance expectations at the median is likely to result in median performance. With a commitment to excellence, operating units are frequently able to achieve upper quartile performance levels despite limitations in funding, facilities, staffing, and technology. Reviewing benchmarking reports in detail to understand the current level of function, identifying areas for potential intervention, and developing strategies to improve performance can result in an excellent learning exercise and builds the foundation for a better business model.

This "reconciliation process" can lead to the development of strategies such as enhanced workforce training, investment in upgrading technology, and revisions of policies and procedures, which can benefit not only the business unit engaged in review but also other units in the organization.

Goals, Rules, Process, and Interpersonal (GRPI) (**FIGURE 12.1**) is an excellent tool to facilitate group performance reviews and questions and items for teams to discuss, and on which teams can vote and come to a consensus.

Project Plan

Performance management also requires organizational skill and project management capabilities. Leaders must marshal and guide the most effective teams to assess

FIGURE 12.1 GRPI Model*

*This model provides a framework for diagnosing and improving team effectiveness. The model is hierarchical: Start with goals, then allocated work/roles, then identify team processes, and finally deal with personalities, styles, and cultural differences to minimize process loss.

and address issues and launch or revise projects to achieve performance outcomes and strategic objectives.

Some key considerations for project development include:

- What are the objectives of the project?
- What steps are necessary to implement the project plan?
- Who will be responsible for oversight and coordination of the plan and its steps?
- When will each step be implemented (timeline)?
- What resources are required for each step?
- What metric will measure success? How often will data be collected?
- If success is not achieved, at what point will the project be reevaluated for a possible revision or course change?

Making Wise Decisions

As team and unit leaders, managers are tasked with making decisions about new strategies and directions to improve performance, often with limited information and data to help guide choices. Some choose to wait for additional input or opt to make incremental decisions with the input available and then monitor the results. Each approach has its pros and cons. Leaders need to keep in mind that decisions made in an effort to improve performance can not only affect the livelihoods of unit employees and the future of the organization as a whole, but also the economy of the geographic region where the organization is located. Therefore, it is important for managers to consider all potential outcomes and consequences in their decision-making process. It is a good idea for leaders to establish ongoing performance metrics to be able to identify negative outcomes and to determine whether a decision was sound or needs review (ReadPeriodicals, 2010).

An effective approach includes these items:

- Understanding that the goal of performance management is to improve the organization
- Identifying areas of concern and analyzing the causes of identified problems and issues
- Focusing efforts on strategies and solutions for these problems
- Using data collected to help drive decisions and recommendations
- Assessing the effectiveness of strategies to address the problems on an ongoing basis and revising these strategies as needed

▶ Management Model

Managers in healthcare organizations are entrusted to deliver high-quality services and programs to their clientele and are accountable for the efficient and effective utilization of resources. Executives must demonstrate that they have been "good stewards" of the organization's resources and have safeguarded the assets of the organization.

Managers must have support for their decision-making; ensure the availability of timely, relevant, and reliable financial information; establish a controlled but supportive environment; and make efficient and effective use of the resources of the organization. Management must also enable the organization to comply with various regulatory bodies and safeguard the assets of the organization.

The management model focuses on managing and directing the organization's resources economically and efficiently to achieve the organization's objectives. It includes strategic planning, analysis, and support for decisions.

Financial Management

Leaders must accurately represent an organization's financial status, including expenditures and revenue. Cash provides the corroboration for financial statements. If more revenue is recorded than cash collected, and the disparity cannot be explained via accounts receivable, there is risk of an overstatement.

Cash

Cash explains and justifies the expenses of the organization, which are generally routine, predictable, and ongoing. Cash is the lifeblood of any organization and must be properly safeguarded through a robust internal control system and monitored to ensure adequate levels are maintained to cover organization expenses.

Budgets

Budget management and review support effective monitoring of financial resources and successful planning for an organization's future. The budget reflects the organization's financial and operational goals. By tracking and analyzing financial performance, management can develop strategic plans that align fiscal resources with the desired goals.

Before the start of the operating year, each organization must establish an accurate budget that integrates the organization's strategic plan into the financial plan. The financial plan documents cash/capital and debt levels, projects the amount and number of resources needed to maintain a sustainable future, and allows the implementation of the strategic plan.

During the operating year, managers should review the budget entries, compare actual expenses and revenue with previous estimates and projections, and analyze the variances between actual and projected data. Variances can also be analyzed against the budget data for earlier intervals. For example, operating units can compare expenditures in the first quarter of this year to the first quarter of the previous year. Managers can be offered incentives to stay within their allocated budgets, be held accountable for unfavorable variances, and tasked to provide corrective action plans when actual results fall outside of the budgeted or planned range.

Variance Analysis

Executives aim to ensure the sustainability of their organizations and strive to increase productivity and performance without increasing expenses and costs. Variance analysis examines the difference, or variance, between projected/budgeted expenses and actual expenses and allows managers to identify areas of concern that need assessment or intervention. Variance data can also be benchmarked against equivalent data from like competitors such as hospitals, and can aid managers in making decisions and developing more effective tactical initiatives that can control excessive spending and improve cost-efficiency and effectiveness. Variance analyses help management to set strategic goals and to explain the utilization of resources in support of those goals, for stakeholders such as the board of directors, staff physicians, insurance companies, and stockholders.

TABLE 12.3 demonstrates an expense variance analysis that examines planned/budgeted expenses versus actual expenses for salary and hours worked.

TABLE 12.3 Salary Variance Analysis	
Actual Expense	$2000
Budgeted Expense	$3200
Actual Hours	400
Budgeted Hours	800
Financial Variance $3200 – $2000 = $1200 Favorable	
There may be two possible causes of the variance between the actual values and the projections:	
Differences in the hourly rate of pay (i.e., a lower salary)	
Differences in the number of hours worked (i.e., fewer hours worked)	
Actual Hourly Expense (salary paid per hour)	$2000/400 = $5.00
Budgeted Hourly Expense (salary projected per hour)	$3200/800 = $4.00
Hourly Variance	
Financial Variance $5.00 – $4.00 = –$1.00 per hour rate of pay Unfavorable	
Price/Rate Analysis:	
Budgeted Hourly Expense	$4.00
Actual Hourly Expense	**$5.00**
Hourly Rate Variance	*<$1.00> Unfavorable*

(continues)

TABLE 12.3 Salary Variance Analysis	*(continued)*
Price/Rate Analysis:	
Actual Hours	**400**
Unfavorable Variance	*<$400>*
Usage/Efficiency Analysis:	
Budgeted Hours Allowed	800
Actual Hours Used	**400**
Usage Variance	400
Budgeted Hourly Expense	$4.00
Favorable Variance	$1600
Variance Analysis Summary	

Price Rate Analysis—Unfavorable <$400>
Usage/Efficiency—Favorable $1600
Total Variance—Favorable $1200

Weekly Projections

Weekly projections are designed to accurately project current month revenue and expenses on a weekly basis to monitor the budget, capture fluctuations, serve as a guide to future financial decisions, and allow financial managers to address concerns in a timely manner.

Monthly Operating Reviews

Financial statements are also produced regularly at longer intervals (e.g., monthly, quarterly, and annually) and summarize the hospital's financial status during designated intervals. Management reviews the information on a monthly basis to ensure the hospital is running effectively and efficiently and to identify any variances between planned and budgeted goals and actual operating results.

The monthly operating review aids managers in pinpointing problems and implementing remediation if there are inconsistencies that deviate from the organization's operating plan. The statement of financial position, or balance sheet, displays the organization's assets, liabilities, and net worth (net assets) during the specific period. The income statement or statement of activities reports the revenue and expenses of the organization during that term. The monthly operating review presents information that allows managers to easily define their progress. It is important for managers to set financial goals in advance of these ongoing assessments, otherwise the data collected is less meaningful.

Net Accounts Receivable Estimates

Funds due from patients or insurance payers that the organization expects to collect within 30–60 days of service are considered accounts receivable. These sums can be large and must be monitored carefully. It can be challenging for financial managers to estimate what percentage of accounts receivable are likely to be collected by the organization—that is, net collectible revenue.

Net Collectible Revenue

A good test of organization solvency is the monitoring of net collectible revenue. Revenue estimates should quantify projected cash collections. A total of 100% of net collectible revenue should be collected in a designated period and monitored via a rolling 6-month trend report. Variances below 100% net collectible should be routinely reconciled and explained. Reconciliation can provide insights into the accounting estimation process, which can then be used to refine future net revenue projections.

Capital Investment and Look-Back

In some cases, additional cash can be generated internally from prior years' capital investments. A Federal Depreciation Look-Back Analysis, which reviews the classification and categorization of assets, has the potential to improve cash flow by reducing current federal and state income tax. This process allows for an organization to accelerate federal tax depreciation into the current year from investments made in buildings and other fixed assets in the past (General Financial and Tax Consulting, LLC, 2009).

Certifications

The Sarbanes-Oxley Act of 2002 introduced major changes in the regulation of corporate governance and financial practice. Section 302 pertains to corporate responsibility and requires certification of financial documents and accountability for the financial reports that organizations produce. To ensure that there is no misrepresentation, a CEO or CFO must review all financial reports and guarantee their accuracy. Any material changes in internal accounting controls, and any deficiencies, accounting misrepresentations, or fraud must be reported immediately to the audit committee. Certification is done quarterly and/or annually and establishes an audit trail, which makes it easier to identify, correct, and track any organizational deficiencies (Sarbanes Oxley 101, 2018).

Senior management is responsible for compliance with these regulations. The signatures of the CEO or CFO signify the accuracy and integrity of the document—that is, that it correctly represents the financial condition of the organization at the time of submission and attests to the effectiveness of the accounting management controls of the organization (Sarbanes Oxley 101, 2018).

▶ Financial Implications of Healthcare Reform and Initiatives

Healthcare Reform

On March 23, 2010, President Obama signed into law the Patient Protection and Affordable Care Act, and 7 days later, the Health Care and Education Reconciliation Act of
2010. The Patient Protection and Affordable Care Act and the Reconciliation measure
(collectively, the "Act") expanded healthcare coverage by providing the following:

- Expanded Medicaid eligibility to enroll an additional 16 million people
- Subsidies for insurance purchase through healthcare exchanges for approxi-
  mately 16 million people
- Health insurance eligibility for individuals with pre-existing conditions
- Extended dependent coverage in insurance programs through age 26
- A ban on lifetime limits and unreasonable annual caps on insurance coverage
- A requirement that states maintain current eligibility levels for a specified period
  for children in Medicaid and the Children's Health Insurance Plan (CHIP)

The Patient Protection and Affordable Care Act (H.R. 3590) was considered
true **healthcare reform**. It enhanced health services for an additional 30 million
Americans and provided new revenue to the healthcare and health insurance industries. However, there were concerns that the Act would deliver significant financial
challenges to healthcare organizations (Dunn, 2010). Some examples of these challenges are listed as follows.

▶ Healthcare Reform Initiatives

As of the time of this revised edition, there have been many challenges to the Affordable Care Act. Some have resulted in modifications to the original act. For example,
in the Tax Cuts and Jobs Act passed by Congress, and signed into law by President Donald Trump in December 2017, the "individual mandate" to obtain health
insurance was eliminated. This mandate required Americans to face a penalty if
they did not have private health insurance, employer-supplied health insurance, or
government-funded insurance such as Medicaid or Medicare. The new tax law elim-
inates this penalty in 2019 (Wharton University, 2018). It is expected that additional
changes to the Act will be considered by legislators over the next several years.

Medicare Reimbursement

As of January 1, 2013, Medicare reimbursements for hospitalized patients decreased
for preventable readmissions. Hospitals with high readmission rates would have
Medicare reimbursements for the original hospitalization reduced by 1% if a patient
was readmitted for a preventable cause within the 7 days after discharge. As a result,
however, to aim for a lower readmission rate, some hospitals considered extending
a patient's initial stay.

Since the beginning of the program on October 1, 2012, hospitals have incurred
nearly $1.9 billion in penalties, including $528 million in fiscal year (FY) 2017. In FY

2013, payment penalties were based on hospital readmissions rates within 30 days for heart attack, heart failure, and pneumonia. In FY 2015, CMS added reviews of readmissions for patients undergoing elective hip or knee replacement, and patients with chronic obstructive pulmonary disease. CMS added readmissions for coronary artery bypass procedures in FY 2017 and likely will add other measures in the future (AHA, n.d.).

Beginning in FY 2019, as required by the 21st Century Cures Act, the Hospital Readmission Reduction Program (HRRP) will use new stratified methodology that evaluates hospital performance relative to other hospitals with similar proportions of patients that are dually eligible for Medicare and full-benefit Medicaid. The Hospital-Level Impact File is designed to provide hospitals information on estimated performance in the HRRP under the new stratified methodology, using data from FY 2018 (CMS, 2017).

Medicare Pilot Program

In 2013, Medicare launched a national pilot program to provide and evaluated bundled payments for acute inpatient hospital services, physician services, outpatient hospital services, and post-acute care services for an episode of care from 3 days prior to hospitalization until 30 days following discharge.

As of January 1, 2018, the Bundled Payments for Care BPCI initiative has 1137 participants in Phase 2, which are comprised of 235 Awardees and 902 Episode Initiators. The breakdown of participants by provider type is as follows: acute care hospitals (287), skilled nursing facilities (540), physician group practices (197), home health agencies (58), inpatient rehabilitation facilities (9), and long-term care hospitals (0). Some awardees are not initiating episodes in BPCI and therefore are not included in the breakdown of participants by provider type (CMS, 2018).

Independent Payment Advisory Board

In 2015, the Act launched an Independent Payment Advisory Board similar to the existing Medicare Payment Advisory Commission (MedPAC), which has Medicare rate-setting authority. Hospitals will be subject to the board's authority in 2019. This reform measure is expected to save $23.4 billion over 10 years (Davis, 2010).

On November 2, 2017, the U.S. House of Representatives passed legislation (H.R. 849) to repeal the provision of the Affordable Care Act (ACA) that authorized the Independent Payment Advisory Board, or IPAB, whose mission was to achieve savings in Medicare with evidence-based guidance. Although the IPAB was authorized under the ACA in 2010, no members had been appointed, and the Board was not operational (Cubanski & Neuman, 2017). In February 2018, the U.S. Senate and the House of Representatives completely repealed the IPAB, as part of the Bipartisan Budget Act of 2018 signed by President Trump.

Medicare and Medicaid Reimbursement Cuts

Beginning in FY 2010, the Affordable Care Act reduced Medicare market basket updates for a number of services and inserted a productivity adjustment.[1] Reimbursements were to be cut by $103 billion over 10 years. Medicare and Medicaid disproportionate-share hospital payments[2] for hospitals that offer services to large cohorts of underserved clients were to be reduced by $44 billion over 10 years, beginning in 2015 (Davis, 2010). As of August 2017, Medicare payments to hospitals for uncompensated care under the Disproportionate Share Hospital program were slated to increase about $800 million over the FY 2017 funding level (Cheney, 2017).

- Market basket adjustments refer to adjustments that reduce reimbursement based on prospective improved productivity.
- Medicaid disproportionate-share hospital (DSH) payments provide financial assistance to hospitals that serve a large number of low-income patients such as the uninsured and individuals covered by Medicaid. Medicaid DSH payments are the largest source of federal funding for uncompensated hospital care (Peters, 2009). Recipients must reduce unnecessary tests and procedures, assess and demonstrate improved quality outcomes, and reduce healthcare costs.

On July 27, 2017, CMS issued a notice of proposed rulemaking (NPRM) regarding Medicaid Disproportionate Share Hospital allotment reductions. This NPRM proposed a methodology to implement the annual reductions to state Medicaid DSH allotments for FY 2018 through FY 2025 as required by the Affordable Care Act. The proposed methodology relies on five factors identified in statute. Taking these factors into account for each state, the proposed methodology will generate a state-specific DSH allotment reduction amount for each fiscal year (Medicaid.gov, n.d.).

Physician Integration

Physicians would like to achieve target incomes while assuming a manageable workload. At the same time, hospitals are experiencing physician shortages, especially in emergency care and specialty services, even as they are facing market challenges from local entrepreneurial physician competitors. Developing partnerships between physicians and hospitals can address the needs of both stakeholder groups, and channel competition into collaboration toward common goals. Integrating physicians and hospitals could help both to share patient information and records, improve quality of care, and avoid undermining each other's efforts.

Collaboration

Hospitals and physicians can work together in several ways, formally and informally. Hospitals can employ physicians or contract with them to provide services. Another type of partnership is a joint venture model, in which selected doctors in a hospital may co-own a hospital service, such as a pharmacy or laboratory. Additionally, physicians and hospitals can collaborate to integrate clinical services and procedures to avoid duplication and incorporate best practices to improve quality of care. However, it is important that such partnerships take great care to comply with state and federal regulations regarding conflict of interest and other legal restrictions.

Summary

The healthcare industry is growing in size and complexity. The value of financial information in leaders' decision-making processes is critical. Financial literacy is essential for healthcare leaders in our constantly changing economic environment. Understanding financial factors and influences will assist leaders in their ongoing assessment and evaluation of these industry changes and allow for preparatory and effective strategic thinking and planning.

Discussion Questions

1. What is the importance of analyzing past and present financial information?
2. What is a key driver in health care?
3. Identify the critical components in a project plan.
4. How does healthcare reform impact healthcare institutions from a financial perspective?

🔍 CASE STUDY: Financial Management

You are the CFO of Amityville Hospital. It is a 250-bed, for-profit hospital renowned for its cardiology unit. The hospital has 300 employees, including 125 physicians with staff privileges.

Amityville is located in a thriving community that represents its primary service region. There are many high-tech companies and industries in the area that attract families and retirees from around the United States. The area has a mild climate and offers an excellent educational environment that includes multiple community colleges and universities.

There are approximately 750,000 residents in the surrounding city, and its population is growing about 4% per year. Approximately 46% of the population is under 18 years of age, 42% is between the ages of 18 and 64 years, 12% is over 65 years of age; 49% of the residents are female and 51% are male.

Amityville has one competitor, Serenity Hospital, which is located 40 miles away. Serenity is a 350-bed not-for-profit hospital with an excellent reputation. It has strong orthopedic and cardiac services and also offers oncology services, which are poorly organized and not accredited. Serenity Hospital's financial performance is stable, and its market share is growing.

Serenity has no formal orthopedic or cardiology departments, though several popular orthopedic surgeons and cardiologists maintain privileges there. The community's premier orthopedic group practices are located near Serenity Hospital, making it inconvenient for surgeons to use Amityville Hospital for surgery except in rare cases. However, a few orthopedic practices are planning to open branch offices near the Amityville facility.

Cardiologists on Serenity's staff restrict their activity to performing consults for Amityville physicians whose patients have been admitted to the facility. Although Amityville Hospital has had moderate success in the burgeoning community, its leaders would like to ensure adequate preparation for the future, especially in the environment of health reform. You will assess key areas in Amityville's operations from a financial perspective and report your results to the board of directors in a PowerPoint presentation. Please address the following questions in your presentation.

Case Study Discussion Questions

1. What areas of Amityville's operations will be critical to review?
2. How will Amityville's financial data be used in the strategic planning and decision-making process?
3. How will healthcare initiatives impact Amityville and its strategic planning?
4. How do the community and Serenity Hospital impact Amityville's strategic planning?

Related Websites

American Hospital Association: https://www.aha.org/other-resources/2016-01-18-aha-fact-sheet
-hospital-readmissions-reduction-programCongress.Gov: https://www.congress.gov/bill/115th
-congress/house-bill/849

Federal Register: https://www.federalregister.gov/documents/2017/07/28/2017-15962/medicaid
-program-state-disproportionate-share-hospital-allotment-reductions

Kaiser Family Foundation: https://www.kff.org/health-reform/issue-brief/the-independent-payment
-advisory-board-a-new/

Sarbanes-Oxley 101: http://www.sarbanes-oxley-101.com/sarbanes-oxley-compliance.htm

Additional Resources

Dydra, L. (2017). 11 thoughts on how the American Health Care Act could affect hospitals. *Becker's Hospital Review*. Retrieved from www.beckershospitalreview.com/hospital-management -administration/11-thoughts-on-how-the-american-health-care-act-could-affect-hospitals.html

Kimmel, P., Weygandt, J., & Kieso, D. (2016). Chapter 8: Reporting and analyzing receivables. *Accounting tools for business decision making* (6th ed., pp. 396–445). Medford, MA: Wiley.

Sarbanes-Oxley Act Presentation—Key Aspects. (n.d.). Retrieved from www.soxtoolkit.com/sox -pres.htm

Sarbanes-Oxley Summary. (2003). A guide to the Sarbanes-Oxley Act: Sarbanes-Oxley Act summary and introduction. Retrieved from www.soxlaw.com/introduction.htm

Belliveau, J. (ed.). What is Healthcare Revenue Cycle Management? *Revenue Cycle Intelligence*. Retrieved from https://revcycleintelligence.com/features/what-is-healthcare-revenue-cycle -management

References

AHA, (n.d). *AHA fact sheet: Hospital readmission reduction program*. Retrieved from www.aha .org/other-resources/2018-01-18-aha-fact-sheet-hospital-readmissions-reduction-program

Cheney, C. (2017, August). *2018 IPPS final rule set to hike hospital reimbursement $2.4 B*. Retrieved from www.healthleadersmedia.com/finance/2018-ipps-final-rule-set-hike-hospital -reimbursement-24b#

CMS. (2017). *New stratified methodology hospital level impact file user guide*. Retrieved March 22, 2018 from www.cms.gov/Medicare/Medicare-Fee-for-Service-Payment/AcuteInpatientPPS /Downloads/HRRP_StratMethod_ImpctFile_UG.PDF

CMS. (2018). *Bundled payments for care improvement (BPCI) initiative: General information*. Retrieved from https://innovation.cms.gov/initiatives/bundled-payments/

Cranfield Centre for Business Performance. (2017). Benefits of performance reporting. *Smart Performance Reporting*. Retrieved from https://cranfieldcbp.wordpress.com/2017/05/24 /benefits-of-performance-reporting/

Cubanski, J., & Neuman, T. (2017). *FAQs: What's the latest on IPAB?* Retrieved March 22, 2018 from www.kff.org/medicare/issue-brief/faqs-whats-the-latest-on-ipab/

Davis, C. (2010). Health reform's financial implications: HFMA details the issues. *Fierce Health Finance*. Retrieved from www.fiercehealthfinance.com/story/health-reforms-financial -implications-hfma-details-issues/2010-03-24

Deeb, C. (2012). Percent of a business budget for salary. *Houston Chronicle*. Retrieved from http:// smallbusiness.chron.com/percent-business-budget-salary-14254.html

Dunn, G. (2010). Healthy financial reporting and disclosure: A summary of the financial reporting and disclosure implications of the health care reform. *Deloitte*. Retrieved from www.deloitte .com/assets/Dcom-UnitedStates/Local%20Assets/Documents/AERS/ASC/us_assur_Heads _Up_040910.pdf

General Financial and Tax Consulting, LLC. (2009). *Federal depreciation look-back analysis*. Retrieved from www.genfitax.com/Resources/GFTC%20-%20Federal%20Depreciation%20 Look%20Back%20Analysis.pdf

Investopedia. (n.d.a). *Contribution margin*. Retrieved from www.investopedia.com/terms/c/contributionmargin.asp#axzz1iq2CL9tT

Investopedia. (n.d.b). *Market share*. Retrieved from www.investopedia.com/terms/m/marketshare.asp#axzz1iq2CL9tT

Investopedia. (n.d.c.). *Operating margin*. Retrieved from www.investopedia.com/terms/o/operatingmargin.asp#axzz1iq2CL9tT

Investopedia. (n.d.d.). *Earnings before interest, taxes, depreciation, and amortization*. Retrieved from www.investopedia.com/terms/e/ebitda.asp

Laurent, W. (2010). Managing and improving quality with key performance drivers. *Dashboard Insight*. Retrieved from www.dashboardinsight.com/articles/business-performance-management/managing-and-improving-quality-with-key-performance-drivers.aspx

Medicaid.gov. (n.d.). *Medicaid disproportionate share (DSH) payments*. Retrieved March 22, 2018 from www.medicaid.gov/medicaid/finance/dsh/index.html

Office of the Auditor General of Canada. (2008). *Financial management capability model*. Retrieved from www.oag-bvg.gc.ca/internet/English/meth_gde_e_19706.html#0.2.2Z141Z1.WKP23M.SXB89F.C

Peters, C. P. (2009). The basics: Medicaid disproportionate share (DSH) payments. *National Health Policy Forum*. Retrieved from www.nhpf.org/library/the-basics/Basics_DSH_06-15-09.pdf

ReadPeriodicals. (2010, January). Hospital strategies for effective performance management. *Healthcare Financial Management*. Retrieved from www.readperiodicals.com/201001/1975387781.html

Sarbanes Oxley 101. (2012). *Sarbanes Oxley Act summary of major sections*. Retrieved from www.sarbanes-oxley-101.com/sarbanes-oxley-compliance.htm

Wharton University. (2018). *Beyond Obamacare: What's ahead for U.S. health care in 2018?* Retrieved from http://knowledge.wharton.upenn.edu/article/the-future-of-the-aca/

Zinner & Co. (n.d.) *Trend Analysis & Benchmarking*. Retrieved from www.zinnerco.com/accounting-tax-services-cleveland/business-advisory-services/trend-analysis—benchmarking

CHAPTER 13

The Physician Leader

Sharon B. Buchbinder and Dale Buchbinder

LEARNING OBJECTIVES

By the end of this chapter, the student will be able to:

- Describe physician education and training, licensure and certification, continuing education, and quality assessment.
- Identify common roles of physician leaders in healthcare organizations.
- Compare and contrast clinical versus nonclinical leadership roles in healthcare organizations.
- Describe the value of physician leaders to a healthcare organization.
- Define sexual harassment and provide strategies for physician leaders to prevent and address it.
- Suggest potential leadership roles for physicians in evolving healthcare organizations.

KEY TERMS

Bell Commission
Board certification
Chief medical officer (CME)
Chief of medical staff
Clinical and educational work
Clinical experience and education
Conflict of interest
Continuing medical education
Corporate practice of medicine (CPOM)
Duty hours

I-PASS
#MeToo
#MedToo
National Practitioner Data Bank
Patient handoffs
Physician credentialing
Physician privileging
Sexual harassment
Transitions of care
Work hours

▶ Introduction

Healthcare organizations employ a wide array of clinical, administrative, and support professionals to deliver services to their patients. The Bureau of Labor Statistics (BLS), which lists more than 40 different categories of healthcare professionals on its website, notes "employment of healthcare occupations is projected to grow 18 percent from 2016 to 2026, adding about 2.4 million new jobs. This projected growth is mainly due to an aging population, leading to greater demand for healthcare services" (Bureau of Labor Statistics, 2018a). In 2016, there were 713,800 physicians employed in the United States; that number is expected to grow by 13% between 2016 and 2026 (Bureau of Labor Statistics, 2018b). While fewer in number than their nursing counterparts at 2.95 million, physicians have a disproportionally greater impact on healthcare organizations (BLS, 2018a). Physicians not only provide critical direct healthcare services but also serve in administrative and leadership roles that significantly contribute to the quality, success, and sustainability of a healthcare organization.

Healthcare administrators can expect to engage and collaborate with physicians who are not only clinicians but also knowledgeable administrative colleagues. Physician leaders, drawing on their extensive training and expertise in medicine and management, can serve as outstanding liaisons and ambassadors between the executive administration and physician stakeholder groups such as employees and contractors. Healthcare organizations reap the benefits of enlisting and utilizing these highly skilled professionals in their strategic workforce.

In this chapter, we will provide you with an overview of physician medical education, licensure and certification, continuing education, and performance management. We will address the recent **#MeToo** and **#MedToo** movements, **sexual harassment** and misconduct in medicine, and the role of physician leaders in addressing these underreported phenomena. Finally, we will provide examples of current roles and functions of physician leaders in healthcare organizations and discuss future leadership opportunities for physicians in this evolving healthcare environment.

▶ Physician Medical Education, Training, Certification, and Continuing Education

Physicians begin their preparation for medical school as undergraduates in a variety of majors, but are often identified and labeled as "premedical students." Premedical students can obtain a degree in any field; however, according to the Association of American Medical Colleges (AAMC), the expectation is that they will graduate from university with a bachelor's degree that includes successfully completed prerequisites in STEM subjects such as mathematics, biology, chemistry, and physics (AAMC, 2018).

Medical schools in the United States generally provide 4 years of academic and clinical instruction. Entry into U.S. medical schools is extremely competitive; successful applicants must earn high grade point averages as undergraduates and high scores on the Medical College Admission Test (MCAT). Some students opt to study medicine at medical schools outside the United States and return to the United States to obtain clinical experience and take the necessary examinations for U.S. licensure and entrance into graduate medical training programs. Other students will seek a post-baccalaureate position or a master's degree prior to medical school entry.

Though some universities offer a shorter, combined Bachelor of Science/Medical Doctor (BS/MD) degree program in the United States, the majority of American medical school graduates will have at least 8 years of post-high school education, including 2 or more years of clinical externships. Some medical students interested in research careers apply for a joint MD/PhD program that will extend their graduate study by 2–3 years. Medical school tuition can be very expensive, and some students will study under scholarship programs that fund medical education, but may require service in the military or underserved communities after licensure.

Medical students seeking U.S. licensure will apply to the National Residency Matching Program in their 4th year of medical school (NRMP, 2018). The NRMP is a process where senior medical students select, apply, interview, and rank their choices for graduate medical education (GME), also known as residencies. The residency training programs also interview and rank their applicants, and program participants are then matched with the highest-ranked choice available. Residency training programs, which provide intensive mentoring and clinical training in a physician's chosen specialty, are sponsored by teaching hospitals, academic medical centers, healthcare systems, and other institutions (Accreditation Council for Graduate Medical Education, ACGME, 2018a).

During their residency training program, physicians are primarily trained by experienced practitioners (attending physicians) in either a general or specialized area of medicine. Depending on the specialty, the length of the residency training program can be as short as 3 years (for family medicine) or as long as 10 years (for general surgery plus cardio-thoracic surgery or neurosurgery). Many fields such as pediatrics, family medicine, and internal medicine offer additional training in sub-specialties such as sports medicine, cardiology, allergy and immunology, etc. via fellowships at teaching hospitals for 2–3 more years. Physicians can be licensed to practice medicine in most states after passing the U.S. Medical Licensing Examination, Part 3 (USMLE), and 1 year of post-medical school training, but are not considered specialists until they complete their residency, when they become "board-eligible."

Completion of an ACGME accredited residency program is one of the criteria that is required for physicians to sit for their specialty **board certification** examinations to become "board-certified" (American Board of Medical Specialties, ABMS, 2018a). Completion of an accredited fellowship allows a physician to sit for sub-specialty board certification examinations.

Residents work extensive hours as part of their specialty training programs. Not long ago, it was common for residents to be on-call every other night, working on duty for 36–48 hours per shift with little or no rest or sleep. Caps on hours of work for residents varied by residency training program, but were typically highest for the surgical specialties, often greater than 100 hours per week.

In 1984, Libby Zion, an 18-year-old college student, died while she was hospitalized at the New York Hospital in Manhattan. Among the factors alleged to have contributed to her tragic death were medical errors, due to a lack of adequate supervision of the hospital residents responsible for her care, as well as the negative effects of overwork and fatigue on the residents' performance (Hoffman, 1995). A criminal grand jury called to review the case did not bring forth an indictment, but did criticize the working conditions in the New York Hospital training program. The New York State Health Commissioner established the **Bell Commission**, which recommended the institution of limits on resident work hours in New York to a maximum of 80 hours per week and 24 hours per shift.

Physician educators and hospital administrators expressed concerns that limiting resident **work hours** would negatively impact resident learning. Residents would no longer be able to stay by a patient's bedside during the critical first 36 hours of a patient's admission and observe the natural course of many acute diseases. However, advocates of limiting resident work hours countered that this "no limits" agenda was also motivated by the active utilization of residents to cover hospital staffing at a pay rate well below the minimum wage.

In 1989, New York became the first state to institute limits on resident work hours and to require the physical presence of supervising attending physicians in the hospital 24 hours a day. Over the past 3 decades, various specialty societies, medical associations, and legislators across the United States have continued to struggle with the definition of "reasonable" work hours for physicians in training. In 2017, the Accreditation Council for Graduate Medical Education (ACGME) adopted new guidelines for residents in U.S.-accredited medical training institutions. While maintaining an emphasis on the need for teamwork and effective **transitions of care**, or **patient handoffs**, the new standards have reversed some of the requirements that were perceived as the most restrictive on resident training. **Clinical experience and education, clinical and educational work**, or work hours have replaced the term **duty hours** (ACGME, 2018b).

Bilimoria et al. (2016) analyzed data from 138,691 patients collected during a national cluster-randomized trial of duty-hour flexibility in surgical training. In what is referred to as the FIRST study, they found "flexible, less-restrictive duty-hour policies were not associated with an increased rate of death or serious complications or of any secondary postoperative outcomes studied" (p. 713). Another study, iCOMPARE, is a "systematic, large-scale cluster-randomized trial comparing the current duty-hour regimen (16-hour maximum continuous work period) against a more flexible regimen" (iCOMPARE, 2018).

Based on findings from the FIRST and early findings from the iCOMPARE studies, as well as in response to various stakeholders, ACGME revised the work hour requirements. Hospitals and residency training program directors are now required to limit resident work hours to no more than 80 hours per week, averaged over 4 weeks. Additionally, PGY-1 residents are now permitted to work 16–24 hours, whereas previously their continuous duty hours could not exceed 16 hours in duration (ACGME, 2018b). Surgical programs support this reversal to allow their residents to have the complete experience of following a patient, rather than "punching out" of a shift, a "time clock mentality" that critics vehemently opposed. In 2017, Asch and colleagues pointed out, however, that the reversal of ACGME's policy on work hours was a return to the previous system of working sleep-deprived residents "into the ground."

Results from a recent multi-site randomized trial comparing the effects of flexible duty hours (i.e., no restriction on duty hours) to standard duty hours (i.e., duty hours restricted to 16-hour shifts) on educational outcomes have been released and have raised some concerns (Desai et al., 2018). The researchers found that primary outcomes (direct patient care and education) were not statistically different between the two groups. The satisfaction levels of the residents, however, were strikingly different. Whereas both groups had a cap of 80 work hours per week, residents in the flexible work hours group were significantly more dissatisfied with their work hours, and more likely to be dissatisfied with important predictors of burnout, such as job satisfaction, morale, fatigue, interpersonal relationships, and personal health. Residency training program directors, on the other hand, were more satisfied with the flexible work hours because, among other items noted, they had more time for bedside teaching. This disconnect between the residents and the program directors is a red flag for anyone concerned about physician dissatisfaction, burnout, and mental health.

McMahon (2018) states, "These alarming differences in the perceptions of the trainees under these controlled conditions cannot be justified by the small positive effects on continuity of care…reported in the flexible programs where residents worked longer shifts" (p. 1).

This generation of residents is educated, informed, and aware that there are restrictions on how much work institutions can eke out of them, but must complete ACGME-accredited residency programs to become board eligible or board certified (Alvin, 2017; Asch, Bilimoria, & Desai, 2017). Their voices—as well as those of patients—will continue to join the debate about physician education in the United States, and the long-term effects of intensive residencies on our physician workforce.

Transitions of care, or patient handoffs, that is, the transference of a caregiver's responsibility for and knowledge of a patient's condition and care at changes in time or place, have been sources of medical errors. More frequent shift changes with reduced residency work hours increase error risks from patient handoffs (Riesenberg, 2012). Therefore, the ACGME increased its emphasis on safer transitions of care.

In 2014, Starmer and her colleagues published the results of a large multisite study of six pediatric residency training programs and more than 10,000 patient admissions which utilized a standardized protocol called the I-PASS Handoff Bundle. **I-PASS** is a mnemonic for Illness severity, Patient summary, Action list, Situation awareness and contingency plans, and Synthesis by receiver. This initiative standardized oral and written handoffs, provided specific handoff and communication training, implemented a faculty development and observation program, and established a sustainability campaign. Researchers observed that medical error rates decreased by 23% and preventable adverse events decreased by 30% (Starmer et al., 2014). Future research will demonstrate whether the return to longer work hours will negatively impact these improvements in transitions of care.

Most physicians trained in the United States are eligible to obtain a license to practice medicine after only 1 year of residency. States can issue an authorization for a graduate of medical school to serve a post-graduate 1–3 years in residency under the supervision of an attending physician. Licenses to practice "medicine and surgery" are granted by state medical boards, and identify a specific, but relatively broad scope of practice. Most licensed physicians limit their scope of practice, however, to the areas in which they have received specialty training. State Boards of Medicine establish the requirements for obtaining medical licenses. These requirements are lengthy and strenuous. For example, among other requirements, the state of Maryland mandates the following (Annotated Code of Maryland, 2016):

- Good moral character
- Minimum age of 18 years
- Payment of a fee
- Documentation of education and training
- Passing scores on one of the following examinations:
  - All parts of the National Board of Medical Examiners' examinations, and/or a score of 75 or better on a FLEX exam, or a passing score on the National Board of Osteopathic Examiners, or a combination of scores and exams; or
  - State Board examination
  - All steps of the U.S. Medical Licensing Examination (USMLE)

Candidates must demonstrate oral and written English-language competency and supply the following:

- A chronological list of activities beginning with the date of completion of medical school, accounting for all periods of time
- All postgraduate training and continuing medical education programs attended, regardless of whether the program was completed or not
- Any disciplinary actions taken by licensing boards, denying application or renewal
- Any investigations, charges, arrests, pleas of guilty or *nolo contendere*, convictions, or receipts of probation before judgment
- Information pertaining to any physical, mental, or emotional condition that impairs the physician's ability to practice medicine
- Copies of any malpractice suits or settlements, or records of any arrests, disciplinary actions, judgments, final orders, or cases of driving while intoxicated or under the influence of a chemical substance or medication
- Results of all medical licensure, certification, and recertification examinations and the dates when taken

Since the last edition of this book, ten more state medical boards, 46 in total, have added criminal background checks (CBCs) as a requirement of initial licensure. Thirty-nine state medical boards require fingerprints as a condition of initial licensure, and 43 state medical boards have access to the Federal Bureau of Investigation database (Federation of State Medical Boards, 2018). The reasons for CBCs are numerous and include, but are not limited to, increasing societal concerns about alcohol and drug abuse, sexual predation, and child and elder abuse. If a CBC contains reports of criminal convictions, the licensure board will closely examine the physician's application and consider approval on a case-by-case basis. Criteria that will determine the board's decision include the extent and frequency of the criminal behavior and the presence of evidence, often submitted by the applicants themselves, of intervention and treatment such as alcohol and drug abuse rehabilitation.

After successful completion of residency or a fellowship, which may require 3 or more years of training in a medical subspecialty, licensed physicians are considered board eligible (that is, prepared to sit for the specialty examinations in their field). Physicians may voluntarily submit documentation of their education, training, and practice to the relevant American Board of Medical Specialists (ABMS) member board for review (ABMS, 2018b). Upon approval of the medical specialty board, the physician is then allowed to take the examination for **board certification**. Successful completion of the examination(s) allows physicians to be granted certification, and designation as board certified in the specialty or subspecialty (e.g., a board-certified pediatrician or a board-certified neonatologist).

Board certification is a form of credentialing a physician's competency in a specific area. This assumption of quality is based on research that more education and training leads to a higher quality of service (Donabedian, 2005; Tamblyn et al., 1998). Most hospitals, HMOs, and other healthcare organizations require a physician to be board certified to be hired or obtain staff privileges because board certification demonstrates the achievement of a designated standard of knowledge and practice. Board eligible physicians may be hired with the proviso that they will achieve board certification or recertification within a designated period of time.

Board certification today is time-limited; medicine is changing rapidly and physicians must demonstrate continued competency in their evolving fields. The purpose of the American Board of Medical Specialties Maintenance of Certification (ABMS MOC) initiative is to ensure that physicians remain up-to-date in their specialties (ABMS, 2018b). In most specialties, physicians are required to take a closed-book examination every 6–10 years to maintain certification plus provide proof of **continuing medical education (CME)** credits earned every 3–5 years, a statement of good standing from a hospital or clinic chief of service, and documentation of clinical activities.

Additionally, most states require that physicians complete a certain number CME credits to maintain state licensure. Some require a special examination or an ABMS MOC examination to demonstrate continued competency for new or selected applicants. Hospitals may also require a minimum number of annual CME credits for their staff, and credential admitting and attending physicians periodically before allowing them to admit and care for patients at their institution (National Institutes of Health, 2015).

Seven organizations—the American Board of Medical Specialists (ABMS), the American Hospital Association (AHA), the American Medical Association (AMA), the Association of American Medical Colleges (AAMC), the Association for Hospital Medical Education (AHME), the Council of Medical Specialty Societies (CMSS), and the Federation of State Medical Boards, Inc. (FSMB)—are members of the Accreditation Council for Continuing Medical Education (ACCME) (ACCME, 2018). ACCME establishes criteria for determining which educational providers are quality providers of CME and gives its seal of approval only to those organizations and programs meeting their standards (ACCME, 2018). "The ACCME's mission is to identify, develop, and promote rigorous national standards for quality CME that improves physician performance and medical care for patients and their communities" (ACCME, 2018, para. 3).

Because of this great investment in education, initial and ongoing training, and CME, physicians are viewed as national resources and are tracked in the American Medical Association Physician Masterfile database from the day they enter medical school. Originally created a century ago to establish biographical records on physicians, the online database stores information on education, training, and certification for each physician throughout his or her professional career and lifetime. The Masterfile serves as a primary resource for professional medical organizations, universities and medical schools, research institutions, governmental agencies, and other health-related groups. It also maintains records on deceased physicians to prevent individuals from attempting to fraudulently assume their credentials (American Medical Association, 2018).

A comprehensive review of a physician's credentials also involves making electronic queries to the **National Practitioner Data Bank** (NPDB). At one time, physicians who were disciplined or lost their license in one state could simply move to another state and obtain a license there. Other than person-to-person contacts, there were few ways to track "bad docs" who moved across state borders. The NPDB was created so that state licensing boards, hospitals, professional societies, and other healthcare entities could more readily identify, discipline, and report those who engage in unprofessional behavior.

The NPDB is "a workforce tool that prevents practitioners from moving state to state without disclosure or discovery of previous damaging performance" (NPDB, n.d., para. 1). One of the main criticisms of the NPDB, however, is that a physician's record can show that he was sued, but not the outcome of the lawsuit. Many lawsuits are unfounded and dropped or dismissed, but only the original suit report remains on the physician's record. Physicians may dispute a report, but correcting the NPDB record can take significant time and effort and be a source of physician stress and distress. The pressure on physicians to remain current and competent in their specialty and scope of practice is enormous. Physician livelihoods can be at stake. However, because patient lives are also at stake, physician leaders and other senior administrators should be vigilant in promoting and facilitating physician active learning, continuing education, and maintenance of certification for the benefit of both physicians and patients.

Despite the intensity and extent of physician training, many physicians have had little or no instruction or mentoring about administrative and logistical changes in healthcare delivery, such as multidisciplinary collaborative team care, team leadership and management, strategic thinking and planning, and effective communications. Physicians who step beyond the traditional doctor–patient dyad into the role of leading an organization at a population-based, or macro-level, face challenges that may require additional training to enhance their skills and expertise. This training can be provided by the healthcare organization, by a graduate/master's-level degree program at a local university, or via continuing education courses and certificate programs from professional organizations such as the American Association for Physician Leadership.

▶ Physicians, Physician Leaders, and Sexual Harassment

(This section will discuss sexual misconduct. If the content will be disturbing to you, please notify your faculty, do not read the following, and skip this section. If you have additional concerns, please notify your faculty, your counseling center, or your campus sexual misconduct advocate. Thank you.)

Movements to identify, address, and prevent sexual misconduct have gained steam in the public discourse. One segment began with reported abuses in Hollywood and expanded to other settings under the hashtag #MeToo. Complainants in other industries such as health care were not as visible in the early stages of this movement (Zacharek, Doctorman, & Sweetland Edwards, 2017). Unfortunately, the healthcare industry has not been devoid of sexual misconduct, which has been unreported or underreported, and, in many cases in the past, unaddressed.

The U.S. Equal Employment Opportunity Commission (EEOC) defines of sexual harassment as below:

> It is unlawful to harass a person (an applicant or employee) because of that person's sex. Harassment can include "sexual harassment" or unwelcome sexual advances, requests for sexual favors, and other verbal or physical harassment of a sexual nature.
>
> Harassment does not have to be of a sexual nature, however, and can include offensive remarks about a person's sex. For example, it is illegal to harass a woman by making offensive comments about women in general.
>
> Both victim and the harasser can be either a woman or a man, and the victim and harasser can be the same sex.
>
> Although the law doesn't prohibit simple teasing, offhand comments, or isolated incidents that are not very serious, harassment is illegal when it is so frequent or severe that it creates a hostile or offensive work environment or when it results in an adverse employment decision (such as the victim being fired or demoted).
>
> The harasser can be the victim's supervisor, a supervisor in another area, a co-worker, or someone who is not an employee of the employer, such as a client or customer.
>
> (EEOC, n.d.)

Multiple scholarly research studies have documented the widespread prevalence of sexual harassment and misconduct in healthcare settings for more than 2 decades (Barberia, Abedin, Berg, & Nunez-Smith, 2012; Quick & McFadyen, 2017; Riska, 2011; Victor, Wichman, & Malakkla, 2017; Wear & Aultman, 2005). Like the complainants in the #MeToo movement, healthcare professionals who have experienced such incidents have been afraid to come forward, fearing negative consequences for their careers and future. Empowered by the #MeToo movement, healthcare professionals (mostly women, but a few men as well) have expressed complaints via the #MedToo movement (Chuck, 2018; Jagsi, 2018; Rege, 2017).

Complainants have provided examples such as:

> From a physician who was a resident at the time of this incident: [She] "... was almost finished spreading apart the patient's staples...the attending physician leaned over so his face was uncomfortably close to hers. 'You know how to spread good,' he whispered ... 'That will teach you how to spread,' (Chuck, 2018, para 3–4)."

> From a Nurse Practitioner who was a student at the time of this incident: "...a professor in a community college's nursing program...pulled her aside to go over a paper during class and told her, 'I've noticed you like to wear shirts that zip down in the front. I really like that.' (Chuck, 2018, para 42)."

> From a physician who was an attending surgeon at the time of this incident: "I spent the evening rebuffing his advances...he accosted me in the coat room...winked at the attendant and said, 'She loves surgeons.' A senior female surgeon happened by... I said, 'I do adore surgeons...I planned to walk home with her.' (Jagsi, 2018, p. 210)."

Retaliation for sexual harassment or misconduct complaints has discouraged others from reporting incidents or serving as witnesses to incidents (Chuck, 2018; Jagsi, 2018; Jagsi et al., 2016). In the case of Doe v Mercy Catholic Medical Center (2017), Doe claimed she was sexually harassed and dismissed in retaliation for complaining about the sexual advances during her residency training. When she complained to Human Resources (HR), Doe was repeatedly told she would have to undergo psychiatric treatment and a remediation plan to be allowed to stay in the residency program—even as her harasser's behaviors increased. She sued under Title IX, the Education Amendment which prohibits discrimination in educational programs based on gender. The defendant (Mercy Catholic Medical Center) claimed the residency was not an educational training program, but a job, and therefore the complainant was subject to the policies and procedures of the HR department just as was any other employee. The court ruled that the residency training program was indeed an educational program and, therefore, subject to Title IX. Unfortunately, by the time Doe's case was adjudicated in court, her ability for due recourse had been cut off, and she was unable to find another residency training program that would accept her. Her opportunities for board eligibility and certification and for her intended career in radiological medicine were damaged. Her case, however, set a precedent for all residency training programs in the United States (Doe v Mercy Catholic Medical Center, 2017).

Sexual harassment has been described as being about "power, aggression, and manipulation" (Quick in Smith, 2018, p. 38). Organizational values and culture can enable sexual harassment (Quick & McFayden, 2017). It can be an underreported phenomenon because victims fear retaliation. Researchers have demonstrated that "harassers and aggressors destroy lives" (Quick & McFayden, 2017, p. 286).

The #MeToo movement has made it clear that organizations that condone or ignore sexual harassment and sexual misconduct will be held up to public scrutiny and may suffer grave legal and financial consequences (Relias, 2016; Wamsley, 2018). All healthcare organizations have the obligation to provide a safe environment for all employees, including healthcare professionals—even if the respondent in a sexual misconduct complaint is a "high value employee" or a "heavy admitter" who brings significant revenues to the healthcare organization. Annual training to update all employees about the expectations of the organization's leadership can provide guidelines for professional behavior; presentation of the organization's sexual misconduct policy, methods to prevent and report sexual misconduct, either experienced or observed; resources for employee assistance and care; consequences for respondents who are found guilty of misconduct; and reassurances that retaliation for incident reports will not be tolerated.

Physician leaders must not only be role models of integrity, they must have zero tolerance for unprofessional behaviors in their healthcare organizations. Organization leaders and Human Resources departments must also take every complaint seriously—or risk suffering the consequences of being found complicit in a criminal or civil suit. Investigations of sexual harassment or sexual misconduct complaints must be thorough, objective, and confidential. Organization leaders and administrators, including physician leaders, would be wise to consider additional training on sexual misconduct prevention and response. A final note: Not all sexual misconduct is from employees to employees. This misconduct can come from patients as well.

▶ Physician Leaders in Healthcare Organizations

In years past, hospital administrators were typically physicians. It was not uncommon in mid-century for hospitals and clinics to be owned and operated by physicians. Their years of medical training, however, did not usually include study in business and finance, which play a critical role in the strategic planning, financial stability, and sustainability of healthcare organizations. The recognition of the value of business skills and expertise led to the development of professional education programs for health administrators who could provide oversight and management of healthcare organizations. Additionally, the expansion of federal and state legislation and regulations over the past few decades required leaders to be well versed in health administration areas such as human and financial resource management, quality control, quality assessment, accountability and compliance, accreditation, and communications and marketing. Health administration graduates become experts in strategic and operational leadership and now serve as hospital CEOs and CFOs. However, health administrators need to work closely and collaboratively with physicians and other clinicians who contribute their expertise to organization leadership as elected or appointed chiefs of medical staff, division chiefs, or department chairs. Physicians who earn degrees such as an MBA, MPH, MHA, or JD can often be found in the C-suite as well.

The **chief of medical staff** often serves both as ambassador and as negotiator between the executive administration and the physicians on staff. A successful chief of medical staff can become a champion for the physician stakeholders in the organization, advocating and representing his or her constituency. The chief of medical staff can also be a valuable contributor of clinical expertise and a conduit from the health administration executives to the staff physicians for strategic planning and change processes. Unfortunately, at times, the chief of the medical staff was viewed with skepticism by other physicians who believed that he or she no longer represented the perspective of the practicing doctor, but instead had been co-opted by ("gone to the dark side") of "administration."

Providing physicians with the necessary business and management skills for successful leadership has helped to avoid these pitfalls and overcome such challenges. The financial and economic pressures that have triggered the breadth of changes in healthcare organizations over the past 30 years demand a skilled team of leaders at the helm, including trained physicians who are "bilingual," that is, who can speak the language of business as well as the language of medicine.

Physician leaders are often drawn from a pool of highly competitive individuals who were trained with a focus on individual patients and one-on-one case examination (i.e., the microlevel of care). Physician leaders must refocus their perspective from the micro to the meta—from the needs of the individual patient to the big picture of a complex healthcare organization and its community. This change of perspective can be challenging for some potential leaders and intuitive for others, especially when additional training and mentoring are provided to encourage skills development.

Clearly, professional experience and training can play a major role in a potential physician leader's perspective. Physicians who graduated from medical school in the 1960s through the 1990s have seen seismic changes in the system of healthcare delivery. Many doctors find these changes frustrating and overwhelming, and are scrambling to cover costs and escape perceived burdens of practice. Some even opt to sell their practices to hospitals with an eye toward retirement rather than address new paradigms of patient care.

A number of organizations that have purchased and/or consolidated practices to increase patient volumes have subsequently faced economic challenges because the buyers had not created a strategic plan for these new acquisitions, or defined post-transition operational changes and productivity expectations with the on-boarded physicians, who are still practicing with a micro-perspective (LeValley, 2010).

On the other hand, recent escalations in purchases of medical practices by hospitals and medical corporations have resurrected fears about the **corporate practice of medicine (CPOM)**, that is, where the corporation dictates how medicine is practiced and overrides physicians' medical judgments (AMA, 2015). These concerns are underscored by the increasing emphasis on the corporate bottom line and the nascent behavior of some non-profits as for-profit organizations, that is, an intense focus on the bottom line and margins. In such a situation, the purchasing organization would be better served if a physician leader with both clinical expertise and business skills worked with the on-boarded MDs to plan and implement a smooth transition from private practice into a consolidated healthcare organization, and to address concerns about how medicine is practiced under the new arrangement.

Physician leaders may not only face challenges communicating with their practicing peers, but with the executive administrators as well. A chief executive officer (CEO) and chief operating officer (COO) may not share the same strategic perspective on how an organization can provide cost-effective, high-quality health care. The use of evidence-based research and guidelines, as well as the implementation of best practices to promote quality improvement in health care and reduce unnecessary expenditures, can bring administrative and clinical leaders together by suggesting effective common strategies to achieve a high quality of care.

Because of their education and training, many physicians tend to gravitate toward clinical leadership roles, wherein they can maximize the use of their medical expertise. Examples of such roles are medical directors of clinics and laboratories. Other physician leaders have moved into roles that demand business as well as medical expertise, such as **chief medical officer** (CMO), CEO, and COO. Research on the 300 best hospitals in the United States found an association between the presence of physician CEOs and higher quality of patient care scores (Goodall, 2011). Additional studies may be able to further identify the skillsets that successful physician leaders provide toward this goal.

Among the leadership opportunities for physicians is service as chairpersons of clinical departments such as Surgery, Medicine, Obstetrics and Gynecology, Pediatrics, etc. Chairs are often responsible for **physician credentialing** and **physician privileging** in their department: developing and updating medical staff bylaws, promoting physician adherence to bylaws and regulations, and ensuring standards of care are met by the unit's doctors through ongoing assessments such as peer review, disciplining physicians whose personal or professional behavior falls below accepted legal and practice standards, and coordinating quality assessment programs that use regular audits and evaluations to engage in continuous quality improvement. Credentialing and privileging must be repeated periodically, as frequently as every 1–2 years for most healthcare organizations, and require a review of the staff physicians' CME, certification, and performance. Some seek assistance for this demanding task from credential verification organizations, which can gather primary verification for credentialing criteria and can collate information from national databases about physicians' professional and performance history.

If a physician's performance or behavior falls below expected standards, chairs may be tasked with intervening to address this disparity. Medical staff bylaws, human resource services guidelines, and state medical board regulations must be adhered to during this process, as the impact of such intervention and possible discipline on a physician's professional career can lead to the loss of privileges to practice in the organization and even the loss of a license to practice medicine.

Spurred by the significant changes in the healthcare landscape, more physicians are pursuing education and training in leadership and management via business courses and executive MBA programs. There are now more than 60 MD/MBA programs in existence in the United States (Association of MD/MBA Programs, 2018). Graduates of these business programs are well prepared to assume a variety of leadership roles in the healthcare industry. Some may choose clinical leadership positions in small or large healthcare organizations, but others may opt for other professional opportunities, for example, with insurance companies or government agencies, such as the Centers for Medicare and Medicaid Services, the Agency for Health Care Research and Quality, and the National Institutes of Health.

Insurance companies and hospitals have long used physicians to perform utilization review, and this role continues to be critical. When physicians in practice request or advocate for insurance payment for specific services, the expertise of a physician employed by the insurance company can be invaluable in helping to assess or determine the medical necessity of those services (American Board of Quality Assurance and Utilization Review Physicians, n.d.).

Some healthcare organizations have established the position of CMO, which is especially suited to candidates with multiple degrees and diverse professional training and expertise, such as an MD/JD (attorney). A CMO's duties may include negotiating the organization's contracts and, in light of our litigious society, supervising patient safety, quality assessment, and risk management programs.

Physician leaders can be an important asset for healthcare organizations. Those physicians who choose to expand their training and expertise into crucial areas such as finance, management, and law will continue to be sought after to help organizations survive and thrive in these challenging times.

▶ Physician Leadership and Conflict Management Skills

Healthcare organizations share common characteristics with other diverse organizations, including similar patterns of communication, collaboration, and conflict. Many healthcare professionals chose their professions because they wanted to help people. Highly educated in their individual fields, each professional brings a different perspective to the healthcare team as to how to provide the best care for a patient or a population of patients. These diverse views can sometimes lead to conflicts. While conflict is often perceived as bad, healthcare managers and physician leaders should not fear or avoid it. With an understanding of individual and group differences that prompt the emergence of conflict, organizations can channel conflict into a positive mechanism that leads to productive change. In healthy, well-run organizations, conflict can be a means to bring fresh ideas to the table, to provide opportunities to air different points of view, and to help the organization evolve and grow.

The high stress environment in which healthcare professionals work can be a breeding ground for tension, miscommunication, and conflict, not only among staff, but among professionals and patients as well. Fires of conflict in healthcare settings can rage out of control and even lead to violence, unless managed properly. The consequences of unmanaged conflict could lead to negative patient outcomes and a drop in the quality of care.

This section will provide an example of a common conflict scenario in a hospital, discuss some of the underlying issues that created the challenges, and demonstrate steps that physician leaders can use to successfully manage conflict.

Scenario: Central Line Protocol

Current standards state that an infected central line should be a "never event," and therefore require a standardized protocol for central line insertion (The Joint Commission, 2018). Cutting Edge Hospital, through its medical executive committee, has approved a policy that mandates a protocol for insertion of central lines. Dr. Quik has been consulted to place a central line for intravenous (IV) access in a very ill patient who is headed to the intensive care unit (ICU). As he inserts the catheter, Dr. Quik omits a major step in the protocol. Agnes Bythebook, RN, attempts to inform Dr. Quik that he has not adequately followed the protocol. Dr. Quik becomes quite indignant and belittles Nurse Bythebook in front of the patient and staff.

Nurse Bythebook reports the incident to her supervisor, who reports it to the Quality Assurance Officer, who, in turn, sends the report to Dr. Quik's department chair and supervisor. Upon questioning, Dr. Quik states, "It was a life-threatening emergency and there was no time to follow the protocol."

Underlying Issues

Dr. Quik was trained as a capable independent practitioner, but is inexperienced in serving as part of a healthcare team. He is a dedicated, responsible physician who deeply cares about his patients, but is not used to answering questions or collaborating in the provision of treatment. Dr. Quik's greatest fear is losing a patient. He believes he did the right thing at the right time for a very sick patient and is the most qualified to make treatment decisions without being questioned or challenged.

Nurse Bythebook is a graduate of an MSN program, who completed an ICU nurse residency training program, and is preparing to take her advanced certification exams as an ICU nurse. Nurse Bythebook wants to avoid unintentionally hurting a patient either directly or indirectly. She believes that advocating for the protocol was the correct action at the right time for a very ill patient.

Healthcare delivery systems now demand that healthcare professionals work together with other health professionals to provide high-quality health care as members of healthcare teams. Clinical research has underscored the importance of excellence in teamwork in the operating room (OR). A multisite retrospective study of 74 Veterans Health Administration (VHA) facilities found that "participation in the

VHA Medical Team Training program was associated with a lower surgical mortality rate" (Neily et al., 2010, p. 1693). The authors reported an 18% *reduction* in annual mortality rates, representing lives saved through teamwork. The findings from this study are significant not only in a research sense but also in a true clinical sense. Dissemination of these findings throughout surgical training programs in the United States will require enormous effort because surgeons often believe "they alone are responsible for patient outcomes" (Pronovost & Freischlag, 2010, p. 1721). It will take a major culture shift to move many physicians and surgeons from this "solo savior" mentality to the "There is no I in teamwork" approach.

Additionally, through collaborative discussion and review, collaborative teams provide a system of checks and balances that reduce the risk of unintentional medical errors that could result in an untoward or tragic patient outcome.

Conflicts between team members often come to the attention of the physician chair of a department, whose role includes serving as a mediator to improve and facilitate the effective communication and work of the team. Educating members of the healthcare team, especially those who have little experience with team function, about the benefits of collaboration for quality of care and patient outcomes can promote buy-in and cooperation by previously reluctant participants.

Management of conflict today, just like the delivery of health care itself, requires a team—a team of skilled managers such as physician and nurse leaders. In the case given, the designated supervisors of the involved team members (e.g., physician department chair and the nursing supervisor) were recruited to assist with reviewing the team members' communications and function and, when indicated, coaching and mentoring the participants in improved team operations. If inappropriate or abusive behavior has been reported, and team members or patients perceive a hostile work environment, human resources professionals may assist physician and nursing leaders in defining and reviewing standards of behavior and, if necessary, implementing disciplinary action.

Physician Leaders' Steps for Conflict Resolution

1. Determine the facts of the case. Such investigations are best done by interviewing all involved parties and witnesses separately and privately.
2. Identify the areas of concern. These may include quality-of-care issues, communications issues, or violations of rules and regulations. Each area should be handled discretely—and discreetly.
3. Use medical expertise to come to a conclusion as to the appropriateness of the medical treatment and deviation from protocols and guidelines. Use management expertise to determine the appropriateness of the behaviors and the possible presence of a hostile work environment.

In the example given, the department chair reviewed the case and agreed with Dr. Quik's medical perspective that his actions were medically appropriate during such an urgent situation. However, the chair also validated the actions of Nurse Bythebook, recognizing that her questioning the deviation from protocol was a valuable contribution toward preventing medical error and ensuring a high standard of care.

Unfortunately, the private interviews conducted by the department chair confirmed that Dr. Quik had communicated inappropriately with his team colleague and that Nurse Bythebook now perceived that she was serving in a hostile work environment. After consulting with Human Resources, the department chair met with Dr. Quik for oral counseling and a written reprimand that clarified expectations for professional behavior and communications, and presented a training program for Dr. Quik to improve his communications, anger management, and team function skills. The chair also supported Nurse Bythebook's supervisor and Human Resources as they explored whether the hostile work environment persisted and additional steps needed to be taken to ensure a safe work environment for Nurse Bythebook. Finally, the chair advised Dr. Quik that repetition of unacceptable behavior may lead to further disciplinary action up to and including loss of hospital privileges and/or termination.

Many healthcare organizations are now proactive in educating and training their healthcare professionals in teamwork and collaborative practice to support a high-quality, patient-centric culture. Some organizations such as the American Association for Physician Leadership, the Center for Creative Leadership, and the Studer Group (2018) provide access to outside resources for coaching and mentoring of physicians. For example, the Center for Creative Leadership (CCL, 2018) conducts week-long on-site training for entire healthcare teams. Though such training may be expensive, the investment can save an organization millions of dollars by staving off grievances and other legal actions down the road.

▶ Future Leadership Roles for Physicians in Evolving Healthcare Organizations

The ancient Greek philosopher Heraclitus wisely advised that "The only constant is change." Just as healthcare organizations constantly change with the times, so do the leadership roles for physicians. The following are some areas where we foresee increasing demands for physician leaders in evolving healthcare organizations.

- *Health Information Technology and Health Informatics:* With the adoption of Electronic Health Records in healthcare organizations, physicians may be involved in the transition from paper charts to electronic records or in the upgrading of practice management software or its transition to the cloud. Physician "superusers" can help administrators select the best software and hardware and cloud storage for this process, promote necessary encryption and security features to ensure HIPAA compliance, as well as design templates that increase clinician efficiency while prompting the documentation necessary for effective reimbursement and quality assurance efforts. Superusers can also be excellent mentors and teachers for physicians new to a system or product.
- *Patient Safety:* The appointment of Donald Berwick, MD, a pediatrician and former CEO of the Institute for Healthcare Improvement (IHI), as the interim head of the Centers for Medicare and Medicaid signaled an important shift in linking patient safety to payments from the country's largest healthcare insurance provider. Although he is no longer at CMS, Dr. Berwick's presence made a major impact on that federal agency.
- *Performance Improvement/Quality Assessment:* Continuous quality improvement has been a staple of healthcare organizations in the past 30 years. Initiatives have included accreditation, audits, peer reviews, morbidity and mortality

review boards, etc. Assessment findings are analyzed and used to "close the loop" in the QI process by informing intentional change in goals, objectives, and strategies. Since the publication of the IOM report, the focus has shifted toward prevention of errors and negative outcomes, and increased use of evidence-based, performance-improvement methods, such as *poka-yokes*. Insertion of these mistake-proof, "fail-safe" mechanisms and backups can prevent errors and reduce patient risks. Physicians trained in quality-improvement methodologies are in high demand.

- *Consulting:* Physicians who have strong administrative and clinical skillsets can serve as independent contractors and private consultants to mentor and coach physician and nonphysician leaders and healthcare staff in organizations. Healthcare consulting firms are increasingly hiring or collaborating with broadly trained physician leaders with MBAs and JDs to expand their resource capabilities.

Summary

Physician leaders play a critical role in successful health services delivery. This chapter has described physician education, training, and continuing education; compared and contrasted clinical versus nonclinical leadership roles in healthcare organizations; defined and discussed sexual harassment and misconduct in medicine; identified common roles of physician leaders in healthcare organizations; analyzed a scenario where conflict management skills are critical to effective physician leadership; and hypothesized future leadership roles for physicians in evolving healthcare organizations. The need for ethical physician leadership will only continue to grow. Wise healthcare managers will recruit, select, and work to retain good physician leaders.[1]

Discussion Questions

1. Delineate the steps in attaining state licensure for physicians for your state.
2. What is the difference between licensure and credentialing?
3. Why is it important to have physician leaders who have both medical and managerial expertise?
4. Define sexual harassment and misconduct and discuss the impact on employees in healthcare organizations.
5. Identify and describe two clinical and two nonclinical leadership roles for physicians.
6. What are the necessary steps that physician leaders can take to address healthcare team conflicts between physicians and other team members?
7. Identify and describe some of the future roles for physician leaders.

---

1 Parts of the "Physician Education, Training, and Continuing Education" and "Physician Leadership and Conflict Management Skills" sections of this chapter were originally published in Introduction to Health Care Management (2nd ed.), 2012 by Sharon B. Buchbinder and Nancy H. Shanks and are reprinted here with permission of the publisher.

🔍 *CASE STUDY: To Be or Not to Be #MeToo?*

Dr. Mary Jane Malone, a 28-year-old general surgery resident, noticed that over the past 6 months, Dr. Ethan Jones, a renowned middle-aged general surgeon at Metropolitan University Hospital, had been giving her a particularly hard time during patient rounds and in the operating room. He had been extremely critical with the care she was delivering to his patients and of her abilities in the operating room. Recently, he gave her a written substandard evaluation. In the past, Dr. Malone had received outstanding evaluations from other surgeons that she had worked with over her first 3 years, and was taken aback by the events surrounding Dr. Jones.

Was it because she refused to go out with him? On several occasions prior to these derogatory comments and evaluations, Dr. Jones had asked Dr. Malone have dinner and drinks with him. It was common knowledge that Dr. Jones was married with three children and was supposedly a devoted husband and family man. One night while performing an emergency appendectomy in the operating room with Dr. Jones, he turned to Dr. Malone and said, "Things would go much better for you if you spent some private time with me." Dr. Malone replied to Dr. Jones that she was engaged and he was married. Dr. Jones pressed her, saying that if she would make time for him, he would see to it that she received better evaluations, be treated better in the residency program, and he would allow her to perform more of his surgeries. This conversation was overheard by the scrub tech, the circulating nurse, and the anesthesiologist.

Case Study Discussion Questions

1. Using the conflict management steps outlined in the scenario earlier in this chapter, what should happen next in this case?
2. What potential consultation(s) should the physician leaders seek?
3. What should the bystanders in the operating room have done? Provide a rationale for your response.
4. Dr. Jones is a heavy admitter. Should he be treated differently from other physicians who do not bring in large revenues for the hospital? Provide a rationale for your response.

🔍 *CASE STUDY: Conflict of Interest or Quality of Patient Care*

Dr. Smith, head of orthopedics at Cutting Edge Hospital, insists on using only products manufactured by BoneMedCo, despite the existence of multiple comparable lines that are manufactured by other companies. If the hospital could shift to a different product line, it could mean a savings of more than $1 million in the next fiscal year. Dr. Smith is adamant: He will not use any other products.

Dr. Richards, the chair of Surgery, reviews the BoneMedCo website, and it is obvious to him that Dr. Smith has been involved in the development of several products and is receiving large royalties on sales. When Dr. Richards and Dr. Justus, the chief medical officer, meet with Dr. Smith, they show him the website and state that they feel this is the reason Dr. Smith is reluctant to use or even evaluate other company products. Dr. Richards and Dr. Justus tell Dr. Smith that they feel this is a

conflict of interest (COI): that is, when individuals can be influenced by money or other considerations to act in a way that is contrary to the good of their employer or the patient for whom they should be advocating.

Dr. Justus points to the Cutting Edge Hospital policy manual and states, "All physicians and employees who make purchasing decisions must complete a COI form disclosing all potential conflicts. Furthermore, you filed a COI form, but did not note your relationship with BoneMedCo."

Dr. Smith replies, "Yes, I helped to develop some of the products, and I just began receiving royalties from BoneMedCo. I planned to update my COI form, but it slipped my mind. Furthermore, these products were developed to my exacting standards. I believe they provide a better quality of care for the patient. Are you saying you want me to give inferior patient care?"

Case Study Discussion Questions

1. Using the conflict management steps outlined in the scenario earlier in this chapter, what should happen next?
2. What potential consultation(s) should the physician leaders seek?
3. If this relationship between Dr. Smith and BoneMedCo was active at the time the COI form was filed, how should that discovery impact the administrator's decisions?
4. At a subsequent meeting, Dr. Smith provides three hot-off-the-presses peer-reviewed articles in prestigious medical journals that conclude the device he helped to create is superior to all others on the market. Do these data change things?
5. What should Drs. Richards and Justus do next? What should Dr. Smith do next?
6. Should conflict of interest be overlooked if doing so could potentially benefit a healthcare organization or its patients?

Related Websites

ABIM Foundation: www.abimfoundation.org/default.aspx
American Association of Medical Colleges: www.aamc.org
American Association for Physician Leadership: www.physicianleaders.org
Association of MD/MBA Programs: www.mdmbaprograms.org
Institute for Healthcare Improvement: www.ihi.org/ihi
Liaison Council on Medical Education: www.lcme.org
Medical College Admissions Test: https://students-residents.aamc.org/applying-medical-school/taking-mcat-exam/
National Board of Medical Examiners: www.nbme.org/
United States Medical Licensing Examination: www.usmle.org/

Additional Resources

ABIM Renewing Professionalism: A Challenge to the Health Care Community. Resetting the Social Contract (Part II)—In the Service of Patients: www.youtube.com/watch?v=A9WcAYrqKBI&feature=related
IHI: Apologizing Effectively to Patients and Families: www.youtube.com/watch?v=kDfoJXq8BRA&feature=relmfu
IHI: Defining Quality: Aiming for a Better Health Care System: www.youtube.com/watch?v=5vOxunpnIsQ
IHI: Open School for Health Professionals: www.ihi.org/IHI/Programs/IHIOpenSchool/
Metoo: https://metoomvmt.org/
Practicing Wise Stewardship of Resources (Part I): Embracing Stewardship in Daily Practice: www.youtube.com/watch?v=P3i2a91HxKA

Renewing Professionalism: A Challenge to the Health Care Community. Why Does Professionalism Matter? (Part I)—Perspectives on Professionalism: www.youtube.com/watch?v=2PIplMOIINg&feature=related

Renewing Professionalism: A Challenge to the Health Care Community. Improving Systems to Deliver High Quality Care (Part II)—Collaborating & Working in Teams: www.youtube.com/watch?v=Glhd7pxyPZg&feature=related

Vo, L. T. (2017, December 5). *We got government data on 20 years of workplace sexual harassment claims: These charts break it down. How prevalent is sexual harassment at your job? We crunched a ton of information — and it's still just the tip of the iceberg.* https://www.buzzfeed.com/lamvo/eeoc-sexual-harassment-data?utm_term=.rayY6ynVd#.lk29WXl6q

Vo, L. T. (2017, December 28). *This is how you defined sexual harassment.* https://www.buzzfeed.com/lamvo/define-sexual-harassment-at-work?utm_term=.vtD8AxnLN#.mvdBN0Jl8

References

Accreditation Council for Continuing Medical Education (ACCME). (2018). *ACCME at a glance.* Retrieved from http://www.accme.org/for-media/accme-at-a-glance

Accreditation Council for Graduate Medical Education (ACGME). (2018a). *The history of duty hours.* Retrieved from http://www.acgme.org/What-We-Do/Accreditation/Clinical-Experience-and-Education-formerly-Duty-Hours/History-of-Duty-Hours

Accreditation Council for Graduate Medical Education (ACGME). (2018b). *Summary of changes to ACGME common program requirements section VI.* Retrieved from http://www.acgme.org/What-We-Do/Accreditation/Common-Program-Requirements/Summary-of-Proposed-Changes-to-ACGME-Common-Program-Requirements-Section-VI

Alvin, M. D. (2017). iCOMPARE: An intern's perspective. *Journal of Graduate Medical Education, 9*(2), 261–262.

American Board of Medical Specialists (ABMS). (2018a). *Frequently asked questions.* Retrieved from http://www.abms.org/about-abms/faqs-abms/

American Board of Medical Specialists (ABMS). (2018b). *Board certification and maintenance of certification.* Retrieved from http://www.abms.org/board-certification/

American Board of Quality Assurance and Utilization Review Physicians (ABQAURP). (n.d.). *About ABQAURP.* Retrieved from https://www.abqaurp.org/ABQMain/About_Us/Mission/ABQMain/Mission.aspx?hkey=698cff8e-c604-4e32-b5e5-1319431aa71a

American Medical Association. (2015). *Issue brief: Corporate practice of medicine.* Retrieved from https://www.ama-assn.org/sites/default/files/media-browser/premium/arc/corporate-practice-of-medicine-issue-brief_1.pdf

American Medical Association. (2018). *AMA Physician Masterfile.* Retrieved from https://www.ama-assn.org/life-career/ama-physician-masterfile

Annotated Code of Maryland (COMAR). (2016). *Licensure: Qualifications for initial licensure.* Retrieved from http://mdrules.elaws.us/comar/10.32.01.03

Asch, D., Bilimoria, K. Y., & Desai, S. V. (2017). Resident duty hours and medical education policy: Raising the evidence bar. *376*(18), 1704. Retrieved from http://www.nejm.org/doi/full/10.1056/NEJMp1703690

Association of American Medical Colleges (AAMC). (2018). *Aspiring docs: The basics.* Retrieved from https://students-residents.aamc.org/choosing-medical-career/medical-careers/aspiring-docs/aspiring-docs-fact-sheets/aspiring-docs-basics/

Association of MD/MBA Programs. (2018). *MD/MBA programs.* Retrieved from http://www.mdmbaprograms.org/md-mba-programs/

Babaria, P., Abedin, S., Berg, D., & Nunez-Smith, M. (2012, April). "I'm too used to it": A longitudinal qualitative study of third year female medical students' experiences of gendered encounters in medical education. *Supports Open Access, 74*(7), 1013–1020. doi:10.1016/j.socscimed.2011.11.043. Epub 2012 Feb 7.

Bilimoria, K. Y., Chung, J. W., Hedges, L. V., Dahlke, A. R., Love, R., Cohen, M. E., ... Lewis, F. R. (2016). National cluster-randomized trial of duty-hour flexibility in surgical training. *New England Journal of Medicine, 374*(8), 713–727.

Bureau of Labor Statistics (BLS). (2018a). *Career guide to industries, healthcare.* Retrieved from https://www.bls.gov/ooh/healthcare/home.htm

Bureau of Labor Statistics (BLS). (2018b). Occupational outlook handbook *physicians and surgeons.* Retrieved from https://www.bls.gov/ooh/healthcare/physicians-and-surgeons.htm

Center for Creative Leadership (CCL). (2018). *About the center for creative leadership.* Retrieved from https://www.ccl.org/about-the-center-for-creative-leadership/

Chuck, E. (2018, February 20). *#MeToo in medicine: Women harassed in hospitals and operating rooms, awaiting reckoning.* Retrieved from https://www.nbcnews.com/storyline/sexual-misconduct/harassed-hospitals-operating-rooms-women-medicine-await-their-metoo-moment-n846031

Desai, S. V., David, A. A., Bellini, L. M., Chaiyachati, K. H., Liu, M., Sternberg, A. L., ... for the iCOMPARE Research Group*. (2018, March 20). Education outcomes in a duty-hour flexibility trial in internal medicine. *New England Journal of Medicine,* doi:10.1056/NEJMoa1800965

Doe v Mercy Catholic Medical Center. (2017, 3rd. Cir.). Retrieved from https://www.justice.gov/crt/case-document/file/947101/download

Donabedian, A. (2005). Evaluating the quality of medical care. *The Milbank Quarterly, 83*(4), 691–729.

Equal Employment Opportunity Commission (EEOC). (n.d.). *Sexual harassment.* Retrieved from https://www.eeoc.gov/laws/types/sexual_harassment.cfm

Federation of State Medical Boards (FSMB). (2018, January 29). *Criminal background checks: Board by board overview.* Retrieved from http://www.fsmb.org/globalassets/advocacy/key-issues/criminal-background-checks-by-state2.pdf

Goodall, A. (2011, July 6). Physician–leaders and hospital performance: Is there an association? *Social Science and Medicine, 73*(4), 535–539. doi:10.1016/j.socscimed.2011.06.025

Hoffman, J. (1995). *Jurors find shared blame in '84 death.* Retrieved from https://www.nytimes.com/1995/02/07/nyregion/jurors-find-shared-blame-in-84-death.html?pagewanted=all

iCOMPARE. (2018). *Individualized comparative effectiveness of models optimizing patient safety and resident education.* Retrieved from http://www.jhcct.org/icompare/

Jagsi, R. (2018). Sexual harassment in medicine–#MeToo. *New England Journal of Medicine, 378*(3), 209–211.

Jagsi, R., Griffith, K. A., Jones, R., Perumalswami, C. R., Ubel, P., & Stewart, A. (2016). Sexual harassment and discrimination experiences of academic medical faculty. *Journal of the American Medical Association, 315*(19), 2120–2121. doi:10.1001/jama.2016.2188

The Joint Commission. (2018). *CLABSI toolkit and monograph.* Retrieved from https://www.jointcommission.org/topics/clabsi_toolkit.aspx

LeValley, C. (2010, September 1). *3 Considerations for hospitals acquiring practices.* Retrieved November 8, 2012 from www.beckershospitalreview.com/hospital-physician-relationships/3-considerations-for-hospitals-acquiring-practices.html

McMahon, G. T. (2018, March 20). Managing the most precious resource in medicine. *New England Journal of Medicine, 378,* 1552–1554. doi:10.1056/NEJMe1802899

National Institutes of Health (NIH). (2015). *Frequently asked questions.* Retrieved from www.nih.gov/news/calendar/calendarfaq.htm#cmecredit

National Practitioner Data Bank. (n.d.). Retrieved from https://www.npdb.hrsa.gov/topNavigation/aboutUs.jsp

National Residency Matching Program (NRMP). (2018). Retrieved from http://www.nrmp.org/about-nrmp/

Neily, J., Mills, P. D., Young-Xu, Y., Careney, B. T., West, P., Berger, D. H., ... Bagian, J. P. (2010). Association between implementation of a medical team training program and surgical mortality. *Journal of the American Medical Association, 304*(15), 1693–1700.

Pronovost, P. J., & Freischlag, J. A. (2010). Improving teamwork to reduce surgical mortality. *Journal of the American Medical Association, 304*(15), 1721–1722.

Quick, J. C., in Smith, B. L. (2018). What it takes to really stop sexual harassment: Psychologists call for a comprehensive approach with a real-world impact. *Monitor on Psychology, 9*(2), 38.

Quick, J. C., & McFadyen, M. A. (2017). Sexual harassment: Have we made any progress? *Journal of Occupational Health Psychology, 22*(3), 286–298. doi:10.1037/ocp0000054

Rege, A. (2017, December 6). *Report: At least 3,085 hospital employees filed sexual harassment claims between 1995 and 2016.* Retrieved from https://www.beckershospitalreview.com /hospital-physician-relationships/report-at-least-3-085-hospital-employees-filed-sexual -harassment-claims-between-1995-and-2016.html

Relias. (2016, April 1). *Hospitals sued — claims of sexual abuse, harassment.* Retrieved from https:// www.ahcmedia.com/articles/137564-hospitals-sued-claims-of-sexual-abuse-harassment

Riesenberg, L. A. (2012). Shift-to-shift handoff research: Where do we go from here? *Journal of Graduate Medical Education, 4*(1), 4–8. doi:10.4300/JGME-D-11-00308.1

Riska, E. (2011). Gender and medical careers. *Maturitas, 68*(3), 264–267.

Starmer, A. J., Spector, N. D., Srivastava, R., West, D. C., Rosenbluth, G., Allen, A. D. … for the I-PASS Study Group*. (2014). Changes in medical errors after implementation of a handoff program. *New England Journal of Medicine, 371*(19), 1803–1812. doi:10.1056/NEJMsa1405556

Studer Group. (2018). *About.* Retrieved from https://www.studergroup.com/who-we-are/about -studer-group

Tamblyn, R., Abrahamowicz, M., Brailovsky, C., Grand'Maison, P., Lescop, J., Norcini, J., … Haggerty, J. (1998). Association between licensing examination scores and resource use and quality of care in primary care practice. *Journal of the American Medical Association, 280*(11), 989–996.

St. Victor, G., Wichman, C. L., & Malakkla, N. (2017). Speaking up: Sexual harassment in the medical setting. *Psychiatric Times, 34*(6), 1–5.

Wamsley, L. (2018, February 26). *Weinstein company will file for bankruptcy after sale talks collapse.* Retrieved from https://www.npr.org/sections/thetwo-way/2018/02/26/588791946 /weinstein-company-will-file-for-bankruptcy-after-sale-talks-collapse

Wear, D., & Aultman, J. (2005). Sexual harassment in academic medicine: Persistence, non-reporting, and institutional response. *Medical Education Online, 10*(1), 4377. doi:10.3402/meo.v10i.4377

Zacharek, S., Doctorman, E., & Sweetland Edwards, H. (2017). *Time person of the year: The silence breakers.* Retrieved from http://time.com/time-person-of-the-year-2017-silence-breakers/

CHAPTER 14

Governance in a New Era

Salvador J. Esparza and Michael L. Wall

LEARNING OBJECTIVES

By the end of this chapter, the student will be able to:

- Understand traditional structures of governance and identify new structures in an environment of healthcare reform.
- Describe the skills and qualifications needed for ideal governance.
- Understand the issue of public scrutiny and its effect on governance.
- Discuss potential strategic alternatives with a quality emphasis.

KEY TERMS

Accountability	Governing body
Fiduciary duty	Trustee/director
Governance	

▶ Introduction

Healthcare organizations (HCOs) today range from not-for-profit, traditional models to corporate and entrepreneurial ventures. The **governance** of modern healthcare enterprises demands increased levels of functioning: one that utilizes the knowledge, skills, and expertise of key individuals to provide the most cost-effective and highest quality of care to target patients and communities. These key individuals frequently make up the organization's governing board or **governing body**, whose responsibility is to govern on behalf of the organization's stakeholders or shareholders (Pointer & Orlikoff, 1999). Effective governance can only result if governing board members clearly understand the broad mission of the HCO, as well as the organization's role as a stand-alone entity or as a part of a larger health or corporate system. To address the enormous number of changes forecast in the years ahead due to healthcare reform initiatives, the governing board must possess highly qualified members, a strong infrastructure, position the organization for success.

Governance can be defined as the state or act of governing and includes the implementation of formal authority and control over an organization. In the United States, most HCOs are not-for-profit and thus are accountable to stakeholders such as the community, employees, management, medical staff, regulators, and other interested parties. HCOs that are for-profit, on the other hand, have shareholders, and thus governance **accountability** is due to the owner or owners of the company (shareholders). Although there are other differences between not-for-profit and for-profit HCOs, both types of organizations share a similar purpose, which is ensuring the deployment of organizational resources in a manner that protects and advances the interests of stakeholders and/or shareholders (Pointer & Orlikoff, 1999). This purpose is also known as **fiduciary duty**.

Board members of not-for-profit HCOs are typically volunteers; they are given the title **trustee** to acknowledge their role in safeguarding community assets held in trust for the benefit of the community at large. For-profit HCO board members are frequently compensated for their service and given the title **director**. However, these titles are often used interchangeably, particularly in the not-for-profit sector. Governing body members in both sectors share common goals and objectives as they discharge their fiduciary duty.

Responsibilities

There are published guidelines that governing boards can adopt to maximize their performance and effectiveness. In more traditional settings, board or governing body responsibilities may include formulating the organization's vision— that is, the future pathway and goals of the organization, making an explicit commitment to high-quality patient care, ensuring the presence of a high-performance executive management team, safeguarding the organization's financial health, and evaluating the board's own effectiveness as a governing body (Pointer & Orlikoff, 1999).

Biggs (2011) described the overall responsibilities of a governing board, which include:

- Creation and/or guardianship of the HCO's mission, vision, and values
- Evaluation of chief executive officer performance
- Ensuring the provision of quality patient care
- Ensuring the organization's financial health
- Assuming some responsibility for the health of the community
- Assuming responsibility for itself

To allow a governing body to function effectively, its members must also assume individual responsibilities. Among these, basic responsibilities are learning about and understanding the organization and its culture, learning about and understanding the target population/clientele, developing a working knowledge of the healthcare industry and the key drivers of the healthcare system, being prepared for and attending meetings regularly, making an active and positive contribution in meetings and toward initiatives, and maintaining confidentiality (Biggs, 2011). Tyler and Biggs (2001) identified five characteristics that individual board members must exhibit for personal effectiveness: (1) demonstrate commitment to their role, (2) set policy and yet not oversee or micromanage daily operations, (3) guard against self-dealing or its appearance, (4) take corrective action as dictated by circumstances, and (5) remain focused on the needs of the community.

Measuring the effectiveness of for-profit boards has been acknowledged as a standard process; governing-body effectiveness is normally reflected in metrics such as the organization's balance sheet, stock price, dividends, and overall return on investment. However, these metrics may not be applicable to not-for-profit organizations, making evaluation of their governing bodies' effectiveness more of a challenge (Bryant & Jacobson, 2006). For-profit board assessment is typically outcome-oriented, whereas not-for-profit board effectiveness is better measured in a process-oriented manner. Examples of process-oriented measurements include achievement of strategic planning initiatives and objectives, utilization and analysis of performance dashboards, development of governance competencies in senior executives and management, adherence to legal requirements; voluntary compliance with corporate conduct regulations, and avoidance of conflicts or dualities of interest (Bryant & Jacobson, 2006).

Legal Basics

The legal guidelines for and the obligations of governing bodies are well documented; there are three basic duties, described as follows. The first legal duty of a governing board member of a HCO is called the *duty of care*. This duty requires the board member to act with due diligence when making decisions for the organization; that is, to do what a reasonable person would do in the same situation with the same information and to act in the best interests of the organization and its clients (Biggs, 2011).

The second legal duty of a board member of a HCO is called *duty of loyalty*. Board members must act in the best interest of the organization and not on behalf of themselves, friends and family, or other organizations with which the board member might be affiliated. Board members must understand *conflict of interest* and *corporate opportunity* (Biggs, 2011). To avoid conflict of interest, board members must acknowledge and remove themselves from decisions that create an integration or conflict between their personal interests and the interests of the organization. Corporate opportunity requires that board members not personally accept business opportunities without making those opportunities available first to the HCO (Biggs, 2011).

The third legal duty of a board member of a HCO is called *duty of obedience*. Board members must comply with all federal, state, and local laws and must support the mission, vision, values, and bylaws of their organizations. Board members should not exceed their delegated authority and violate the trust of their organizations; such actions could endanger the tax-exempt status of nonprofits (Biggs, 2011).

▶ Structures in Governance: What Should We Look Like?

Many federal, state, and municipal laws and regulations impact HCOs, and can influence or determine their bylaws, configuration, and operations. HCOs are frequently structured as business corporations, for-profit (taxable) or not-for-profit (nontaxable). Corporations are expensive to establish and operate under strict guidelines and reporting requirements. However, the advantages of incorporation include limited liability for stakeholders (community, not-for-profit) and shareholders (proprietary, for-profit); ease of transfer of ownership; and unlimited life.

Hospital Structures

As HCOs have merged with or acquired other healthcare entities, several variations in HCO governance structures have evolved. Pointer and Orlikoff (1999) have described these varying structures as *decentralized, centralized*, or *modified centralized*. Decentralized structures (see **FIGURE 14.1**) typically have multiple boards or layers of governance, with a parent board retaining designated authority, oversight, control, and coordination over subsidiary boards that govern "operating units." Clear delineation of functions, authority, and scope, along with fruitful information-sharing and communication among all the boards, is critical if the parent board is to be effective as a governing body (Pointer & Orlikoff, 1999).

In a centralized structure (see **FIGURE 14.2**), the parent board has the ultimate authority over its subsidiary entities, which are themselves considered the operating units. These subsidiary organizations are not formally governed by subsidiary boards, as in Figure 14.1, but they may establish their own advisory bodies, which, however, do not exercise any fiduciary or legal authority (Pointer & Orlikoff, 1999).

A modified centralized structure (see **FIGURE 14.3**) is a compound of the first two. In this model, the parent board will oversee some subsidiary entities that are managed as operating units, and some subsidiary entities that are decentralized boards and serve as subsidiary fiduciary governing bodies.

The governance of HCOs in both modified centralized and centralized structures is complicated by the fact that, typically, an entire HCO is:

- Licensed by the state.
- Certified by the federal government to provide care to Medicare and Medicaid patients.
- Accredited by national agencies such as The Joint Commission.

Licensing, certification, and accreditation requirements hold the healthcare entity as a whole accountable for its operational components. Each unit must meet

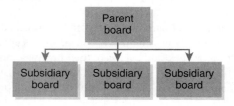

FIGURE 14.1 Decentralized Structure

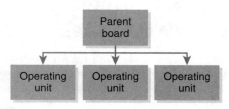

FIGURE 14.2 Centralized Structure

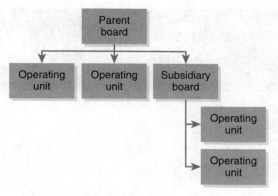

FIGURE 14.3 Modified Centralized Structure

regulations and standards in areas such as quality of care and community service. The advisory bodies of these operating units may play a critical role in supporting organization-wide accountability initiatives by overseeing policy development and approval and provider credentialing and privileging. Pointer and Orlikoff (1999, p. 116) state that "the right structure is necessary to provide a liberating framework for the creativity, imagination, focus, big-picture thinking, and timely and meaningful action that is the hallmark of good governance."

HCOs that retain local boards should practice shared governance—that is, to grant these local boards sufficient jurisdiction and authority to make decisions affecting their target communities and promote achievement of legal and accreditation standards (Center for Healthcare Governance, 2010). Elements of effective shared governance include informed and inclusive decision-making, transparency and clarity of operations, open lines of communication, accountability, and mutual trust and respect.

Physician Structures

Physicians also have traditionally provided services through a variety of structures, such as:

- Sole proprietorship/solo practice.
- Partnerships.
- Professional corporation or professional association.
- Professional limited liability partnership.
- Professional limited liability company.

Which of these medical practice structures is adopted by a healthcare provider or organization is usually determined by factors such as the size of the entity, its anticipated growth, its tax goals, and the liability concerns of its owners or principals (Medical Group Management Association, 2009). **TABLE 14.1** outlines the advantages and disadvantages of the various types of medical practice structures.

Emerging Forms of Governance

Historically, there have been several regulatory barriers or limitations for hospitals and physicians who have endeavored to align themselves structurally, financially, or operationally. One of the federal statutes that has had the most significant impact

TABLE 14.1 Medical Practice Structures

Type of Structure	Advantages	Disadvantages
Proprietorships and Partnerships	Ease of formation Subject to few regulations Physician–owner has total control over money and decisions No corporate taxes	Limited life Cash flow stops if physician–owner is absent Difficult to transfer ownership Unlimited liability Difficult to raise capital
Professional Corporation (PC) or Professional Association (PA)	Unlimited life Easy transfer of ownership Limited liability Ease of raising capital Tax deductible benefit expenses Often used by individual clinicians	Cost of formation and reporting Requires a governance structure with a board and elected officers Dual taxation for investor-owned corporations
Professional Limited Liability Partnerships (PLLP) and Professional Limited Liability Companies (PLLC)	Treated as a partnership for tax purposes Revenues and losses passed through to owners Not subject to dual taxation Partners liable for their own malpractice (PLLP) Liability like that of stockholders (PLLC)	Difficult to establish strong governance Physicians are not its employees and are not entitled to same benefits as with a PC Requires special financial practices Not all states allow creation for medical practices

Modified from Medical Group Management Association. (2009). *Body of knowledge—Governance*. Englewood, CO: Author.

in this area is known collectively as the Stark Law. This statute is actually three separate provisions that govern physician self-referral for Medicare and Medicaid patients (see www.starklaw.org) and is named after U.S. House Representative Pete Stark, who authored the initial bill. According to the Stark Law website, physician self-referral is defined as "the practice of referring a patient to a medical facility in which he or she has a financial interest, be it ownership, investment, or a structured compensation arrangement." Proponents of the Stark Law allege that physician self-referral is a conflict of interest and may encourage overutilization of services, which provide increased revenue or reimbursement that would increase the cost of care.

Another barrier to alignment is "corporate practice of medicine" statutes, such as those in California, which prohibit nearly all hospitals from directly employing physicians. Restrictions implemented by these federal and state laws spurred health-care providers to develop work-around strategies and creative governance structures, such as tax-exempt foundations and independent practice associations (IPAs).

In states where such prohibitions did not exist, hospitals began hiring physicians or purchasing physician practices. These approaches flourished during the early 1990s as an effort to protect revenue and market share in response to managed care penetration and anticipation of Clinton health reform initiatives (Menninger, 2010). Although some of these newer healthcare entities remained successful, the majority did not survive due to their utilization of only market-driven strategies, ineffective governance structures, and poor communication and collaboration between hospital executives and physicians (Menninger, 2010).

The enactment of the Patient Protection and Affordable Health Care Act in 2010 has once again opened the door to physician–hospital integration via specific *clinical integration* strategies. Today, the emphasis throughout these partnerships is on the provision of quality of care through the practice of evidenced-based medicine, care coordination, and population and disease management. One of the vehicles for creating this clinical integration is through an *Accountable Care Organization* (ACO). An ACO brings together various healthcare entities—primary care physicians, specialists, hospitals, ambulatory surgery centers, diagnostic centers, and home health agencies—to oversee and coordinate care for a defined patient population. ACOs promote access to care and value of care and are rewarded for meeting outcomes and benchmarks for quality of care and cost-effectiveness.

According to Michael Peregrine (2011), partner with the healthcare law firm of McDermott, Will, & Emery, a critical success factor of any ACO is the creation of an effective governance structure. In addition to the traditional board responsibilities mentioned previously, Peregrine indicates that an ACO board must perform these 10 unique duties:

1. Development of performance criteria for the chief executive officer.
2. Evaluation of network provider performance against plans and budgets.
3. Approval of the clinical integration program.
4. Establishment of network provider criteria for participation.
5. Oversight of performance incentive programs for participating providers.
6. Monitoring network provider performance against benchmarks.
7. Review and approval of payer contracts against standards.
8. Oversight of quality reporting and auditing activity.
9. Oversight of compliance plans and substandard care concerns.
10. Oversight of implementation programs to meet external standards.

Another critical success factor for ACOs is their ability to adapt to changing circumstances and new regulations; these are currently evolving and will continue to do so in the near future. Peregrine (2011) warns that it is imperative for ACO governance to be ever-vigilant regarding the mission and operations of the organization and to develop and implement strong conflict disclosure and resolution processes.

Additionally, which type of legal entity is chosen for ACO formation will affect the governance structure and related fiduciary considerations (Peregrine, 2011). How the ACO's structure will form and develop may vary depending on its history of alliances, partnerships, mergers, and joint ventures.

Regardless of the governance structure established, healthcare leaders must learn from the failures of previous hospital–physician integration strategies and avoid repeating the errors of the past. **BOX 14.1** provides an outline developed by Menninger (2010) for the California Health Care Foundation to promote successful HCO–provider integration in today's era of reform.

BOX 14.1 Key Elements of Successful HCO–Provider Integration

- A shared strategic vision that identifies the longer-term goals of the ACO within the contexts of community health, provider capabilities, and overall health policy.
- An organizational structure that supports ACO strategy through shared hospital–physician leadership, transparent decision-making, and clarity about participants' roles.
- Respectful and trusting relations among ACO participants, with open channels of communication.
- Appropriate clinical and organizational infrastructure to implement coordination of medical care, information technology, and financial systems.
- Aligning provider financial incentives with achievement of ACO strategic goals and objectives, while simultaneously addressing issues of cost, quality, access, and choice.
- Sufficient capital and clinical/financial management capabilities to support the assumption of risk and plans to move from lower-risk payment models (i.e., shared savings) to higher-risk models (i.e., capitation).

Modified from Menninger, B. (2010). *Accountable care organizations: Avoiding the pitfalls of the past.* Oakland, CA: California HealthCare Foundation.

▶ Board Composition: Whom Do You Want?

As Pointer and Orlikoff (1999) indicated over a decade ago, the individual members of a board can make the difference between mediocre governance and great governance. It is imperative for a governing body to retain a good balance of individuals with the requisite personal characteristics, experience, and skills that will contribute effectively to the organization. Tyler and Biggs (2001) add that respected community stature, volunteer experience, and excellent references from other board members are key criteria.

The American Hospital Association's Center for Healthcare Governance (CHG) has published a series of monographs on a wide range of governance topics. In its blue-ribbon report, "Building an Exceptional Board: Effective Practices for Healthcare Governance" (2007), the CHG outlines personal characteristics and experience considered important for board members (see **TABLE 14.2**).

Leaders should also make the case for diversity. Data from a 2011 survey by the American Hospital Association and the CHG showed that HCO governing boards are less diverse than the communities they serve. The CHG (2007) recommends that organizations strive to achieve board diversity in age, gender, and ethnicity in order to reflect the community and patients served and, even more importantly, to promote a diversity of thoughts and ideas. Biggs (2011) expands on this notion of diversity by including individuals who have demonstrated achievement, the ability to be a team player, integrity, receptivity to training and evaluation, the resources to contribute, and a willingness to devote their time.

Selection

In most cases, board members can join the governing body via three basic methods or models: election, appointment, and self-perpetuation (Pointer & Orlikoff,

TABLE 14.2 Effective Board Characteristics and Experience

Personal Characteristics	Reputable Big-picture thinker Intelligent Objective Open to new ideas Proactive Highly engaged Able to ask tough questions and challenge others in a non-disruptive way Embraces organization's values Ability to collaborate or work with others
Experience	Demonstrated leadership Board experience Community involvement Particular business experience Some members should have clinical experience (physicians and nurses)

Modified from Center for Healthcare Governance. (2007). Building and exceptional board: Effective practices for health care governance. Chicago, IL: Author.

1999). Elected board members are selected by a vote of stakeholders. Stakeholders can include taxpayers in the county or district the HCO serves. Advantages of the election model include opportunities for constituents to exert control over the governing body and to demand accountability. The major disadvantage of this model is that the board position becomes politicized.

In the appointment model, board members are selected and appointed by another entity, such as a parent board or government body (e.g., board of supervisors). An advantage of this method is that board members who are appointed can advance the goals and objectives of the larger entity or governing body. One major disadvantage, however, is that appointees may be reluctant to make decisions that may be in the best interest of the local organization but conflict with aims of the larger entity (Pointer & Orlikoff, 1999).

A self-perpetuating board selects its own members and therefore perpetuates itself. In this process, a current board member or nominating committee recommends a new member for selection as a member of the governing body. This model allows the board to ensure membership continuity, expertise, and qualifications that best meet the needs of the organization (Pointer & Orlikoff, 1999). Unfortunately, without outside influences, there is also a potential risk that a mediocre board will remain mediocre or that *groupthink* can become the dominant culture of the governing body.

Keeping the Board Engaged

Board engagement is a two-way street. The board chair and chief executive officer have a responsibility to create an atmosphere that encourages attendance and participation while remaining sensitive to members' time demands. Effective board leaders implement a well-defined governance process that is aligned with the organization's strategic focus, provide appropriate and ongoing education, inspire and motivate excellent performance, and create a culture of respect that survives professional disagreement and dissent.

Board members also have a responsibility to effectively promote the mission and goals of the organization by being prepared, understanding the organization in its larger context, respecting the other board members and the executive team, and appreciating the backgrounds and expertise of their colleagues and leaders. Finally, they have the responsibility to be actively engaged in the governance process and dialog or discussions and not just rubber-stamp management decisions.

▶ Governance Skills: What Do You Need?

The CHG (2007) has indicated that boards should recruit and appoint members who have the specific skills and abilities needed to help govern effectively. Necessary skills may include expertise in developing and managing quality initiatives, business partnerships, and financial and legal issues. Emotional intelligence and proficiency in building and maintaining collaborative professional relationships are also critical.

HCOs that anticipate growth in strategic partnerships are wise to seek board members with backgrounds in mergers and acquisitions and in enterprise-wide risk management (CHG, 2010). Organizations whose clinical integrations result in the assumption of clinical and financial accountability for the health of defined populations should consider finding board members with expertise in public health, population health management, and health disparities (CHG, 2010). These new strategic partnerships will also demand that board members bring a systems-thinking mindset and objectivity to their governance activities.

Strategic Change Management

No skill is in greater demand during this turbulent era than the ability to strategically manage change for an organization. As Heraclitus said, "The only constant is change." The governing body has a responsibility to prepare and position the organization to adapt and respond to changes in the environment. Organizations with a high adaptive orientation, which includes taking advantage of new opportunities and innovation whenever possible, have a better chance of succeeding than those that take a wait-and-see approach (Brown, 2011).

This adaptation can only occur effectively through the use of a systems model, which acknowledges the organization as an open system influenced by the environment (Brown, 2011). A *system* is a set of interrelated and interdependent parts that are brought together by design to achieve a goal or purpose. Organizations are in continuous interaction with their environment (see **FIGURE 14.4**). The environment continuously influences the resource *inputs* (the items needed to create or launch a process), the transformational *processes* (the activities or functions performed to produce products or services), and *outputs* (the products and services produced) (Brown, 2011).

Change can be radical or incremental. *Radical change* is an acute and major *revolutionary* change, whereas *incremental change* is slower, more limited, and *evolutionary* in nature. Regardless of the type of change introduced, however,

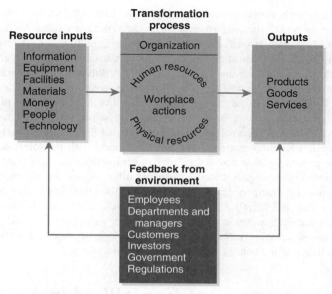

FIGURE 14.4 The Open System Organization

Courtesy of Brown, Donald R, *Experiential Approach To Organization Development*, 8th Edition, © 2011. Printed and Electronically reproduced by permission of Pearson Education, Inc., Upper Saddle River, New Jersey.

resistance to change is a typical response. The greatest resistance will come from changes that have a high impact on the culture of the organization and demand a major degree of change (Brown, 2011). The organizational changes that are anticipated under healthcare reform fall into this category, and governing boards should be fully prepared for this challenge. The governing body of a healthcare entity can support the executive management team and increase the chances of a successful change process (Brown, 2011) by ensuring that their organization has:

1. Created a climate that is conducive to change.
2. Clearly articulated a vision for the change.
3. Provided the appropriate leadership for the change.
4. Understood the politics of the change and negotiated with appropriate stakeholders.
5. Effectively and continuously communicated the change to all stakeholders.
6. Allowed for participation of appropriate organizational members in the change process.
7. Developed reward systems to promote and reinforce the change process.

The Chief Executive Officer: The Pivotal Point Person

One cannot discuss the roles and responsibilities of a governing body without acknowledging the key individual who represents the board to the organization and represents the organization to the board—the chief executive officer (CEO).

The relationship between the board and the CEO cannot be underestimated, and can "make or break" the performance of the governing body and the institution (Biggs, 2011; Pointer & Orlikoff, 1999; Tyler & Biggs, 2001). For effective governance, this relationship must be based on mutual trust and respect. Open lines of communication should be maintained; the chair of the governing board and the CEO should meet regularly to keep the relationship reliable and productive.

The CEO's role is to run the organization in a manner consistent with its mission, vision, values, policies, and procedures, as approved by the governing body. Because of their skills, knowledge, and expertise, CEOs can be a crucial source of information for their boards about industry trends; with the information provided, the governing body can make better-informed decisions regarding the strategic direction of the organization. Boards may often request the presence of other experts from the executive team as well, such as the chief financial officer, chief nursing officer, and chief medical officer, to provide additional information and insight. Ultimately, however, it is the CEO alone who is accountable to the governing body for the effective and efficient operation of the organization and for the appropriate execution of the board's short- and long-term strategies.

▶ Transparency: Everyone Is Watching!

Triggered by the less-than-stellar governance of some institutions, primarily in financial and for-profit healthcare sectors, increased government and public scrutiny has resulted in regulatory changes that "shine a spotlight on board practices and accountability" (Orlikoff, 2009, p. 72). The not-for-profit healthcare sector has not been immune to this scrutiny. For example, recent legislation now requires not-for-profit HCOs to complete the newly revised Internal Revenue Service (IRS) Form 990. Form 990 not only asks for reports of income but also for disclosures of governance information, including an organization's number of voting board members and specific organizational or governing body policies addressing issues such as conflict of interest and whistleblower protection.

In health care, transparency allows stakeholders and shareholders to remain aware of hospital quality, safety, pricing, and financial performance (Totten, 2011). Organizations promote transparency by publishing quarterly financials for investor agencies, by providing internal monthly financial reports to department heads and medical staff, by publicly reporting clinical quality/patient safety outcomes and patient satisfaction data, and by quantifying the level of community benefit provided each year (CHG, 2007).

However, transparency encompasses much more than data reporting. A transparent organization is honest, open, and accountable with regard to how its business is conducted. Transparency is reflected by an organization's willingness to allow greater internal and external visibility and to communicate effectively with the people it serves (Totten, 2011). The tone for transparent behavior must be clearly set by the governing body.

Transparency carries risks and benefits. According to Totten (2011), the benefits of transparency include the opportunity for:

- Patients to make informed decisions about the organization.
- Payers to make accurate determinations regarding cost-effectiveness.

- Staff and physicians to monitor their organizations' performance.
- Organizations to develop best practices to improve care.

There are also risks that exist with increased transparency (Totten, 2011). These risks include:

- Leaders and organizations being held to higher expectations.
- "Once the door is open, there is no turning back."
- Demands for information continue to grow.
- Leaders can no longer shun accountability.

Measuring and Monitoring What Matters

HCOs, particularly hospitals, are tasked with a multitude of mandatory reporting requirements. These requirements are driven primarily by the federal government via the Centers for Medicare and Medicaid Services (CMS), and, to a lesser extent, by state legislatures and public health departments. For example, hospitals must report hospital-acquired conditions and present-on-admission information for all diagnoses of Medicare patients admitted to the hospital. Additionally, hospitals are required to annually report quality-of-care data so that reimbursement rates can be updated and readjusted. Board members should understand their organization's reporting requirements and how these reports reflect on the organization's performance and reputation.

Clearly, boards should be kept apprised of their organizations' performance and quality of care through rigorous assessments and reports, which provide a breadth of information and data. Without adequate information, the governing body may not be able to provide the necessary leadership to ensure the organization is achieving its mission. Sometimes, however, boards may be inundated with information that is peripheral or irrelevant to their tasks (Biggs, 2011). Boards should receive information critical to governance rather than management information more relevant to day-to-day operations, such as daily staffing reports, monthly operating reports, risk-management reports, and unit accounting summaries. Governance reports should focus on strategic information, which, according to the CHG (2010, p. 18), may include:

> …trends, forecasts, emerging technologies, regulatory and legislative requirements, and other environmental issues, threats, and opportunities …[and] organization-specific information in the context of local and broader environmental issues …in a manner that allows decisions to be made regarding the organization's audit and financial statements, executive compensation, and clinical quality and patient safety.

One way to organize governance information is through the use of standardized reporting formats such as balanced scorecards and dashboards, which can display the organization's performance as compared to established targets or metrics. Balanced scorecards should ideally focus on four primary dimensions: organizational, executive, quality of care, and financial (CHG, 2010). **TABLE 14.3** shows the various elements that may be included in these dimensions. By spotlighting and monitoring these four dimensions of performance, the governing body can focus on issues that are most critical for the organization's success (CHG, 2010).

TABLE 14.3 Elements of a Balanced Governance Scorecard

Dimension	Intent	Elements
Organizational Performance	To ensure the organization is achieving its mission, goals, and objectives	Formulating a mission and vision to maximize stakeholder and client benefit Developing key goals the organization must achieve Assuring that management strategies align with these goals
Executive Performance (fiduciary boards only)	To ensure that C-level executives such as the CEO are empowered and able to contribute to organizational success	Recruiting and selecting the CEO Assessing CEO performance Determining CEO compensation Overseeing CEO succession planning If necessary, terminating the CEO
Quality of Care Performance	To ensure that the organization provides excellent service and a high quality of care in a safe environment to its patients/clients	Developing clinical quality, safety, and service objectives Credentialing and privileging members of the medical staff Ensuring effective quality management and improvement systems are implemented and regularly assessed Monitoring all aspects of quality and ensuring corrective action is implemented if needed
Financial Performance	To ensure the organization is financially sound and remains so in the future	Specify financial objectives Review management's financial plans and budgets, ensuring alignment with strategic goals Ensure effective capital allocation Ensure the accuracy of financial statements Ensure the creditworthiness of the organization Monitor financial performance and implement corrective action as needed

Modified from Center for Healthcare Governance. (2011). AHA health care governance survey report. Chicago, IL: Author.

▶ Quality: Is There Skin in The Game?

Renowned investor Warren Buffett coined the term "skin in the game" to describe a situation in which high-ranking executives use their own money to buy stock in their company. This personal investment (and assumed risk) will increase the chances that these executives will remain committed to promoting the success of their business. Inviting the board of a HCO to make a personal investment in the quality initiatives of their organization can have a similar positive effect.

Unfortunately, of the four dimensions of organizational performance, *quality* can be the most vexing for board members, particularly those who lack a clinical background or knowledge base. Although most board members see themselves as unqualified to pass judgment on matters of patient care or quality, changing regulations and accreditation standards have made it clear that hospital board members are now being held accountable for the quality of care delivered in their organization (CHG, 2010). Governing boards must embrace this change, assume the responsibility of overseeing quality, and ensure that their organizations' services are delivered in a safe, effective, and reliable manner (Biggs, 2011).

Even though many board members will not become experts in clinical care, they can still contribute to quality improvement within their organizations via a number of strategies. In some organizations, governing boards acknowledge and accept responsibility for the care and safety of their organizations' clients (Biggs, 2011). These boards facilitate close relationships among board members, the medical staff, and executive management, which allows for open, honest, respectful, and productive discussion about quality initiatives and patient care outcomes—even when outcomes are negative.

Another effective strategy for board members striving to interpret and analyze quality data is to educate themselves about the main drivers of quality, to understand data provided as they relate to those drivers, and to ask executives and medical professionals to clarify queries that may arise.

A third strategy is to determine specific outcomes, as guided by appropriate benchmarks, for medical, nursing, and other clinical staff. These targets should be aggressive in order to dramatically improve the quality of care and reduce potential harm to patients (Biggs, 2011).

A fourth strategy is to demand clear and unambiguous accountability for quality outcomes. Many organizations are holding CEOs accountable for quality outcomes and tying a large portion of executive compensation to their achievement. Governing boards must make quality a priority and address quality issues as comprehensively as they do financial and operational issues (Biggs, 2011).

Healthcare reform trends include the promotion of greater accountability for quality of care through *pay for performance* or P4P (CHG, 2010). HCOs are being rewarded, by both public and private payers, for achieving quality outcomes. Conversely, organizations are also being penalized financially for reporting hospital-acquired conditions, errors, or poor outcomes. These "never events" are monitored by the CMS and, if recurrent, can cause a hospital to lose its Medicare certification—and even its operating license.

One of the greatest challenges to quality improvement is variability and misalignment in the reimbursement process, which limits collaboration toward a common goal. For example, hospitals are paid a lump sum by Medicare per case or diagnosis, whereas physicians are paid on a fee-for-service or piecemeal basis. If a patient's condition worsens and discharge is delayed, the hospital is placed at economic risk; the patient stays in the hospital extra days and consumes additional resources without additional reimbursement. The physician, on the other hand, can continue to bill Medicare for his or her daily visits to the patient. As long as hospitals and physicians are not partnered financially in the quest to provide excellent care and service to patients, there will be little progress in dramatically improving quality.

Nevertheless, at no time in the history of health care has there been a stronger business case for improving healthcare quality. Not only are hospitals pursuing improved quality because it's "the right thing to do," but also because their enhanced reputations are becoming a competitive advantage in the healthcare marketplace. Better quality, fewer errors, and less harm mean greater cost savings; improving quality may be the "most powerful value strategy on the board governance scorecard" (Biggs, 2011). In this era of reform, governing bodies are implementing clinical integration to align hospitals and physicians and improve outcomes by fully sharing risks and rewards, through more effective reimbursement methods such as bundled payments, shared savings, and other benefit-sharing arrangements.

Summary

All elaborate organizations require some form of governance, and, in light of their size and complexity, HCOs are no exception. Traditional forms of governance have been effective in the past, but now, as a result of changes in the industry, government regulation, and market forces, we are seeing new, nontraditional forms emerge.

Governing bodies play a critical role in ensuring the success and quality of HCOs. The responsibilities of governing boards in this regard have been well articulated by researchers, consultants, and legal experts. Measuring and evaluating organizational performance is a key collective function for boards of both not-for-profit and for-profit entities. As individuals, board members have specific obligations and accountabilities as well, including fiduciary duty, duty of loyalty, duty of obedience, and avoidance of conflict of interest.

The composition of the board or governing body will be critical for navigating the turbulent waters of a new era in health care. Recruiting board members with the requisite characteristics and experience via the most effective selection method is essential for governance effectiveness.

Different HCOs have different governance structures. Hospitals that follow a corporate model can be stand-alone entities or part of a larger, multihospital/health system. Medical groups tend to structure themselves as traditional and hybrid business entities. As a result of health reform legislation, HCOs must learn to adapt to changing circumstances and develop structures that provide opportunities for provider/clinical integration to promote more efficient and effective healthcare delivery. ACOs are an example of this evolving governance structure.

The governing board will be required to lead the organization in making the strategic changes necessary for adaptation and response to this new environment. Boards must take a systems approach to facilitating the changes needed, whether they be incremental or radical. Resistance to change is common; successful change management requires a positive and trusting relationship between the governing body, the executive leadership, and the medical staff to effectively develop successful change strategies for the organization.

Finally, transparency is the name of the new game. Information about quality of care, patient safety, and pricing is now publicly available via the Internet and other sources. The demands for efficiency and effectiveness by stakeholders, regulatory agencies, and clients fall on the shoulders of the governing body; HCO boards must know how and what performance measures to monitor and assess to promote and ensure success.

Governance is facing an exciting and challenging future in this era of reform. Understanding the roles, responsibilities, and value of governance is critical for competence in the field of modern health administration.

Discussion Questions

1. How are nontraditional forms of governance affecting the efficiency and effectiveness of organizational performance?
2. Have the demands for quality and accountability changed in governance? Why and how?
3. How can members of the governing body assist the organization to prepare for change in the new environment?
4. There are many types of agencies that oversee HCOs. Do you think there will be more agencies created or do you anticipate a consolidation of these agencies? Why or why not?

🔍 CASE STUDY: Conflicts in Governance

(This case study was contributed by Hildy Aquinaldo, JD, MPH.)

Approximately 10 years ago, South Bridge Health System (SBHS) allocated Noble Regional Medical Center (NRMC) a capital budget that was commensurate with its poor financial performance. The medical staff at NRMC believed that if the hospital became more profitable, SBHS would likewise make more funding available. Accordingly, the medical staff worked in concert with NRMC's leadership to improve the hospital's financial situation and, in the meantime, got by with what they had.

Today, NRMC is one of the strongest cogs in the SBHS wheel. However, SBHS has not lived up to its end of the bargain. In fact, total capital expenditures at NRMC rose only 2% between 2002 and 2012. On the ground, this meant that many of the medical staff's requests for the purchase of new or replacement medical equipment had been deferred to "next year." The medical staff commented that it felt unappreciated and dis-incentivized from future improvement.

In light of this sentiment, the medical staff drafted a letter to SBHS, but wisely sought the advice of NRMC's president and CEO, Raymond Collins, before sending it off to the powers that be. Mr. Collins suggested that because the medical staff reported to the hospital's Community Board, that they should seek the latter's support, and indeed they did. As a result of their efforts, the chair of the Community Board, Bridget Andrade, drafted a letter to Ethan Christiansen, SBHS's chief operating officer. Her letter detailed the medical staff's concern over capital budget allocations and invited Mr. Christiansen to meet with the Board the following month.

(continues)

Prior to that meeting with the Board, however, Mr. Christiansen took an unusual step by meeting with the medical staff. Following their frank discussions, Mr. Christiansen volunteered to dip into his own reserves to grant the hospital $200,000, with consideration for additional funds. He also agreed to revisit the issue of SBHS's distribution formula so that the system's high performers would be encouraged to continue their progress. By the time the board meeting came around, the fire had been extinguished.

Case Study Discussion Questions

1. When hospitals are part of a larger system that must allocate its capital equitably among its other entities, what would be considered a "fair" formula for allocation? What criteria might be included?
2. Why might the medical staff of a hospital organization feel that they have some say in the distribution of capital?
3. What is the responsibility of the Board in this case? Whose interests must they be concerned about and why?

Related Websites

Center for Healthcare Governance: www.americangovernance.com/
Great Boards: www.greatboards.org
Stark Law: www.starklaw.org
Trustee Magazine: www.trusteemag.com

References

Biggs, E. L. (2011). *Healthcare governance: A guide for effective boards* (2nd ed.). Chicago, IL: Health Administration Press.

Brown, D. R. (2011). *An experiential approach to organization development* (8th ed.). Upper Saddle River, NJ: Pearson Prentice Hall.

Bryant, E. L., & Jacobson, P. D. (2006, December). Ten best practices for measuring the effectiveness of nonprofit healthcare boards. *Bulletin of the National Center for Healthcare Leadership.* Supplement to *Modern Healthcare, 36*(48), 9–17.

Center for Healthcare Governance. (2007). *Building an exceptional board: Effective practices for health care governance.* Chicago, IL: Author.

Center for Healthcare Governance. (2010, November). Governance implications of healthcare reform. *Great Boards Newsletter.* Retrieved from www.greatboards.org/newsletter/2010 /Governance_Implications_of_Healthcare_Reform.pdf

Center for Healthcare Governance. (2011). *AHA health care governance survey report.* Chicago, IL: Author.

Medical Group Management Association. (2009). *Body of knowledge—Governance.* Englewood, CO: Author.

Menninger, B. (2010). *Accountable care organizations: Avoiding the pitfalls of the past.* Oakland, CA: California Health Care Foundation.

Orlikoff, J. E. (2009, May/June). Are you ready for greater transparency and accountability? *Healthcare Executive, 24*(3), 72–73.

Peregrine, M. (2011, February 15). ACO formation and operation: Principal governance issues [Podcast]. *McDermott Will & Emery, LLP.*

Pointer, D. O., & Orlikoff, J. E. (1999). *Board work: Governing health care organizations.* San Francisco, CA: Jossey-Bass.

Totten, M. K. (2011, September/October). Transparency: Considerations for CEOs and boards. *Healthcare Executive, 26*(5), 76–77.

Tyler, J. L., & Biggs, E. L. (2001). *Practical governance.* Chicago, IL: Health Administration Press.

CHAPTER 15

Leadership and Community Outreach

David Cockley and Timothy Putnam

LEARNING OBJECTIVES

By the end of this chapter, the student will be able to:

- Delineate the role of leadership in outreach to small/rural communities.
- Identify outreach roles of community-based health organizations.
- Understand transitions from stand-alone community facilities to networked partners.
- Provide models and methods of outreach leadership.

KEY TERMS

Collaborations
Community benefit
Community needs assessments
Community outreach

Critical access hospital
Federally qualified health center
Partnerships

▶ Introduction

Leaders in healthcare organizations (HCOs) are expected to be involved in strategic activities within the organization. For several important reasons, executives and managers should also be aware of and involved in community-oriented outreach activities beyond the HCO. Such outreach activities enhance the HCO's networking, augment the organization's role and reputation in the community, and serve to promote marketing for the HCO, its service line, and its mission.

The reputation and image of an entity can be influenced by a variety of issues, including customer satisfaction, workforce development, and recruitment of patients and insurance plans. **Community outreach** increases opportunities for partnerships with other organizations and extends the HCO's footprint and mission. The local media as well as business and educational communities also recognize HCOs by their community-wide reputation. Organizations often expend substantial resources to enhance the public image of their facility in the wider community.

Where does the responsibility of a healthcare leader end? Is it at the threshold of the facility? Is it to the organization's primary service area, to the local or extended community?

A profit-motivated leader might utilize every opportunity to drive profitable business to the HCO. An altruistic leader might simply answer that the HCO would continue to promote, provide, and improve healthcare services in any way it could, regardless of the financial impact on the organization. Outreach activities can allow leaders to carve a middle ground between these two positions by leveraging the resources of an organization to serve the health needs of a community without compromising the financial viability of the HCO.

Organizations and Communities

All HCOs exist within the milieu of one or more specific communities. Some smaller facilities, such as community hospitals or small physician groups, may have been established and developed through the efforts of a specific locality or city. Their business and services are typically branded with the culture, values, and local politics of those localities, and their staff and patients are generally residents of those communities. Even in larger, more urban areas, healthcare facilities are still molded by local or regional characteristics. Additional neighborhood influences that have an impact on HCOs include the existence of adjacent health-related training academies (such as medical schools, nursing programs, and specialized ancillary training programs), the proximity to one or more military bases with active duty or retired personnel, or the presence of special populations (such as university students, immigrants, or "snowbird" populations). A general adage in government is that "all politics are local." Understanding the demographics, expectations, and challenges of a local population is also necessary to develop outreach opportunities and to fully serve the community's health needs.

The mission of an HCO is one prominent place wherein this local flavor can be displayed. Although most HCOs have mission statements that acknowledge the patient populations that will be served by the organization, many statements also speak to the role of the community and its unique patient subpopulations. This is especially true of many freestanding community hospitals or community clinics that were initiated as county, city, or district facilities and may answer to local governmental bodies. The mission statements of such HCOs set the strategic parameters that guide the operations of the organizations, which include outreach efforts with community-based partners.

The laudable goal of addressing the health-related needs of a local community can be promoted through involvement in specific community-oriented programs and by allowing representatives or administrators from these community stakeholders to have a voice in addressing healthcare concerns. Various types of **collaborations** can be established, from one-time **partnerships** with community groups to address a particular community need, to ongoing formal linkages of organizations, including program affiliations or joint ownership of a community resource.

A community-oriented vision can also provide a way for an HCO to test and market its services. Successful outreach endeavors can blossom into new services or full-blown service lines for the HCO. Innovative programs or modes of service delivery catch the attention of the public, area media publicity, and monitoring groups such as state governments or The Joint Commission. Community outreach projects can also build or improve organizational reputation, and demonstrate **community benefit** required for the not-for-profit status of many HCOs.

An outreach orientation also helps the HCO become a significant leader in broader networks of medical, healthcare, and social service providers in an area. Organizations such as county health departments, senior centers, and long-term care facilities may become network partners and expand an HCO's service delivery options. With the recent federal focus on transitions of care for patients who receive health and social services from multiple organizations, such multidisciplinary collaborations are paramount.

As health organizations are increasingly advised to link with other providers in their region, the leaders of these organizations benefit from adopting such a collaborative perspective. The positive results for the organization and its leadership include favorable community publicity, opportunities for inter-organizational leadership in the local health environment, and achievement of the organization's mission of serving the healthcare needs of the community.

Providing healthcare services in nontraditional sites (i.e., schools, industrial workplaces, mobile health units, or long-term care facilities) can address both the identified health-related concerns of the locality and increase the community esteem for the HCO and its partners. In a community with, for example, elevated adolescent obesity rates or an excessively high incidence of Type 2 diabetes, a local hospital may take a leadership role in sponsoring a community-wide weight monitoring program. A smaller physician group practice may provide influenza vaccines at multiple community sites, such as schools, places of worship, community centers, or workplaces. In each case, the HCO moves beyond its physical location into the community to address a particular community need.

▶ Outreach Roles of Health Organizations

Outreach includes the many ways that organizations go beyond their organizational walls to address population needs or expand services. Many of the healthcare conditions that bring patients to HCOs have their antecedents or causes in environmental or community factors. Addressing those causal factors may require the HCO to move outside its borders.

One widely noted outreach activity involves organizations that offer treatments for cancer. The HCO and sponsors support annual or periodic community-based initiatives or "walks" to highlight their concern for patients and families impacted by this health condition. Many other outreach programs are initiated by an organizational marketing campaign and provide critical services in a new venue. The services provided may not be unique, but the places where they are provided may be new for the HCO. School-based health centers are no longer novel, but have become a widely accepted way to address the physical, chronic, and behavioral concerns of children and adolescents at a location convenient to children. Many workplaces have been transformed in a similar way by offering workplace healthcare and wellness programs, exercise facilities, and breastfeeding support for employees.

Outreach programs can also allow HCOs to reach new populations of patients. Although the healthcare industry has widely assumed that patients who need healthcare services will arrive at a facility's door, a more proactive approach is to extend needed healthcare services to the patients in accessible locations, such as schools, workplaces, community centers, and shopping malls. Studies have shown the value of such healthcare initiatives, often led and directed by executives of local HCOs, in the positive development of communities (Alexander, Comfort, Weiner, & Bogue, 2001). Because the provision of healthcare services is central to the robust economic and service infrastructure of a community, organizational leaders will continue to be drafted for input or oversight of such community initiatives.

Examples of successful outreach partnerships include:

- A large statewide hospital system has an agreement with the state's Department of Health to manage many of the state's local public health clinics.
- A small physician practice operates the only pharmacy in a large rural county.
- A **federally qualified health center (FQHC)** partners with the local school system to offer in-school health centers to provide primary care and behavioral health services to county adolescents.
- A regional public health district promotes annual flu shots at a large number of workplaces to increase the rate of immunization and reduce the incidence of influenza and employee absences.
- Urgent care or primary care clinics are temporarily or permanently located in shopping malls to provide easy access for clients/patients with health concerns.

Even if a local health organization is not leading an outreach initiative, it may play a role in supporting the initiative's financing. If funding is needed, the HCO, as a major stakeholder and employer, will often be asked to provide approval or endorsement for the project and to contribute available resources. HCOs may also have fundraising or marketing expertise that can assist the outreach endeavor and its partners.

This collaboration can provide benefits within organizations as well. Smaller HCOs or health-related businesses that join these efforts can access the training, skills, and experience of leaders in larger HCOs. Through this mutual effort, the smaller entity can potentially gain valuable expertise, and the larger HCO can enhance recognition or enlist allies in outreach and marketing.

▶ The Role of Leadership in Outreach Initiatives

Healthcare industry leaders recognize that outreach is essential to the success of not only health services organizations but also large corporate networks. "Money matters" has become a truism throughout the American business world. In the altruistic milieu of health care, the common adage is "no margin, no mission." Even smaller HCOs need to generate adequate revenues for survival and sustainability. Without the proven value of outreach initiatives, HCOs may face drops in revenue that result in "no mission, no margin." Effective HCO leaders should be aware of this risk and should strive to enhance their organizations' economic and mission "fitness" by remaining engaged in their communities and addressing their neighbors' needs and concerns.

HCOs such as hospitals, physician practices, or skilled nursing facilities typically play a significant leadership role in their neighborhoods, especially in small or rural communities where HCOs may not only be the area's primary healthcare providers but also the primary employers. For that reason, city planners often strive to include HCOs in local community-planning initiatives (Alexander et al., 2001).

Involvement of HCO leaders is often a critical factor in the success and sustainability of outreach programs. HCO leaders bring the positive reputation of their organizations to the table, adding value to the initiative and its objectives, and inspiring and motivating the program participants. Healthcare providers, administrators, or ancillary staff may be the implementers of a successful HCO outreach program, but the organization's top managers or executives can guide its development and strategic planning, and can facilitate the coordination of key program elements. Leaders' involvement can also draw greater media attention, build the reputation of the participant stakeholders, and enhance internal and external collaboration and networking to promote program success.

HCO leaders can bring their partners and competitors to the table to address a mutually agreed-upon health concern and can encourage and support initiative participants in the discussion and resolution of common problems. Even highly competitive organizations understand the value of putting aside their differences and working together to serve the community's greater needs. Larger HCOs are often viewed as the dominant players in such multi-participant groups, but the directors or leaders of smaller HCOs can also contribute critical data or skills to positively influence the partnership and play pivotal roles in building consensus and developing mutually agreed-upon solutions.

In many communities, HCO leaders have formalized partnerships to address community needs with local or regional associates and continue to inform and support them on an ongoing basis.

Greater Cincinnati Health Council

One example is the Greater Cincinnati Health Council (GCHC; www.gchc.org), a network of HCOs within 50 miles of Cincinnati. GCHC members range from academic medical centers such as Cincinnati Children's Hospital and the University of Cincinnati to community hospitals such as Dearborn County Hospital in Lawrenceburg, Indiana. Although individual council member institutions typically compete with each other on a variety of fronts, including staff recruiting and client marketing, the council has developed outreach initiatives that address common goals and objectives and benefit the participants in the group and the patients that they serve. An example of a successful GCHC initiative was the development of HealthBridge, a health information exchange that allowed all member healthcare providers to electronically share patients' personal health information. As a result, the GCHC network of member institutions has implemented an integrated model for patient records management ahead of the timeline proposed in the 2010 Patient Protection and Affordable Care Act.

Remote Area Medical Clinic

Another example of a successful outreach partnership is the large annual Wise County Remote Area Medical Clinic. The clinic, located in southwest Virginia, is sponsored by multiple providers of health and health-related services. These partners include local health, dental, and vision providers; the state medical schools and their students; and social service agencies for uninsured and low-income families in the region. Each year, the clinic, which runs Friday through Sunday, reaches thousands of underserved low-income patients in this economically challenged region (Huttlinger, Schaller-Ayers, & Lawson, 2004; Merwin, Snyder, & Katz, 2006).

▶ Outreach and Collaboration

Outreach efforts to address community-based health concerns may require more resources than a single organization such as a community hospital can provide. In these circumstances, organizations may need to collaborate temporarily (or on an ongoing basis) to address a mutually identified concern. For example, overweight and obesity intervention in a local population is not typically within a single organization's scope. Goal-focused partnerships can draw discrete organizations together around a particular issue, such as obesity rates in the community, and engage them in both short-term and long-term collaboration to benefit their clientele.

When multiple independent or linked organizations collaborate to address an identified outreach project, leadership skills that facilitate effective team operation and function are required (Alexander et al., 2001). Leaders can help participants overcome barriers to collaboration, such as divergent missions or populations, or issues regarding competition, and help collaborators build formal and informal networks for implementing and providing services.

Some examples include:

- To address behavioral health needs in the community, a mid-sized community hospital facilitated the launch of a collaborative network of area safety-net providers.
- After a natural disaster ravaged a community, local public health services became unavailable. Under the leadership of the state Department of Health, healthcare providers in adjacent communities stepped forward temporarily to fill in the service gaps.
- To monitor high-risk pregnancies in a small community, its Community Health Center instituted a telehealth link with a medical center over an hour's drive away, saving time and reducing necessary travel for pregnant women for prenatal care.

Skillsets for Outreach Leadership

The leadership skillsets required to accomplish successful outreach goals include looking strategically beyond the organization, categorizing the wider community as the customer, and understanding the central role of needs assessment in that community. Additionally, team-building skills that enhance collaboration across disciplines and organizations are of great value.

Population Orientation

When an organization turns its attention to groups beyond its typical patient population, its leaders must adopt a different perspective, a population orientation distinct from the patient or consumer orientation central to most healthcare facilities (Huttlinger et al., 2004). Leaders need to learn about, understand, and empathize with the specific needs and challenges of the larger group the HCO is aiming to serve. Public health agencies function with this broader population perspective, and their operational models can be adopted by private HCOs for outreach initiatives. The following list presents examples of the ways in which HCOs can partner with public health agencies.

- A nursing home wishes to identify and address the home healthcare needs of its region. To make a judicious decision about expanding into home health services, the nursing home examines the population data for its county or region to assess the demand for regional home health care.
- A community health center wishes to provide additional services to the homeless population in a midsized city. It assesses the specific healthcare needs of this population, identifies those needs not being currently or adequately addressed, and partners with other service providers such as public health and social service agencies to help fill in the gaps.
- A **critical access hospital**, in partnership with a regional hospital, develops a Stroke Response Initiative that coordinates rural emergency department services to regional stroke specialists via telehealth and transportation networks.

HCOs have traditionally relied on individual patients, either by choice or by referral, to come to the HCO doors and access the services provided. A population orientation sends the HCO or a collaboration of organizations to the community first to assess unmet needs and then to strategize how services can be figuratively or literally delivered to the patient. Data analysis of population assessments, available from local and state public health departments, and national agencies such as the Centers for Disease Control and Prevention, can allow the identification of specific characteristics or needs within a subset of the larger population and can drive the development of interventions that more appropriately address the needs of that discrete group.

The health needs of populations or communities will be formulated differently than those of an individual. For example, to address the rapidly escalating problem of Type 2 diabetes, an individual healthcare provider treating an individual patient might focus on diet, exercise, and prescription medication. An HCO with a population orientation, on the other hand, might build community exercise facilities, monitor school lunch programs, provide nutrition education sessions, and advocate for improved food labeling at the supermarket. Both the individual and population efforts address Type 2 diabetes, but the outreach initiative has the potential to improve the health of many individuals in a community and facilitate a population-wide response.

Collaboration and Negotiation

Outreach activities of HCOs often involve partnerships with other organizations, including those outside the healthcare industry, which come together to implement an initiative or achieve a short- or long-term goal. Outreach partners may be direct competitors (e.g., two hospitals within a small city), healthcare providers of different types (e.g., home health agencies, physician group practices, or long-term care facilities), or they may be social service agencies or private businesses that do not provide direct healthcare services.

Interagency collaboration in the healthcare arena can develop referral networks and linkages for patient care. Most HCOs already have established linkages with other health providers (e.g., specialists, therapy practitioners, the regional tertiary-care facility) to facilitate additional care for patients with specific health needs in areas beyond the scope of the specific HCO.

These linkages with ancillary providers may be formal or informal and involve multiple organizations. For example, a community hospital facility may offer state-of-the-art cardiac imaging and establish a secure communications pathway with the private cardiology practices in the region to transfer patient test results quickly and confidentially.

Not every HCO manager has the skills necessary for successfully building a team of such diverse partners. HCO leaders may opt to recruit capable members of their management team or other HCO professionals with these skillsets to implement collaborative outreach programs, or may purchase these services through external contractors qualified and experienced in operationalizing strategic plans. Training in team-building and facilitation skills can allow leaders to successfully navigate the challenges of guiding a multifaceted group. This investment by an HCO that promotes successful outreach partnerships can provide valuable returns in enhancing both the organization's reputation and its bottom line.

Multidisciplinary clinical teams, led by a capable manager trained and skilled in negotiation and mediation, are being promoted as a method for bridging the array of disciplines providing health care. But multidisciplinary administrative groups are also recommended to manage complex administrative problems in and across organizations and disciplines (Anderson & McDaniel, 2000; McDaniel & Driebe, 2001). Though these internal teams share many aspects in common with outreach partnerships, they are distinct from teams built from multiple organizations, especially those representing diverse industries. Setting up a management team within a community hospital, for example, is different from engineering a multi-entity task force spanning a hospital, several independent physician practices, and an elder retirement community.

Alexander et al. (2001) identified specific leadership skillsets necessary to successfully develop partnership arrangements across organizations. They identified five categories of factors necessary for effective community partnership. These included a systems perspective, the ability to promote vision-based leadership, collateral leadership, power sharing, and process-based leadership.

Trauma Project for the University of Mississippi Medical Center

Advanced trauma centers across the country offer lifesaving multispecialty resources for critical patient treatment. Unfortunately, not all traumatic injuries occur in locations close to an academic medical center and its trauma unit. In Mississippi, for example, rural hospitals receiving trauma cases would often transport their injured patients over long distances at high risk to the trauma center at the University of Mississippi Medical Center in Jackson (UMMC). UMMC leaders realized that many of the patients transferred could be best stabilized and treated at their local hospital if trauma evaluations could be performed locally with a high level of confidence. UMMC developed a plan to partner with seven rural hospitals throughout the state via a telemedicine service, which allows the local emergency department team to consult with the trauma team at UMMC to evaluate patients remotely and determine the most appropriate care.

The study of the telemedicine trauma project at UMMC (Duchesne et al., 2008) demonstrated some dramatic results. In the 30 months prior to the implementation of the telemedicine service, 351 patients were transferred from these seven hospitals for trauma care. In the next 30 months, the UMMC team evaluated 463 trauma patients through the Internet-based telemedicine system; only 51 patients required transfer to the trauma center at UMMC. Additionally, the study found that there was a dramatic decrease in the total cost of care for patients treated in the telemedicine era.

It is important to recognize that such an outreach program is not successful solely due to the use of modern technology. The vital ingredient in the program's success is the relationship developed among the medical professionals and healthcare leaders in the participating organizations. Constant refinement of processes and procedures are critical to maintain and improve the success of such a program. If the team at UMMC were to lose confidence in the capabilities of a rural hospital's staff, they would have little choice but to recommend more patients be transferred for trauma care. Ongoing active communication and education can promote and enhance the quality of care provided via this outreach partnership.

Clearly, UMMC realized that its responsibility to care for patients did not end at its emergency department door or even at the city limits of Jackson. As the leader in trauma care for Mississippi, UMMC recognized the need to reach out to rural areas and develop a partnership that better met the needs of patients throughout the state. However, few other programs have attempted to duplicate this telemedicine trauma program. For this type of outreach to expand around the country, healthcare leaders will need to accept that their responsibility to patients extends far beyond the front door of their facility.

Excellent communication skills become a heightened priority when leaders work with multiple organizations in collaborative networks. The HCO leader can mentor staff in how to best communicate and collaborate with other organizations. Clear communication among organizations prevents misunderstandings and promotes program success, especially in the delicate but critical area of resource allocation. Partners must clearly understand and agree on the contributions of personnel, time, and funding toward the project, before and during its implementation.

Needs Assessment

Many community-based HCOs incorporate periodic **community needs assessments** to identify areas of unmet need, new opportunities for organizational collaboration, and new directions for strategic planning and service delivery. Additionally, many HCOs, independently or in collaboration with other local/regional organizations, carry out such assessments to evaluate how the HCO is meeting the healthcare needs of the locality.

The value of needs assessment for leaders and HCOs is underscored by requirements within the Patient Protection and Affordable Care Act (ACA). The ACA stipulates that hospitals conduct a community health needs assessment at least once every 3 years beginning in 2012 (PPACA, 2010). The purpose of this requirement is to identify the healthcare needs in the community served by the HCO and to stimulate the development of strategies through which the HCO can address these community health needs. HCOs are being tasked with the responsibility to serve their communities, and their action plans and strategic outcomes will be assessed in the future to document implementation and effectiveness.

Needs assessment can be performed as an internal exercise for individual organizations to identify potential markets for new or expanded services, evaluate client satisfaction, or guide future organizational mission and goals. Needs assessment may also be undertaken by external groups, including collaborations of multiple community organizations, seeking to assess healthcare or social service needs and identify healthcare gaps.

Such assessments are an excellent means for multiple health-related organizations within one locality or region to pool resources to obtain a mutually beneficial product. A needs assessment coordinated by a specific community group, such as a community mental health center, would typically assess the community from one perspective (mental health) and not identify unmet health needs for, say, acute care providers or other interests in the community. A broadly targeted needs assessment, sponsored by a partnership of health-related groups or community-based resources, such as the Chamber of Commerce or a community action agency, can develop an assessment that spans multiple areas of interest and identifies new areas where HCOs may direct their attention and efforts.

The process of bringing multiple organizations together to formulate the assessment instrument and collect and analyze the results is in itself a significant outreach endeavor. Distinct and unaffiliated organizations can learn the various skillsets and strengths of community partners, resources that lay the groundwork for future joint activities. Coordinating needs assessment projects with other healthcare providers can also help eliminate duplication of effort and help develop a common vision and "message." Some examples are:

- A small group practice partners with a continuing care retirement community (CCRC) to open a satellite clinic at the CCRC that expands direct service delivery to a larger population of retired individuals.
- A community hospital sponsors radio talk shows by local physicians on local health issues to educate the general public.
- A university's student health center contracts with a primary care practice in the college town to provide extended services to the university's student and employee populations.
- **Critical access hospital** and affiliated healthcare practices develop telemedicine connections with a large tertiary medical center to increase community-based specialty services.

▶ Models and Methods of Outreach Leadership

HCOs are involved in a wide variety of outreach activities. Models for outreach programs include individual HCOs intent on building alliances within a local community or expanding services by partnering with other agencies, and multiple organizations seeking to achieve common missions and objectives. Two specific examples of successful ongoing outreach activities are presented later.

Critical access hospitals

Throughout much of the rural United States, small hospitals serve as the main source of health care, including emergency services (see **FIGURE 15.1**). Leaders of these institutions face specific challenges such as a lack of human and financial resources, overwhelming patient demand, time-intensive and difficult-to-implement government regulations, and falling reimbursements. Historically, small hospitals have struggled to survive; from 1980 to 1990, some 330 rural hospitals closed in the United States. Hospitals with fewer than 100 beds demonstrated less profitability than larger hospitals, and outreach efforts were often seen as an unaffordable luxury. The failure rate for rural hospitals was 29% higher than for urban facilities, often creating an additional healthcare void that was left unfilled (Drain, Godkin, & Valentine, 2001).

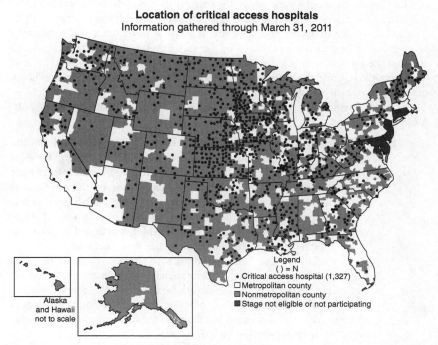

Location of critical access hospitals
Information gathered through March 31, 2011

Legend
( ) = N
• Critical access hospital (1,327)
☐ Metropolitan county
▦ Nonmetropolitan county
■ Stage not eligible or not participating

Alaska and Hawaii not to scale

FIGURE 15.1 2011 Distribution of Critical Access Hospitals
Courtesy of the Rural Assistance Center.

Location of Critical Access Hospitals

Information Gathered Through March 31, 2011

Analysis Center, Cecil G. Sheps Center for Health Services Research, University or North Carolina at Chapel Hill.

In an effort to help stem the rising tide of rural hospital closures, the federal government implemented the Critical Access Hospital (CAH) program in 1997 (Roop, 2008). The CAH program allowed small rural hospitals to be reimbursed 101% of their allowable costs for Medicare patients, that is, a cost-based reimbursement. The program was offered to healthcare facilities that were typically the only hospital in their region and had fewer than 25 inpatient beds. Today, more than 1300 CAHs are in existence. These facilities are often the sole hospital in their community, and the CAH program has stabilized their financial performance and reduced the closure rate seen in previous decades (Holmes, Pink, & Slifkin, 2006).

The CAH program also provided common guidelines for the operations of the member institutions. Although services varied from hospital to hospital, the program encouraged consistency in areas such as bed capacity and length of patient stay. Hospitals that had functioned like solitary islands now felt they became part of an archipelago in which there is a level of interdependence and information-sharing. Participants not only communicated informally, but also formalized cross-hospital groups into networks to develop programs and services of use to all. One such organization is the Illinois Critical Access Hospital Network (ICAHN; www.ICAHN.org). This network of more than 50 CAHs has worked together to accomplish several projects that would have been very difficult for any of its hospitals to accomplish individually. The network does not function like a traditional healthcare system with its standard corporate hierarchy and structure. ICAHN is governed and directed by a small group of hospital leaders elected by the entire group; this governance council oversees the operation of the network and the work of the employed ICAHN staff (see www.ICAHN.org). Each hospital retains its own level of local control that is not encumbered or usurped by the governing council.

ICAHN is empowered to develop services of value to the group as a whole. A few examples include:

1. *Information technology expertise:* The Illinois CAHs identified that the technological revolution in health care augmented the demand for electronic health records, telehealth linkages, and other health information technology (HIT) advances. Unfortunately, managing these technologies demanded a broad HIT skillset with part-time availability that was difficult for most participants to obtain in their small towns. ICAHN was charged with developing an IT team, which is assigned to assist and support the needs of the individual hospitals in the network.

2. *Sharing best practices:* Small hospitals with limited resources fazed by operational challenges used to hire expensive outside experts to consult and help develop solutions. Today, these hospitals can query the other members of the network (many of whom have faced similar challenges and have developed successful solutions) for advice and recommendations. Methods for sharing include:

   a. Computerized listservs that allow hospital leaders to communicate with their counterparts at other ICAHN hospitals.

      b.   User groups that communicate online and meet in person to share ideas and exchange information.

      c.   Annual conferences that focus on educational and operational needs as well as updating members on relevant industry trends and projections.

  3. *Physician peer review:* For reaccreditation and licensure, as well as if a concern arises regarding the care provided by a physician to a patient, HCOs set up formal peer-review programs within their institutions. Peer providers review selected cases and render an opinion about the care and treatment provided and, if necessary, offer recommendations for future care.

Unfortunately, in small hospitals, there may not be a physician peer available to review cases in certain specialties. For example, even if there are several family medicine/primary care providers in local practice, a community may have only one cardiologist or neurologist, whose cases would need review by another specialist in those fields. Additionally, in the interdependent environment of a small hospital, physicians are often hesitant to scrutinize or criticize their close colleagues, so smaller hospitals often utilize national firms to perform peer reviews. Unfortunately, there are drawbacks with this process; first, external review is expensive and may limit the number of cases submitted for review. Second, the external reviewers, who are often located in large urban areas, are not always aware of the challenges and limitations their peers face in CAHs; they may provide recommendations that are difficult to implement in a small hospital.

For ICAHN hospitals, a better option was to utilize physicians across the ICAHN network to peer review cases from sister CAHs. This option was not only more affordable for the member hospitals but, because the reviewers hailed from similar smaller institutions, it also resulted in more relevant and helpful recommendations.

The ICAHN network is an excellent example of the value of collaboration in enhancing healthcare delivery and addressing challenges that could overwhelm an individual institution. HCO leaders in the ICAHN network have been able to organize and develop their network and promote cooperation among its members by demonstrating the benefits of this partnership for all the involved institutions. The key to its success is the development of trust among the members. A hospital would hesitate to share information or engage in collaborative initiatives if it sees its partners as competitors. Building trust among members and demonstrating the benefits of working together is the primary task of the effective HCO leader.

Pendleton Community Care

Pendleton Community Care (PCC) is a comprehensive primary care clinic located in rural West Virginia. PCC began as a small private nonprofit practice in the early 1980s, evolved into a Rural Health Clinic (1986), and, in 1998, became a federally qualified health center. Because the providers who launched the practice wanted to address the health concerns of the broader community, they began assessing the healthcare needs of their community early in the clinic's history.

PCC initiated several community-based outreach projects to address these identified community needs. Funding for these projects came from sources such as grant funding, direct reimbursement, or the clinic's operational budget. Another PCC goal was to ensure the initiatives' financial sustainability (see www.pcc-nfc.org/history.htm). Initiated from an assessment of their community populations, specific new healthcare services were provided external to the health center's normal operations.

- PCC's clientele included many noninstitutionalized community elders as well as their adult children caregivers. Clinicians observed that the elders' health status was directly related to the health condition of the caregiver. Overburdened and exhausted caregivers were unable to provide the best care for either their parents or themselves. To address this issue, PCC launched a community-based program to train and support homemaker aides for elders who needed home services, which also allowed routine monitoring of the elders' conditions. In addition to easing the caregivers' burdens and providing additional elder care, these aides could keep clinicians apprised of their patients' home situations and functional status between office encounters. After its launch, the state Medicaid program offered financing for the initiative in the hopes of reducing early nursing home admissions for Medicaid-eligible adults.
- Working with the county school system and parental contacts, PCC proposed and developed a series of school-based health centers (SBHCs). PCC now operates four school sites staffed by physician or nurse practitioners for regular hours each week. This outreach endeavor has proven successful at bringing primary care services to the students' location. The current SBHCs are addressing comprehensive primary care and behavioral health needs in this vulnerable population.
- PCC partnered with county employers to begin a series of worksite wellness initiatives, which provided health assessment exams for workers and offered a series of worksite health initiatives, including exercise competitions, diet and weight-loss classes, and health education modules on food and exercise. Initially funded from the PCC budget, this project evolved into a statewide health initiative for public employees.

▶ Outreach Challenges

Despite the acknowledged value of outreach initiatives for HCOs, challenges to participation remain. These include organizational factors such as limitations of resources or shortages of specialized personnel, regulatory obstacles in the industry, or issues in the community. HCO leaders must face and overcome challenges to build a successful outreach program.

Healthcare managers and organizations often cite a lack of sufficient resources to undertake outreach initiatives. HCO leaders owe a fiduciary loyalty to their organization and understandably focus on attaining the mission and goals set forth by the organization's governing body and/or owners. Outreach proposals that could eventually enhance the organization's reputation or financial stability may be met by confusion and resistance from organization executives and governing boards. The leader trying to focus attention on community needs or collaborative efforts with other organizations may hear "this is not our core purpose," from the Board. Demonstrating the value of outreach initiatives in achieving organization goals, along with the advantages for the organization of reaching out beyond its property line and expanding its footprint, is critical to assuaging such concerns and gaining acceptance and support.

The value of outreach activities and network development should be viewed in a longer-term strategic environment—positive results and revenue returns may not be immediate, but should be visible over the medium- to long-term. Among the demonstrable benefits that can improve acceptance of outreach initiatives are evidence that separate community groups, including actual or potential competitors, build ongoing relationships or partnerships that provide partner organizations with new service lines or revenue streams; barriers to service availability and utilization are weakened; new referral patterns for existing services are built; and the community or subpopulations within the community see improved health.

Another challenge for HCO leaders aiming to tackle community-wide or non-traditional initiatives is the need for specialized management expertise that may be lacking in all but the largest organizations. A community hospital, for example, may not have the experienced personnel to forge meaningful linkages with a nearby skilled nursing facility or home health agency.

The field of healthcare management has evolved to the stage wherein multiple layers of management expertise may be necessary within a single HCO to maximize its revenue or service lines. Many health services administrators begin their careers as management generalists, but the increasing pressure to specialize has influenced healthcare executives just as it has physicians and nurses. In fact, one of the key drivers for standalone HCOs to join larger networks or chains is the opportunity to tap into specialized management expertise.

In addition to shortages of management specialists, local HCOs, especially those in smaller communities and rural areas, may also face shortages of clinical staff such as nurses, ancillary personnel, and specialty physicians. A nursing shortage, for example, will negatively impact the delivery of specific hospital services in the area, as well as put the hospital in direct competition with skilled nursing facilities, home health agencies, and local physician practices. Though sharing of resources may help alleviate a shortage, competition to recruit new hires may hamper attempts at organizational collaboration among these separate healthcare groups.

HCO leaders should be prepared for such challenges as they develop and implement outreach initiatives. Collaboration among HCO leaders to exchange best practices and skillsets that can help overcome challenges can promote greater success in facilitating outreach collaborations.

Summary

Leaders of HCOs often become involved in outreach activities through their strategic planning initiatives in their HCO. An organization's specific goal may be to enhance its image or to market services to new populations of users. Strategically designed outreach activities, involving organizational leadership, employees, and the community, can provide marketing and partnership prospects for the HCO.

HCO leaders are influential in creating partnerships and in encouraging colleagues in their community to construct partnerships to address identified healthcare needs. However, the specific management skillsets required to build and sustain such partnerships and collaborations may be distinct from the skills taught traditionally in management. A population orientation, skills for building collaborations across multiple disciplines or provider groups, and methodologies to assess the healthcare needs of populations and communities are critical.

Multiple examples of outreach activities by distinct types of HCOs help exemplify the range of opportunities available to HCOs and their leaders. Among them are the Critical Access Hospital program, outreach endeavors of specific federally qualified health centers, and initiatives of specific academic medical centers. These examples highlight both the range of programs and the best-practice opportunities available to HCOs.

Engaging in nontraditional and innovative initiatives is not without challenges for leaders of HCOs. Obtaining the different management skills needed, understanding effective resource allocation, and recruiting the necessary stakeholders and partners will allow leaders to successfully sustain outreach activities beyond an initial pilot phase, for the benefit of the HCO and its community.

▶ Conclusions

Many HCOs become providers of outreach activities, either as part of their declared mission to meet the healthcare needs of a community or through short- and long-term partnerships to address specific goals and objectives with other HCOs. Understanding the value of outreach initiatives and the benefits of successful collaboration is critical for successful HCO leaders. Effective healthcare leaders will understand how to make use of all the organizational, financial, and collegial resources at their disposal to provide outreach to serve their communities via synergistic collaborations.

A shift in focus beyond a facility or organization may be necessary for healthcare leaders as they move to include outreach in their strategic planning efforts. Participation in a variety of collaborative linkages and partnerships will expand the vision of the organization beyond the focus on its internal operations. The managerial skillsets necessary to lead an organization's involvement in outreach initiatives may differ from the skillsets required to manage an organization internally. A successful outreach orientation will require knowledge about how to assess and analyze the healthcare needs of a community, a willingness to look beyond one's organizational boundaries for partners and delivery sites, team-building and facilitation skills, negotiation skills effective across multiple organizations and industries, and the ability to facilitate creative solutions for fiscal and other challenges.

Many industries pursue outreach initiatives to enhance market share and revenue streams. Yet, in health care, outreach and collaboration can have a profoundly positive impact, not only on organizations, but on the lives of individuals and communities. This reality motivates HCOs to consider and develop outreach programs that improve health and quality of life for individuals and populations, even at a cost to the bottom line. As they engage in strategic planning decisions, HCO leaders must consider and include the benefits of outreach programs on human lives.

Discussion Questions

1. Why should HCOs consider outreach programs to address identified healthcare needs in their communities? What are the strategic and marketing benefits of outreach efforts?

2. Hospitals in urban markets routinely compete, sometimes aggressively, for market share and workforce. What are some specific outcomes from HCO collaboration that would benefit a community's health status?

3. In what ways do outreach challenges differ for hospitals in highly competitive urban markets versus sole hospitals in smaller communities?
4. What skills are necessary for leaders in competing organizations to practice to be able to work together and share resources to benefit the health of the community?
5. Why is a partnership with other community organizations necessary for many successful outreach initiatives? What are some of the potential pitfalls of initiating an outreach project without the support of other community organizations?
6. Answer the following questions as an HCO leader who understands the value and benefits of outreach:
   a. If your HCO develops a new procedure that significantly reduces nosocomial (hospital) infections, should you as its leader share that information with other HCOs, or parlay your improved outcomes for competitive advantage to increase market share?
   b. Your HCO's primary service area has a new and growing population of non-English speaking individuals with little ability to pay for healthcare services. What responsibility do you have as a leader to serve the health needs of this population?

🔍 *CASE STUDY: Mobile Dental Services*

St. Mary's Medical Center is a tertiary-care hospital located in Evansville, Indiana. For several years, the hospital has coordinated a novel outreach program—Mobile Dental Care for Kids—which provides full-service dental care for children who would otherwise have little or no access to dentists (see **FIGURE 15.2**). This program reports more than 3000 patient contacts in 2010, primarily from elementary school-age children at the rotating school sites.

St. Mary's is an acute care medical center that does not provide any other dental services. Why have they chosen to coordinate an outreach program in a field in which they have little expertise? The steps below provide a pathway toward the implementation of this successful initiative.

Identification of the problem:

- An existing partnership with area schools and school nurses identified a problem that could not be readily solved given limited school-district resources. Low-income elementary school children would come to school with acute tooth pain, unable to be cured by the school nurse. The lack of dental care often allowed these acute problems to become chronic, and students in constant pain were unable to study and learn effectively.
- Many of the affected children were eligible for Indiana Medicaid dental services. Research showed that few dentists in the area accepted Medicaid patients because
  - Medicaid reimbursement rates were significantly lower than private insurance reimbursement rates.
  - Transportation and accessibility challenges for Medicaid patients resulted in a high incidence of patient late arrivals and no-shows, costing dental practices vital revenue.

(continues)

FIGURE 15.2 St. Mary's Mobile Dental Care for Kids

Courtesy of St. Mary's Medical Center.

Resources available in the community:

- St. Mary's, the local acute care medical center, offered to help and worked with leaders in the schools to coordinate resources.
- School nurses and support staff worked with parents to:
  - Ensure eligible students were registered for Medicaid dental services.
  - Obtain the necessary consents for treatment.
  - Schedule students for exams during the school day to make the best use of the dental unit and staff.
- Area civic organizations and churches offered to help families with care logistics when school was not in session.
- A mobile dental service van was outfitted and launched to improve accessibility of dental care.
- Area dentists agreed to work shifts to provide care when the mobile unit's full-time dentist was unavailable.

The success of this program is due to the effective partnership among St. Mary's and the other partner organizations. Together, the collaborators identified a problem (health concern), researched the causative factors, and developed creative strategies to address these factors. Each partner contributed different resources to the initiative, allowing the development of a successful solution to address this challenge.

Case Study Discussion Questions

1. What information and personnel resources are available to St. Mary's Medical Center to aid in planning and development of this outreach program?
2. Ongoing partnerships were developed with key stakeholders in the community. How can the leadership at the Medical Center sustain these partnerships with the school personnel, area dentists, and multiple civic organizations?
3. What other benefits does St. Mary's Medical Center gain from this outreach endeavor? Are there financial, marketing, or promotional benefits that can accrue to the Medical Center?

⌕ *CASE STUDY: The Opioid Crisis*

The opioid crisis has become a significant community health concern of the 2010s. This multifaceted problem requires healthcare leaders to develop solid community partnerships to have an impact on the problem, as no single entity will be able to address the many issues of the opioid challenge our society faces. Among the multiple factors associated with this crisis include:

- *Physician prescribing practices:* In 2001, The Joint Commission, the primary accrediting body for hospitals, in an attempt to address the under-treatment of pain, introduced standards for organizations to improve their care for patients with pain. Coincidentally, the prescribing practices for prescription opioids, a common drug used to treat acute pain (e.g., oxycodone and hydrocodone), quadrupled from 1999 to 2014.[1]

- *Transition from prescription opioids to illicit drugs*—It has become clear that many of the people who become addicted to illicit drugs such as heroin began drug use with prescription opioids. In a study of young adult heroin users, it was found that 86% had used prescription opioids "non-medically" prior to their use of heroin.[2] The transition to illicit drugs may be promoted by several factors: the individual's finite supply of prescription opioids, the expense of purchasing prescription opioids, legally or illegally, and the desire for increased potency of illicit drugs, as compared to the majority of prescription opioids.

- *Overdose death rate*—From 2000 to 2014, the deaths related to drug overdose increased 200%, with 47,055 people dying in the United States in 2014. 61% of overdose deaths involved some type of opioid. These 2014 data reveal a 15-year trend in increases of overdose deaths involving both prescription opioid pain relievers and illicit opioids.[3] The unregulated/illicit opioid market, by definition, offers extremely high variability in product. Users may assume that they are injecting heroin, but may actually be taking a more potent synthetic opioid such as fentanyl or the elephant tranquilizer carfentanil, which can be 5000 times more potent than heroin. When a very potent or "bad batch" of heroin, mixed with or replaced with fentanyl or carfentanil, enters a region, a high volume of overdoses over a short period of time may be observed.

- *Rescue efforts*—Emergency response teams including EMS, police, and firefighters are called to respond to opioid overdoses. Unlike with other illicit drugs such as the stimulant methamphetamine, users overdosing on opioids experience a significant decrease in respiratory efforts. In many cases, the respiratory effort ceases completely, depriving the brain of oxygen. Rescue efforts must therefore take place rapidly. In addition to establishing a patent airway, emergency responders may use the opioid antagonist medication naloxone to counter and reverse the sedative effects of the opioid.

- *Neonatal Abstinence Syndrome (NAS)*—Perhaps the biggest lifelong impact of opioid abuse will be felt by infants who are born addicted. Virtually in parallel with the rise in opioid use, NAS has nearly tripled from 1.6 per 1000 live births in 1999 to 6 per 1000 in 2013. Some U.S. regions, such as West Virginia, have rates of over 30 NAS babies born per 1000 births.[4] The average cost of newborn care for an NAS baby in 2015 ranged from $159,000 to $238,000.[5] These infants can be inconsolable in their first days of life, as they suffer the effects of withdrawal. Clearly, the long-term

(continues)

financial, developmental, and social impacts of being born with a dependence on drugs may be felt for years after infants recover from their acute addiction.

■ *Addiction treatment*—The volume of people addicted to opioids has created the need for far more addiction treatment services than currently exist. Most healthcare systems have found their existing resources inadequate to meet the need presented in their local communities. Additionally, reimbursement for services generally falls short of the cost for providing addiction treatment, and many of the addicted patients lack coverage or the ability to pay for care.

References

1. Centers for Disease Control and Prevention. Vital Signs: Overdoses of Prescription Opioid Pain Relievers United States, 1999–2008. *MMWR* 2011; 60(43):1487–1492.
2. Lankenau SE, Teti M, Silva K, Jackson Bloom J, Harocopos A, Treese M. Initiation into prescription opioid misuse amongst young injection drug users. *Int J Drug Policy*. 2012; 23(1):37–44.
3. CDC Morbidity and Mortality Weekly Report, January 1, 2016; 64(50):1378–1382.
4. CDC Morbidity and Mortality Weekly Report, August 12, 2016; 65(31):799–802.
5. Mihaly R. Medical Costs of Addicted Newborns: Neonatal Abstinence Syndrome, www.ncdrugtreatmentcourts.com/NAS.html

Discussion Questions

1. In what ways can a healthcare leader in a community ravaged by opioid addiction address individuals' and community needs?
   A. A physician employed by a HCO for many years has been found to have an opioid prescribing rate quadruple that of the national average. This physician is also very popular in the community and has the highest patient satisfaction scores.
   B. The increase in NAS babies in the community has tripled in the last decade.
   C. Addiction is rated in the community needs assessment as the highest health concern by the community and local healthcare professionals.
   D. Adding an addiction treatment center would cost approximately $500,000 a year, approximately 2% of the overall HCO operating budget.
2. What actions would you take to address these issues?

Related Websites

AHA annual survey, American Hospital Association: https://www.aha.org/data-insights/aha-data-products

Caring for Communities (AHA program of community outreach): http://www.ahacommunityconnections.org

Center for Disease Control and Prevention: www.cdc.gov/datastatistics/

Center for Medicare and Medicaid Services (CMS) Critical Access Hospitals Certification and Compliance Guidelines: www.cms.gov/Medicare/Provider-Enrollment-and-Certification/CertificationandComplianc/CAHs.html

Guidelines for Community Benefit: https://www.irs.gov/charities-non-profits/charitable-organizations/new-requirements-for-501c3-hospitals-under-the-affordable-care-act

Health Resources and Service Administration (HRSA) Federally Qualified Health Center Guidelines: http://bphc.hrsa.gov/about/requirements/index.html

PPACA Needs Assessment Guidelines: www.ruralcenter.org/tasc/resources/ppaca-tax-exempt-hospital-status-requirements-9007

Rural Health Clinic Guidelines: www.cms.gov/Center/provider-Type/Rural-Health-Clinics-Center.html

Rural Health Clinic Program: www.hrsa.gov/ruralhealth/

References

Alexander, J. A., Comfort, M. E., Weiner, B. J., & Bogue, R. (2001). Leadership in collaborative community health partnerships. *Nonprofit Management & Leadership, 12*(2), 159–175.

Anderson, R. A., & McDaniel, R. R. (2000). Managing healthcare organizations: Where professionalism meets complexity science. *Healthcare Management Review, 25*(1), 83–92.

Drain, M., Godkin, L., & Valentine, S. (2001, Fall). Examining closure rates of rural hospitals: An assessment of a strategic taxonomy. *Health Care Management Review, 26*(4), 27–51.

Duchesne, J. C., Kyle, A., Simmons, J., Islam, S., Schmieg, R. E., Jr., & McSwain, N. E., Jr. (2008). Impact of telemedicine upon rural trauma care. *Journal of Trauma, 64*(1), 92–97.

Holmes, M., Pink, G. H., & Slifkin, R. T. (2006, November). Impact of conversion to critical access hospital status on hospital financial performance and condition. Retrieved from www.flexmonitoring.org/documents/PolicyBrief1.pdf

Huttlinger, K., Schaller-Ayers, J., & Lawson, T. (2004). Healthcare in Appalachia: A population-based approach. *Public Health Nursing, 21*(2), 103–110.

McDaniel, R. R., & Driebe, D. J. (2001). Complexity science and healthcare management. *Advances in Healthcare Management, 2*, 11–36.

Merwin, E., Snyder, A., & Katz, E. (2006). Differential access to quality healthcare: Professional and policy challenges. *Family and Community Health, 29*(3), 186–194.

Patient Protection and Affordable Care Act (PPACA). (2010). Pub. L. No. 111148, 124 Stat. 119. Retrieved from www.healthcare.gov /law/full/

Roop, E. S. (2008, January). A litmus test for critical access. *Hospital Health Network, 82*(1), 42–44.

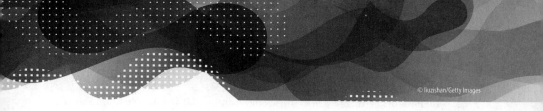

CHAPTER 16

Global Healthcare Leadership

Carrie A. Pullen EdD and Frankline Augustin DPPD

LEARNING OBJECTIVES

By the end of this chapter, the student will be able to:

- Understand the importance of considering global health care.
- Describe recent advances and challenges in global health.
- Understand the role of the World Health Organization and the requirements of the International Health Regulations in improving global health care.
- Explain factors impacting health disparities both among and within countries.
- Discuss some of the current challenges facing global healthcare leaders today.
- Describe how cultural competence is an important tool in addressing global health care and ethics/human rights.
- Explain how future leaders can engage in and contribute to global health.

KEY TERMS

Cultural competence
Cultural relativism
Ethnocentrism
Global health
Health inequities
Medical tourism
Organization for Economic Co-operation and Development (OECD)

Public health
United Nations (UN)
United Nations Educational, Scientific and Cultural Organization (UNESCO)
World Health Organization (WHO)

▶ Introduction

A review of healthcare leadership today cannot fail to include attention to **global health** and health care. The health of residents living in the United States can be impacted by what goes on in other countries, both positively and negatively. Leaders who seek to improve U.S. patient outcomes must, at a minimum, consider global **public health** issues, such as risks from communicable diseases and benefits from medications and treatments around the world. As Dr. Margaret Hamburg, the 21st commissioner of the U.S. Food and Drug Commission, emphasized "Today we must recognize, to successfully protect U.S. public health, we must think, act, and engage globally. Our interests must be broader than simply those within our borders" (McGuire, 2013). Conscientious healthcare leaders will seek to adopt and share best practices that can improve health both nationally and globally. This chapter examines the history of global health administration, as well as issues and challenges prominent in today's practice of international public health. The ongoing efforts of national leaders to address the impact of these issues on health care in the United States will also be explored.

▶ Defining and Understanding Global Health

Global health has been defined by the U.S. Institute of Medicine (1997) as "health problems, issues and concerns that transcend national boundaries and may best be addressed by cooperative actions." In the past 30 years, the world has seen significant improvement in benchmarks of human health, with life expectancies rising and infant mortality rates dropping significantly. Vaccination initiatives have made great inroads in controlling, and in some cases eradicating, life-threatening diseases. Significant challenges, nonetheless, remain.

- Disparities in access to quality care across populations continue to be glaring. Such disparities negatively impact nations' economic development, the quality of life of residents of these nations, and the prospects of improved health for future generations. Uneven access to and distribution of health resources due to differences in socioeconomic status can lead to less optimal health outcomes, that is, **health inequities**. Death and suffering due to lack of resources could and should be preventable. For example, in sub-Saharan Africa, children are 14 times more likely to die before the age of 5 of pneumonia, malaria, diarrhea, etc., than children from the rest of the world (World Health Organization, n.d.).
- Failure to protect the environment has also negatively impacted public health in many regions; local and international responses to natural disasters may not be sufficient to minimize morbidity and mortality.
- Disparities in care received are not solely tied to an individual's nationality, but can also be affected by one's gender, race, class, home location, and income. The **World Health Organization** (WHO, n.d.) reports that nearly 1 billion of our world's population resides in low-income housing or are homeless. Health services for these individuals are frequently inaccessible and unaffordable.
- Though praiseworthy, improvements in health-related treatments and outcomes have, in some cases, raised new concerns. Longer lifespans and growing populations of elderly individuals have created a need for new approaches to

effectively manage chronic conditions, such as diabetes and Alzheimer's disease. The advent of new and expensive drug treatments and technologies, combined with efforts to improve access to care, have improved health outcomes, but have also increased pressures globally to provide ongoing and chronic care more efficiently and at a lower cost.

■ Current and future global healthcare leaders will need to address these developments, create actionable and sustainable goals, marshal the resources needed to achieve high-quality outcomes, and accurately measure the progress of local and global collaborative initiatives to provide effective interventions and solutions.

▶ The History of Global Health

To understand the evolution of global health in the last 200 years, it is helpful to examine how the concept developed, as well as the major factors that have guided our efforts to address global health needs today. Health advances spread slowly and sporadically, if at all, through the developing world, until the 19th century, when churches and faith groups began mounting medical missions. These missions used health interventions at first as vehicles for religious evangelism, but eventually came to view the health services themselves as their mission (Foege, 2005). Missionaries from different faith groups initially competed with each other, but, before long, adopted cooperation amongst themselves and with the governments of impacted countries to share resources and coordinate efforts. In addition to positively impacting the health of individuals in the targeted nations, this outreach served to educate and galvanize the public in the United States regarding the scope and severity of the problems faced by many developing nations, which host a majority of the world's population.

The military of European nations, and, eventually, that of the United States, also contributed to the development of a concerted effort to improve world health by conducting research initially designed to protect their own service members stationed overseas (Foege, 2005). This focus on international diseases led to data collection, analysis, and evidence-based practices that were useful to protect the inhabitants of the countries impacted as well as the soldiers abroad. It must be pointed out, however, that colonization has also been held responsible for creating epidemics due to factors such as extensive travel and exposure of indigenous and immigrant populations to new communicable pathogens (Palilnois, 2015).

During the 1950s, the WHO was formed, which launched a strategic and formalized approach to tracking and improving global health. Non-governmental organizations (NGOs) and private citizens also began efforts to support health care in specific countries or to address specific health concerns. As the described efforts coalesced, progress was made in the control of infectious diseases, and the modern world saw an overall improvement in global health. Developed countries were more able to focus on addressing increasing longevity and associated chronic disease. Unfortunately, vast disparities in health services and outcomes remained.

The second half of the 20th century saw the eruption of the HIV/AIDS epidemic and the initial coordinated international attempts to respond with research, education, infection control measures, and treatment. Outbreaks of disease in animals threatened human health as well; avian flu and mad cow disease required similar coordinated responses among governments, industry regulators and their stakeholders, consumers, and healthcare professionals worldwide.

Funding in the United States for global health rose dramatically during the 1990s and early 2000s as Americans embraced their role as healthcare leaders on the global front (Palilnois, 2015). It began to be understood that developing countries have an unfair burden of disease and that more developed countries have the practical and moral responsibility to use their resources to help address these disparities. The question has been posed, however, whether that trend will continue, as many nations who have led the fight to improve health conditions across the globe recently appear to be embracing nationalism. This change threatens the appetite for, and therefore the funding of, much of the work that has resulted in the described advances in global health that have been observed.

Privatization of healthcare services has recently begun to diminish hard-won gains in health outcomes. For example, China previously had a well-developed public health system. During the 30 years between the 1950s and 1980s, the infant mortality rate in China dropped substantially, and life expectancy nearly doubled. The 1980s, however, saw a radical change as the government quickly dismantled the previously existing health system (Blumenthal & Hsiao, 2005). As a consequence, health care in China became available predominantly to those who could afford it. Privatization has been reducing access to quality care in many countries, leading to debates around the question: "Is health care a human right?"

▶ The World Health Organization

That global health is considered important is not new. The WHO was established in 1948, to work within the framework of the **United Nations (UN)** to create a healthier world by coordinating and leading the charge to improve global heath. The WHO continues to combat diseases and works to improve the health of world populations by promoting improved regulating air, food, and water quality, and by supporting the availability of vaccines and other medicines. The WHO has five published priorities that have been established to positively impact global health. Those priorities are listed in **BOX 16.1**.

In 2000, the UN created the Millennium Development Goals (MDGs). There are eight MDGs, four of which relate directly to addressing and improving public health. The first goal is to eradicate extreme hunger and poverty. The fourth is to reduce child mortality. The fifth is to improve maternal health, and the sixth is to combat HIV/AIDS, malaria, and other diseases. Unfortunately, it must be noted, that we are not yet on-track to meet the MDGs (Gostin, 2012).

BOX 16.1 WHO Priorities

Published WHO Priorities
1. Providing leadership
2. Helping to shape international research agendas
3. Setting standards in international health
4. Providing technical support to member countries
5. Monitoring health situations and trends

In 2007, the WHO created the International Health Regulations (IHR), a binding international legal instrument that sets out requirements for member countries regarding the reporting of disease outbreaks and public health events. The regulations specify, however, that the reporting should be done in a way that will "avoid unnecessary interference with international traffic and trade" (Gostin, Lucey, & Phelan, 2014, p. 265). This effort attempts to limit the potential damage to a region's economy while endeavoring to protect public health for residents and visitors. Long-term damage to a nation's economy could set back progress made in providing health services to its population.

▶ Understanding What Impacts Global Health and How It Is Measured

Leaders in global health should understand the factors that impact the health of individuals, as well as the general public as a whole. The health of an individual is based upon factors such as age, sex, and genetic history. Epigenetic and environmental factors also influence health; these include the local environment, and access to clean air, water, proper sanitation, good nutrition, and quality healthcare services. Factors that can impede access to health services include inconvenient or inaccessible location of services, unaffordable cost, language and cultural barriers, limited education, poverty, political and economic instability, and violence or war.

Political instability and lack of economic resources are among the greatest barriers to improving the health of populations in developing countries. Health improvement initiatives must be weighed against economic impacts, as programs that aim to improve health, yet result in negative economic impacts for a population, can fail to result in the overall desired improvement in the long term. Improving the economic health of a country is closely tied to improving the health of its citizens, and peace is essential to stabilizing and improving economic conditions and is also a crucial ingredient of improving health conditions. Poverty and inequities in wealth distribution are factors that contribute significantly to political instability. Improving all of these intertwined factors in tandem must be a goal when aiming for enhanced global health.

In order to understand, follow, and positively impact global health, healthcare leaders depend upon data to assess, track, and analyze the health of populations. Key indicators used to assess a country's level of health include infant mortality, life expectancy, and mortality rates of children under 5 years of age. Data, however, are only as accurate as the sources utilized and are not always reliable. Accurate data are needed with regard to births, deaths, and causes of death in order to inform and support effective intervention efforts.

▶ International Comparisons of Healthcare Spending

The United States spends more on health care than any other country; more than 18% of its annual gross domestic product is spent on health (Galea, 2017). According to the Peterson-Kaiser Health System Tracker, U.S. healthcare spending per

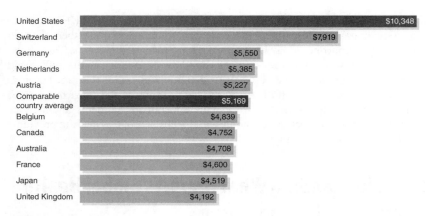

FIGURE 16.1 Health Expenditures per Capita

Kaiser Family Foundation analysis of data from OECD (2017), "OECD Health Data: Health expenditure and financing: Health expenditure indicators", OECD Health Statistics (database) (Accessed on March 19, 2017).

person was $10,348 in 2016 (Sawyer & Cox, 2018). Switzerland was the next developed country on the list, with a per capita expenditure of $7,919 (**FIGURE 16.1**).

Factors causing elevated healthcare spending in the United States include the high cost of technological interventions, the high price of services, the high administrative cost of insurance plans, and unrestrained pharmaceutical drug spending. These costs are higher than in the average **Organization for Economic Co-operation and Development (OECD)** member country. OECD is an international economic organization comprised of 35 member countries who promote policies that advance social and fiscal well-being (Fuchs, 2014). Wealthy countries whose governments play a pivotal role in regulating health care are able to keep costs down by regulating cost control over services (e.g., limiting the number and reimbursement of specialists), pharmaceuticals, and technology.

It is natural to expect a positive correlation between high healthcare spending and favorable health outcomes, but this is not the case for the United States. OECD claims that the U.S. ranks 27th in life expectancy (78.8 years), has the fourth-highest infant mortality rate, the sixth-highest maternal mortality rate, and is the most obese country (Meisler, 2017). OECD notes that Japan has the highest life expectancy at 83.9 years, with health expenditures of only $4519 per capita (Meisler, 2017). Thus, high healthcare costs do not necessarily equate to positive health outcomes.

▶ Addressing Threats and Adopting Best Practices

As referred to previously in this chapter, engaging in the world health arena provides important benefits to the United States. Elimination or reduction of long-standing diseases such as tuberculosis and polio, and early identification and control of outbreaks of new diseases globally have obvious benefits in preventing outbreaks in the United States, as well as abroad. Additionally, because data show that other countries are spending less on health care with better outcome results, the United States has significant opportunities to learn about and adopt their best practices in order to improve our domestic health outcomes.

A recent example of an outbreak of significant international concern was from the virus Ebola, which appeared in West Africa in late 2013 and spread to other countries, including the United States via international travel and the infection of international aid workers. The WHO did respond to the crises, but resources to quickly and adequately address emergencies of this nature were observed to be less than ideal (Gostin & Freidman, 2014). Part of the reason for that gap has been lack of funding. The WHO has a budget that is generally agreed to be insufficient to address the identified needs around the world. Participating countries are tasked to contribute, but there are insufficient penalties for failing to do so.

The Ebola crisis also demonstrated ethical concerns about healthcare inequities; healthcare workers were treated differently than the patients they were serving. For example, during the height of the crisis, two American healthcare workers infected with Ebola virus were transported to Atlanta, Georgia, and treated with an experimental drug that had limited availability. Concerns understandably arose about the appropriateness of this action because African patients had little or no access to the drug.

This crisis also illustrated the connections between addressing health in developing countries and concerns about political and economic impact. As the outbreak mounted, some countries called for travel bans in an attempt to prevent virus spread, whereas others decried that measure as detrimental for tourism to the affected countries that had recently begun making strides to recover from devastating civil wars.

An example of an opportunity to benefit from advances in other countries is related to care for the elderly, especially for those with dementia or Alzheimer's disease. The U.S. model for caring for the elderly is based on a medical/hospital model that is both unnecessary and undesirable for individuals who have declines or deficits in neurological functioning, but are otherwise healthy. The Dutch have developed a concept that allows elders with memory difficulties to live in a controlled "town" environment, maintaining access to independent functioning while simultaneously offering the relative safety of a monitored and supported space (Henley, 2012). This model offers considerable potential for the United States, in which individuals with similar levels of functioning, once unable to live independently, are instead left with traditional skilled nursing care facilities as their only option.

▶ Cultural Competence, Ethics, and Human Rights

It is likely not surprising that working across cultures inevitably comes with challenges and ethical dilemmas. Effective global healthcare leaders ensure that their cross-cultural interventions follow practices that are culturally competent and morally defensible. **Cultural competence** is defined by the Department of Health and Human Services Office of Minority Health as "a set of congruent behaviors, attitudes, and policies that come together in a system, agency, or among professionals that enables effective work in cross-cultural situations" (U.S. Department of Health and Human Services Office of Minority Health, 2016).

The application of cultural competence begins with self-awareness of any personal biases (Fowler & Prickett, 2010; Gurchiek, 2017; Negi et al., 2010). Oxford Dictionary describes bias as a "prejudice in favor of or against one thing, person, or group compared with another, usually in a way considered to be unfair" (Bias, n.d., para. 1). In a culturally diverse setting, it is essential that global healthcare leaders engage in deliberate proactive self-reflection about their attitudes, opinions, and/ or behaviors that may be perceived as negative towards any culture that is different from their own. Without such self-exploration and insight, unaddressed biases can block a leader's perspective and potentially negatively affect the outcomes of encounters and services for the various cultures they serve.

Global healthcare leaders must also be aware of **ethnocentrism**. Ethnocentrism is defined by Myers (as cited in Raden, 2003) as the "belief in the superiority of one's own group and a corresponding disdain for all other groups" (p. 804). Throughout the world, ethnocentric beliefs are common. Ethnocentrism can instill a positive sense of community, loyalty, and pride within nations. However, ethnocentrism can cause dissension among interactive groups or nations that believe that those outside the group do not tolerate or welcome their culture, belief system, and values.

A possible alternative to ethnocentrism for the global healthcare leader is **cultural relativism**. Cultural relativism is an anthropological concept that supports the principle that understanding people's values, beliefs, and practices requires being considerate of their cultural context (Howsen, 2009). Esikot (2012) defines cultural relativism as the "view that different cultures have different moral standards which regulate human actions and these actions are or should be assessed or evaluated by these standards" (p. 131). Practicing the principles of cultural relativism can be complicated, particularly when the values and standards of different cultures clash with Western values.

One complication is the intersection of cultural relativism with human rights. For example, Karen Musalo (Markkula Center for Applied Ethics, 2015), an attorney from the United States, represented Fauziya Kassindja, a West African woman who sought political asylum to flee from her tribe's custom of female genital mutilation (PBS, n.d.). When Musalo took Kassindja's case, she was accused of unethically foisting her Western perspectives of human rights onto a culturally accepted practice in continents like Africa, Middle East, and Asia. Musalo contends that cultural relativism in this matter would be in conflict with the practice of universal human rights.

Is the idea of human rights a universal standard? And, if so, what criteria are covered under that label? The UN, an international organization founded in 1945 and made up of 193 member states, has been guided by principles established in its charter (United Nations, n.d.a). The UN is thereby positioned to respond to issues facing humankind, such as terrorism, gender equality, food production, and human rights.

In 1948, the UN produced the Universal Declaration of Human Rights, which was formulated by representatives from diverse cultural backgrounds from different parts of the world (United Nations, n.d.b). The declaration states that fundamental human rights are to be universally protected. The **United Nations Educational, Scientific and Cultural Organization (UNESCO)**, a specialized agency for the

UN, emphasizes that human rights do include the choice of adopting cultural rights as long as they do not infringe "on another human right" (UNESCO Culture for Sustainable Development, n.d.).

Research has shown an association between human rights and positive health outcomes (Mann, 2006). The promotion of human rights as an effective basis for improving health has been assessed and demonstrated (Dyer, 2015; Mullany et al., 2007; Porsdam-Mann, Bradley, & Sahakian, 2016). However, despite treaties and international declarations that seek to protect human rights, countries remain that fail to ensure the rights of their citizens.

Another alternative to ethnocentrism is the transformational practice of cultural humility. Cultural humility is "the lifelong commitment to self-evaluation and critique, to redressing the power imbalances ... and to developing mutually beneficial and non-paternalistic partnerships with communities on behalf of individuals and populations" (Tervalon & Murray-García, 1998, p. 123). Cultural humility distinguishes itself from cultural competence in that it characteristically focuses on power in relationships. Exercising cultural humility requires an in-depth analysis and understanding of one's personal blind spots through the implementation of a "process-oriented approach to competency" (Rincon, 2009; Waters & Asbill, 2013). Cultural humility as a practice requires intentional effort because it can be personally challenging. Generally speaking, few individuals want to acknowledge that they may be biased or unwelcoming to different groups. Cultural humility requires a commitment to the gradual learning process that helps to eliminate bias and ethnocentrism.

▶ Current and Future Challenges

The world has made progress in focusing resources on underserved populations in the arena of public health, but many challenges remain. This section will describe some of the most pressing challenges facing the world health community today. These challenges include threats such as rising nationalism, risks to peace, and the growing refugee crisis. Addressing the opportunities associated with new technology and maximizing potential economic gains from evidence-based clinical practice will create challenges as well. Leaders will need to consider new approaches that include international collaboration, such as partnerships in testing and approval of new medications and treatments across borders. U.S. health will become more interdependent on international health, and U.S. health leaders will need to maintain a global perspective to achieve their goals for domestic and international health.

The Threat of Rising Nationalism

As noted previously, the rising tide of nationalism in many developed countries is currently threatening to negatively impact the resolve of those countries to provide resources to improve the health of global populations (Gostin & Friedman, 2014). The United States has been a leader in shaping global health policy and allocating resources to meet healthcare goals and address international health disparities. It is feared, however, that ongoing progress may be derailed by ethnocentric sentiments in resource-rich nations.

Migration

Wars and violence in many countries have led to waves of refugees seeking to escape to safety. Many countries to which refugees flee are not equipped to handle the migration, and are unable to provide safe and healthy environments for the large numbers of adults and children arriving. Unsanitary conditions that breed infection and illness can develop when absorption of immigrants into a new community or repatriation is difficult or impossible (Gushulak, Weekers, & MacPherson, 2009).

Migration in and of itself carries significant risks. Transportation has become faster and more reliable, and humans are increasingly mobile. Unfortunately, this mobility creates health challenges in the spread of communicable diseases, even in developed countries, now only separated by a flight of several hours.

Technological Advances

Globalization has been effective in advancing healthcare technology. The internet has narrowed the distance between countries, and allowed innovative software, medical equipment and products, research data and evidence, and treatment approaches to rapidly spread across national borders. The healthcare marketplace has become truly global. Unfortunately, Internet penetrance is not 100%, and some developing countries are not able to access health information and technologies or afford them, resulting in a financial barrier to health.

A prudent response has been the growing use of low-cost mobile health applications. GSMA Intelligence, which represents the interests of mobile operators worldwide, reports in their research that 2017 was a global milestone (Sivakumaran & Iacopino, 2018). The number of people connected to mobile services exceeded "5 billion globally, with 3.7 billion in developing markets…two out of three people in the world had a mobile subscription at the end of 2017" (Sivakumaran & Iacopino, 2018, p. 11). To put these data into perspective, there are more people in the world who have access to mobile phones than to running water, toilets, or electricity (Parke, 2016; Wang, 2013). The growth of mobile service around the world, especially in developing countries, is an opportunity and valid tool for global healthcare leaders to use to increase health promotion and augment healthcare delivery services. As examples, SMS (short message service) technology has been used in Uganda to track malnutrition; has sent reminders to patients in Kenya to take their medication; has served as a health promotion tool to educate pregnant mothers in India about best health practices; and has empowered patients in Ghana to report the selling of counterfeit medication (Chachoua, 2015).

Mobile health has great potential for low-income and middle-income countries to improve health outcomes. But more research must be done to determine its impact and its effectiveness.

Standardizing Pharmaceutical Approvals

One of the biggest current opportunities for reducing health costs involves standardizing and creating reciprocal agreements for common approvals for new drugs and treatments (Gebelhoff, 2017). Currently, the United States requires that new drugs go through a separate approval process through the U.S. Food and Drug Administration. Most other developed countries require a similar review.

These parallel processes can create unnecessary duplication of efforts; costs may be eliminated through reciprocal agreements. Concerns understandably exist, however, that such agreements hold all parties to the highest standards and ensures the protection of consumers. Because the costs of pharmaceuticals continue to be expensive in the United States, contributing to the high cost of health care, reducing healthcare costs by avoiding duplication of research could provide a significant source of savings.

Medical Tourism and Traveling Medical Teams

Quality of care and access to services continue to vary widely across countries. Residents of other countries have historically come to the United States to access otherwise unavailable resources, technology, and expertise. Unfortunately, countries with limited resources may have a large population with economic and environmental barriers to care who are unable to travel. Wealthy individuals, typically from developed countries, may be in a better position to obtain services abroad at a lower cost than domestically; even as those services remain unaffordable for the local population. This process has been termed "**medical tourism**," in which Americans seek more economical procedures or treatments in other countries, options which are unavailable or very expensive in the United States.

An example is the recent flow of U.S. citizens to Mexico for reduced-cost dental care. Residents of San Diego can simply walk across the border to obtain dental care that is significantly less expensive than similar services provided in the United States. While the medical tourists are there, they can also pick up antibiotics and other medications at a local pharmacy at a much lower price without the doctor's prescription that is needed in the United States. Also notable is the observation that San Diego is now launching a marketing campaign designed to attract both national and international medical tourists to the city to bolster tourism spending. The advertised attraction, in this case, is not the low cost of services, but rather the high quality of care and the ease of recovery in the picturesque seaside environment of southern California (Weisberg, 2017). Other examples of medical tourism include Brazil, which has long been known for its niche as a leader in the cosmetic surgery market, as well as European countries for potentially lifesaving drugs or treatments that are not currently available in the United States.

In addition to patients traveling to access care, it is also common for care to travel across international borders to access patients. Operation Smile is an example of an organization that provides reconstructive surgery to residents of developing countries without such resources. This organization, founded in 1982, sends surgical teams to provide cleft palate correction surgery to children around the world. Initially, the surgical teams traveled to the locations where the children lived, operated on as many children as was feasible in 4 or 5 days, and then returned to their home countries. Demand, however, always exceeded supply, and efforts are now underway to establish sustainable clinics in locations such as Guwahati, a province in Northern India (Coll, 2011). Other examples of this model include Doctors without Borders, Timmy Global Health, and Floating Doctors, all NGOs that provide medical services to isolated or distressed areas. These organizations serve important needs but are expensive to operate. Finding ways to make these services more sustainable is an ongoing challenge. Cooperation with local government agencies is crucial to the success and sustainability of such efforts.

▶ The Future Role of Healthcare Leaders in Global Health

So how can today's global healthcare leaders address these issues, opportunities, and challenges? First, by establishing measures and tracking global trends and outcomes, which provide the data necessary to create sound interventions and evaluate their effectiveness. Encouraging humanitarian efforts by governments and charitable institutions can make measurable inroads towards improving health outcomes. Providing enhanced education and resources are proven methods to positively impact health outcomes as well; adequate funding will be key to meeting global health goals.

Finally, by ensuring that our leaders are exposed to and involved in international health care, we can promote improved global health and simultaneously benefit from the efforts and innovations of other nations. Elizabeth Bradley, a professor of public health at Yale and a noted leader in global health strategy development, advises that would-be health leaders spend time in international locales, with the goals of learning how to help and how to be helped. She states that we have a lot to learn from engaging with patients and caregivers living and working in resource-limited areas because they are often exceptionally creative when working to solve problems. These innovations can then be applied to similar issues that arise in the United States.

Author Mark Twain wrote, "Travel is fatal to prejudice, bigotry, and narrow-mindedness. Many Americans would benefit from new experiences to broaden their horizons. Broad, wholesome, charitable views of people and things cannot be acquired by vegetating in one little corner of the earth all of one's lifetime," (Twain & Cardwell, 1984).

Healthcare administrators with the goal of improving global health should seek out opportunities to travel to, work in, and experience other locales and cultures. American universities and corporations should invest in providing access to those opportunities for its students, faculty, and staff.

Summary

As this chapter has pointed out, some health problems are bigger than any one country or government can address alone. International cooperation is needed to identify, track, and treat both existing, and, as yet unrealized, threats. NGOs, educational institutions, and prominent public figures also play an important role in improving global health. Their efforts have enhanced public health worldwide, but continued allocations of resources are needed to ensure that recent hard-won gains in health outcomes are not lost, that inequities are addressed, that suffering is reduced, and quality of life is improved for all global citizens. The United States is facing many demands to reduce costs and improve access to health care and quality of care domestically, but has both a moral and pragmatic imperative as well to lead the mission to improve public health abroad and create a healthier future around the world.

Discussion Questions

1. Why is the health of people in other nations important for the U.S. population?
2. How do we define and measure global health?
3. What is WHO and what do they do?

4. What is the impact of human rights on health?
5. How does the United States measure up against other developed countries with regards to health costs and outcomes?
6. Define and contrast ethnocentrism and cultural relativism and their implications as related to global health.
7. What are some of the biggest challenges facing leaders who are attempting to positively impact global health today?
8. What actions are recommended for the global health leaders of tomorrow?

🔍 CASE STUDY: Story of Dr. Junzhang Tian, a Chinese Healthcare Leader

by Donghai Wei, PhD and Louis Rubino, PhD, FACHE

Junzhang Tian's educational background began in China's Military Medical Universities, from which he received his doctor of medicine degree with a specialty in imaging and nuclear medicine in 2003. Over the past 15 years, Dr. Tian has demonstrated his medical, as well as his administrative skills, as the vice director of the Imaging Department of the Guangdong 177th Hospital, and then as the director of the Imaging Department of the Guangdong Second Provincial General Hospital.

Dr. Tian's supervisors recognized his leadership potential and sent Dr. Tian to the United States as a visiting scholar for 1 year at California State University, Northridge, under the mentorship of Dr. Louis Rubino, the program director for Health Administration in the College of Health and Human Development. Dr. Tian audited Health Administration department classes and worked with Dr. Rubino to research and compare U.S. and international healthcare delivery systems. Dr. Tian believes this experience helped him to learn about effective health care and quality improvement on a broader level, beyond just one department.

Dr. Tian became president of the Guangdong Second Provincial General Hospital (GSPGH) soon after returning to China and has served in that capacity for the last 9 years. Dr. Tian has transformed this hospital into a very successful and unique medical care facility, not only in Guangdong Province, but in more remote areas, through its telemedicine program. In fact, GSPGH has been named the first "Internet Hospital," due to its provision of remote medical services and outreach. The hospital has offered the first dynamic community model to address chronic disease by utilizing "health huts" to provide diagnosis and treatment for more than one million villagers. This program has greatly improved access to medical services for rural communities and has lowered healthcare costs (e.g., medications) for the patients in the villages.

Dr. Tian developed and implemented many innovative procedures at GSPGH to enhance services and promote quality and cost-effectiveness. He pioneered an appointment registration service and implemented an after-care payment system, which allowed patients to pay for their services after receiving their diagnosis and treatment, as opposed to the Chinese business practice of requiring payment prior to rendering services. His hospital launched the use of "robots" to guide patients with hospital rules and procedures and smart devices to promote greater efficiency. A new supply processing distribution system and an intelligent pharmacy were created. These changes greatly improved the quality of care rendered and the level of patient satisfaction and at the same time reduced costs. As a result, Dr. Tian was awarded the

Innovative Persons in Health Service Reform award in 2013 by the Chinese National Health and Family Planning Commission.

Emergency management always attracted Dr. Tian as well, so he led the National Emergency Medical Rescue Team, which was certified by the WHO in 2017. This team is only one of nine emergency medical teams in the world, and introduced emergency operations procedures in China that meet international emergency rescue standards. An emergency medical rescue volunteer training system was also developed to call upon first responders when a disaster occurs. Successful rescue missions have included aiding in the recovery from the Ya'an earthquake in Sichuan in 2008 and the massive mudslide in Guangming New District of Shenzhen in 2015.

While overseeing this acclaimed modernized healthcare system, Dr. Tian remained active in scientific research. Having begun his practice with radiologic imaging, Dr. Tian continued his studies in that field, examining the relationship between insomnia and damaged white brain matter. He also continued his efforts as an inventor, taking the lead in developing a new type of portable oxygen machine and other rescue equipment. For his research efforts, he was honored as a Hero of the Provincial Party Committee and the Provincial Government.

The latest area of interest for Dr. Tian has been the utilization of artificial intelligence in the hospital outpatient setting. Through the use of sophisticated computer technology, medical "big data," the mobile internet, and cloud computing, his hospital is reengineering and optimizing the outpatient process. An intelligent payment system, consultant system, facial-recognition system, logistic system, emergency command system, and image diagnostic system have been developed for use at his hospital. "The future is now" at GSPGH.

Dr. Tian continues to explore ways to improve GSPGH hospital operations and care provided. To accommodate and support the advancements noted previously, Dr. Tian has endeavored to redesign hospital facilities within a sustainable and environmentally friendly model. He is also working with government leaders engaged in China's national healthcare reform to develop new policies and to obtain additional financial support that would allow GSPGH to further expand its reach. He is also working on a new method of performance evaluation to allow for better accountability.

In sum, Dr. Tian has demonstrated his leadership skills through his efforts to transform Guangdong Second Provincial General Hospital into an emergency hospital, then a network hospital, and now the first intelligent hospital. He has fully embraced the Chinese national government's strategy of "Internet +" and has made GSPGH a model for all of China. Dr. Tian has accomplished these goals as a result of having had both clinical and management training and experience. This relatively new concept provides a pathway for healthcare leaders in China to transform its hospitals.

Case Study Discussion Questions

1. Why do you think coming to the United States for 1 year as a scholar helped Dr. Tian's leadership at GSPGH?
2. GSPGH development occurred in stages. What outside forces might be considered drivers to these changes?
3. It is unusual for Chinese healthcare leaders to be trained in management. Instead, clinical directors are promoted into the C-suite. Describe the pros and cons associated with this practice.

Related Websites

Doctors Without Borders: http://www.doctorswithoutborders.com
Floating Doctors: http://www.floatingdoctors.com
Operation Smile: http://www.operationsmile.com
Timmy Global Health: http://www.timmyglobalhealth.org
World Health Organization: http://who.int

References

Bias. (n.d.). In *Oxford dictionaries*. Retrieved from http://oxforddictionaries.com/us/definition/american_english/bias

Blumenthal, D., & Hsiao, W. (2005). Privatization and its discontents: The evolving Chinese health care system. *New England Journal of Medicine, 353*, 1165–1170. doi:10.1056/NEJMhpr051133

Chachoua, E. (2015, March). How mobile technology could change healthcare in developing countries. *World Economic Forum*. Retrieved from https://www.weforum.org/agenda/2015/03/how-mobile-technology-could-change-healthcare-in-developing-countries/

Coll, A. (2011). International plastic surgery: Leaving a legacy. *RCS Bulletin, 93*(10), 348–349. doi:10.1308/147363511X13158258989712

Dyer, L. (2015). A review of the impact of the human rights in healthcare programme in England and Wales. *Health & Human Rights: An International Journal, 17*(2), 111–122.

Esikot, I. F. (2012). Globalization versus relativism: The imperative of a universal ethics. *Journal of Politics and Law, 5*(4), 129–135. doi:10.5539/jpl.v5n4p129

Foege, W. H. (2005). *Global health leadership and management*. San Francisco, CA: Jossey-Bass.

Fuchs, V. R. (2014). Why do other rich nations spend so much less on healthcare? *The Atlantic*. Retrieved from https://www.theatlantic.com/business/archive/2014/07/why-do-other-rich-nations-spend-so-much-less-on-healthcare/374576/

Galea, S. (2017, May 24). America spends the most on healthcare but isn't the healthiest country. *Fortune*. Retrieved from http://fortune.com/2017/05/24/us-health-care-spending/

Gebelhoff, R. (2017, February 14). Why people should be able to buy drugs approved in other countries. *The Washington Post*. Retrieved from https://www.washingtonpost.com

Gostin, L. O. (2012). A framework convention on global health: Health for all, justice for all. *JAMA, 307*(19), 2087–2092. doi:10.1001/jama.2012.4395

Gostin, L. O., & Friedman, E. (2014). Ebola: A crisis in global health leadership. *The Lancet, 384*(9951), 1323–1325. doi:10.1016/S0140-6736(14)61791-8

Gostin, L. O., Lucey, D., & Phelan, A. (2014). The Ebola epidemic: A global health emergency. *JAMA, 312*(11), 1095–1096. doi:10.1001/jama.2014.11176

Gurchiek, K. (2017). Embracing diversity starts with self-awareness, D&I expert says. Retrieved from https://www.shrm.org/resourcesandtools/hr-topics/behavioral-competencies/global-and-cultural-effectiveness/pages/embracing-diversity-starts-with-self-awareness,-di-expert-says.aspx

Gushulak, B. D., Weekers, J., & MacPherson, D. W. (2009). Migrants and emerging public health issues in a globalized world: Threats, risks and challenges, an evidence-based framework. *Emerging Health Threats Journal, 2*(1), 7091.

Henley, J. (2012, August 28). G2: Village people: How is society to look after the ever-growing numbers of people with dementia? Jon Henley visits a curiously uplifting Dutch care home that may have the answers. *The Guardian*. Retrieved from https://www.theguardian.com/us

Howsen, A. (2009). Cultural relativism. Retrieved from https://www.ebscohost.com/uploads/imported/thisTopic-dbTopic-1247.pdf

Markkula Center for Applied Ethics. (2015). When rights and cultures collide. Retrieved from https://www.scu.edu/ethics/ethics-resources/ethical-decision-making/when-rights-and-cultures-collide/

Mann, J. (2006). Health and human rights. *American Journal of Public Health, 96*(11), 1941–1943. doi:10.2105/AJPH.96.11.1940

McGuire, S. (2013). U.S. food and drug administration. Global engagement. *Advances in Nutrition, 4*(2), 265–266. doi:10.3945/an.112.003590

Meisler, L. (2017). Americans die younger despite spending the most on health care. Retrieved from https://www.bloomberg.com/graphics/2017-health-care-spending/

Mullany, L. C., Richards, A. K., Lee, C. I., Suwanvanichkij, V., Maung, C., Mahn, M., ... Lee, T. J. (2007). Population-based survey methods to quantify associations between human rights violations and health outcomes among internally displaced persons in eastern Burma. *Journal of Epidemiology & Community Health, 61*(10), 908–914. doi:10.1136/jech.2006.055087

Negi, N. J., Bender, K. A., Furman, R., Fowler, D. N., & Prickett, J. C. (2010). Enhancing self-awareness: A practical strategy to train culturally responsive social work students. *Advances in Social Work, 11*(2), 223–234. Retrieved from https://journals.iupui.edu/index.php/advancesinsocialwork

Palilnois, M. (2015). An introduction to global health and global health ethics. Retrieved from http://bioethics.wfu.edu/wp-content/uploads/2015/09/Topic-3-A-Brief-History-of-Global-Health.pdf

Parke, P. (2016). More Africans have access to cell phone service than piped water. *CNN Africa View.* Retrieved from https://www.cnn.com/2016/01/19/africa/africa-afrobarometer-infrastructure-report/index.html

PBS. (n.d.). Female genital mutilation and immigration abuse. Retrieved from http://www.pbs.org/speaktruthtopower/fauziya.html

Porsdam-Mann, S., Bradley, V. J., & Sahakian, B. J. (2016). Human rights-based approaches to mental health: A review of programs. *Health and Human Rights, 18*(1), 263–276. Retrieved from https://www.hhrjournal.org

Raden, D. (2003). Ingroup bias, classic ethnocentrism, and non-ethnocentrism among American whites. *Political Psychology, 24*(4), 803–828. doi:10.1046/j.1467-9221.2003.00355.x

Rincon, A. (2009). Practicing cultural humility. In T. Berthold, A. Avila-Esparza, & J. Miller (Eds.), *Foundation for community health workers* (pp. 136–137). San Francisco, CA: John Wiley & Sons.

Sawyer, B., & Cox, C. (2018). How does health spending in the U.S. compare to other countries? Retrieved from https://www.healthsystemtracker.org/chart-collection/health-spending-u-s-compare-countries/#item-average-wealthy-countries-spend-half-much-per-person-health-u-s-spends

Sivakumaran, M., & Iacopino, P. (2018). The mobile economy 2018. Retrieved from https://www.gsmaintelligence.com/research/2018/02/the-mobile-economy-2018/660/

Tervalon, M., & Murray-García, J. (1998). Cultural humility versus cultural competency: A critical distinction in defining physician training outcomes in multicultural education. *Journal of Health Care for the Poor and Underserved, 9*(2), 117–125. doi:10.1353/hpu.2010.0233

Twain, M., & Cardwell, G. (1984). *The innocents abroad: Roughing it.* New York, NY: Literary Classics.

UNESCO Culture for Sustainable Development. (n.d.). Culture and human rights. Retrieved from http://www.unesco.org/new/en/culture/themes/culture-and-development/the-future-we-want-the-role-of-culture/culture-and-human-rights/

United Nations. (n.d.a). Overview. Retrieved from http://www.un.org/en/sections/about-un/overview/index.html

United Nations. (n.d.b). Universal declaration of human rights. Retrieved from http://www.un.org/en/universal-declaration-human-rights/

U.S. Department of Health and Human Services Office of Minority Health. (2016). What is cultural competency? Retrieved from https://minorityhealth.hhs.gov/omh/content.aspx?ID=2804

U.S. Institute of Medicine. (1997). *America's vital interest in global health: Protecting our people, enhancing our economy, and advancing our international interests.* Washington, DC: National Academy Press.

Wang, Y. (2013, March 25). More people have cell phones than toilets, U.N. study shows. *Time.* Retrieved from http://newsfeed.time.com/2013/03/25/more-people-have-cell-phones-than-toilets-u-n-study-shows/

Waters, A., & Asbill, L. (2013, August). Reflections on cultural humility. *CYF News.* Retrieved from http://www.apa.org/pi/families/resources/newsletter/2013/08/cultural-humility.aspx

Weisberg, L. (2017, November 15). San Diego's new selling point: Medical tourism. *Los Angeles Times.* Retrieved from http://www.latimes.com/

World Health Organization. (n.d.). 10 facts on health inequities and their causes. Retrieved from http://www.who.int/features/factfiles/health_inequities/facts/en/

CHAPTER 17

Future Trends: Implications for Leadership

Andrew N. Garman, Christy Harris Lemak, and Melanie P. Standish

LEARNING OBJECTIVES

By the end of this chapter, the student will be able to:

- Identify macro trends in the U.S. health sectors that have implications for healthcare leadership.
- Describe key trends in healthcare leadership development.

KEY TERMS

Future trends   Leadership development
Leadership competencies   Population health improvement

▶ Introduction

As we write this chapter, the health services sector in the United States is evolving at an unprecedented pace. Health systems are consolidating, and organizations are beginning to emerge that transcend historical boundaries between payers, providers, suppliers, and consumer services. A wave of technology solutions is also spreading, providing new ways to address long-standing challenges related to access, affordability, and self-management.

We can get a clearer sense of future directions—and their implications for healthcare leaders and administrators—by taking a longer-term view of the industry's fundamental trends. Part of the work of the non-profit National Center for Healthcare Leadership (NCHL) focuses on understanding these trends and assessing their impact to better inform current and future leaders. In this chapter, we discuss **future trends** and their potential impact on the healthcare industry and its leadership. In addition, we provide a glimpse of how organizational approaches to leadership training and development are evolving as a result of scientific advances in industrial psychology and education.

▶ High-Level Trends Affecting Health Care

Change in the healthcare sector is highly complex and multifaceted. Our goal in this section is not to comprehensively document the changes that are likely to take place over the coming years—such a task would easily fill volumes. Instead, we will describe six trends that we believe will have the greatest impact on the learning needs of healthcare leaders entering the field in the years to come.

Trend 1: Growing Emphasis on Cost Constraints, Transparency, and Value-Based Reimbursement

Despite many uncertainties about how various health reforms will unfold, it is widely accepted that growth in reimbursement for care will flatten, if not decline. There will be considerable pressure to move health services to settings where they can be provided most efficiently. Additional savings in the system will be pursued through financial incentives for improving the quality of care. Value-based purchasing approaches are creating increased interest in clinical and other systems that can meaningfully improve patient outcomes. For hospitals, these outcomes include 30-day readmission rates, healthcare-associated infections, and other markers of safe and high-quality care. Healthcare systems will continue to publicly report their performance on a variety of metrics, including clinical quality, patient experience, and access to care. Leaders will spend more time understanding the perspectives of patients and their families and designing systems that simultaneously improve quality, lower costs, and enhance patient satisfaction.

Trend 2: Moving Toward Population Health Improvement

There is growing recognition that the high costs of health care in the United States have not been associated with better health outcomes. Although inefficiencies in the system are partly to blame, we have also historically underinvested in the prevention of illness and the management of chronic diseases. There is some truth to the old saying that "an ounce of prevention is worth a pound of cure." In the future, we are likely to see greater attention to systematic investment in preventing and more effectively managing chronic conditions such as diabetes and asthma. For health systems, this may mean that work addressing social determinants could begin taking on the characteristics of its own service line, with its own "payer mix" of community, government, and foundation support, in addition to the contributions of traditional insurers and other payers.

Improving population health will also require leaders from across the health and social sectors to work together in new ways. This collaboration will include health systems, clinics, social service agencies, public health leaders, policy-makers and, increasingly, organizations from other sectors. In particular, organizations with broad and established consumer bases have begun evolving new platforms for meeting their consumers' health-related needs. In the last several years, technology companies such as Amazon, Apple, and Google have each introduced major new products and services with consumer health as focal components. Additionally, retail chains such as CVS and Walmart, as well as all of the major health insurers in the United States, have made announcements about mergers, partnerships, and business models evolving to meet health-related needs.

Trend 3: Increasing Importance of Organizational Learning

The availability and depth of electronic health information is likely to expand at a rapid pace, creating new opportunities for evidence-based practice as well as challenges in effectively managing information storage, retrieval, and use. The Institute of Medicine has called for health systems to transform themselves into "learning healthcare systems," capable of routinely working with data from electronic health information systems to continuously improve care (Institute of Medicine, 2012). At the same time, advances in the capabilities supporting machine learning are creating increasingly powerful predictive tools that can help healthcare leaders more effectively anticipate needs and more efficiently deploy resource to meet them.

Beyond information management comes the challenge of *knowledge management*—processes for turning information and experience into accessible "inputs" to support more effective decision-making. Knowledge management requires mastery of dissemination techniques such as *positive deviance*—identifying and facilitating the spread of locally created solutions to common challenges (Pascale, Sternin, & Sternin, 2010) and building a culture that values and supports professionals in actively sharing lessons learned. Advances in artificial intelligence, in particular, will open new avenues and opportunities for accelerating these organizational learning processes (National Academy of Medicine, 2017).

Trend 4: Changing Demographics and Needs of Patients

The U.S. population is expected to grow by a total of 63 million people (20%) between 2010 and 2030 (U.S. Census Bureau, 2008). By 2050, the 65-and-older population is projected to double, representing 21% of the total population (Ortman, Velkoff, & Hogan, 2014). The number of the "oldest old" (age 85 and older), a group associated with multiple complex health and social support needs, is also projected to more than double. In addition to the aging population, the number and severity of chronic conditions is also expected to increase, due in part to lifestyle factors. Conditions such as diabetes, heart disease, stroke, high blood pressure, and some cancers, will increase, exacerbated by unhealthy diets and poor nutrition, sedentary lifestyles, and smoking. Diabetes alone is projected to increase 54% between 2015 and 2030, with costs rising at a similar pace (Rowley, Bezold, Arikan, Byrne,

& Krohe, 2017). This will put new strains on healthcare leaders to improve the ability to manage patients with complex needs and provide care coordination and care management services to support patient needs across the care continuum.

In addition to these growing needs, approaches to treatment as well as patients' levels of participation in healthcare decision-making are also evolving. Advances in genetics are leading rapidly to new approaches to treating cancer and other diseases, giving some patients new hope but also increasing financial pressures on the system (Dzau et al., 2016). As the emphasis on population health management continues to grow, clinicians and system leaders are recognizing the need to more actively engage patients in accepting greater responsibility for their own health, as well as redesigning the care systems with which patients will engage.

Trend 5: Changing Demands on the Healthcare Workforce

Heightened demands on the system are also predicted to worsen shortages in the clinical workforce, particularly in rural and underserved areas. These domestic shortfalls could also be exacerbated by the modernization of health systems in other countries. International medical graduates, i.e., physicians who received their training outside the United States and Canada, comprise 24% of the U.S. physician workforce (AAMC, 2016). Although U.S. nurses and general practitioners earn the highest incomes in the world (Fujisawa & Lafortune, 2007; Peterson & Burton, 2007), other countries are catching up, particularly the home countries of many of these immigrants (Garman, Johnson, & Royer, 2011), suggesting that, in the future, immigration trends may slow or even reverse. Fortunately, the U.S. market-driven system has shown itself to be remarkably adaptable to shortages (Auerbach, Buerhaus, & Staiger, 2011). With growing pressures on both the supply and demand sides, however, the limits of this adaptability may be tested in the years to come. Healthcare leaders will need to pay close attention to population-based estimates of need for various clinical services and the resulting workforce required to serve these populations.

Trend 6: Increasing Globalization and Global Innovation

A recent analysis of global trends in health service delivery concluded that most of the macro trends affecting health services in the United States are also affecting other countries (Garman & Johnson, 2018). To fully benefit from the innovative solutions and best practices other countries develop to address these challenges, healthcare leaders will need to monitor what is going on outside of the United States. Historically, differences in regulations across borders significantly slowed the diffusion of innovations globally, but recent years have brought increased efforts to align international regulatory requirements. For example, the International Conference on Harmonisation of Technical Requirements for Registration of Pharmaceuticals for Human Use is a collaboration between the United States, Japan, and Europe to reduce duplicative testing that is currently required for research and development and to bring new products to market in multiple countries in a more timely manner (Cortez, 2009). These trends will require health system leaders to have an awareness of global perspectives and the skills to operate and collaborate across borders.

▶ Leadership Competency Implications

The trends outlined previously are likely to substantively affect the **leadership competencies** needed for successful healthcare administrators. Here we consider some of the competencies future leadership roles will require in order to help manage and capitalize on these trends. More information about each of the competencies mentioned can be found in the National Center for Healthcare Leadership's Competency Model Version 3.0, which can be downloaded from the NCHL website (www.nchl.org).

The trend toward transparency and value-based purchasing suggests that leaders will need to be particularly strong in *Accountability* (setting clear expectations and holding people to them). At the senior level, leaders will need to establish management systems that help ensure a culture of accountability throughout the organization. Pressures for higher value (quality outcomes per resources expended) suggest that health systems are going to need leaders who are particularly skilled in performance improvement, and in the application of *Quality and Process Improvement*—the continuous improvement of system reliability and efficiency (Grossman, Goolsby, Olsen, & McGinnis, 2011; Valdez, Ramly, & Brennan, 2010). These system redesign efforts are also likely to promote an increased focus on engaging patients in the redesign process. Leaders will need to learn effective skills for collecting patient input through patient advisory councils, and integrating that input into strategic thinking and design processes. Future leaders will also have greater opportunities, as well as responsibilities, to leverage *Information Technology Management* to facilitate efficient, evidence-informed practices. The complementary competency *Change Leadership* (i.e., helping others to see change as imperative, and building the will within them to take the steps needed to redesign their work) will also be important for successful management in this arena of complex, multifaceted change. Important components of this competency include the ability to proactively identify high-priority areas for change and to communicate a clear and compelling vision for the desired future state. It also involves ensuring that communications about the change process reach intended employees and other stakeholders, who are thereby provided the opportunity to support the process as participants.

The trend toward **population health improvement** suggests that health system leaders will need to develop new competencies in *Community Collaboration* to pro-actively engage their communities in addressing public health needs. Leaders will need to be able to effectively develop and facilitate diverse stakeholder coalitions and groups, which may include community centers, social services providers, religious organizations, businesses, as well as government organizations such as park districts and school systems. There will also be a greater need for "*collaborative competition*," that is, developing and managing relationships with organizations to create efficiencies, while still competing with these organizations for market share.

Trends toward increased globalization and more broadly accessible innovation suggest future leaders will need to have particularly well-honed skills in *Information-Seeking*. High-performing leaders will be those who become adept at systematically scanning for promising emerging innovations that may benefit their organizations. Equally important will be the capacity to rapidly and critically assess these innovations, to maximize the attention spent on those with the greatest real potential, and minimize the time spent on those that may ultimately not pan out.

Taken together, these trends also suggest that healthcare providers in the future will need leaders who have a strong *Strategic Orientation*: that is, the ability to identify the 5–10 year trends that are likely to affect health services delivery and assess their implications through approaches such as futures task forces and scenario-planning. To convert these efforts into meaningful action, leaders will also need competency in both *Self Development* and *Talent Management*, a capacity and orientation toward continuous improvement of the skills of oneself and others. Given the magnitude of evolution we are forecasting for the future of health care, we will need to learn new ways to approach our work, and methodical and efficient retraining will be essential to success.

At the same time, as the workforce continues to diversify, leaders will need to develop greater *Interpersonal Understanding*: that is, sensitivity to and appreciation for the unique talents and needs each individual brings to the table. Lastly, as health systems continue to evolve away from providers of treatments and procedures and toward facilitators and mentors for total health and wellness, leaders may be increasingly called on to become role-models in *Well-being* (creating a climate and working conditions that are conducive to employees' long-term emotional, mental, spiritual, and financial health).

With these requirements in mind, we now turn to a discussion of how future leaders are likely to be developed and supported in their learning, training, and careers.

▶ Emerging Trends in Leadership Development

As the scientific underpinnings of effective **leadership development** continue to strengthen (Anderson & Garman, 2014; Day, Fleenor, Atwater, Sturm, & McKee, 2014; Lacerenza, Reyes, Marlow, Joseph, & Salas, 2017), organizations' approaches to developing leaders are likely to change in some of the following ways.

Leadership development will be increasingly tied to corporate strategy. Health systems will need to align their leadership development agendas to their corporate goals and outcomes, such as quality of clinical care and patient satisfaction (Crowe et al., 2017; Garman, McAlearney, Harrison, Song, & McHugh, 2011; Li, Barth, Garman, Anderson, & Butler, 2017). Successful alignment requires that training and development include human resource operational leaders at a strategic level within an organization; however, this still does not happen reliably in healthcare settings. Hospitals and health systems in which training is viewed primarily as a regulatory compliance function may focus leadership development on basic supervisory training. Organizations with a more strategically aligned training and development operation, in contrast, will have a systematic approach to aligning corporate strategy with learning and performance management practices, such as those depicted in **FIGURE 17.1**.

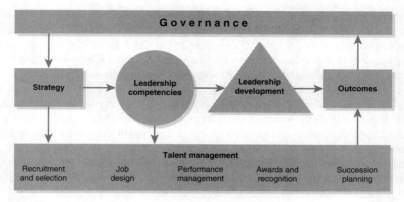

FIGURE 17.1 The NCHL Catalyst™ Model of Leadership Development

Reprinted with permission from the National Center for Health Leadership (www.nhcl.org), Chicago, IL.

Greater emphasis on team- and systems-based development rather than individual leader development. Throughout most of modern healthcare's existence, formal leadership development activities have focused on the individual leader. A leader might join a professional association, go offsite to attend conferences, and bring lessons learned back to their team. In recent years, there has been growing recognition that the off-site, individual-focused approach has limited impact—particularly when leadership goals involve the need for intense collaborative leadership efforts (Lacerenza et al., 2017). Increasingly, health systems are providing internal leadership academies that include a focus on leadership teams, particularly among academic medical centers (Lucas, Goldman, Scott, & Dandar, 2018). This is likely to grow in the future, given the substantial team leadership efforts required by the trends described previously in this review.

Increasing emphasis on enhancing on-the-job learning. Healthcare organizations are starting to shift away from an emphasis on classroom training and toward more "learning by doing." Many organizations with formal leadership training programs now require participants to complete one or more applied projects, which can comprise half or more of the total hours spent in the program. Identification of "stretch assignments" is also becoming a more routine part of talent management programs. Such assignments are typically matched to leaders based on specific competencies they need to develop. Coaching, mentoring, and peer-learning approaches are also being used to ensure participants gain the maximum learning benefit from their experiences (Anderson & Garman, 2014).

Greater use of simulation-enhanced education. For many types of health services, particularly those for which errors pose significant risk of life or health, a student clinician's first experiences are with simulated rather than actual patients. Simulated patients allow a clinician to practice in an environment free from the potential for patient harm until the procedure can be performed with a high degree of reliability. There are many leadership development activities as well in which direct experience may be less desirable, either because it is too expensive, relatively unavailable, or potentially risky. With advances in technology, simulations are becoming increasingly viable alternatives to direct experience in leadership development as well. The widespread availability of internet and mobile technologies has helped drive down the cost of computer-based simulations. Evidence supporting their effectiveness has been accumulating rapidly, to the point where they now compare favorably to other types of training, particularly when added to traditional courses (Sitzmann, 2011).

In addition to helping student leaders gain experience in risky or rare contexts, simulations may also help develop leaders prepare for environments that do not yet exist. In other industries, simulations have been used to test out possible future strategic directions, as well as the implications of impending changes in a given market. They can also be used to examine alternatives to currently entrenched operating models, as well as the potential impact of competitive threats coming from outside of currently established health sector organizations.

Summary

Regardless of the specifics of what the future holds for health care in the United States, it is safe to assume that all healthcare leaders will be called on to help the system work more reliably and efficiently to deliver higher value care for an increasingly diverse population. It is also safe to assume that leadership expectations will be different 5 and 10 years from now. Change is imperative, and, as a future leader, you will need to actively continue to develop your skills, through participation in continuing education, on-the-job learning, and ongoing self-reflection and improvement. Doing so will help ensure that you stay current and relevant, and that you are helping to build and improve a health system that provide the very best care possible for all of the people and communities we serve.

Discussion Questions

1. Have major technology and/or retail companies changed the way you find health information or seek out care? How do you think these and other changes in consumer behavior may affect the health sector in the future?
2. What other trends can you identify that were not addressed in the chapter that may affect health care in the future?
3. How might changes in other countries affect the U.S. healthcare system?
4. As a future healthcare leader, what skills do you think you might need to develop further after you graduate?
5. How might the relationship between health systems and universities need to evolve in the future?

Related Websites

Global Infobase, World Health Organization: https://apps.who.int/infobase/
Institute for Healthcare Improvement: www.ihi.org
Kaiser Health Reform Source: http://healthreform.kff.org/
National Academy of Medicine, Health and Medicine Division: www.nationalacademies.org/hmd/
National Center for Healthcare Leadership: http://www.nchl.org
TEDMED: http://www.tedmed.com/home
U.S. Census, population projections: https://www.census.gov/library/working-papers/2009/demo/us-pop-proj-2000-2050.html

References

AAMC. (2016). *2016 physician specialty data report.* Retrieved from www.aamc.org/data/workforce /reports/458506/1-7-chart.html

Anderson, M. M., & Garman, A. N. (2014). *Leadership development in healthcare systems: Toward an evidence-based approach.* White paper, National Center for Healthcare Leadership. Retrieved from http://www.nchl.org/Documents/Ctrl_Hyperlink/doccopy6464_uid9192016443322.pdf

Auerbach, D. I., Buerhaus, P. I., & Staiger, D. O. (2011). Registered nurse supply grows faster than projected amid surge in new entrants ages 23–26. *Health Affairs, 30*(12), 2286–2292.

Cortez, N. (2009). International health care convergence: The benefits and burdens of market -driven standardization. *Wisconsin International Law Journal, 26*(3), 646–704.

Crowe, D., Garman, A. N., Li, C., Helton, J., Anderson, M. A., & Butler, P. W. (2017). Leadership development practices and health system financial outcomes. *Health Services Management Research, 30*(3), 140–147.

Day, D. V., Fleenor, J. W., Atwater, L. E., Sturm, R. E., & McKee, R. A. (2014). Advances in leader and leadership development: A review of 25 years of research and theory. *The Leadership Quarterly, 25*(1), 63–82.

Dzau, V. J., Ginsburg, G. S., Chopra, A., Goldman, D., Green, E. D., Leonard, D. G. B., ... Yamamoto, K. R. (2016). Realizing the full potential of precision medicine in health and health care: A vital direction for health and health care. *National Academy of Medicine.* Retrieved from https:// nam.edu/wp-content/uploads/2016/09/Realizing-the-Full-Potential-of-Precision-Medicine -in-Health-and-Health-Care.pdf

Fujisawa, R., & Lafortune, G. (2007). *The remuneration of general practitioners and specialists in 14 OECD countries: What are the factors influencing variations across countries?* Working paper, Organisation for Economic Co-operation and Development. Retrieved from rwww.oecd.org /dataoecd/51/48/41925333.pdf

Garman, A. N., & Johnson, T. J. (2018, May). *The future of medical travel: Emerging trends and their potential impact.* Athens, Greece: IMTJ Academic Forum.

Garman, A. N., Johnson, T. J., & Royer, T. C. (2011). *The future of healthcare: Global trends worth watching.* Chicago, IL: Health Administration Press.

Garman, A. N., McAlearney, A. S., Harrison, M. I., Song, P. H., & McHugh, M. (2011). High -performance work systems in healthcare, Part 1: Development of an evidence-informed model. *Health Care Management Review, 36*(3), 201–213.

Grossman, C., Goolsby, W. A., Olsen, L., & McGinnis, J. M. (2011). *Engineering a learning healthcare system: A look at the future.* Washington, DC: National Academies Press.

Institute of Medicine. (2012). *Best care at lower cost: The path to continuously learning health care in America.* Washington, DC: National Academies Press.

Lacerenza, C. N., Reyes, D. L., Marlow, S. L., Joseph, D. L., & Salas, E. (2017). Leadership training design, delivery, and implementation: A meta-analysis. *Journal of Applied Psychology, 102*(12), 1686–1718.

Li, C., Barth, P., Garman, A. N., Anderson, M. A., & Butler, P. (2017). Leadership development practices and patient satisfaction: A study of U.S. academic medical centers. *Patient Experience Journal, 4*(1), 97–102.

Lucas, R., Goldman, E. F., Scott, A. R., & Dandar, V. (2018). Leadership development programs at academic health centers: Results of a national survey. *Academic Medicine, 93*(2), 229–236.

National Academy of Medicine. (2017, November). *Digital collaborative meeting highlights.* Retrieved from https://nam.edu/wp-content/uploads/2017/12/DLCNov30MeetingHighlights_FINAL.pdf

Ortman, J. M, Velkoff, V. A., & Hogan, H. (2014). *An aging nation: The older population in the United States.* Washington, DC: U.S. Census Bureau.

Pascale, R., Sternin, J., & Sternin, M. (2010). *The power of positive deviance: How unlikely innovators solve the world's toughest problems.* Cambridge, MA: Harvard Business Review Press.

Peterson, C. L., & Burton, R. (2007). *U.S. health care spending: Comparison with other OECD countries.* Washington, DC: U.S. Congressional Research Service. Retrieved from http://assets .opencrs.com/rpts/RL34175_20070917.pdf

Rowley, W. R., Bezold, C., Arikan, Y., Byrne, E., & Krohe, S. (2017). Diabetes 2030: Insights from yesterday, today, and future trends. *Population Health Management, 20*(1), 6–12.

Sitzmann, T. (2011). A meta-analytic examination of the instructional effectiveness of computer
-based simulation games. *Personnel Psychology, 64,* 489–528.

U.S. Census Bureau. (2008). Projections of the population by selected age groups and sex for the
United States: 2010 to 2050 (NP2008-T2). Retrieved from http://www.census.gov/population
/www/projections/summarytables.html

Valdez, R. S., Ramly, E., & Brennan, P. F. (2010). *Industrial and systems engineering and health care:
Critical areas of research–Final Report.* AHRQ Publication No. 10-0079. Rockville, MD: Agency
for Healthcare Research and Quality.

Glossary

360-degree evaluation: An assessment of skills and competencies that is performed by individual employees and all or a subset of stakeholders with whom they interact, such as direct reports, peers, supervisors, clients, vendors, patients, and the like, in order to obtain multiple perspectives on abilities and demonstrated behaviors. Paired with coaching to debrief and identify employee development plans and follow-through.

Accountability: Assumption and acknowledgment of responsibility for decisions and actions by setting clear expectations for employees to address and achieve.

Accountable Care Organization (ACO): An organization that can provide primary care, specialty care, and inpatient care for a population of patients. An ACO and its physicians are collectively willing and able to take responsibility for the overall costs and quality of care for a population.

Agendas: A list of things to be done, especially in a program or meeting.

Aims for improvement: In their landmark publication, *Crossing the Quality Chasm*, the Institute of Medicine called for a shared vision of six aims for healthcare quality improvement: safe, effective, patient-centered, timely, efficient, and equitable.

ANCC Nursing Magnet Recognition Program: A program established by the American Nurses Credentialing Center to recognize healthcare organizations for quality patient care, nursing excellence, and innovations in professional nursing practice.

Balanced scorecard: A strategic performance management tool, first described by Kaplan and Norton, that presents a mixture of financial and nonfinancial performance measures reflecting an organization's strategic priorities.

Bell Commission: A New York State appointed panel of experts led by Bertrand Bell, MD, which was convened to examine the circumstances surrounding the death of Libby Zion. The recommendations of the Bell Commission led to the Accreditation Council on Graduate Medical Education (ACGME) reforms of medical resident work hours. All postgraduate residency training programs are required to adhere to designated requirements for employee work hours, or risk major consequences, up to and including loss of accreditation status.

Benchmarking: The process of comparing one's performance metrics or business processes to the best practices of peers in the industry.

Bench strength: A term used to refer to an organization's development of new leaders who can provide backup and eventually replace the current leaders in charge

Board certification: Formal documentation of proficiency in a specific specialty or specialties within the practice of medicine. Prior to sitting for a board certification examination, physicians must complete a residency training program in a specialty or subspecialty. Surgeons must provide documentation of successful completion of an adequate number of cases for their specific board certification. The American Board of Medical Specialties' (ABMS) Maintenance of Certification (ABMS MOC) requires physicians and surgeons to demonstrate continuing education, ongoing continuous quality improvement, monitoring of patient outcomes, and objective assessment of knowledge and skills at periodic intervals.

C-suite: The designation of a literal or figurative area from which an organization's senior executives work. In a hospital, the C-suite can include examples such as CEO (Chief Executive Officer), COO (Chief Operation Officer), CNO (Chief Nursing Officer), CIO (Chief

Information Officer), CMO (Chief Medical Officer), and CFO (Chief Financial Officer).

Care delivery model: Method by which an organization delivers care to patients and families.

Character: A combination of qualities or features that emphasize one's values and ethics and distinguish individuals and organizations from a larger group.

Chief medical officer (CMO): A physician who serves at the executive level in a healthcare organization, and whose duties may include negotiating contracts and supervising patient safety, quality assessment, and risk management programs. CMOs often have graduate degrees in law (JD) or business administration (MBA).

Chief of medical staff: An individual typically elected by the staff physicians of a healthcare organization, or appointed by the senior leadership. The Chief of Medical Staff acts as the advocate for physicians and as a liaison to the organization's senior administration regarding physician issues and concerns.

Clinical experience and education; Clinical and educational work: Interchangable terms for the number of hours residents work in residency training programs.

Co-design: A way to identify both problems and solutions together with patients and thereby improve the quality of care experience.

Collaborations: A process in which two or more individuals or organizations work together to achieve a common goal.

Collaborative alliances: Creating interdependence among organizations for complex problem-solving.

Collaborative leadership: Leadership skills and attributes needed to successfully develop and manage inter-organizational strategic alliances and other forms of partnership.

Community benefit: The provision of charity care that distinguishes not-for-profit hospitals and health systems from for-profit healthcare organizations.

Community collaborators: Leaders who can influence diverse groups of stakeholders to work together.

Community needs assessments: A method of gathering information about a community's opinions, needs, concerns, and challenges that is used to determine which projects or services

can be implemented or adapted to meet the needs of the community.

Community outreach: The process of providing services or resources to benefit a community in an effort to improve the quality of life for community residents.

Competency: The ability of a person to perform a job appropriately.

Conduct: Professional behavior in the workplace.

Conflict of interest (COI): A situation in which individuals may be influenced by money or other considerations to act in a way that is contrary to the good of the organization for whom they work or of the patient for whose best interests they should be advocating.

Consensus: Collective opinion or agreement.

Continuing medical education (CME): Lifelong learning undertaken by physicians through a variety of delivery modes to stay current in their specialties, sustain clinical proficiency, adhere to professional organization requirements, and maintain their state licensure and hospital privileges.

Core values: Internal principles that make up the underlying foundation of a person or agency and guide relationships with others.

Corporate practice of medicine (CPOM): Where a corporation dictates how medicine is practiced and overrides physicians' medical judgments.

Creative thinking: The visualization or development of something new or original.

Critical access hospitals: Small, geographically remote facilities that provide outpatient and inpatient hospital services to people in rural areas.

Cultural competence: The ability and willingness to communicate respectfully and effectively with individuals of all ethnic, cultural, and religious backgrounds.

Cultural relativism: An anthropological concept that supports the principle that understanding people's values, beliefs, and practices requires being considerate of their cultural context. The view that different cultures have different moral standards which regulate human actions and these actions are or should be assessed or evaluated by these standards

Culture of safety: The creation and promotion of an environment providing high quality of care and minimized risks for medical errors and patient injuries and negative outcomes.

Diversity: The inclusion of different entities in a group, e.g. different demographics, ethnicities, etc.

Duty hours: Old term for resident work hours; replaced by the term work hours.

Emotional intelligence: Ability to identify, assess, and manage the emotions of oneself, of others, and of groups.

Empowerment: The sharing of information, knowledge, skills, rewards, authority, and responsibility with employees and direct reports. This process promotes improved employee initiative and morale.

Ethics: The study of standards of conduct (behavior) and moral judgments.

Ethnocentrism: The "belief in the superiority of one's own group and a corresponding disdain for all other groups."

Executive coaching: A confidential set of consultations between a qualified coach and a senior leader, which focuses on enhancing or improving the executive's leadership skills.

External environment: Entities that exist outside an organization's physical or functional boundary, but which may have a significant influence on the organization's survival and growth.

Federally Qualified Health Center (FQHC): A healthcare entity that has entered into an agreement with CMS and is receiving a grant under §330 of the Public Health Service (PHS) Act; or is an outpatient health program or facility operated by a tribe or tribal organization under the Indian Self-Determination Act, or by an Urban Indian organization receiving funds under Title V of the Indian Health Care Improvement Act.

Fiduciary duty: Ensuring the deployment and utilization of organizational resources in a manner that protects and advances the interests of the organization and its stakeholders and/or shareholders.

Financial management: The planning, organizing, directing, and controlling of the financial activities of a business enterprise.

Future trends: Changes in the healthcare sector that are likely to take place over the coming years.

Global health: Health problems, issues and concerns that transcend national boundaries and may best be addressed by cooperative actions.

Governance: The state or act of governing; includes the implementation of formal authority and control over an organization.

Governing body: A group of individuals who make up the panel designated to administer or supervise an organization.

Groupthink: A phenomenon in which group members tend to agree with one another.

Healthcare Executive Competencies Assessment Tool: A self-assessment instrument developed by the American College of Healthcare Executives to assist managers in identifying areas of leadership strength, as well as areas in which they may wish to improve their performance.

Healthcare Leadership Alliance: A consortium of six major professional organizations, which identifies and facilitates competencies that promote excellence in healthcare management across diverse professional roles.

Healthcare reform: A reference to developments or changes in health policy on a national or state level, which can affect regulations, reimbursements, scope of services, and other aspects of healthcare delivery.

Healthcare teams: Small groups brought together to achieve an identified goal.

Healthcare value: Cost-effective, high-quality health services.

Health inequities: Uneven access to and distribution of health resources due to differences in socioeconomic status which can lead to less optimal health outcomes.

High potentials: Employees identified as strong candidates to develop for promotion to upper management levels. May often be identified in succession plans.

High reliability organization: One which focuses on developing new, improved, and more reliable quality improvement practices by removing impediments generated by hierarchical authority; utilizing standardized protocols and checklists; pre- and post-procedural briefings; incident reporting; and huddles.

Human resources metrics: A set of measurements used to determine effectiveness and value of implemented human resource strategies.

Implicit/unconscious bias: A cognitive perspective developed to guide human behavior as a protective response to a stressful environment.

Inclusive leadership: A leadership style that values and accepts the uniqueness of each individual and treats diverse individuals and groups fairly.

Interdisciplinary care teams: Care teams which include members from a variety of healthcare disciplines, such as nursing, medicine, pharmacy, respiratory technology, etc.

I-PASS: The acronym (Illness severity, Patient summary, Action list, Situation awareness and contingency plans, and Synthesis) for a standardized transitions of care program for oral and written patient handoffs.

Key drivers: Factors that influence and direct the outcome of a process, mission, program, or strategic plan.

Leadership: The process whereby a designated individual influences individuals or teams to accomplish a specified goal.

Leadership competencies: The skills and abilities necessary to guide individuals and groups towards the achievement of a designated goal. Skills needed may include problem solving, effective communication, and strategic thinking.

Leadership development: The required education and training of a leader to gain necessary skills for effective leadership in a rapidly changing industry.

Leadership models: Algorithms for leadership function and behavior.

Leadership pipeline: The selection and development of leaders for upper management positions.

Lean: A methodology to increase value and efficiency through a reduction of waste; based on the Toyota Production System.

Learning organization: An organization that is skilled at acquiring, creating, and transferring knowledge and modifying its behavior to reflect new insights and adapt to ongoing change.

Malcolm Baldrige National Quality Award: A national recognition awarded to U.S. organizations for performance excellence through the Baldrige Program, which was established by Congress in 1987 to recognize U.S. companies for their achievements in quality and business performance.

Management models: A model that plans to direct and use the organization's resources economically and efficiently to achieve the organization's objectives.

Medicaid: A health insurance program for eligible low-income and needy individuals and families supported by federal, state, and county dollars.

Medical tourism: A process through which individuals seek more economical procedures or treatments in other countries, options which are unavailable or very expensive in their home country.

Medicare: A federally sponsored health insurance program for individuals age 65 and older, and for individuals of all ages with specific conditions and disabilities.

#MedToo: A national movement for health professional survivors of sexual harassment and abuse.

Mental models: Images, stories, and assumptions about aspects of the world, which determine our perspectives of what we see, how we see it, and how we act.

Mentoring: Serving as a teacher, advisor, or trainer for another, typically a younger colleague.

#MeToo: A national movement for survivors of sexual harassment and abuse.

Mission, vision, and values: Statements of organizational purpose, future, ethics, and philosophy that provide guidance to the organization.

Multicultural workforce: Diversity among employees; may include a variety of factors such as ethnicity, race, gender identity, socioeconomic background, etc.

Multidisciplinary team: In healthcare, groups whose members are drawn from various professional disciplines.

Multigenerational workers: Employees in a workforce composed of multiple generations/ages.

Multigenerational workforce: A group of employees composed of multiple generations/ages. These differences may bring different experiences and perspectives to the work setting.

National Practitioner Data Bank (NPDB): A central repository of information on physicians, dentists, and other healthcare providers through which state licensing boards, hospitals, professional societies, and other healthcare entities can identify, discipline, and report those who engage in unprofessional behavior, negligence, or malpractice.

Obligation: A course of action that one is required to take. May be legal or moral.

Organization for Economic Cooperation and Development (OECD): The Organisation for Economic Co-operation and Development (OECD) promotes policies that will improve the economic and social well-being of people around the world.

Organizational culture: Shared values and norms that guide how individuals and teams in an organization function and communicate within and beyond.

Paid time off: Leave which is funded, e.g. vacation, sabbaticals.

Partnerships: An arrangement whereby two parties agree to cooperate with one another to advance their mutual interests.

Patient activation: Advocacy by patients for a transparent and collaborative relationship with their healthcare providers

Patient engagement: When individuals use their skills, knowledge, and confidence to manage their health and health care with interventions designed to promote positive health behaviors.

Patient family advisors: Participants in organizations' advisement councils who provide input and feedback on health care based on their experiences and perspectives.

Patient Family Advisory Council: A committee that enables current and former patients to serve as part of care teams and offer their input and perspectives regarding their care and help to uncover barriers that negatively impact the patient experience.

Patient- and family-centered care (PFCC): An approach to the planning, delivery, and assessment of healthcare, grounded in mutually beneficial partnerships among healthcare providers, patients, and families. Four concepts comprise PFCC: (1) dignity and respect, (2) information sharing, (3) participation, and (4) collaboration.

Patient- and family-centered leaders: Individuals in formal or informal positions who are able to implement positive change and who are patient- and family-centered. They listen to and value the individual and collective voice of patients and families, empower patients and their families to take charge of their own health and welfare, and recognize that patient and family partnerships inform and shape the healthcare organization's operational policies, staff interactions, facilities, services, and programs.

Patient and family partnerships: True and equal collaboration between patients, families, providers, and administrators in the planning, implementation, and delivery of care at the individual and organizational levels.

Patient handoffs: The transference of a caregiver's responsibility for and knowledge of a patient's condition and care at changes in time or place.

Patient Protection and Affordable Care Act (ACA): Enacted in 2010, the ACA was a series of reforms of the U.S healthcare delivery system. The Act went fully into effect in 2014, with the main goals of increasing the availability and accessibility of health insurance for US citizens and providing better coordinated, high-quality, cost-effective care.

Performance evaluation: The process of a formal, systematic assessment of how well employees are performing in their jobs in relation to established standards.

Performance reporting: Documentation that communicates the results obtained in a performance evaluation. Often compared with prior reports to assess trends in achievement of goals and objectives.

Person-centered care: In settings where healthcare is provided, the care focus is only on the individual person.

Person-family centered leadership: A process of partnership with patients and families which helps to identify both problems and solutions together and thereby improve the quality of care experience

Physician credentialing: The process of verifying information that a physician supplies on an application for staff privileges at a hospital, health maintenance organization (HMO), or other healthcare organization. Most healthcare organizations have protocols that they have established, which include obtaining primary (i.e., first-hand and original) verification and documentation of credentials from transcripts with raised seals, by contacting each place of education, training, and employment recorded.

Physician privileging: When physicians apply for privileges at a hospital, HMO, or other healthcare organization, they must specify the scope of their practice, not only by specialty but also by procedure. Using extensive documentation, the physician must demonstrate competency for the requested privileges, before they can be granted.

PIE2: Personal (internal and external) and professional (internal and external) professionalism.

Population health improvement: Improving the health status of a group of individuals, inclusive of health outcomes and disease burden. Its scope exceeds traditional, individual-level medicine by focusing on factors that affect entire populations such as communities' environment, social structure, and economic wellbeing.

Priority populations: Groups identified by the AHRQ which demonstrate a poorer quality of healthcare, e.g. ethnic and racial minorities, older adults, LGBT, etc.

Process improvement: A systematic approach to improving the performance of a process or system through streamlining and cycle time reduction, and via the identification and elimination of the causes of substandard quality, process variation, activities that do not add value.

Professional practice model: A practice system comprised of specific structures, processes, and values that support registered nurse control over the delivery of nursing care and the environment in which the nursing care is delivered.

Professionalism: Quality, character, or conduct expected of a member of a specific profession. The conduct or qualities that characterize or mark a profession.

Psychological contract: A person's beliefs, formed by the organization, regarding the terms and conditions of a reciprocal agreement between that person and his or her organization.

Public health: Public health promotes and protects the health of people and the communities where they live, learn, work, and play.

Recruitment: The process of attracting, interviewing, and hiring new employees.

Relationships: Professional and collegial associations and collaborations.

Retention: A set of activities designed to reduce turnover and retain the talent necessary for effective organization performance.

Rounding: Communicating face-to-face with employees for the purpose of gathering information in a structured, consistent manner.

Selection: The process of identifying an individual or group of individuals who are a good fit for a position or team within an organization.

Servant leadership: A leadership model in which the leader supports and facilitates the goals, mission, and work of the employees and the organization.

Sexual harassment: Unwelcome sexual advances, requests for sexual favors, and other verbal or physical harassment of a sexual nature. This includes offensive remarks about a person's gender identity or sex. The complainant and the respondent can be either a woman or a man, and the both can be the same gender. Sexual harassment is illegal when it is so frequent or severe that it creates a hostile or offensive work environment or when it results in an adverse employment decision (such as the victim being fired or demoted).

Sexual orientation: The sexual attraction of one individual to individuals in another group or groups, e.g. to the same gender, a different gender, or all genders or non-binary individuals.

Shadowing: A formal technique that invites a high-potential employee to follow a leader for a designated period of time, observing and learning about the leader's daily duties.

Single-payer: A government sponsored health insurance program for all of a country's population, e.g. UK: National Health Service, US: "Medicare for all".

Situation analysis: Analyzing an active situation by evaluating factors such as the strengths and weaknesses internal to the organization and the opportunities and threats in the external environment.

Six Sigma: A data-driven statistical methodology that focuses on improving quality by identifying and eliminating defects in a process.

Strategic management: The process of assigning responsibility to implement and monitor the activities that must be accomplished to reach an organization's goals.

Strategic planning: A method used to define the tasks and to operationalize activities that must be accomplished to reach an identified or agreed-upon goal.

Strategic thinking: A mental process of synthesizing and analyzing information to envision the strategies and tactics needed to achieve an ultimate goal.

Strategy formulation: The process of determining appropriate courses of action for achieving organizational goals and objectives.

Strategy implementation: The effective execution of strategic goals and objectives.

Stretch assignment: A form of on-the-job learning that requires employees to extend beyond their comfort zone and develop new skills or strengthen existing competencies.

Succession plan: A strategic plan that outlines how leadership roles will effectively transition with the departure of one or more leaders.

Succession plan(ning): The process taken to ensure that qualified employees are in place and ready to fill key roles in an organization as needed for smooth transitions in leadership.

Talent management: An internal structure and process for developing and nurturing leaders within an organization.

Team charter: A document that outlines the purpose and function of a team.

Theory X: A theory of motivation introduced by Douglas McGregor in the 1960s which implies that people are generally lazy, do not really enjoy work, and only work for the paycheck.

Theory Y: A theory of motivation introduced by Douglas McGregor in the 1960s to describe the idea that employees are ambitious, self-motivated, and self-controlled, and work because they wish to do so.

Top box achievement: Achieving the highest performance level possible.

Total rewards model: A set of strategies to attract, motivate, and retain employees.

Training and development: A set of activities designed to assist employees in maintaining and enhancing their knowledge, skills, and abilities.

Transactional leader: A person whose leadership style promotes his or her own interests and who assumes that all employees are motivated similarly, e.g. by pay raises.

Transformational leaders: Individuals who possess and communicate a compelling vision that inspires followers to adjust expectations, perceptions, and motivations to work towards common goals.

Transitions of care: The transference of a caregiver's responsibility for and knowledge of a patient's condition and care at changes in time or place.

Transparency: The act of being open, honest, and providing full disclosure.

Trustee/director: A legal term describing a person who holds property, authority, or a position of trust or responsibility for the benefit of another.

United Nations: An organization of representative countries from around the world which meet to discuss and promote international cooperation and order.

United Nations Educational, Scientific and Cultural Organization (UNESCO): An agency of the United Nations which promotes international collaboration through educational, scientific, and cultural reforms.

Value-based purchasing: A payment methodology that bases inpatient hospital reimbursement on the provider's performance results in clinical quality, patient experience, and the cost of care provided.

Virtual teams: A group of individuals who work across time, space, and organizational boundaries with links strengthened by webs of communication technology.

Will-Ideas-Execution: The core elements of a framework to achieve better performance as suggested by the Institute for Healthcare Improvement. Successful leaders must develop the organizational will to achieve results, generate or identify effective ideas or strategies for improvement, and then execute those ideas.

Workforce planning: A process used to align the needs of the organization with the availability of human and financial resources.

Work hours: The hours a healthcare provider is "on duty", "on shift", or "on call". Replaces the term duty hours for residency training, i.e., the number of hours a resident is permitted to work.

Work-life balance: A healthy allocation of an individual's time between work and other aspects of their lives.

World Health Organization (WHO): An agency of the United Nations which directs international health within the United Nations' system and leads partners in global health responses.

Index

Note: Page numbers followed by *f*, *t* and *b* indicate figures, tables and boxes, respectively.

O

Z